# IMPROVING
# READING
# COMPREHENSION
# SKILLS

---

## JOHN LANGAN
ATLANTIC COMMUNITY COLLEGE

## CAROL H. BADER
MIDDLE TENNESSEE STATE UNIVERSITY

## HARLEY F. ANTON
MIDDLE TENNESSEE STATE UNIVERSITY

**TOWNSEND PRESS**     Marlton, NJ 08053

The Other Books in the Townsend Press Reading Series:

GROUNDWORK FOR COLLEGE READING
GROUNDWORK FOR COLLEGE READING II
TEN STEPS TO BUILDING COLLEGE READING SKILLS
TEN STEPS TO IMPROVING COLLEGE READING SKILLS
TEN STEPS TO ADVANCING COLLEGE READING SKILLS

Books in the Townsend Press Vocabulary Series:

GROUNDWORK FOR A BETTER VOCABULARY
BUILDING VOCABULARY SKILLS
IMPROVING VOCABULARY SKILLS
ADVANCING VOCABULARY SKILLS
BUILDING VOCABULARY SKILLS, SHORT VERSION
IMPROVING VOCABULARY SKILLS, SHORT VERSION
ADVANCING VOCABULARY SKILLS, SHORT VERSION

Supplements Available for Each Book:

Instructor's Manual
Test Bank and Computer Guide
Set of Computer Disks (Apple, IBM, or Macintosh)

Copyright © 1992 by Townsend Press, Inc.
Printed in the United States of America
ISBN 0-944210-54-6

Send book orders and requests for desk copies or supplements to:

**Townsend Press Book Center**
**RD # 11, Box 192A**
**Mt. Penn Road**
**Reading, PA  19607**

For even faster service, telephone our toll-free number:

**1-800-772-6410**

Or fax your request to:

**1-215-796-1491**

ISBN 0-944210-54-6

# CONTENTS

Preface to the Instructor    vii

How to Become a Better Reader and Thinker    1

1  **Vocabulary in Context**    **5**
   Mastery Tests    13

2  **Main Ideas**    **43**
   Mastery Tests    61

3  **Supporting Details**    **91**
   Mastery Tests    105

4  **Transitions**    **135**
   Mastery Tests    145

5  **Patterns of Organization**    **175**
   Mastery Tests    193

6  **Fact and Opinion**    **223**
   Mastery Tests    233

7  **Inferences**    **263**
   Mastery Tests    275

8  **Purpose and Tone**    **305**
   Mastery Tests    315

9  **Propaganda**    **345**
   Mastery Tests    355

10  **Argument**    **385**
    Mastery Tests    399

**Combined Skills Mastery Tests**    **429**

Limited Answer Key    459

Acknowledgments    465

Index    467

Performance Chart    *Inside back cover*

# Preface to the Instructor

We all know that many students entering college today do not have the reading skills needed to do effective work in their courses. A related problem, apparent even in class discussions, is that students often lack the skills required to think in a clear and logical way.

The purpose of IMPROVING READING COMPREHENSION SKILLS is to develop effective reading *and* clear thinking. To do so, the book presents a sequence of ten reading skills that are widely recognized as essential for basic and advanced comprehension. The first five skills concern the more literal levels of comprehension:

- Using vocabulary in context
- Recognizing main ideas
- Identifying supporting details
- Understanding transitions
- Understanding patterns of organization

The remaining five skills cover the more advanced, critical levels of comprehension:

- Distinguishing facts from opinions
- Making inferences
- Identifying purpose and tone
- Detecting propaganda
- Evaluating arguments

In each chapter, the key aspects of a skill are explained and illustrated clearly and simply. Explanations are accompanied by practices, and each chapter ends with a brief review.

Following each chapter are fifteen mastery tests. The tests progress in difficulty: there are three tests on reading level A, three tests on reading level B, three tests on reading level C, three tests on reading level D, and three tests on reading level E. (The grade equivalents for A, B, C, D, and E are given on the inside front cover of the *Instructor's Edition* of the book.)

While designed for quick grading, the tests ensure that students must think carefully before answering each question. Moreover, the sequence of tests, from easy to difficult, enables students to gradually strengthen each skill. As they continue to work, they proceed step by step up the comprehension ladder. Their motivation often builds along with their skill as they clearly see their progress in moving from tests on one level of difficulty to the next.

## Important Features of the Book

• **Focus on the basics.** The book seeks to explain in an extremely clear, step-by-step way the essential elements of each skill. Many examples are provided to ensure that students understand each point. In general, the focus is on *teaching* the skills—not just on explaining them and not just on testing them.

• **Frequent practice and feedback.** In the belief that it is largely through abundant practice and careful feedback that progress is made, this book includes numerous activities and tests. Students can get immediate feedback on the practice exercises in each chapter by turning to the limited answer key at the back. The answers to the review at the end of each chapter and to all of the mastery tests are in the *Instructor's Edition*.

The limited answer key increases the active role that students take in their own learning. They are likely to use the answer key in an honest and positive way when they realize they will be evaluated on the mastery tests, for which answers are not provided. (Answers to the mastery tests can be easily copied from the *Instructor's Edition* and passed out at the teacher's discretion.)

• **High interest level.** Dull and unvaried exercises work against learning. Students need to experience genuine interest and enjoyment in what they read. Teachers as well should be able to take pleasure in the materials, for their own good feeling can carry over favorably into class work. The exercises in the book, then, have been chosen not only for the appropriateness of their reading level but also for their compelling content. They should engage teachers and students alike.

• **Ease of use.** The straightforward sequence in each chapter—from explanation to example to practice to review—helps make the skills easy to teach. The limited answer key at the back of the text also makes for versatility: it means that the teacher can assign some chapters for self-teaching. Finally, the mastery and combined skills tests—each on its own clear-cut grade level and on its own tear-out page—make it a simple matter for teachers to evaluate student progress.

• **Integration of skills.** In addition to learning the skills individually in each chapter, students also learn to apply the skills together through a series of combined skills tests (see pages 429-458). They become effective readers and thinkers through a good deal of practice in applying a combination of skills. An added benefit is that the combined skills tests approximate the reading passages and questions that are typically used in standardized reading tests. Students, then, both master essential reading skills and also prepare themselves for the standarized reading test required in many college programs.

• **Focus on thinking.** The mastery tests cannot be done mechanically; students must truly *think* to answer the questions. As they work through the wide range of tests for the ten reading skills, their cognitive abilities and performance are sure to improve. While the mastery tests demand attention and hard work, they also repay that work. Students who progress through the entire sequence of skills and tests are substantially more equipped to do the independent reading and thinking required in a typical college curriculum.

• **Supplementary materials.** The three helpful supplements listed below are available at no charge to instructors using the text. Any or all can be obtained by writing Townsend Press (Pavilions at Greentree—408, Marlton, New Jersey 08053) or by calling a toll-free number: 800-772-6410.

1   An *Instructor's Edition*—you are probably holding it in your hand— is identical to the student book except that it provides a "Notes to the Instructor" on the inside front cover and answers to all the practices and tests.

2   A combined *Instructor's Manual, Test Bank, and Computer Guide* consists of the following:

    a   Hints for teaching the course, a suggested syllabus, and information on readability levels.

    b   Five additional mastery tests for each of the ten skills (with one test on each of the five levels of difficulty) and five additional combined skills tests.  Note that all of these tests are on letter-sized sheets so they can be copied easily for use with students.

    c   A computer guide that reproduces the two additional mastery tests for each skill that are on the computer disks available with the book

3   A *set of computer disks* (available in Apple, IBM, and Macintosh formats) that contain two additional mastery tests for each of the ten skill chapters in the book. The disks are self-booting and include a number of other user- and instructor-friendly features: brief explanations of answers, a sound option, frequent mention of the user's first name, a running score at the bottom of the screen, and a record-keeping score file. (Note that these disks are identical to the ones for TEN STEPS TO IMPROVING COLLEGE READING SKILLS, Second Edition.)

    Since the disk tests are reproduced in the *Computer Guide*, teachers can readily decide just how to use the materials without having to work through each test on the computer. And teachers without a computer lab can copy these tests for use in class as additional mastery tests.

• **One of a sequence of books.** IMPROVING READING COMPREHENSION SKILLS is part of a series that includes three other books. TEN STEPS TO BUILDING COLLEGE READING SKILLS is the basic book in the series; IMPROVING READING COMPREHENSION SKILLS and TEN STEPS TO IMPROVING COLLEGE READING SKILLS, Second Edition, are the intermediate books; and TEN STEPS TO ADVANCING COLLEGE READING SKILLS is an advanced text.

The BUILDING book is a lower-level book suited for a first college reading course. The two IMPROVING books are appropriate for the core developmental reading course offered at most colleges. The ADVANCING book is a slightly higher developmental text than the two IMPROVING books. It can be used as the core book for a more advanced class, as a sequel to the intermediate book, or as a second-semester alternative to it.

A companion set of vocabulary books, listed on page iv, has been designed to go with the TEN STEPS books. The vocabulary books help students cope with the problem that, very often, they simply don't know enough words to understand what they read. Recommended to accompany this book is IMPROVING VOCABULARY SKILLS, SHORT VERSION.

To summarize, then, IMPROVING READING COMPREHENSION SKILLS teaches ten key reading skills that help developmental college students become independent readers and thinkers. Through a carefully sequenced series of tests, students receive extensive guided practice in the skills. The result is a progressive approach to learning that will, by the end of a course, produce better readers and stronger thinkers.

## Acknowledgments

We are grateful to several people who helped us prepare and test some of the practice materials in the book: Elaine J. Lessig, Rick Robinson, and Beth Johnson Ruth. We are especially indebted to two editors at Townsend Press. Thanks to the exceptional design, editing, and computing skills of Janet M. Goldstein, this book enjoys a remarkably clear and user-friendly format. Her work also made possible the creation of the *Instructor's Edition* that accompanies the book. We value equally the exceptional editorial role played by Carole Mohr, who has worked closely with us for many months on every page of the book. Thanks to her many insights into the nature of each skill and her unfailing sensitivity to the needs of students, the text is significantly better than it would have been otherwise. It has been a special pleasure to work with colleagues who aspire toward excellence. With them, we have been able to create a much better book than we ever could have managed otherwise.

*John Langan*
*Carol H. Bader*
*Harley F. Anton*

# How to Become a Better Reader and Thinker

The chances are you are not as good a reader as you should be to do well in college. If so, it's not surprising. You live in a culture where people watch on the average of *over seven hours of television every day!!!* All that passive viewing does not allow much time for reading. Reading is a skill that must be actively practiced. The simple fact is that people who do not read very often are not likely to be strong readers.

• How much TV do you guess you watch on an average day? _____

Another reason besides TV for not reading much is that you may have a lot of responsibilities. You may be going to school and working at the same time, and you may have a lot of family duties as well. Given a hectic schedule, you're not going to have much time to read. When you have free time, you're exhausted, and it's easier to turn on the TV than to open up a book.

• Do you do any regular reading (for example, a daily newspaper, weekly magazines, occasional novels)? _____

• When are you most likely to do your reading? _____

A third reason for not reading is that our public school system may have soured you on it. One government study after another has said that our schools have not done a good job of turning people on to the rewards of reading. If you had to read a lot of uninteresting and irrelevant material in grade and high school, you may have decided (mistakenly) that reading in general is not for you.

• Do you think that school made you dislike reading, rather than enjoy it?

_____

Here are three final questions to ask yourself.

• Do you feel that perhaps you don't need a reading course, since you "already know how to read"? _____

• If you had a choice, would you be taking a reading course? (It's OK to be honest.) _____

• Do you think that a bit of speed reading may be all you need? _____

Chances are that you don't need to read *faster* as much as you need to read *smarter.* And it's a safe bet that if you don't read much, you can benefit enormously from the reading course in which you are using this book.

One goal of the book is to help you become a better reader. You will learn and practice ten key reading comprehension skills. As a result, you'll be able to read and understand more easily the many materials in your other college courses. The skills in this book have direct and practical value: they can help you perform better and more quickly—giving you an edge for success—in all of your college work.

The book is also concerned with helping you become a stronger thinker, a person able not just to understand what is read but to analyze and evaluate it as well. In fact, reading and thinking are closely related skills, and practice in thoughtful reading will also strengthen your ability to think clearly and logically. To find out just how the book will help you achieve these goals, read the next several pages and do the brief activities as well. The activities are easily completed and will give you a quick, helpful overview of the book.

## HOW THE BOOK IS ORGANIZED

To help you become a more effective reader and thinker, this book presents a series of ten key reading skills. They are listed in the table of contents on page v. Turn to that page to fill in the skills missing below:

## Ten Reading Skill Chapters

1    Vocabulary in Context

2    _____

3    Supporting Details

4    _____

5    Patterns of Organization

6    Fact and Opinion

7    Inferences

**8** _____

**9** Propaganda

**10** _____

Each chapter is developed in the same way. First of all, clear explanations and examples help you *understand* each skill. Practices then give you the "hands-on" experience needed to *master* the skill.

• How many practices are there for the second skill, "Main Ideas" (pages 43-60)? _____

Closing each chapter is a short review.

• On which page is the review for "Main Ideas"? _____

## Mastery Tests

Following each chapter is a series of fifteen mastery tests. The tests are arranged on five levels of difficulty:

3 tests on level A, the first level of difficulty
3 tests on level B, the next level of difficulty
3 tests on level C, the third level of difficulty
3 tests on level D, the fourth level of difficulty
3 tests on level E, the highest level of difficulty

• On which pages are the three highest level of difficulty tests for "Main Ideas"? _____

The test pages are perforated and can be torn out and given to your instructor. There is a scorebox at the start of each test so you can track your progress. Your score can also be entered on the "Performance Chart" at the back of the book.

## HELPFUL FEATURES OF THE BOOK

1    The book centers on *what you really need to know* to become a better reader and thinker. It presents ten key comprehension skills, and it explains the most important points about each skill.

2    The book gives you *lots of practice*. We seldom learn a skill only by hearing or reading about it; we make it part of us by repeated practice. There is, then, a series of mastery tests in the book. These tests are not "busy work," but carefully designed materials that should help you truly learn each skill.

As part of this design, certain passages are repeated at times. For example, a passage on main ideas may appear in a test for supporting details or patterns of organization. Such repetition will sharpen your awareness of the variety of skills a reader often brings to bear in a single reading situation.

3    The book provides *a sequence of tests*, from easy to difficult. You therefore have a chance to build your understanding and to strengthen your reading and thinking skills a step at a time. If you persist, you will climb steadily up the ladder of comprehension.

## HOW TO USE THE BOOK

1    A good way to proceed is to read and reread the explanations and examples in a given chapter until you feel you understand the ideas presented. Then carefully work through the practices. As you finish each one, check your answers with the "Limited Answer Key" that starts on page 459.

For your own sake, don't just copy in the answers without trying to do the practices! The only way to learn a skill is to practice it first and *then* use the answer key to give yourself feedback. Also, take whatever time is needed to figure out just why you got some answers wrong. By using the answer key to help teach yourself the skills, you will prepare yourself for the progressive mastery tests that follow.

If you have trouble catching on to a particular skill, stick with it. In time, you will learn each one.

2    Then start working through the mastery tests. Start with the first level and gradually move your way up, one sure step at time. As needed, your instructor will provide you with the answers to the tests on each level.

3    Keep clear track of your progress by entering your test scores into the "Performance Chart" at the back of the book.

In summary, IMPROVING READING COMPREHENSION SKILLS has been designed to interest and benefit you as much as possible. Its format is straightforward, its explanations are clear, its content is appealing, and its many practices will help you learn through doing. *It is a book that has been created to reward effort*, and if you provide that effort, you will make yourself a better reader and a stronger thinker. We wish you success.

*John Langan*
*Carol H. Bader*
*Harley F. Anton*

# 1

# Vocabulary in Context

If you were asked to define the words *torrid*, *ascertain*, and *euphoria*, you might have some difficulty. On the other hand, if you saw these words in the sentences, chances are you could come up with fairly accurate definitions. To illustrate, see if you can define the words in *italics* in the three sentences below. Circle the letter of the meaning you think is correct.

To avoid the burning sun in *torrid* climates such as deserts, many animals come out only at night.

*Torrid* means
a. familiar        b. extremely hot and dry        c. very bright

The officer tried to *ascertain* the truth about the accident by questioning each witness separately.

*Ascertain* means
a. create        b. avoid        c. find out

In their *euphoria,* the fans of the winning team danced in the stadium aisles and chanted victory songs, until their intense joy was dampened by a sudden downpour.

*Euphoria* means
a. intense joy        b. hurry        c. disappointment

In the sentences above, the *context*—the words surrounding the unfamiliar word—provides clues to each word's meaning. You may have guessed from the context that a *torrid* climate is an extremely hot and dry one, that *ascertain* means "find out," and that *euphoria* is "intense joy."

Using context clues to understand the meaning of unfamiliar words will help you in several ways:

- It will save you time when reading. You will not have to stop to look up words in the dictionary. (Of course, you won't always be able to understand a word from its context, so you should always have a dictionary nearby as you read.)

- After you figure out the meaning of the same word more than once through its context, it may become a part of your working vocabulary. You will therefore add to your vocabulary simply by reading thoughtfully.

- You will get a good sense of how a word is actually used, including its shades of meaning.

## TYPES OF CONTEXT CLUES

There are four common types of context clues:

1   Examples

2   Synonyms

3   Antonyms

4   General Sense of the Sentence or Passage

In the following sections, you will read about and practice using each type. The practices will sharpen your skills in recognizing and using context clues. They will also help you add new words to your vocabulary.

## 1   Examples

If you are given *examples* of an unknown word, you can often figure out its meaning. To understand how this type of clue works, read the sentences below. An *italicized* word in each sentence is followed by examples that serve as context clues for that word. These examples, which are in **boldfaced** type, will help you figure out the meaning of each word. Circle the letter of each meaning you think is correct.

Note that examples are often introduced with such signal words and phrases as *including* and *such as*.

1.   *Nocturnal* creatures, such as **bats and owls**, have highly developed senses that enable them to function in the dark.

*Nocturnal* means
a. feathery          b. flying          c. active at night

2.  The *adverse* effects of this drug, including **dizziness, nausea, and headaches,** have caused it to be withdrawn from the market.

    *Adverse* means
    a. deadly              b. harmful              c. expensive

3.  Common *euphemisms* include **"final resting place"** (for *grave*), **"intoxicated"** (for *drunk*), **and "comfort station"** (for *toilet*).

    *Euphemisms* means
    a. unpleasant reactions        b. answers      c. substitutes for offensive terms

    In the first sentence, the examples given of nocturnal creatures—bats and owls—may have helped you to guess that nocturnal creatures are those that are active at night, since bats and owls do come out at night. In the second sentence, the unpleasant side effects mentioned are clues to the meaning of *adverse*, which is "harmful." Finally, as the examples in sentence three indicate, *euphemisms* means "substitutes for offensive terms."

## ➤ *Practice 1*

In each of the sentences below, underline the examples of the italicized word. Then circle the letter of the meaning of the word in italics.

1.  The *meager* meal, consisting of only a spoonful of rice and a few beans, was the most the neglected boy had eaten all day.

    *Meager* means
    a. small              b. sweet              c. filling

2.  Some mentally ill people have *bizarre* ideas. For instance, they may think the TV is talking to them or that others can steal their thoughts.

    *Bizarre* means
    a. very strange        b. realistic          c. creative

3.  There are several common *gambits* used in singles bars, such as "What sign are you?" "How do you like this place?" and "You remind me of someone."

    *Gambits* means
    a. questions          b. conversation starters      c. steps

4.  Since my grandfather retired, he has developed such *avocations* as gardening and long-distance bike riding.

    *Avocations* means
    a. hobbies            b. vacations          c. jobs

5.  In biology class today, the teacher discussed such *anomalies* as two heads and webbed toes.

    *Anomalies* means
    a. groups          b. illnesses          c. abnormalities

## 2  Synonyms

Context clues are often found in the form of *synonyms*: words that mean the same as the unknown word. Synonyms may be purposely included by an author to help readers understand a less familiar word. In such cases, the synonyms are usually set off by special punctuation within the sentence, such as commas, dashes, or parentheses; and they may be introduced by *or* ("Nuptials, or weddings, . . .") and *that is* ("Woolies, that is, knitted wool underwear . . ."). A synonym may also appear anywhere in a sentence as a restatement of the meaning of the unknown word.

In each of the following sentences, the word to be defined is italicized. Underline the synonym for the italicized word in each sentence.

1.  Are you *averse*—opposed to—the decision?

2.  His *naivete*, or innocence, was obvious.

3.  The salesperson tried to *assuage* the angry customer's feelings, but there was no way to soothe her. (*Hint:* Here, a synonym of the italicized word is used later in the sentence to restate the word's meaning.)

You should have underlined "opposed to" as a synonym for *averse*, "innocence" as a synonym for *naivete*, and "soothe" as a synonym for *assuage*. (Remember, by the way, that you can turn to your dictionary whenever you want to learn to pronounce an unfamiliar word.)

## ➤ *Practice 2*

Each sentence below includes a word or phrase that is a synonym of the italicized word. Underline the synonym of the italicized word in each case.

1.  My friend Julie is a great *procrastinator*—she's a person who habitually postpones doing things, from household chores to homework.

2.  Because my father had advised me to *scrutinize* the lease, I took time to carefully examine all the fine print.

3.  The presidential candidate vowed to discuss *pragmatic* solutions to the nation's problems; the American people, he claimed, want practical answers, not empty theory.

4.  A common public-health measure is *quarantine*, or isolating infected patients to prevent their diseases from spreading.

5. Father Gordon decided to lecture on *euthanasia* to the Nurses' Association because there is a great deal of interest in mercy-killing these days.

## 3 Antonyms

*Antonyms*—words and phrases that mean the opposite of a word—are also useful as context clues. Antonyms are often signaled by words and phrases such as *however, but, yet, on the other hand,* and *in contrast.*

In the sentences below, underline the words that mean the *opposite* of the italicized words; then circle the letter of the meaning of each word in italics.

1. My sister Kathy is lively and outgoing; however, I am rather *introverted.*

   *Introverted* means
   a. friendly and helpful     b. quiet and withdrawn     c. strong and athletic

2. Religions in America are not *static*, but changing, especially in this period of shifting values.

   *Static* means
   a. unchanging                b. unknown                c. shifting

3. Many people have pointed out the harmful effects that a working mother may have on the family, yet there are many *salutary* effects as well.

   *Salutary* means
   a. well-known                b. beneficial                c. hurtful

In the first sentence, *introverted* is the opposite of "lively and outgoing"; *introverted* means "quiet and withdrawn." In the second sentence, the opposite of *static* is "changing"; *static* means "unchanging." Last, *salutary effects* are the opposite of "harmful effects"; *salutary* means "beneficial."

## ➤ Practice 3

Each sentence below includes a word or phrase that is an antonym of the italicized word. Underline the antonym of the italicized word in each case. Then, based on these clues, circle the letter of the meaning of the word in italics.

1. He was born to a family that possessed great wealth, but he died in *indigence.*

   *Indigence* means
   a. a hospital                b. an accident                c. poverty

2. Many politicians do not give *succinct* answers to questions, but long, vague ones.

   *Succinct* means
   a. brief and to the point     b. accurate                c. complete

3. "I've caught several students *surreptitiously* checking answer sheets during my exams," said the professor. "However, until today I never saw one openly lay out a cheat sheet on his desk."

   *Surreptitiously* means
   a. legally              b. secretly              c. loudly

4. In the early days of automobile manufacturing, *stringent* laws controlled motorists' speed; in contrast, the laws designed to protect consumers from faulty products were extremely weak.

   *Stringent* means
   a. informal             b. not effective         c. strong

5. While Irma's house is decorated plainly, her clothing is very *flamboyant*.

   *Flamboyant* means
   a. inexpensive          b. flashy                c. washable

# 4   General Sense of the Sentence or Passage

Sometimes it takes a bit more detective work to puzzle out the meaning of an unfamiliar word. In such cases, you must draw conclusions based on the information given with the word. Asking yourself questions about the passage may help you make a fairly accurate guess about the meaning of the unfamiliar word.

Each of the sentences below is followed by a question. Think about the answer to each question, and then circle the letter of the meaning you think is correct.

1. A former employee, *irate* over having been fired, broke into the plant and deliberately wrecked several machines.
   (What would be the employee's state of mind?)

   *Irate* means
   a. relieved             b. very angry            c. undecided

2. Despite the *proximity* of Ron's house to his sister's, he rarely sees her.
   (What about Ron's house would make it surprising that he didn't see his sister more often?)

   *Proximity* means
   a. similarity           b. nearness              c. superiority

3. The car wash we organized to raise funds was a *fiasco*, for it rained all day.
   (How successful would a car wash be on a rainy day?)

   *Fiasco* means
   a. great financial success    b. welcome surprise    c. complete disaster

The first sentence provides enough evidence for you to guess that *irate* means "very angry." *Proximity* in the second sentence means "nearness." And a *fiasco* is a complete disaster. (You may not hit on the exact dictionary definition of a word by using context clues, but you will often be accurate enough to make good sense of what you are reading.)

## ➤ *Practice 4*

Try to answer the question that follows each item below. Then use logical guesses based on each answer to help you circle the letter of the meaning you think is correct.

1. Larry didn't want to take the time to tell Anne the entire plot of the movie so far, so he just gave her the *gist* of the story.
   (What kind of information would Larry give Anne?)

   *Gist* means
   a. ending                b. title                c. main idea

2. The lizard was so *lethargic* that I wasn't sure if it was alive or dead. It didn't even blink.
   (How active is this lizard?)

   *Lethargic* means
   a. green                 b. inactive             c. big

3. After the accident, I was angered when the other driver told the police officer a complete *fabrication* about what happened. He made it seem that I was the only person at fault.
   (How truthful was the other driver's information?)

   *Fabrication* means
   a. lie                   b. description          c. confession

4. The public knows very little about the *covert* activities of CIA spies.
   (What kind of activities would the CIA spies be involved in that the public wouldn't know much about?)

   *Covert* means
   a. public                b. secret               c. family

5. Whether or not there is life in outer space is an *enigma*. We will never know for sure until we are capable of space travel or aliens actually land on our planet.
   (What would we call something to which we have no answer?)

   *Enigma* means
   a. reason                b. certainty            c. mystery

## A NOTE ON TEXTBOOK DEFINITIONS

You don't always have to use context clues or the dictionary to find definitions. Very often, textbook authors provide definitions of important terms. They usually follow a definition with one or more examples to ensure that you understand the word being defined. Here is a short textbook passage that includes a definition and example:

> People do not always satisfy their needs directly; sometimes they use a substitute object. Use of a substitute is known as *displacement*. This is the process that takes place, for instance, when you control your impulse to yell at your boss and then go home and yell at the first member of your family who is unlucky enough to cross your path.

Textbook authors, then, often do more than provide context clues: they define a word and provide examples as well. When they take the time to define and illustrate a word, you should assume that the material is important enough to learn.

More about textbook definitions and examples appears in the "Patterns of Organization" chapter on page 189.

➤ *Review*

To review what you've learned in this chapter, complete each of the following sentences.

1.  Often, a reader can figure out the meaning of a new word without using the dictionary—by paying attention to the word's _____.

2.  One type of clue that helps readers figure out the meaning of a new word is the general sense of a _____.

3.  In the sentence below, which type of context clue is used for the italicized word?

    a. example                 b. antonym                 c. synonym

    You can't take certain courses unless you've taken a *prerequisite*; for instance, you can't take Spanish Literature I unless you've taken Spanish III.

4.  In the sentence below, which type of context clue is used for the italicized word?

    a. example                 b. antonym                 c. synonym

    There are thick pine forests at the foot of the mountain, but higher up, the trees become *sparse*.

5.  Often when textbook authors introduce a new word, they provide you with a _____ and follow it with _____ that help make the meaning of the word clear.

## VOCABULARY IN CONTEXT: Test A-1

Figure out the meanings of the following five words by studying them in context. Then complete the matching and fill-in test that follows.

| | | |
|---|---|---|
| 1 | **elicit**<br>(i-lis′-it) | Elizabeth Taylor's violet eyes always **elicit** admiration and wonder.<br><br>Peter's jokes are in such bad taste that they **elicit** looks of disgust instead of laughter. |
| 2 | **fortify**<br>(fôr′-tə-fī′) | Babies need milk to **fortify** their bones.<br><br>The builders plan to **fortify** the old tower with steel beams. |
| 3 | **indolent**<br>(in′-də-lənt) | Sue is so **indolent** that she thinks if she works five minutes, she deserves a coffee break.<br><br>My uncle has been fired from three jobs for being **indolent**. He shows up on time, but he does little work and leaves early. |
| 4 | **persistent**<br>(pər-sis′-tənt) | At first Tony wouldn't go out with Lola, but she was **persistent** in asking him. Now they're engaged.<br><br>I am a very **persistent** salesman. I work with customers for as long as it takes for them to buy something. |
| 5 | **skeptical**<br>(skep′-ti-kəl) | Jessica's family is so rich that she is **skeptical** about any man who asks her out. She wonders if he's interested in her or in her money.<br><br>I am **skeptical** about the articles on movie stars and space aliens in supermarket newspapers. My brother, however, believes every word he reads in those papers. |

**A.** Match each word with its definition.

1. elicit    _____ refusing to quit; stubbornly continuing

2. fortify    _____ to draw forth

3. indolent    _____ to strengthen

4. persistent    _____ doubting; questioning

5. skeptical    _____ lazy; avoiding or disliking work

*(Continues on next page)*

B. Fill in each blank with one of the words in the box. Use each word once.

| | | |
|---|---|---|
| elicit | fortify | indolent |
| persistent | skeptical | |

6. The night before running the marathon, Elsa will probably
_____ herself by eating a large plate of pasta.

7. My mother's rose garden is so gorgeous that it _____s
compliments from strangers who pass by.

8. When the roofer gave us an estimate that was much lower than what others
charged, we became _____ about the quality of his
work.

9. My sister is so _____ that the most work she ever does
is pushing the remote control to switch the TV channel.

10. Abby was _____ in her efforts to change the Little
League's boys-only rule. After seven months of trying, she was finally
allowed to join the team.

# VOCABULARY IN CONTEXT: Test A-2

Figure out the meanings of the following five words by studying them in context. Then complete the matching and fill-in test that follows.

1 **blunt**
(blunt)

"I'll be **blunt**," Phil said, as plainspoken as ever. "You're a jerk."

Kay can be **blunt** to the point of cruelty. She once told a guy that she'd never date him because he's so short.

2 **deplore**
(di-plōr′)

Martin Luther King, Jr., **deplored** all bigotry.

Some people who **deplore** child pornography are working for stricter laws against the practice.

3 **provoke**
(prə-vōk′)

"Mr. Jackson **provoked** me by saying nasty things about my mother, so I hit him," Terry told the judge.

My father is slow to anger, but this morning my sister's wisecracks began to **provoke** him.

4 **revitalize**
(rē-vīt′-ə-līz′)

If Dwight is tired after work, he finds a brief nap will **revitalize** him for a night on the town with friends.

The City Council hopes to **revitalize** the currently lifeless shopping district by offering tax breaks for new businesses.

5 **scrutiny**
(scroōt′-ə-nē)

Store security guards keep people with large bags under careful **scrutiny**, since the bags may be used to shoplift.

Before being published, a book comes under the **scrutiny** of a proofreader, who examines it for grammar and spelling errors.

A. Match each word with its definition.

1. blunt _____ to feel or express disapproval of

2. deplore _____ close inspection; careful examination

3. provoke _____ to renew the strength and energy of; to restore to a vigorous, active condition

4. revitalize _____ rudely brief and straightforward

5. scrutiny _____ to stir up anger or resentment in someone

*(Continues on next page)*

**B.** Fill in each blank with one of the words in the box. Use each word once.

| | | |
|---|---|---|
| blunt | deplore | provoke |
| revitalize | scrutiny | |

6. If the teacher had been _____, she would have told Kevin his essay was terrible. Instead, she politely said, "It could use much more work."

7. Dusty usually doesn't let his older sister's teasing _____ him, but he gets angry whenever she calls him "baby."

8. Federal agents kept the house of the suspected terrorists under _____ for weeks, but no unusual behavior was seen.

9. No one _____s drinking and driving more than Elena, whose son was killed by a drunk driver.

10. The African violets in my kitchen aren't doing well. Do you think some fertilizer would _____ them?

## VOCABULARY IN CONTEXT: Test A-3

Figure out the meanings of the following five words by studying them in context. Then complete the matching and fill-in test that follows.

1  **apathy**
   (ap′-ə-thē)

Since voter **apathy** was high, the turnout on election day was very low.

Student **apathy** turned to intense interest when the psychology teacher discussed Freud's views on sex.

2  **ecstatic**
   (ek-stat′-ik)

I wouldn't be just glad if I won the lottery; I'd be **ecstatic**.

The smallest thing, like a cherry popsicle on a hot day or a ladybug in the grass, can make a child **ecstatic**.

3  **longevity**
   (lon-jev′-i-tē)

The animal with the greatest **longevity** is the giant land tortoise, which can live several hundred years.

Volvos and Hondas, known for their **longevity**, outlast more expensive cars.

4  **prone**
   (prōn)

Mr. Walker is **prone** to high blood pressure, so he limits his salt intake.

**Prone** to fits of laughter during class, Chris sometimes controls the impulse by biting into his pen.

5  **revert**
   (ri-vûrt′)

After his release from jail, Sam **reverted** to his old habit of stealing.

Helene gave up smoking while she was pregnant, but she **reverted** to smoking a pack a day after her daughter was born.

A. Match each word with its definition.

1. apathy          _____ having a tendency; inclined

2. ecstatic        _____ a long span of life

3. longevity       _____ lack of interest and concern

4. prone (to)      _____ to return to a previous habit, opinion, or condition

5. revert (to)     _____ extremely joyful

*(Continues on next page)*

**B.** Fill in each blank with one of the words in the box. Use each word once.

| | | |
|---|---|---|
| apathy | ecstatic | longevity |
| prone | revert | |

6. Nan is _____ to accidents, so her car insurance rates are quite high.

7. My brother vowed to eat only one Oreo a day, but I'm afraid he'll _____ to his old habit of eating the entire bag of cookies at one sitting.

8. Research suggests that our parents' _____ doesn't necessarily affect how long we will live.

9. Sidewalk litter is a sign of _____, showing that people don't care about a clean environment.

10. "I'm _____," said Dinah on the day of her divorce. "I wasn't even this happy on my wedding day."

# VOCABULARY IN CONTEXT: Test B-1

Figure out the meanings of the following five words by studying them in context. Then complete the matching and fill-in test that follows.

1 **condone**
(kən-dōn′)

The reason I don't **condone** Barb's habit of smoking is that it hurts those around her as well as herself.

I can overlook it when you're five minutes late. But how can I **condone** your coming to work an hour late?

2 **inept**
(in-ept′)

I am so **inept** at carpentry that a hammer in my hand is a dangerous weapon.

Since the actress was **inept** at playing comic characters, she tried out only for dramatic roles.

3 **innovation**
(in′-ə-vā′-shən)

When commercial bakers first offered sliced bread, it was considered an exciting **innovation**.

A medical **innovation** called a PET scan can show which parts of a person's brain are most active.

4 **relevant**
(rel′-ə-vənt)

Your statement isn't **relevant**—it has nothing to do with our conversation.

"The weather is not **relevant** to my question," Yvonne's mother said. "Don't change the subject when I bring up your speeding tickets."

5 **venture**
(ven′-chər)

Instead of hiring a lawyer, the defendant will **venture** pleading her own case in court.

"I'll **venture** going on any ride in this amusement park except the Twister," said Nick. "I'll risk getting sick to my stomach, but I won't risk my life."

A. Match each word with its definition.

1. condone _____ related to the matter at hand; to the point

2. inept _____ to forgive or overlook

3. innovation _____ to dare; to risk

4. relevant _____ a new custom, method, or invention; something newly introduced

5. venture _____ unskillful

*(Continues on next page)*

**B.** Fill in each blank with one of the words in the box. Use each word once.

| | | |
|---|---|---|
| condone | inept | innovation |
| relevant | venture | |

6. At tomorrow's staff meeting, I will _____ to say what I really think and cross my fingers that I don't get fired.

7. When you do a research paper, you need to find _____ evidence—evidence that relates to the points you are trying to make.

8. An interesting _____ in food packaging is a bottle from which salad dressing is squirted, rather than poured.

9. "I can't stop you," Ms. Mather told her daughter, "but neither can I _____ your plan to live with Allen without being married to him."

10. I'm so _____ at bowling that I usually roll the ball into the gutter. Once I actually released the ball behind me, and it rolled onto someone's toes.

# VOCABULARY IN CONTEXT: Test B-2

Figure out the meanings of the following five words by studying them in context. Then complete the matching and fill-in test that follows.

1 **aloof**
(ə-lōof′)

Some people say that the English are **aloof,** but the ones I've met seem warm and open.

I knew that Taylor was upset with me about something because he was **aloof** even when I tried to be friendly.

2 **enhance**
(en-hans′)

Our gym teacher **enhanced** her appearance with a more attractive haircut.

The college catalogue stated that the writing course would "**enhance** all students' writing skills" by improving their grammar and style.

3 **ironic**
(ī-ron′-ik)

Isn't it **ironic** that the richest man in town should win the million dollar lottery?

It's **ironic** that Loretta is such a strict mother because she was certainly wild in her youth.

4 **oblivious**
(ə-bliv′-ē-əs)

It's easy to spot two people in love. They are the ones who, **oblivious** to everyone else present, see only each other.

The chatty, slow-moving sales clerk seemed **oblivious** to the long line of impatient customers at his checkout.

5 **sedentary**
(sed′-ən-ter′-ē)

Bus drivers, writers, and others in **sedentary** occupations need to make a special effort to exercise.

My **sedentary** girlfriend jokes that the most exercise she ever gets is between her front door and the car.

A. Match each word with its definition.

1. aloof        _____ being opposite to what might be expected

2. enhance       _____ cool and reserved; distant in personal relations

3. ironic        _____ unaware of; failing to notice

4. oblivious     _____ characterized by much sitting; accustomed to much sitting

5. sedentary     _____ to improve; to strengthen

*(Continues on next page)*

**B.** Fill in each blank with one of the words in the box. Use each word once.

| | | |
|---|---|---|
| aloof | enhance | ironic |
| oblivious | sedentary | |

6. Balancing a book on one's head is supposed to _____ one's posture.

7. When I'm frightened, I try to appear _____—looking cool and distant helps me feel in control.

8. Since Granddad retired, he's been interested only in _____ activities. Grandma wants to get up and do things, but he wants to read and watch TV.

9. The driver continued into the intersection, apparently _____ to the fact that the light had turned red.

10. "The Gift of the Magi" is a short story with a(n) _____ twist: A woman sells her long hair to buy a chain for her husband's watch, and her husband sells his watch to buy combs for her hair.

# VOCABULARY IN CONTEXT: Test B-3

Figure out the meanings of the following five words by studying them in context. Then complete the matching and fill-in test that follows.

1 **benign**
(bi-nīn')

In his usual **benign** manner, my neighbor carefully picked up the ant in his kitchen, brought it outside, and gently put it down on the sidewalk.

Finding a stranger on our doorstep startled me, but the **benign** expression on his face told me not to worry.

2 **detract**
(di-trakt')

Julius thinks the scar on his cheek **detracts** from his good looks, but it's barely noticeable.

All of the litter in the park certainly **detracts** from the beauty of the trees and flowers.

3 **implore**
(im-plōr')

The princess **implored** the evil magician to spare the handsome prince's life.

Victor **implored** his parents over and over to let him buy a motorcycle, but they consider motorcycles too dangerous.

4 **pathetic**
(pə-thet'-ik)

That plumber's work was **pathetic**. Not only does the faucet still drip, but now the pipe is leaking.

Health care in some areas of the world is **pathetic**. People are dying of diseases that are easily treatable with modern medicine.

5 **rationale**
(rash'-ə-nal')

Danielle's **rationale** for majoring in business was simple. "I want to make a lot of money," she said.

The **rationale** for raising the drinking age to 21 is that self-control and good judgment usually increase with age.

A. Match each word with its definition.

1. benign    _____ pitifully lacking or unsuccessful; so inadequate as to be ridiculous

2. detract   _____ to beg or plead

3. implore   _____ kindly; gentle; not harmful

4. pathetic  _____ the reasons for something; logical basis

5. rationale _____ to lessen what is admirable or worthwhile about something

*(Continues on next page)*

**B.** Fill in each blank with one of the words in the box. Use each word once.

| | | |
|---|---|---|
| benign | detract | implore |
| pathetic | rationale | |

6. My sit-ups are _____. They're so weak that they look like neck-ups.

7. People talking in a movie theater greatly _____ from the experience of watching a film.

8. Please hide those Hershey bars, and don't tell me where they are no matter how much I _____ you.

9. Gorilla mothers, usually loving and _____, can become abusive to their babies when caged with them.

10. When asked to explain the _____ behind his decision to divorce, Ed had two strong reasons—his wife's two affairs.

# VOCABULARY IN CONTEXT: Test C-1

Figure out the meanings of the following five words by studying them in context.
Then complete the matching and fill-in test that follows.

1 **gape**
(gāp)

Everyone stopped to **gape** at the odd-looking sculpture in front of the library.

Because drivers slowed to **gape** at an accident in the southbound lanes, northbound traffic backed up for miles.

2 **intricate**
(in′-trə-kit)

It was amazing to see the **intricate** gold and silver jewelry that ancient Indians made with only simple tools. It obviously required great patience and skill to create such complex ornaments.

*War and Peace* is a long, **intricate** novel that weaves together the detailed life stories of many individuals.

3 **mobile**
(mō′-bəl)

My parents own a **mobile** home, which can be moved from place to place on a long truck.

When I was a bedridden hospital patient, the highlight of my days was the **mobile** library that a volunteer wheeled into my room each morning.

4 **persevere**
(pûr′-sə-vēr′)

"I know you're tired," Jack said, "but we've got to **persevere** and get to the camp before the storm hits."

It was not easy to attend English classes while working two jobs, but Nina **persevered** until she could speak English well.

5 **squander**
(skwon′-dər)

It's sad to see such a wonderful artist **squander** her talent designing labels for baked bean cans.

By examining her recent expenses, Coretta realized that she had **squandered** money on too many expensive meals.

**A.** Match each word with its definition.

1. gape _____ having many parts arranged in a complicated way; complex

2. intricate _____ to waste

3. mobile _____ to continue with an effort or plan despite difficulties

4. persevere _____ to stare in wonder or amazement

5. squander _____ moving or able to move from place to place

*(Continues on next page)*

B. Fill in each blank with one of the words in the box. Use each word once.

| | | |
|---|---|---|
| gape | intricate | mobile |
| persevere | squander | |

6. The company lunchroom now closes promptly at one o'clock so that workers can't _____ time on long lunch breaks.

7. Several pedestrians stopped to _____ at the homeless man and his small shelter, made of cardboard and a torn blanket.

8. At the concert, I sat behind a woman with a(n) _____ hairstyle. Numerous intertwined braids wound about the back of her head.

9. Learning the computer program was difficult, but when Maria realized how useful it would be in her work, she was glad she had _____(e)d.

10. My mother is unable to walk, but with her wheelchair she is _____ enough to get around her one-story home, move along a sidewalk, and even shop at a mall.

# VOCABULARY IN CONTEXT: Test C-2

Figure out the meanings of the following five words by studying them in context. Then complete the matching and fill-in test that follows.

1 **benevolent**
(bə-nev′-ə-lənt)

My grandmother is one of the most **benevolent** people I know. She's always doing something kind.

Henry Burton, in a poem, gave good advice on being **benevolent**: "Have you had a kindness shown? Pass it on."

2 **esteem**
(e-stēm′)

The critics held the play in such high **esteem** that they voted it "Best Play of the Year."

When Mr. Crane retired after teaching gym and coaching for thirty years, his admiring students gave him a gold whistle as a sign of their **esteem**.

3 **incorporate**
(in-kôr′-pə-rāt′)

Jerry **incorporated** all of his favorite desserts into one: a chocolate-covered banana-cream pecan pie.

Since my brother and I live next door to each other, we've **incorporated** our backyards into one big playground for our children.

4 **rupture**
(rup′-chər)

When the pressure in the gas pipe became too great, the pipe **ruptured**.

The bulge in the baby's stomach was caused by a muscle wall that **ruptured** and would have to be repaired.

5 **wary**
(wâr′-ē)

It's wise to be **wary** when walking through an unfamiliar neighborhood at night.

I'm a little **wary** of people who, when they first meet me, treat me as if I'm their best friend.

A. Match each word with its definition.

1. benevolent _____ to burst or break apart

2. esteem _____ kind; charitable

3. incorporate _____ cautious; on one's guard; careful

4. rupture _____ to unite into a single whole; combine

5. wary _____ a high regard; respect; favorable opinion

*(Continues on next page)*

**B.** Fill in each blank with one of the words in the box. Use each word once.

| benevolent | esteem | incorporate |
|---|---|---|
| rupture | wary | |

6. Someone has managed to _____ a tomato and a potato into one plant.

7. People don't really know how _____ Mr. Wallace is since he tries to help others in private.

8. If the dam were to _____, the town would disappear under many feet of water.

9. To show his _____ for her singing, the talent agent sent Mary lilacs after she performed in a local theatre.

10. Whoever said "There's no such thing as a free lunch" was telling us to be _____ about promises of something for nothing.

# VOCABULARY IN CONTEXT: Test C-3

Figure out the meanings of the following five words by studying them in context. Then complete the matching and fill-in test that follows.

1 **ambivalent**
(am-biv′-ə-lənt)

"Because I'm **ambivalent** about marriage," Earl said, "I keep swinging back and forth between wanting to set the date and wanting to break off my engagement."

I'm **ambivalent** about my mother-in-law. I appreciate her desire to help, but I dislike her efforts to run our lives.

2 **cursory**
(kûr′-sə-rē)

Most people do only a **cursory** job of brushing their teeth. But to avoid cavities, you must take time to brush carefully.

Because I had to work late, I had only enough time to give my apartment a **cursory** cleaning before my parents arrived.

3 **empathy**
(em′-pə-thē)

Families who have lost loved ones in Vietnam have **empathy** for one another because of their shared grief.

Ms. Allan is an excellent career counselor partly because of her great **empathy**. She understands each student's feelings and point of view.

4 **lucrative**
(lōō′-krə-tiv)

Investments in the stock market can be **lucrative**. However, they can also result in great financial loss.

"Teaching at a small college isn't **lucrative**," Professor Baum admitted, "but I never cared to make much money."

5 **quest**
(kwest)

During Carlos' **quest** for the perfect pizza, he sampled the cheese pizza at twenty-seven different restaurants.

Ponce de Leon's **quest** was for the the Fountain of Youth; what he found instead was Florida.

A. Match each word with its definition.

1. ambivalent _____ profitable; well-paying

2. cursory _____ the ability to share in someone else's feelings or thoughts

3. empathy _____ done quickly and without attention to detail

4. lucrative _____ a search; hunt

5. quest _____ having conflicting feelings about someone or something

*(Continues on next page)*

**B.** Fill in each blank with one of the words in the box. Use each word once.

| | | |
|---|---|---|
| ambivalent | cursory | empathy |
| lucrative | quest | |

6. Acting is _____ for only a small percentage of performers. The rest need additional sources of income, such as waiting on tables or driving a cab.

7. "I'm _____ about the dress," Anita said. "I like the style, but not that green-yellow color."

8. Many scientists worldwide are active in the _____ for a cure for cancer.

9. Margo couldn't identify the driver of the car. She'd given him only a _____ glance at the time of the accident.

10. Because adults were once kids, they often have _____ for children. Kids, on the other hand, rarely identify with adults.

## VOCABULARY IN CONTEXT: Test D-1

Figure out the meanings of the following five words by studying them in context. Then complete the matching and fill-in test that follows.

1  **deter**
(di-tûr′)

To **deter** burglars, my father put a sign on our lawns that says, "Beware of German shepherd."

Being totally deaf did not **deter** Beethoven from composing one of his most loved works, his *Ninth Symphony.*

2  **escalate**
(es′-kə-lāt′)

As George's anger increases, his blood pressure also **escalates**.

The fight between the two hockey players **escalated** into an all-out battle among members of both teams.

3  **mandatory**
(man′-də-tōr′-ē)

"A research paper isn't **mandatory**," the instructor said, "but if you write one, you'll get extra credit."

"Since automobile insurance is **mandatory**," Dad said, "you have no choice but to pay the high rates."

4  **perception**
(pər-sep′-shən)

Brenda's **perceptions** of others are usually accurate. She is able to size people up quickly.

Our **perceptions** of the problem differ. Rob thinks money is the main issue, but I believe it's a question of who controls the purse strings.

5  **recession**
(ri-sesh′-ən)

The department store laid off twenty workers during the **recession**, but it rehired them when business improved.

While seashore businesses suffer a **recession** in the winter, they do very well from spring to fall.

**A.** Match each word with its definition.

1. deter       _____ to increase or intensify

2. escalate       _____ a temporary decline in business

3. mandatory       _____ to prevent from doing something; to discourage

4. perception       _____ required

5. recession       _____ an impression; the way someone or something is viewed

*(Continues on next page)*

**B.** Fill in each blank with one of the words in the box. Use each word once.

| | | |
|---|---|---|
| deter | escalate | mandatory |
| perception | recession | |

6. Opponents of the death penalty say it does not actually _____ anyone from committing murder.

7. An entrance fee wasn't _____, but a sign suggested that visitors make a donation.

8. The shouting match between Rose and her brother _____(e)d until it was so loud that the neighbors complained.

9. Floyd's _____ of human nature is strongly colored by some bad experiences. He thinks everyone is basically selfish.

10. The whole town went into a(n) _____ when the shoe factory closed because the laid-off workers had no money to spend in local businesses.

## VOCABULARY IN CONTEXT: Test D-2

Figure out the meanings of the following five words by studying them in context. Then complete the matching and fill-in test that follows.

1  **elation**
   (i-lā′-shən)

The principal shouted with **elation** when the school team scored the winning touchdown.

Although Gene was overjoyed and proud to have won the Senate race, he was too tired to show **elation**.

2  **intrinsic**
   (in-trin′-sik)

Trust is **intrinsic** to any good friendship.

Because Lee Ann has an **intrinsic** desire to learn, she doesn't need the reward of good grades to motivate her studies.

3  **mortify**
   (môr′-tə-fī′)

It would **mortify** me if my voice were to crack during my choir solo.

James was completely **mortified** when he proposed and Carla just laughed in his face.

4  **redundant**
   (ri-dun′-dənt)

Eric's teacher wrote "**redundant**" in several spots in his essay which were wordy and too repetitive.

My aunt's letters are annoyingly **redundant**, always repeating the "news" of previous letters.

5  **waive**
   (wāv)

The defendant decided to **waive** his right to an attorney and, instead, speak for himself in court.

Since Lin had studied so much math on her own, the school **waived** the requirement that she take high school algebra.

A.  Match each word with its definition.

1.  elation       _____  to humiliate or embarrass

2.  intrinsic     _____  a feeling of great joy or pride

3.  mortify       _____  wordy or needlessly repetitive

4.  redundant     _____  to willingly give up (as a claim, privilege, or right); do without

5.  waive         _____  belonging to a person or thing by its very nature (and thus not dependent on circumstances)

*(Continues on next page)*

**B.** Fill in each blank with one of the words in the box. Use each word once.

| | | |
|---|---|---|
| elation | intrinsic | mortify |
| redundant | waive | |

6. The TV ad for a headache medicine was so _____ that it gave me a headache! The name of the product was repeated at least a dozen times.

7. When he received the college scholarship, my brother felt such _____ that he wept with joy.

8. Lassie has the qualities of loyalty and affection that seem _____ to most dogs.

9. The old man decided to _____ any claim he had to the family fortune, preferring to see the money go to the younger generation.

10. I doubt if anything will ever _____ me more than the streamer of toilet paper that clung to my shoe as I returned from the ladies' room to rejoin my date in a fancy restaurant.

## VOCABULARY IN CONTEXT: Test D-3

Figure out the meanings of the following five words by studying them in context. Then complete the matching and fill-in test that follows.

1 **bizarre**
(bi-zär′)

The woman's **bizarre** makeup included white lipstick and eyebrow pencil lines that could have been drawn on with Magic Markers.

Wally's outfits may seem **bizarre**, but if you see him with his stranger-looking friends, his dress looks quite ordinary.

2 **detrimental**
(de′-trə-men′-təl)

Do you think all television is **detrimental** to children or that some programs are good for kids?

Even something as healthy-sounding as vitamins can be **detrimental** to your health when taken in large quantities.

3 **encounter**
(en-koun′-ter)

Some people claim to have **encountered** space aliens, but there is no convincing evidence of such meetings.

My brothers had planned to meet in the department store, but they **encountered** each other in the parking lot.

4 **interim**
(in′-tər-im)

Our secretary left last week, and the new one arrives next month. In the **interim**, we have to do our own typing.

The baby takes her nap between 2 to 4 p.m. During that **interim**, the house is fairly peaceful.

5 **pseudonym**
(sood′-ə-nim)

When writing a personal story for a family magazine, Bev used a **pseudonym.** She didn't want everyone in town to know about her problems.

Samuel Langhorne Clemens wasn't the first author to use the **pseudonym** Mark Twain. A newspaper writer of the time used the same pen name.

A. Match each word with its definition.

1. bizarre          _____   to meet unexpectedly; come upon

2. detrimental    _____   dramatically unusual, as in manner or appearance; odd

3. encounter      _____   the period of time in between; meantime

4. interim          _____   a false name used by an author

5. pseudonym    _____   harmful

*(Continues on next page)*

**B.** Fill in each blank with one of the words in the box. Use each word once.

| | | |
|---|---|---|
| bizarre | detrimental | encounter |
| interim | pseudonym | |

6. Halloween offers everyone the chance to look as _____ as possible.

7. I dislike returning to my small hometown, where I am likely to _____ people who knew me as a troubled kid.

8. The gases from automobiles and factories have been so _____ to the environment that some of the damage may be permanent.

9. Cassie hadn't seen her nephews for years. During that long _____, they had grown from rascals into serious young men.

10. A well-known political writer signed a humorous essay he wrote with a _____. He didn't want readers who knew him to expect a serious piece.

## VOCABULARY IN CONTEXT: Test E-1

Figure out the meanings of the following five words by studying them in context. Then complete the matching and fill-in test that follows.

1 **alleviate**
(ə-lē′-vē-āt′)

I took some aspirin to **alleviate** my pounding headache.

To **alleviate** his loneliness, the widower moved closer to his daughter and her family.

2 **evoke**
(i-vōk′)

The smells of cider, pumpkin pie, and burning leaves all **evoke** thoughts of autumn.

Although the horror movie was meant to **evoke** fear, Jon found the purple monsters only laughable.

3 **flagrant**
(flā′-grənt)

The congressman's use of campaign funds for his private business was a **flagrant** violation of the law.

In **flagrant** disregard of his parents' wishes, Art wore a T-shirt and jeans to the dinner party.

4 **gist**
(jist)

The **gist** of the novel is that a family got stranded on an island and had to struggle to survive.

We asked Alex to skip the details and get right to the **gist** of the argument he had with his boss.

5 **paradox**
(par′-ə-doks′)

My mother used to recite this **paradox** to my father: "When a husband brings his wife flowers for no reason, there's a reason."

When Joan kept postponing her decision about whether or not to go back to school, I reminded her of the **paradox** "No decision is also a decision."

A. Match each word with its definition.

1. alleviate _____ to draw forth, as a mental image or a feeling

2. evoke _____ a statement that seems contradictory yet may be true

3. flagrant _____ to relieve; make easier to bear

4. gist _____ shockingly obvious; outrageous

5. paradox _____ the main point or essential part of a matter; central idea

*(Continues on next page)*

**B.** Fill in each blank with one of the words in the box. Use each word once.

| | | |
|---|---|---|
| alleviate | evoke | flagrant |
| gist | paradox | |

6. When Charlene lost her job because she spoke up for a fellow employee, it was a(n) _____ violation of her union rights.

7. Ron has decided to become a nurse; it appeals to him to help people _____ their pain.

8. The photos in my album _____ many fond memories of my high school friends.

9. When Chun's parents said they worried when he didn't call them, he said, "Remember that well-known _____—no news is good news."

10. The _____ of Kelly's essay was that school should be open only four days a week, from 8 a.m. to 6 p.m.

## VOCABULARY IN CONTEXT: Test E-2

Figure out the meanings of the following five words by studying them in context. Then complete the matching and fill-in test that follows.

1  **conventional**
   (kən-ven′-shə-nəl)

Barb's work is hardly **conventional**—she owns and operates a day-care center for pets.

If the **conventional** method of opening a jar doesn't work, try first wrapping a rubber band around the lid.

2  **designate**
   (dez′-ig-nāt′)

At the party, Betty drank soda rather than beer, so her friends **designated** her driver for the trip home.

The presidential candidate gets to **designate** who will run for vice president.

3  **intimidate**
   (in-tim′-i-dāt′)

"Don't try to **intimidate** me with your threats of blackmail," said Bugsy. "I don't frighten easily."

Will's huge size **intimidates** strangers, but anyone who knows him realizes that he's a very gentle man.

4  **precedent**
   (pres′-i–dənt)

When Jean's employer gave her three months off after her baby was born, a **precedent** was set for any other woman in the firm who became pregnant.

Lawyers can strengthen a case by citing a useful **precedent** among previous similar cases.

5  **subjective**
   (səb-jek′-tiv)

Mary, a highly **subjective** judge of her son's abilities, feels he's brilliant in every respect. The boy's father, however, has a more unbiased view of him.

The reporter refused to write about his friend's trial. He knew any story he wrote would be too **subjective** to be published as an unbiased article.

A.  Match each word with its definition.

1.  conventional _____ based on personal opinions, feelings, and attitudes; biased; not objective

2.  designate _____ anything that may serve as an example in dealing with later similar circumstances

3.  intimidate _____ customary; ordinary

4.  precedent _____ to make timid, or afraid; frighten

5.  subjective _____ to name to an office or duty; appoint

*(Continues on next page)*

**B.** Fill in each blank with one of the words in the box. Use each word once.

| | | |
|---|---|---|
| conventional | designate | intimidate |
| precedent | subjective | |

6. No matter how knowledgeable the critics may be, movie reviews are always

   _____ because they represent the critics' personal
   choices.

7. A co-worker was _____(e)d to give Vonnie the
   "Employee of the Year" award at the banquet.

8. It's better to get children's cooperation through setting shared goals than by

   trying to _____ them with threats of punishment.

9. Dad had wanted to propose to my mother in the _____
   manner, so in the middle of a restaurant, he got down on his knees.

10. "I'd like to give you a day off to go to the World Series," said Calvin's boss.

    "But I'd be setting a(n) _____ that other
    employees would use to go to events they'd want to see."

# VOCABULARY IN CONTEXT: Test E-3

Figure out the meanings of the following five words by studying them in context. Then complete the matching and fill-in test that follows.

| | | |
|---|---|---|
| 1 | **altruistic**<br>(al'-trōō-is'-tik) | "I'm not often **altruistic**," Brett admitted. "I usually put my own welfare first."<br><br>When an enemy approaches, ground squirrels show **altruistic** behavior. They risk their own lives to give alarm calls to nearby relatives. |
| 2 | **charisma**<br>(kə-riz'-mə) | John Kennedy's **charisma**, perhaps even more than his policies, brought him widespread support.<br><br>Though some movie stars are short on talent, they have a **charisma** that makes people want to see their films. |
| 3 | **dilemma**<br>(di-lem'-ə) | The manager faced a **dilemma**: should she arrest an elderly, needy man or ignore store rules about shoplifters?<br><br>In old romantic stories, the heroine's **dilemma** often involves choosing between a rich boyfriend and the poor man she really loves. |
| 4 | **flippant**<br>(flip'-ənt) | Kim stayed after school a half hour for not bringing her homework and another half hour for her **flippant** excuse—"My goldfish ate it."<br><br>My brother hides his lack of confidence by being **flippant**. He rarely treats anything seriously. |
| 5 | **sinister**<br>(sin'-i-stər) | In the movie, a mad scientist thought up the **sinister** scheme of releasing a deadly virus. His evil plot failed when he died from the virus himself.<br><br>The Joker's name is misleading, for he's a **sinister** man who takes pleasure in doing evil, including trying to get rid of Batman. |

A. Match each word with its definition.

1. altruistic   _____ a situation requiring a difficult choice

2. charisma   _____ unselfishly concerned for the welfare of others

3. dilemma   _____ evil; wicked

4. flippant   _____ the quality of a leader which captures great popular devotion; personal magnetism; charm

5. sinister   _____ disrespectful and not serious enough

*(Continues on next page)*

**B.** Fill in each blank with one of the words in the box. Use each word once.

| | | |
|---|---|---|
| altruistic | charisma | dilemma |
| flippant | sinister | |

6. When, for the third time, I told my son to clean his room, he gave this
_____ response: "Why should I? I just cleaned it last
month."

7. Her numerous fans worldwide show that Great Britain's Princess Diana
certainly has _____.

8. The novel *Rosemary's Baby* concerns the _____ plans of a
group of devil-worshippers.

9. I'm facing a(n) _____. Do I tell the truth and risk losing
Lori's friendship, or do I conceal the fact that her boyfriend has been asking
me out?

10. A(n) _____ person might prefer a low-paying job with a
charitable organization over a high-paying corporate job.

# 2

# Main Ideas

Read the following paragraph:

> Many bosses share two weaknesses. First, they are often poor communicators. They tell people what to do and how and when to do it, without explaining the reasons for their rules, and they do not welcome feedback or questions. In addition, many bosses are not well-rounded people. Their jobs tend to be their lives, and they expect everybody who works for them to think and act the way they do. These bosses frown upon hearing that a family matter will keep an employee from working late, and they come out of their office looking irritated if there is too much talk or laughter during a coffee break.

More than any other skill, the key to good comprehension is recognizing the main idea. The basic question you must ask about any selection that you read is, "What is the main point the author is trying to make?" To answer such a question, it is often useful first to determine what topic is being discussed. In the above paragraph, for example, the topic is "many bosses"; the main idea about the topic "many bosses" is that they "share two weaknesses." The rest of the paragraph then supports that idea by detailing the two weaknesses.

The purpose of this and the following chapter is to give you a solid sense of the key parts in any communication: the *topic*, the *main idea* about the topic, and the *supporting details* that develop the main idea.

## AN OVERVIEW: TOPIC, MAIN IDEA, SUPPORTING DETAILS

To fully understand any selection that you read, it is important to find the main idea and its supporting details. One way to find the main idea is to use a two-step process:

1　Find the topic.

2　Then find the writer's primary point about that topic. You will now have the main idea.

Any selection that you read will be about a particular *topic*. The topic is a selection's general subject. The topic of a paragraph, for example, might be "My Roommate."

*Topic:* My Roommate

In contrast, the *main idea* is the writer's primary point *about* the subject. The main idea of the paragraph on the roommate might be that the roommate is messy.

*Topic:* My Roommate
*Main idea:* My roommate is messy.

The rest of the paragraph might be a few sentences that give examples of the messiness. Imagine that you have a sloppy roommate. Write down in the space below two examples of his or her behavior:

*Topic:* My Roommate
*Main idea:* My roommate is messy.
*Supporting details:*

_____

_____

Compare what you have written with my experience. I had a messy dorm roommate in my first year at college. He threw his dirty laundry under his bed and let it stay there for weeks. He brought with him to school his collection of a hundred-plus copies of *Playboy* magazines, and they were everywhere in the room: on the bed, chairs, his desk, chest of drawers, the floor. He also piled on any horizontal surface his clothes, empty soda cans, notebooks, crumpled pizza boxes, letters, newspapers, and so on. He was a nice enough guy who did not quite have his life under control, and he disappeared from school by mid-semester.

I could easily write a paragraph about my roommate. The topic would be my roommate, the main idea would be that he was messy, and the evidence would be supporting details such as the ones I provide above. My paragraph would be typical of paragraphs in general: it would have a topic, a main idea about the topic, and details that develop the main idea.

Note that in longer selections made up of many paragraphs, such as articles or textbook chapters, there is an overall main idea called the *central point* or *thesis*. There will also be a number of intermediate and smaller main ideas within a long selection.

This chapter focuses on finding the main idea in a paragraph, and the next chapter focuses on identifying supporting details. Once you can identify main ideas and details on the level of the paragraph, you can begin to identify them as well in the longer selections that are included in this book.

## MORE ON USING THE TOPIC TO FIND THE MAIN IDEA

Remember that the *topic* is the subject of a selection. It is a general term that can usually be expressed in a few words. Textbooks typically give the overall topic of each chapter in the title of the chapter; they also provide many topics and subtopics in boldface headings within the chapter. Most magazine and journal articles, as well, give you the topic in the title of the piece.

To find the topic of a selection for which there is no title, ask the simple question, "Who or what is the selection about?" Ask this question as you read carefully the paragraph that follows. Then write, on the line below, what you think the topic is.

*Topic:* _____

Extrasensory perception, or ESP, is an area that fascinates people. However, ESP is not documented by any convincing evidence. For instance, it would seem that ESP would be an excellent way of winning at games of chance, such as are played at gambling casinos. But casino owners in Las Vegas and Atlantic City report no problem with "psychics" winning great sums of money. For another thing, although great publicity is generated when a psychic helps police solve a crime, such a thing rarely happens. Much more often, psychic tips are worthless, and a case is solved through traditional police work. And while audiences may be amazed at the feats of "mind readers," there is rarely any ESP at work there. Instead, mind readers use simple psychological tricks to exploit their audiences' willingness to believe.

The first sentence suggests that the topic of this paragraph is extrasensory perception. And as you read the paragraph, you see that everything has to do with ESP. Thus your first impression in this case was correct—the topic is ESP. Once you have the topic, your next step is to ask, "What is the author's primary point about the topic?" The answer will be the main idea of the paragraph. Read the ESP paragraph again, and then write down in the space below the author's point about ESP:

*Main idea:* _____

The main idea about the topic, ESP, is that it is not documented by any convincing evidence. Here as in other paragraphs, the main idea is a general idea that summarizes what the entire paragraph is about. In other words, the main idea is an "umbrella" statement under which the other material in the paragraph fits. In this case, the other material is in the form of several examples that back up the main idea. The parts of the paragraph can be shown as follows:

*Topic:* ESP

*Main idea:* The evidence for ESP has not been convincing.

*Supporting details:*

1. There have been no reports of "psychics" winning great sums at casinos.

2. Most crimes are solved by police work, not psychic tips.

3. Mind readers use simple psychological tricks, not psychic ability.

The following activities will sharpen your sense of the difference between the topic of a selection and the main idea of that selection.

## ➤ *Practice 1*

Circle the letter of the correct topic of each paragraph. (To find the topic, remember to ask yourself, "Who or what is the paragraph about?") Then circle the letter of the main idea—the author's main point about the topic.

1.    According to one scientist who has studied aging, there are ways to remain healthy in old age. The key, he believes, is to continue to find mental and physical challenges. In addition, he recommends that people stick to a balanced, low-cholesterol diet and a reasonable exercise program throughout their lives. He also cautions people about the dangers of smoking.

*Topic:*
a. Science
b. Mental and Physical Challenges
c. Health in Old Age
d. A Balanced Diet

*Main idea:*
a. A balanced diet helps the elderly stay healthy.
b. According to one researcher, health in old age can be achieved in various ways.
c. Science includes the study of aging.
d. A scientist who has studied aging cautions people about the dangers of smoking.

2. A good way to find a part-time job is to create one yourself. Two high school students, for example, realized that many people prefer not to leave their pets at a kennel. Those students started a business of feeding and exercising pets while their owners are on vacation. And a housewife runs her own pet-taxi service, for which she drives people's caged pets to the vet or the kennel.

   *Topic:*
   a. Finding a Part-time Job     c. Animal Care
   b. Student Jobs     d. A Pet-Taxi Service

   *Main idea:*
   a. Many people work in animal care.
   b. One good part-time job is running a pet-taxi service.
   c. Many students as well as people in general need part-time jobs.
   d. One way to get a part-time job is to create one that fills a need.

3. Some people believe that if you spill salt, you must toss a pinch of salt over your left shoulder "into the Devil's face" in order to avoid bad luck. That is just one of many superstitions that cover everyday events. Others are the beliefs that umbrellas should not be opened indoors and that people should leave a friend's house by the same door they entered.

   *Topic:*
   a. Spilling Salt     c. Superstitions
   b. Umbrellas     d. Bad Luck

   *Main idea:*
   a. People are afraid of bad luck.
   b. Some people consider opening an umbrella indoors to be bad luck.
   c. Many superstitions are about everyday events.
   d. According to one superstition, if you spill salt, you should toss a pinch of salt over your shoulder.

4. Instinct, rather than learning, is the strongest influence on animals' behavior. One common example of instinct is the spider's spinning of its intricate web. No one teaches a spider how to spin; its inborn instinct allows it to accomplish the task. Another example of instinctive behavior is the salmon's struggle to swim upstream to lay its eggs. It would be much easier for the salmon to follow the current downstream, but instinct overrides all other considerations.

   *Topic:*
   a. Learned Behavior     c. The Salmon's Upstream Struggle
   b. Spiders     d. Instinct

*Main idea:*
a. One type of behavior is learned behavior.
b. Spiders spin intricate webs without being taught to do so.
c. Salmon swim upstream to lay their eggs.
d. Instinct is the strongest influence on animal behavior.

## THE TOPIC SENTENCE

In a paragraph, authors often give readers the main idea in a single sentence called the *topic sentence*. For example, look again at the paragraph on bosses:

> Many bosses share two weaknesses. First, they are often poor communicators. They tell people what to do and how and when to do it, without explaining the reasons for their rules, and they do not welcome feedback or questions. In addition, many bosses are not well-rounded people. Their jobs tend to be their lives, and they expect everybody who works for them to think and act the way they do. These bosses frown upon hearing that a family matter will keep an employee from working late, and they come out of their office looking irritated if there is too much talk or laughter during a coffee break.

As we have already seen, the topic of this paragraph is "many bosses," and the primary point about bosses is that they "share two weaknesses." Both the topic and the point about the topic are expressed in the opening sentence, which is therefore the topic sentence. All the sentences that follow provide details about the weaknesses which bosses share. The parts of the paragraph can be shown as follows:

*Topic:* Many bosses

*Main idea (expressed in the topic sentence):* Many bosses share two weaknesses.

*Supporting details:*
1. They are poor communicators.
2. They are not well-rounded people.

Now read the paragraph on the next page and try to find the topic sentence that states its main idea. Test a statement that you think is the main idea by asking, "Is this statement supported by all or most of the other material in the paragraph?" Write the number of the sentence you choose in the space provided. Then read the explanation that follows.

*Topic sentence:* _____

> [1]Bad health habits can persist for a number of reasons. [2]One is childhood fears; if people are afraid as children to go to the dentist, they might avoid dental checkups when they are adults. [3]In addition, poor health habits may persist if they are defense mechanisms. [4]An overweight teenager, for example, could be holding onto that baby fat to avoid the pressure of competing for dates. [5]It's easier to blame loneliness on twenty extra pounds than to slim down and face potential rejection. [6]A third reason is low self-esteem. [7]People who smoke or subsist on junk foods may simply not care enough about themselves to go to the trouble of improving their habits.

After thinking about the paragraph, you may have decided that the first sentence is the topic sentence. If so, you should have checked yourself by asking, "Does the other material in the paragraph support the idea that 'Bad health habits can persist for a number of reasons?'" In fact, the rest of the paragraph does provide three reasons why bad health habits may persist. The specific details about childhood fears, defense mechanisms, and low self-esteem all develop the general idea expressed in the first sentence. By asking and answering a basic question, you have made it clear that the first sentence is indeed the topic sentence.

The important hint given above for finding the topic sentence and main idea is worth repeating: *Always test yourself on an idea you think is the main idea by asking the question, "Is this statement supported by all or most of the other material in the paragraph?"*

## ➤ Practice 2

This exercise will give you more practice in distinguishing between a topic (the general subject), a main idea (the primary point being made about the subject), and the specific ideas that support and develop the main idea. Each group of statements on the next page includes one topic, one main idea (topic sentence), and two supporting ideas. In the space provided, label each item with one of the following:

| | |
|---|---|
| *T* | (for *Topic*) |
| *MI* | (for *Main Idea, expressed in a topic sentence*) |
| *SD* | (for *Supporting Detail*) |

*Group 1*

_____ a.  Teachers cause stress by asking children to copy and recopy their work until it is perfect.

_____ b.  The children are afraid of getting a low grade for their work.

_____ c.  Children's fears of writing in school.

_____ d.  Children's fears of writing in school have several causes.

*Group 2*

_____ a.  The horned toad and the glass snake are both really lizards, and the crayfish isn't a fish, but a relative of the lobster.

_____ b.  The names of some animals.

_____ c.  Neither the ring-tailed cat nor the civet cat are actually cats: the ring-tailed cat is related to the raccoon, and the civet cat is related to the mongoose.

_____ d.  Some animals' names are misleading.

*Group 3*

_____ a.  Antibiotics have helped cure children of certain infectious diseases.

_____ b.  Childhood diseases that used to be fatal.

_____ c.  Better hygiene has helped to control infectious diseases from spreading.

_____ d.  Many childhood diseases that used to be fatal are now almost unknown in the United States because of scientific advances.

*Group 4*

_____ a.  Taking large amounts of vitamin C.

_____ b.  When a person takes large doses of vitamin C, the body speeds up its process of eliminating the excess.

_____ c.  Taking large amounts of vitamin C and quitting suddenly can cause scurvy, a vitamin-deficiency disease.

_____ d.  The body continues to rid itself of the vitamin for some time even after the large dose is discontinued, and a shortage results.

## LOCATIONS OF THE TOPIC SENTENCE

In two of the paragraphs considered in this chapter, the topic sentence has been the first sentence of the paragraph: "Many bosses share two weaknesses" and "Bad health habits can persist for a number of reasons." That is a common pattern, but not the only one. Topic sentences may also appear within the paragraph. For example, the topic sentence of the ESP paragraph ("However, ESP is not documented by any convincing evidence") is the second sentence. Topic sentences may also appear at the very end of a paragraph. Or they may even appear twice—at the beginning and the end.

### Within a Paragraph

```
Introductory Detail
Topic Sentence
Supporting Detail
Supporting Detail
Supporting Detail
```

When the topic sentence appears somewhere *within* a paragraph, it is preceded by one or more introductory sentences that may relate the main idea to the previous paragraph, arouse the reader's interest, or give background for the main idea. Here is an example of a paragraph in which the topic sentence is somewhere in the middle. Try to find it, and then write its number in the space provided. Then read the explanation that follows.

*Topic sentence:* _____

[1]Many of us are annoyed by telephone solicitors who call us day and night, trying to sell us everything from magazine subscriptions to vacation homes. [2]These electronic intruders don't seem to care how much they are inconveniencing us and refuse to take "no" for an answer. [3]However, these nuisance callers can be stopped if we take charge of the conversation. [4]As soon as one of them asks if we are Mr. or Ms. X, we should respond, "Yes, and are you a telephone solicitor?" [5]This technique puts them on the defensive. [6]We then have an opening to say that we don't accept solicitations over the phone, only through the mail. [7]This puts a quick end to the conversation.

If you thought the third sentence gives the main idea, you were correct. The two sentences before the topic sentence introduce the problem; the topic sentence then gives the writer's main idea, which is that we can stop nuisance callers from going on by taking charge of the conversation. The rest of the paragraph develops that idea.

## End of a Paragraph

```
Supporting Detail
Supporting Detail
Supporting Detail
Supporting Detail
Topic Sentence
```

When the topic sentence is at the end of a paragraph, the previous sentences build up to the main idea. Here is an example of a paragraph in which the topic sentence comes last.

A study at one prison showed that owning a pet can change a hardened prison inmate into a more caring person. Another study discovered that senior citizens, both those living alone and those in nursing homes, became more interested in life when they were given pets to care for. Even emotionally disturbed children have been observed to smile and react with interest if there is a cuddly kitten or puppy to hold. **Animals, then, can be a means of therapy for many kinds of individuals.**

## Beginning and End of a Paragraph

```
Topic Sentence
Supporting Detail
Supporting Detail
Supporting Detail
Topic Sentence
```

Even though paragraphs have only one main idea, they may include two topic sentences, with each providing the main idea in different words. In such cases, the topic sentences are usually at the beginning and the end. In these cases, the author has chosen to introduce the main idea at the start of the paragraph and then emphasize it by restating it in other words at the end. Such is the case in the following paragraph.

**We are on our way to becoming a cashless, checkless society, a trend that began with the credit card.** Now some banks are offering "debit cards" instead of credit cards. The costs of purchases made with these cards are deducted from the holder's bank account instead of being added to a monthly bill. And checking accounts, which are mainly used for paying bills, are going electronic. Now some people can make computer transactions over their pushbutton phones to pay bills by transferring money from their account to the account of whomever they owe. **Soon we may be able to conduct most of our business without signing a check or actually seeing the money we earn and spend.**

Note that the main idea of the first sentence of this paragraph—that "we are on our way to becoming a cashless, checkless society"—is restated in other words in the final sentence.

## ➤ Practice 3

The topic sentences of the following paragraphs appear at different locations. Identify each topic sentence by filling in its sentence number in the space provided. In the one case where the paragraph has a topic sentence at both the beginning and the end, write in both sentence numbers.

A.   ¹Serious depression, as opposed to the fleeting kind we all feel at times, has several warning signs. ²One symptom of depression is a change in sleep patterns—either sleeplessness or sleeping too much. ³Another sign is abnormal eating patterns; a person either may begin to eat a great deal or may almost stop eating. ⁴Finally, a general feeling of hopelessness may signal depression. ⁵People feel indifferent to their families and jobs and may begin to think that life is not worth living.

*Topic sentence(s):* _____

B.   ¹School officials complain about vandalism that leaves classrooms wrecked and damages expensive equipment. ²Teachers complain about the low salaries they get for their difficult and important jobs. ³And parents complain that their children's test scores are dropping, that their children can't read or do math. ⁴The problems within our school systems are varied and affect almost everyone involved.

*Topic sentence(s):* _____

C.   ¹Every thirty-seven seconds, a car is stolen somewhere in the United States. ²Although this statistic is frightening, it is possible for drivers to prevent car theft if they take a few simple precautions. ³When they leave their cars, they should lock all valuables in the trunk or glove compartment to avoid tempting a thief to break in. ⁴Parking in the middle of the block on a busy, well-lighted street will deter would-be thieves. ⁵The most obvious precaution, of course, is always to lock the car and take the keys—even if the driver is stopping for just a minute. ⁶One out of every five stolen cars was left unlocked with the keys in the ignition.

*Topic sentence(s):* _____

D.  [1]One of the most significant factors in selling a product is how it is packaged. [2]When Stuart Hall Company, which manufactures notebooks and paper products for students, realized its sales were declining because fewer children were being born, it decided to change its products' appearance. [3]So, beginning in 1968, the company replaced its plain tablets with colored paper and decorated the covers of its notebooks with the Pink Panther and other cartoon characters. [4]Students loved the new designs, and sales soared. [5]Packaging, therefore, can be a method of solving marketing problems.

*Topic sentence(s):* _____

## Topic Sentences That Cover More Than One Paragraph

At times you will find that a topic sentence does double duty—it provides the main idea for more than one paragraph. This occurs when an author considers the development of the main idea to be too lengthy for one paragraph. He or she then breaks up the material into one or more added paragraphs to make it easier to read.

See if you can find and write down the number of the topic sentence for the paragraphs below. They are taken from an essay on factors involved in highway accidents. Then read the explanation that follows.

*Topic sentence:* _____

[1]In addition to poor highway and automobile design, people's attitudes about driving also contribute to the high rate of traffic accidents. [2]Some people persist in believing that they can drink and be alert drivers. [3]Yet alcohol is estimated to be a factor in at least half of all fatal highway accidents. [4]Refusing or forgetting to wear safety belts also increases fatalities. [5]A negative attitude about wearing seat belts is inconsistent with statistics showing that the chances of being seriously hurt or dying in a car accident are greater when a seat belt is not worn.

[6]Another potentially deadly attitude is the point of view that the best driving is fast driving. [7]Again, statistics contradict this attitude—fast driving is more likely to be deadly driving. [8]After the speed limit was lowered in 1973 to fifty-five miles per hour, traffic fatalities fell significantly. [9]Evidence on speed limits in other countries is just as telling. [10]Where high-speed driving is permitted, a higher rate of accidents occurs.

After you read the first paragraph, it becomes clear that sentence 1 includes the main idea: "people's attitudes about driving also contribute to the high rate of traffic accidents." Sentences 2 and 3 deal with the attitude of those who feel that drinking does not interfere with driving. Sentences 4 and 5 deal with not wearing seat belts.

By beginning with the words "another potentially deadly attitude," the first sentence of the next paragraph tells us that it will continue to develop the topic sentence of the previous paragraph. The author has simply chosen to break the subject down into two smaller paragraphs rather than include all the information in one long paragraph. This relationship between the two paragraphs can be seen clearly in the following outline:

*Main idea:* Some attitudes about driving contribute to traffic accidents.

1. Drinking does not interfere with driving.
2. Seat belts are not important.
3. Good driving is fast driving.

## IMPLIED MAIN IDEAS

Sometimes a selection lacks a topic sentence, but that does not mean it lacks a main idea. The author has simply decided to let the details of the selection suggest the main idea. You must figure out what that implied main idea is by deciding upon the point of all the details. For example, read the following paragraph.

> In ancient times, irrational behavior was considered the result of demons and evil spirits taking possession of a person. Later, the Greeks looked upon irrational behavior as a physical problem—caused by an imbalance of body fluids called "humors"—or by displacement of an organ. In the highly superstitious Middle Ages, the theory of possession by demons was revived. It reached a high point again in the witch hunts of eighteenth-century Europe and America. Only in the last one hundred years did true medical explanations of mental illness gain wide acceptance.

You can see that no sentence in the paragraph is a good "umbrella" statement that covers all the others. We can decide on the main idea by considering all the details and asking, "What is the topic of this paragraph?" (in other words, "Who or what is this paragraph about?"). Once we have the topic in mind, we can ask, "What is the primary point the author is trying to make about that topic?" When we think we know the main point, we can test it out by asking, "Does all or most of the material in the paragraph support this idea?"

In the paragraph above, all of the details are about mental illness, so that must be the topic. And what is the general idea all the details are making about mental illness? The details show that people have explained mental illness in many different ways over the years. Although this idea is not stated, you can see that it is a broad enough summary to include all the other material in the paragraph—it is the main idea.

Now read the paragraph below, and see if you can pick out which of the four statements that follow it expresses the main idea. Circle the letter of the statement you choose, and then read the explanation that follows.

> More and more commuters are forming car-pools to save money in gas, tolls, and wear and tear on their cars. Also, the special (and often faster) lanes many expressways provide for cars with three or more passengers during the rush hours can make the commute shorter and more hassle-free. Finally, car-pooling can reduce the boredom of the daily drive back and forth to work. Members who are not driving can talk, eat breakfast, read the paper, or get a head start on the day's work.

a. Car-pooling saves commuters money.
b. Car-pooling can mean shorter, easier commuter rides.
c. Everyone should join a car-pool.
d. There are several reasons that more commuters are forming car-pools.

As we begin to read this paragraph, we might think the first sentence is the topic sentence. If that were the main idea, however, then the details in the paragraph would have to be about the savings in money. Such details might focus on how much money can be saved by buying less gas, sharing tolls, and saving on the wear and tear of cars. But as we continue to read, we find that the paragraph, instead, goes on to give more reasons for people car-pooling, and so answer *a* is incorrect—it is too narrow to be the main idea.

Answer *b* is also too narrow to be the main idea—it also covers only a single reason for forming car-pools.

Answer *c* is incorrect because the details of the paragraph do not include any judgment about what people should do.

Answer *d* is a correct statement of the main idea. The phrase "several reasons that more commuters are forming car-pools" is a general reference to the three specific reasons listed in the paragraph: 1) Car-pooling saves money, 2) Car-pooling can make for a shorter, easier ride, and 3) Car-pool members who aren't driving can use the time riding to work to do something else.

## ➤ *Practice 4*

The following paragraphs have unstated main ideas, and each is followed by four sentences. In each case, circle the letter of the sentence that best expresses the unstated main idea.

Remember to consider carefully all of the details and ask yourself, "Who or what is the paragraph about?" Once you discover the topic of the paragraph, ask, "What is the author's main point about the topic?" Then test your answer by asking, "Does all or most of the material in the paragraph support this idea?"

1.  One misconception about exercise is that if women lift weights, they will develop large muscles. Without male hormones, however, women cannot increase their muscle bulk as much as a man's. Another myth about exercise is that it increases the appetite. Actually, regular exercise stabilizes the blood sugar level and prevents hunger pains. Some people also think that a few minutes of exercise a day or one session a week is enough, but at least three solid workouts a week are needed for muscular and cardiovascular fitness.

    a.  Women who lift weights cannot become as muscular as men.
    b.  There are several myths about exercise.
    c.  Exercise is beneficial to everyone.
    d.  People use many different excuses to avoid exercising.

2.  Since anti-smoking campaigns made teens aware of the risks of smoking, the percentage of teens smoking has dropped from 28 to 20 percent over the last ten years. Additionally, in schools where students have access to health clinics which provide birth control information and devices, pregnancy rates have declined by 30 percent. Furthermore, another study demonstrated that students in schools with comprehensive health education were less likely to use alcohol, to try drugs, or to attempt suicide.

    a.  If more schools would conduct anti-smoking campaigns, the number of teens smoking would greatly decline.
    b.  Evidence suggests that health education programs have a favorable effect on teen behavior.
    c.  Health education clinics are a positive influence on how people of all ages take care of themselves.
    d.  One study found that students in schools with comprehensive health education were less likely to use drugs or to attempt suicide.

3.  The work homemakers do is essential to the economy. The estimated value of the cleaning, cooking, nursing, shopping, child care, home maintenance, money management, errands, entertaining, and other services homemakers perform has been estimated at equal to roughly one-fourth of the gross national product. In fact, the Commerce Department's Bureau of Economic Analysis has proposed a revision of the gross national product that would take into account the value of the homemaker's services. But homemaking is not formal employment that brings money or prestige. No financial compensation is associated with this position, and the *Dictionary of Occupational Titles* places mothering and homemaking skills in the lowest category of skills, lower than the occupation of "dog trainer."

    a. We no longer value the work done by homemakers.

    b. Housewives should receive salaries for their work.

    c. Because homemaking is unpaid labor, its true value is often ignored.

    d. It's better to be a dog trainer than a homemaker.

## Putting Implied Main Ideas Into Words

When you read, you often have to *infer*—figure out on your own—an author's unstated main idea, and no one will give you a list of statements to choose from. So you must be able to decide on implied main ideas on your own. The implied main idea that you come up with must not be too narrow to cover all the details in the paragraph, and it also must not be too broad. See if you can find the unstated main idea in the following paragraph. Then read the explanation below.

> Some actors and rock stars are paid more than 100 times as much per year as school teachers are. We enjoy such performers, but certainly they do not do work that is many times more important than those who teach and guide our nation's students. Indeed, the reverse is true. As another example, professional athletes earn vastly more than firefighters. The first group may bring enjoyable diversion to our lives, but the latter literally saves lives. Again, there can be little doubt that the lower-paid group, firefighters, makes the more important, indeed essential, contribution to society. As a last example, most high-fashion designers, who can make up to $50,000 for a single gown, far out-earn police officers. Now, we can easily live without sophisticated clothes (and probably about 99.9 percent of us do), but a society without law-enforcement officers would be unlivable for all of us.

What is the implied main idea of this paragraph? _____

_____

To find an implied main idea, consider all of the supporting details. In this case, the supporting details are three comparisons between highly paid occupations in our society and lesser paid, but more important occupations. The pairs of occupations are 1) rock stars and teachers, 2) professional athletes and firefighters, and 3) high-fashion designers and police officers. Thus the main idea is a general idea about these examples. One way of wording that general idea is: Workers in our society are not necessarily paid according to how important their work is.

➤*Practice 5*

Write the implied main ideas of the following paragraphs in your own words.

1.  Many people think sleepwalkers drift about in a ghost-like way, with arms extended. The fact is most sleepwalkers walk around quite normally, though their eyes are usually closed or glazed. It is also commonly believed that one should never wake a sleepwalker. But it is advisable to do so if the walker seems in imminent danger—for example, going toward an open window or handling sharp objects. Another popular misconception is that sleepwalkers are not "really" sleeping or are only half-asleep. In fact, they are in a very deep state of sleep. A last commonly held belief is that sleepwalkers are easy to spot because they're in nighties or pajamas. Often this isn't true, because sleepwalkers can do routine tasks, including getting completely dressed.

    *Implied main idea:* _____

    _____

2.  Many people think that only children are lucky because of the material goods and attention they receive. But consider that only children have no privacy. Parents always feel entitled to know everything that's going on in an only child's life. Another drawback of only children is they lack the advantages that children with brothers and sisters have. They can never blame a sibling for something that goes wrong, or ask for a privilege that an older brother or sister was given earlier. In addition, only children miss the companionship of siblings. Not only can they be lonely, but they may have trouble making friends later in life because they never learned to get along with a brother or sister.

    *Implied main idea:* _____

    _____

3.  After a stressful day it's restful to just put your feet up and enjoy a favorite program. And, of course, TV is entertaining for all ages. Videotaped movies, video games and special cable offerings, as well as regular network programming, provide a choice of amusements for the whole family. TV is deservedly famous for being our best source of up-to-the-minute news. When history is being made, we are often there, thanks to TV. Most importantly, television is a real educational tool. From *Sesame Street* to public television's nature programs, it teaches in a colorful and interesting fashion.

    *Implied main idea:* _____

    _____

## ➤ *Review*

To review what you've learned in this chapter, complete each of the following sentences about main ideas.

1.  The umbrella statement that covers all of the material in a paragraph is its *(topic, topic sentence, supporting detail)* _____

2.  The main idea of a longer selection is often called its *(topic, central point, implied main idea)* _____

3.  To locate the main idea of a selection, you may find it helpful to first decide on its *(topic, central point, implied main idea)* _____
    _____

4.  When a paragraph has no topic sentence, we say that its main idea is
    _____

5.  To help you decide if a certain sentence is the topic sentence, ask yourself, "Is this statement supported by all or most of the _____
    _____?"

# MAIN IDEAS: Test A-1

A. Circle the letter of the correct topic of each paragraph. Then circle the letter of the main idea—the author's primary point about the topic.

1.  People interested in physical fitness need not spend hundreds of dollars on fancy exercise equipment or health club memberships. Anyone can get into good shape simply by climbing stairs. Stair-climbing helps in weight loss; just walking up and down two flights of stairs a day instead of riding an elevator will take off six pounds a year. Climbing stairs is also good for the heart and can prevent heart attacks. And frequent stair-climbing strengthens the muscles of the legs and buttocks.

    *Topic:*   a. Exercise Equipment         c. Weight Loss
               b. Stair-climbing             d. Health Club Memberships

    *Main idea:* a. Exercise equipment can help in weight loss.
                 b. People can get into good shape with stair-climbing.
                 c. Some people spend hundreds of dollars on fancy exercise equipment or health club memberships.
                 d. Stair-climbing can strengthen the muscles of the legs and the buttocks.

2.  If you want productivity to improve, improve quality. Think about it. If every person and machine did things right the first time, the same number of people could handle more work. High costs of inspection could be channeled into greater production, and managers could take all the time they spend checking and devote it to productive tasks. Wasted materials would become a thing of the past. In fact, it's been estimated that attention to quality can reduce the total cost of operations anywhere from 10 to 50 percent. As Philip Crosby said: "Quality is free. What costs money are the unquality things—all the actions that involve not doing jobs right the first time."

    *Topic:*   a. Quality            c. High Costs of Inspection
               b. Business           d. Philip Crosby

    *Main idea:* a. Philip Crosby is an expert in quality in business.
                 b. It is wasteful to spend so much money on plant inspections.
                 c. Businesses can improve their sales in several ways.
                 d. Productivity can be improved if quality is improved.

*(Continues on next page)*

B. Each of the following groups of items includes one main idea (topic sentence) and two supporting details. In the spaces provided, label each item with one of the following:

**MI** (for *Main Idea*)
**SD** (for *Supporting Detail*)

### Group 1

_____ a.  Driving at night is less safe than in the daytime.

_____ b.  In 1981, 62 percent of all traffic deaths took place at night.

_____ c.  The chances of being in a fatal accident are nearly four times greater at night than during the day.

### Group 2

_____ a.  The sand-dune cat's feet are thickly padded, which helps it walk over sand.

_____ b.  The sand-dune cat gets along without drinking by getting enough liquid from the bodies of the animals it eats.

_____ c.  The sand-dune cat is well suited for the deserts it lives in.

# MAIN IDEAS: Test A-2

Topic sentences appear at various locations within the following paragraphs. Identify each topic sentence by writing its sentence number in the space provided. In the one case where the paragraph has a topic sentence at both the beginning and the end, write in both sentence numbers.

1. [1]Scientists believe that tropical rain forests contain large numbers of plant and animal species still unknown to science. [2]Nevertheless, the rain forests of the world are being recklessly destroyed. [3]In order to grow more food, farmers burn down the forests and plant crops. [4]The nutrients in rain-forest soil, however, are quickly exhausted by farming. [5]Also, trees are cut down for their timber faster than new trees can grow to replace them.

   *Topic sentence(s):* _____

2. [1]Falling in love involves enormous risks which can result in heartbreak. [2]First, there is the risk of rejection if the object of one's affection does not return the sentiment or is the first to fall out of love. [3]Then, there is the chance that a loved one will die and leave the lover alone and forlorn. [4]Even worse is the risk of betrayal, if the loved one is dishonest, or reveals confidences or takes on a new lover. [5]Yes, unfortunately, not even love is risk-free.

   *Topic sentence(s):* _____

3. [1]"It took us years to teach Junior not to be left-handed, but we finally cured him!" [2]Many parents think it's part of their job to "teach" their children to be right-handed. [3]Not only is it not necessary for a child to be right-handed; it is actually harmful to force a natural "lefty" to use the other hand. [4]When adults force a child to use the hand he does not naturally prefer, it frustrates the child badly. [5]Many children who are made to use their right hands develop speech problems, such as stuttering. [6]Others may have trouble learning to read or may be bothered by other learning disabilities.

   *Topic sentence(s):* _____

*(Continues on next page)*

4.    [1]It contains an old Pullman railroad car spittoon, Ray Bolger's *Wizard of Oz* scarecrow costume, a giant Pacific octopus, 14 condom vending machines, 50 parking meters and 1,272 specimens of lice. [2]Can you guess what this is? [3]Okay, here are more clues. [4]It also houses an Air Force cargo plane, an ancient Chinese scroll and thousands of World's Fair souvenirs dating to 1850. [5]Still not sure? [6]Would it help if we added that it also contains 2,500 fossils imprinted with ferns and insects that lived in an Illinois swamp more than 300 million years ago? [7]I admit, this is a toughie, so I'll just tell you the answer. [8]All of the above are in the famous, Washington-based Smithsonian Institution, where America stores its odds and ends—mostly odd!

*Topic sentence(s):* _____

5.    [1]Snoring is the number one complaint in marriages all around the world. [2]The honks, hoots, and snorts created by snorers annoy their mates and deprive them of sleep. [3]Fortunately, there are some means of preventing snoring. [4]First, the snorer should avoid breathing through his mouth. [5]Mouth-breathing can be discouraged if the snorer sleeps on his side with his forearm under his chin—effectively pressing his mouth shut. [6]Secondly, the snorer should increase the humidity in his bedroom. [7]A humidifier or even a pot of water in the room may help. [8]In addition, snoring may disappear if an overweight snorer loses some pounds. [9]And finally, a snorer should avoid drinking alcohol in the evening.

*Topic sentence(s):* _____

## MAIN IDEAS: Test A-3

**A.** Topic sentences appear at different locations within the following two paragraphs. Identify each topic sentence by writing the sentence number in the space provided.

1.  [1]Would you like to have your cake—and get no cavities from it, too? [2]Maybe you can. [3]According to a dental researcher, drinking plain tea while eating sweets helps block the sugar in food from forming cavities. [4]The researcher found that when tannin, a natural substance found in tea, combines with sugar, it interferes with sugar's conversion into plaque, a sticky film that forms on teeth. [5]Although it may look innocent—if you can even see it at all—plaque eats tiny holes in teeth, which is what cavities are.

    *Topic sentence:* _____

2.  [1]Hollywood directors will sometimes go to great lengths to achieve the effects they want. [2]When Cecil B. deMille was filming *The Ten Commandments* in 1956, he was not satisfied with the crowd of actors playing Israelites as they heard the Commandments from Moses. [3]The actors, he felt, did not display the correct degree of emotion. [4]So deMille announced that a member of the movie cast had died that morning, leaving eight children behind. [5]He asked that the actors observe two minutes of silence out of respect for their dead colleague. [6]The actors stood quietly, expressions of shock and sadness on their faces. [7]DeMille kept the cameras rolling and got exactly what he wanted on film. [8]Afterwards he told them he had made up the story about the cast member's death.

    *Topic sentence:* _____

**B.** Circle the letter of the sentence that best expresses the implied main idea of each of the following two paragraphs.

3.  As you speak with someone, you can easily gather clues about how much he understands or agrees with you and adjust your conversation accordingly. But when you write, you must try to anticipate the reader's reactions without those verbal clues. You also have to provide stronger evidence in writing than in conversation. A friend may accept an unsupported statement such as "He's a lousy boss." But in writing, the reader expects you to back up such a statement with proof.

    *Implied main idea:*
    a.  There are special techniques to communicating verbally with others.
    b.  Effective writing is more difficult than effective conversation.
    c.  Speaking and writing are both challenging ways of communicating.
    d.  When conversing, you get feedback about a person's reaction that helps you to make your conversation more effective.

*(Continues on next page)*

4.    A chemistry professor wished to demonstrate the harmful effects of alcohol to her class. On the lab table, she set two beakers—one containing water and the other filled with grain alcohol. Then she dropped an earthworm into each. The worm in the alcohol beaker wriggled violently in a vain attempt to escape and quickly died. The other worm, in the water beaker, moved slowly and gracefully, seeming to enjoy its new environment. The professor smiled with satisfaction and looked at the roomful of students. Then she asked, "What lesson can be learned from this demonstration?" One student quickly answered, "If you drink alcohol, you'll never have worms."

*Implied main idea:*
a.  Teaching chemistry is extremely difficult.
b.  The teacher should not have sacrificed a worm for her lesson.
c.  More schools should be teaching students about the harmful effects of alcohol.
d.  Sometimes what a student learns in class is not what the teacher had in mind.

C. Write out the implied main idea of paragraph 5.

5.    Americans' favorite pizza toppings include sausage and mushrooms. But in Tokyo, the natives favor pizza topped with tuna. Australians often make another fishy choice: shrimp. In Germany, salami (which is close to our prized pepperoni) gets many best-topping votes. Israelis, believe it or not, sometimes order fried-egg pizza. And in England, many palates are pleased by pizza topped with sweet corn.

*Implied main idea:*

_____

_____

# MAIN IDEAS: Test B-1

A. Circle the letter of the correct topic of each paragraph. Then circle the letter of the main idea—the author's primary point about the topic.

1. Why do people get married? According to pollster Louis Harris, there are three popular reasons for getting married. The most popular reason is for love, cited by 83 percent of both men and women as good grounds for getting married. The next most popular reason for getting married is "to be with a particular person," which was stated by 55 percent of the population. Finally, according to 44 percent, "to have children" is another compelling reason to get married.

   *Topic:*    a. Love                          c. Getting Married
                    b. Desire to Be with a Particular Person   d. Having Children

   *Main idea:*  a. The most popular reason for getting married is love.
                   b. People get married for three main reasons, according to pollster Louis Harris.
                   c. The desire to be with a particular person is the second most popular reason for getting married.
                   d. Many people get married in order to have children.

2. Baseball enthusiasts hold softball in low esteem. It's a picnic game, they argue, with a big, soft ball, shorter base paths, and a pitcher who throws underhand. Yet fast-pitch softball can be as intense and dramatic as any baseball game, perhaps more so. True, the base paths are shorter, but ask any third baseman how quickly a well-met groundball reaches him on softball's smaller diamond. True, the pitcher throws underhand, but he stands 15 feet closer to the plate, and he might hit speeds exceeding 80 miles per hour. True, the ball is softer than a baseball, but catch a hard one in the ribs just once, and such knowledge is small comfort. Baseball might be America's favorite pastime, but for speed, action and raw drama, softball is its equal.

   *Topic:*    a. Baseball Enthusiasts        c. A Well-met Groundball
                    b. Fast-pitch Softball            d. America's Favorite Pastime

   *Main idea:*  a. Baseball fans have a low opinion of softball.
                   b. Baseball might be America's favorite pastime.
                   c. Fast-pitch softball can be at least as intense and dramatic as baseball.
                   d. The softball pitcher throws 15 feet closer to the plate than the baseball pitcher.

*(Continues on next page)*

B. Each of the following groups of items includes one main idea (topic sentence) and two supporting details. In the spaces provided, label each item with one of the following:

**MI** (for *Main Idea*)
**SD** (for *Supporting Detail*)

### Group 1

_____ a. It is said that the antidote to walking under a ladder is to quickly make a wish or cross your fingers.

_____ b. If a black cat crosses your path, go back home.

_____ c. For the superstitious, there are remedies for worrisome accidents.

### Group 2

_____ a. Washoe thought up the term "drink-fruit" for watermelon.

_____ b. Washoe, a female chimpanzee who has been taught sign language, has created some words on her own.

_____ c. Washoe, who has called an enemy "dirty jack," calls the swan "water-bird."

# MAIN IDEAS: Test B-2

Topic sentences appear at various locations within the following paragraphs. Identify each topic sentence by writing its sentence number in the space provided. In the one case where the paragraph has a topic sentence at both the beginning and the end, write in both sentence numbers.

1.  [1]Some interior designers seem to think plastic plants are superior to real ones. [2]Real plants, however, can do much that even the most realistic plastic ones can't. [3]Plants, for instance, improve the quality of the air by giving off oxygen and absorbing certain air pollutants. [4]Also, they cool the air as water evaporates from their leaves. [5]Large plants—trees and shrubs—can even muffle the otherwise harsh sounds of construction work and street traffic.

    *Topic sentence(s):* _____

2.  [1]Bugs are the curse of the gardener, the blight of the picnic, the bane of the kitchen. [2]They are rarely thought of as deserving much respect, much less gratitude. [3]But the tiny carrion beetle serves as an honored employee of a distinguished American university. [4]Thousands of the little flesh-eating insects live in a basement room of Yale University's Peabody Museum of Natural History. [5]Their job is to strip the flesh from animal skeletons being prepared for display at the museum. [6]The ravenous insects do a better job of cleaning tiny shreds of flesh from delicate animal bones than any other known method. [7]They can strip a small animal carcass clean in just a few hours.

    *Topic sentence(s):* _____

3.  [1]Creatures that are particularly sensitive to a drop in barometric pressure, which happens before a storm, can "predict" a change in the weather. [2]Birds, for example, sense the pressure change and fly lower to compensate. [3]Low-flying birds, then, indicate that rain is coming. [4]Similarly, houseflies detect this change and move indoors to avoid the downpour. [5]And cats are known to groom themselves just before a storm. [6]In doing so, they are reacting to the static electricity that enters the air before a thunderstorm. [7]The electricity separates their fur and makes them feel dirty, so they lick themselves to make the fur smooth and "clean" again.

    *Topic sentence(s):* _____

*(Continues on next page)*

4.    [1]Taking good care of a pet is not only good for the animal—it's also good for the pet owner. [2]The American Heart Association has said that pet owners are more likely to survive during the first year after a heart attack than people who don't own pets. [3]Also, owning a dog that needs a daily walk can encourage a senior citizen to get some much-needed exercise. [4]People living alone are even likely to eat better when they have a pet. [5]Apparently the act of feeding the cat or dog reminds them that they need nourishment as well. [6]And before-and-after studies have shown that petting an animal causes a decrease in many people's blood pressure. [7]These facts are just some of the evidence that owning a pet is good for one's health.

*Topic sentence(s):* _____

5.    [1]In Western society, adolescence is an often stormy period that frequently places parents and their children in conflict. [2]Adolescents are told to "act like adults," but they are often treated as children. [3]The Mbuti tribe of East Africa provides a practical solution to the problem of how to become an adult. [4]Mbuti boys and girls are taken from their homes to separate "marriage and adulthood" camps. [5]During the three months that the camps last, the children are taught about the responsibilities of adulthood. [6]They learn about sharing, conflict, and respecting others. [7]The elders of the community talk to them about spiritual and moral values. [8]When the "campers" return to their village, they are no longer boys and girls. [9]They are men and women entitled to marry and set up their own homes.

*Topic sentence(s):* _____

# MAIN IDEAS: Test B-3

**A.** Topic sentences appear at different locations within the following two paragraphs. Identify each topic sentence by writing the sentence number in the space provided.

1.  [1]The stages of life, from birth to death, may seem fixed by biology. [2]But the way we think about life's stages is shaped by society. [3]During the Middle Ages, for example, children dressed—and were expected to act—just like little adults. [4]Adolescence became a distinct stage of life only fairly recently, when a separate teenage subculture began to appear. [5]Until then, young people were "children" until about age 16. [6]Then they went to work, married, and had their own children. [7]Today, "young adulthood" has become a new stage of life, stretching from about age 20 to 30.

    *Topic sentence:* _____

2.  [1]The eruption of volcanoes has caused death and misery throughout the centuries. [2]Yet in parts of Italy, Iceland, Chile, and Bolivia, volcanic steam is used to run heat and power plants. [3]Pumice, which is made from volcanic lava, is used as a grinder and polisher. [4]Sulfur produced by volcanoes is useful to the chemical industry. [5]Hawaiian farmers grow crops on land made rich by decayed volcanic material. [6]Thus, in spite of all the damage they cause, volcanoes do benefit us in various ways.

    *Topic sentence:* _____

**B.** Circle the letter of the sentence that best expresses the implied main idea of each of the following two paragraphs.

3.  You don't have to scare your family with statistics about heart attacks. To get them to exercise more often, emphasize instead how good they'll feel and how much better they'll look if they do daily calisthenics. Another method that works is to set an example. If they see you walking to the convenience store instead of driving, they might be encouraged to do likewise the next time they have errands in the neighborhood. Finally, make exercise a family activity. Suggest that the whole family go swimming together, take up early morning jogging, or join the Y at the group rate.

    *Implied main idea:*
    a. Statistics on heart attacks may scare your family into exercising.
    b. Exercise is good for the whole family.
    c. There are several ways to get your family to exercise.
    d. Most American families are in poor physical condition.

*(Continues on next page)*

4.   The earliest humans probably used the lengthening and shortening of shadows on the ground to measure the passage of time. Later, the sundial was invented to tell time more precisely, but still by using the shadow principle. The hourglass, a slightly more recent invention, measured time by allowing grains of sand to fall from one container to another. In about the year 1300, a primitive clock was invented. It had only an hour hand, but it became the most exact way yet to tell the time. Since then, clocks have been so improved technically that today's clocks and watches can be depended upon to be quite precise.

*Implied main idea:*
a. Throughout history, people have found better and better ways to measure the passing of time.
b. The hourglass is a slightly more recent invention than the sundial.
c. The first methods of measuring the passing of time took advantage of the changing shadows cast by the sun throughout a day.
d. A primitive clock invented in about 1300 was the most exact way to tell time up to that point.

C. Write out the implied main idea of paragraph 5.

5.   There are plenty of jokes about the trials of being married. And we all know that being married doesn't necessarily mean living happily ever after. But did you know that married people live longer and suffer fewer chronic illnesses than single people do? In contrast, divorced people have a greater risk of dying early than people in any other category. Widowed people, too, tend to die younger than married folks. In addition, single men are much more likely than married men to experience serious emotional breakdowns.

*Implied main idea:*

_____

_____

# MAIN IDEAS: Test C-1

A. Circle the letter of the correct topic of each paragraph. Then circle the letter of the main idea—the author's primary point about the topic.

1.    Hospices are a special type of health-care institution. They differ from hospitals and nursing homes in several ways. First of all, hospices treat patients suffering from incurable diseases who are not expected to live for more than a year. Hospitals, however, aim to help patients recover from disease, and nursing homes provide long-term care for the handicapped and elderly. Also, the hospice's purpose is to help the dying and their families. In contrast, hospitals and nursing homes have limited resources for helping patients' families.

*Topic:*    a. Patients           c. Long-term Care
          b. Hospices         d. Incurable Diseases

*Main idea:* a. Patients may have curable or incurable diseases.
           b. Hospices differ from hospitals and nursing homes in a few ways.
           c. For long-term care, nursing homes are better than hospices and hospitals.
           d. Hospitals have limited resources for helping patients' families.

2.    For many years, there has been a section in *Reader's Digest* magazine called "Laughter, the Best Medicine." The name may be accurate. Medical studies show that laughter is good for one's physical and emotional health. A hearty laugh exercises the internal organs, including the heart and lungs. The deep breathing that accompanies laughter supplies your body with extra oxygen. Many diseases deplete the body's supply of oxygen, so getting extra oxygen is important. Laughter may also stimulate the body's production of endorphins, which act as painkillers and anti-depressants.

*Topic*:    a. *Reader's Digest*    c. Endorphins
         b. Deep Breathing     d. Laughter

*Main idea:* a. *Reader's Digest* has a long-lived section titled "Laughter is the Best Medicine."
           b. Deep breathing can supply the body with extra oxygen, which can be important for people with certain diseases.
           c. Endorphins act as painkillers and anti-depressants.
           d. Laughter, according to medical studies, is good for our physical and emotional health.

*(Continues on next page)*

**B.** Each of the following groups of items includes one main idea (topic sentence) and two supporting details. In the spaces provided, label each item with one of the following:

**MI** (for *Main Idea*)
**SD** (for *Supporting Detail*)

*Group 1*

_____ a.  A drive-in church in Daytona Beach, Florida, has unusual services.

_____ b.  The church's members, nearly 1800, come to services dressed in shorts.

_____ c.  Members stay in their cars during services, which take place in a former drive-in movie.

*Group 2*

_____ a.  Curved streets discourage speeding cars.

_____ b.  For residential neighborhoods, curved streets have advantages.

_____ c.  The graceful lines of curved streets are more attractive than straight lines.

# MAIN IDEAS: Test C-2

Topic sentences appear at various locations within the following paragraphs. Identify each topic sentence by writing its sentence number in the space provided. In the one case where the paragraph has a topic sentence at both the beginning and the end, write in both sentence numbers.

1.  ¹It may seem as if Rudolph the Red-Nosed Reindeer has been part of Santa Claus's team forever. ²In fact, although Rudolph is one of the most popular holiday figures, he is a fairly recent addition to our Christmas celebration. ³It all began in 1939, when Robert May worked as an advertising writer for a Montgomery Ward department store. ⁴His store manager wanted something for Santa to hand out to parents shopping at Christmastime, so May came up with a Christmas poem. ⁵He first wanted to call the shiny-nosed reindeer "Rollo," and then "Reginald," but finally stuck with Rudolph. ⁶The poem about Rudolph was part of Christmas at Montgomery Ward until 1947, when songwriter Johnny Marks wrote music to accompany it. ⁷Two years later, singing cowboy Gene Autry recorded the song. ⁸Since then, the musical version of "Rudolph, the Red-Nosed Reindeer" has sold more than eighty million recordings.

    *Topic sentence(s):* _____

2.  ¹There is a tendency in our society to turn important decisions over to groups. ²In the business world, most important decisions are made around a conference table rather than behind one person's desk. ³In politics, major policy decisions are seldom vested in just one person. ⁴Groups of advisers, cabinet officers, committee members, or aides meet to deliberate and decide. ⁵In the courts, a defendant may request a trial by jury, and for some serious crimes, a jury trial is required by law. ⁶And of course, the U.S. Supreme Court renders group decisions on issues of major importance.

    *Topic sentence(s):* _____

3.  ¹Meditation provides several physical benefits. ²For example, it has been found to change the brain-wave patterns of the meditator. ³Specifically, it increases the occurrence of "alpha waves," which are associated with relaxation. ⁴During meditation, a person usually consumes less oxygen than normal. ⁵Decreased oxygen use indicates a very deep state of relaxation. ⁶In some cases meditation has even been shown to lower a person's high blood pressure. ⁷These and other effects of meditation show it can be a valuable part of a general health-care plan.

    *Topic sentence(s):* _____

*(Continues on next page)*

4.   [1]Fire extended humans' geographical boundaries by allowing them to travel into regions that were previously too cold to explore. [2]It also kept predators away, allowing early humans to sleep securely. [3]Fire, in fact, has been a significant factor in human development and progress in many ways. [4]Obvious benefits of fire are its uses in cooking and in hunting. [5]Probably even more important, however, is that learning to control fire allowed people to change the very rhythm of their lives. [6]Before fire, the human daily cycle coincided with the rising and setting of the sun. [7]With fire, though, man gained time to think and talk about the day's events and to prepare strategies for coping with tomorrow.

*Topic sentence(s):* _____

5.   [1]By the end of the first series of Sherlock Holmes stories, the author, Sir Arthur Conan Doyle, had become tired of writing detective stories. [2]So at the end of his second book of Holmes stories, he decided to have the detective die. [3]The last story in the collection, "The Final Problem," ends with Holmes and his arch-enemy, Moriarty, plunging to their deaths from a high cliff overlooking a waterfall. [4]After that, hundreds of letters poured in to Conan Doyle, begging him to bring Holmes back. [5]Also, magazines offered him huge sums of money for additional Sherlock Holmes adventures. [6]Finally, after nine years, Conan Doyle wrote a new story in which Holmes reappears and tells Dr. Watson that he did not die after all. [7]Sometimes it is the reader, not the author, who determines how long fictional heroes will live.

*Topic sentence(s):* _____

# MAIN IDEAS: Test C-3

A. Topic sentences appear at different locations within the following two paragraphs. Identify each topic sentence by writing the sentence number in the space provided.

1.  [1]Adult children who move back home can avoid family conflicts by following some helpful tips. [2]First, they should contribute what they can—and it doesn't necessarily have to be in terms of money: [3]Being productive family members will help them earn their keep. [4]This can involve tutoring or coaching younger sisters or brothers, or helping Mom and Dad with household chores and errands. [5]Second, these "returnees" should not expect their parents to rescue them from difficulties. [6]As adults, they are responsible for getting out of their own scrapes—and for trying to avoid them in the first place. [7]Last, they must respect their parents' lifestyles and own needs for independence. [8]It is unrealistic to expect parents' lives to revolve around the needs of a grown child, as they may have when the child was younger.

    *Topic sentence:* _____

2.  [1]1Through our telescopes we can see billions of galaxies, each of which has billions of stars. [2]And according to scientists, the probability is good that many of these stars have planets orbiting them. [3]Some astronomers believe that they have actually detected planets orbiting other stars, but these sightings have not been confirmed. [4]We do not know what the chance is that any one planet would have life on it. [5]But with so many billions of stars to choose from, it is probable that many millions of them are orbited by planets that support life forms. [6]And where there is life, there is the possibility that it might evolve to intelligence and civilization. [7]Thus there are probably numerous civilizations scattered around the universe.

    *Topic sentence:* _____

*(Continues on next page)*

**B.** Circle the letter of the sentence that best expresses the implied main idea of each of the following two paragraphs.

3.    A puddle of dark liquid under a car indicates a leak in the oil or transmission fluid. Another warning sign of car trouble is uneven wear on tire treads. If the outer edge of the tire tread wears out before the center, the tire is under-inflated. The most significant early warning signal, however, is lower mileage readings every time the tank is filled. Lower fuel economy is caused by a variety of problems ranging from a clogged filter to ignition or carburetor trouble.

*Implied main idea:*
a.  Several warning signs can indicate car problems.
b.  A puddle of dark liquid under a car is a sign that a car has an oil or transmission-fluid leak.
c.  The most significant warning signal of a car problem is getting lower mileage per gallon of gas.
d.  Various problems may cause a car's fuel economy to decrease.

4.    People with normal vision can perceive an infinite number of colors. They can experience the color blue, for example, ranging from the palest robin's-egg color to the deepest midnight hue. It is estimated, however, that 5,000 people in the United States do not experience color at all; rather, they see the world only in shades of gray. Even more—about 1.5 million Americans—are affected by partial color blindness. While most of them are unable to distinguish red and green colors, others cannot see blues or yellows.

*Implied main idea:*
a.  Many Americans are affected by partial color blindness.
b.  People with normal vision can see a wide range of colors.
c.  Total or partial color blindness robs many Americans of the ability to perceive color.
d.  Numerous Americans have a physical handicap of some kind.

**C.** Write out the implied main idea of paragraph 5.

5.    People who wish to reduce the salt in their diets should read labels carefully, looking for telltale ingredients like sodium and monosodium glutamate (MSG). Also, they should avoid salt-coated snacks such as potato chips, pretzels, and corn chips. Canned fish should be drained to removed the salted liquid it is packed in. Finally, the salt shaker should be removed from the table and replaced by onion powder, garlic powder, herbs, or lemon juice, all of which give food added taste.

*Implied main idea:*

_____

_____

# MAIN IDEAS: Test D-1

**A.** Circle the letter of the correct topic of each paragraph. Then circle the letter of the main idea—the author's primary point about the topic.

1.  Because the achieving of adulthood is a significant time in a young person's life, many traditional cultures mark the event in some ceremonial way. In some cultures, the ceremony is primarily a religious one. Jewish 13-year-olds are welcomed into the adult community through a bar or bat mitzvah, in which they read from the Torah during a synagogue service. Other ceremonies emphasize the taking on of adult characteristics. When a Northern Shoshone Indian girl begins menstruating for the first time, she is isolated and kept very busy so that she will become an industrious woman. And some ceremonies involve a painful coming-of-age rite. A boy of the Andaman Islands is welcomed to manhood by having sixty or more cuts made in his back with a sharpened arrowhead.

    *Topic:*  a. Young People          c. Painful Coming-of-Age Ceremonies
             b. Religious Ceremonies  d. The Achieving of Adulthood

    *Main idea:* a. To young people, achieving of adulthood is a significant time.
                b. Religious ceremonies vary from culture to culture.
                c. Painful coming-of-age ceremonies include cutting the back of a boy of the Andaman Islands with a sharpened arrowhead.
                d. The achieving of adulthood is marked in traditional cultures in ceremonial ways.

2.  Though natural-fiber purists may turn up their noses at it, polyester-and-cotton-blend clothing has advantages over all-cotton garments. For one thing, polyester, which is man-made, costs less than cotton, which grows naturally, but is expensive to process. Therefore, cotton/polyester clothing is more economical than pure cotton garments. Also, the polyester content of cotton clothing helps the garments retain their shape after repeated washings. That's because this synthetic does not share cotton's tendency to shrink or stretch after immersion. But perhaps polyester's most endearing quality is its "no-wrinkle policy." Unlike pure cotton, polyester blends require little or no ironing—hooray!

    *Topic:*  a. Polyester-and-Cotton Blend Clothing  c. Synthetic Fabrics
             b. Fabrics                              d. Ironing

    *Main idea:* a. Ironing is unnecessary with polyester-blend fabrics.
                b. Synthetic fabrics have several advantages over natural fabrics.
                c. Polyster-and-cotton blend clothing has advantages over all-cotton garments.
                d. All fabrics, either synthetic or natural, have advantages and disadvantages.

*(Continues on next page)*

B. Each of the following groups of items includes one main idea (topic sentence) and two supporting details. In the spaces provided, label each item with one of the following:

**MI** (for *Main Idea*)
**SD** (for *Supporting Detail*)

*Group 1*

_____ a. Since powerwalkers always have one foot on the ground, they feel only half as much impact when they touch down.

_____ b. For the city dweller, powerwalking—or walking briskly—has several advantages over jogging.

_____ c. The hard surfaces in our cities are much better suited to walking than to running.

*Group 2*

_____ a. During the Middle Ages, wearing garlic was thought to protect people against werewolves and vampires.

_____ b. The Romans believed that eating garlic gives strength and courage.

_____ c. Throughout the ages, people have believed that garlic has special powers.

# MAIN IDEAS: Test D-2

Topic sentences appear at various locations within the following paragraphs. Identify each topic sentence by writing its sentence number in the space provided. In the one case where the paragraph has a topic sentence both *near* the beginning and *at* the end, write in both sentence numbers.

1.  [1]Procrastinators put off unpleasant or burdensome tasks for different reasons. [2]"Perfectionist" procrastinators fear criticism or failure. [3]"Action-junkie" procrastinators enjoy the drama of putting things off until the very last moment. [4]"Crazy-making" procrastinators stall as a way to manipulate others. [5]"Feeling good" procrastinators feel obligated to have fun rather than to do what they should. [6]And "Don't Rely on Me" procrastinators don't want to be responsible for anyone or anything.

    *Topic sentence(s):* _____

2.  [1]An author doing research for a book asked thousands of Americans what made them happy. [2]Among the popular responses she received were eating ice-cream sandwiches and candy, being offered a football ticket, and visiting city parks. [3]Other common responses included eating ravioli, feeling the cool underside of a pillow, and rereading old love letters. [4]Almost no one gave the answer of owning flashy jewelry, showy cars or other expensive things. [5]The author concluded that most of the things that put a smile on our face are simple, free or inexpensive.

    *Topic sentence(s):* _____

3.  [1]Plastic trash bags were once considered a major menace to the environment. [2]The makers of plastic trash bags responded to the environmental concerns and made several positive changes in their product. [3]First, they made use of a new additive—actually, potato peels—to make the bags biodegradable (that is, capable of breaking down and being absorbed by the environment). [4]Next, they removed any ingredients in their plastic formula which would contaminate soil in a landfill. [5]Finally, they determined that the bags can be burned safely, providing more fuel value than wood or coal.

    *Topic sentence(s):* _____

*(Continues on next page)*

4.    [1]According to a study of firstborn children, an amazing 21 of the country's first 23 astronauts were firstborn in their families. [2]Also, slightly more than half—52 percent—of our presidents were firstborn. [3]Less positive is the fact that firstborns are under a lot of pressure to succeed because their families often pin their hopes and dreams on them. [4]Also, as the eldest, they are expected to "set an example" for their younger siblings. [5]Furthermore, these firstborns sometimes have trouble with personal relationships because they learned to be very independent and to enjoy doing things on their own—since they were the only child in their families until their younger brothers and sisters were born. [6]The conclusion of the study is that being a firstborn child is a mixed blessing, having positive and some negative aspects.

*Topic sentence(s):* _____

5.    [1]Job-related illnesses and injuries in certain professions are well known. [2]No one is surprised, for example, to hear of knee or back problems in a professional football player. [3]Lately, however, occupation-caused injuries have become a virtual epidemic among professional musicians. [4]As many as three-fourths of the individuals who earn a living by playing an instrument have become disabled, and for some instruments virtually all players eventually are affected. [5]Trumpeters typically develop neck strain, throat problems and spine curvature. [6]Pianists often wind up with crippled right hands as well as back problems. [7]Even such a gentle instrument as the harp puts its players at risk for back and neck injuries. [8]Obviously, being a musician is a risky profession.

*Topic sentence(s):* _____

## MAIN IDEAS: Test D-3

**A.** Topic sentences appear at different locations within the following two paragraphs. Identify each topic sentence by writing the sentence number in the space provided.

1.  [1]With so many young, single people having babies, the question arises as to how happy they are being young parents. [2]A national survey of young, single mothers and fathers reveals that most were happier before they became parents. [3]Sixty-seven percent of the 9,000 new parents, aged 16 to 22, who responded to the survey said having a baby presented more problems than they envisioned. [4]Fifty-six percent of the respondents said they had to drop out of school, despite their hopes that they could manage schoolwork plus rearing a baby. [5]A majority (73 percent) said they were forced to seek financial help from family, friends and/or government agencies, and 37 percent said they accepted low-paying, unsatisfying jobs out of necessity. [6]Also, 70 percent said they missed the "good times" with friends that they enjoyed before their babies were born.

    *Topic sentence:* _____

2.  [1]The evidence that tobacco smoke kills is beyond dispute, yet millions of Americans continue to smoke. [2]There are several reasons why people still smoke, reasons which differ from one person to the next. [3]One of the primary reasons is that smoking is highly addictive, some say as addictive as heroin. [4]Smokers trying to quit may suffer from withdrawal symptoms which they cannot overcome. [5]A second reason for continued smoking is that it becomes a social habit. [6]For example, some smokers don't feel comfortable at a party without a cigarette. [7]These habits are hard to break and become even more difficult if others in the same social group continue to smoke. [8]A third reason for many to continue smoking is that they just don't believe reports that smoking is dangerous. [9]They see tobacco advertisements with attractive people doing interesting and exciting things. [10]They listen to tobacco companies deny the evidence that cigarettes are harmful, and they read that the government continues to subsidize tobacco farmers. [11]Faced with contradictory information, they choose to believe that smoking will not hurt them.

    *Topic sentence:* _____

*(Continues on next page)*

**B.** Circle the letter of the sentence that best expresses the implied main idea of each of the following two paragraphs.

3. For every thirteen Anglo-Americans and thirty-three blacks that do not complete high school, there are forty Mexican-Americans who do not. Eight times as many Mexican-Americans as Anglo-Americans are held back at least one year in school. And Mexican-Americans and Puerto Ricans are twice as likely to be expelled from school as are Anglo-Americans.

*Implied main idea:*
a. More Anglo-Americans and blacks graduate high school than Hispanics.
b. Our educational system seems to be failing its Hispanic students.
c. Hispanics are much more likely to be held back at least one year in school than Anglo-Americans are.
d. Our educational system compares very poorly with other countries in the ways we educate minorities.

4. After *The Deer Hunter* first appeared in movie theaters, more than two dozen people reenacted the Russian roulette scene in the movie and killed themselves with a bullet through the brain. Similarly, a San Diego high-school student killed his parents and sister with an ax after watching a television movie about Lizzie Borden, the ax murderer. And then there's John Hinckley, Jr., who after seeing the movie *Taxi Driver*, became obsessed with actress Jodie Foster. In the movie, a psychopath tries to "protect" Foster's character by killing people. Hinckley, of course, tried to kill President Reagan.

*Implied main idea:*
a. The Russian roulette scene should not have been included in *The Deer Hunter*.
b. A television movie on Lizzie Borden influenced a high-school student to kill his parents and sister.
c. Violence in movies can cause or influence violent behavior.
d. The man who tried to kill President Reagan had watched the violent movie *Taxi Driver*.

**C.** Write out the implied main idea of paragraph 5.

5. In America, the "A-Okay" gesture—made by joining the thumb and fore-finger in a circle—means that everything is fine. An American tourist will find that this positive sign in the United States has an insulting connotation in France and in Belgium. There the sign means: "You're worth zero!" In southern Italy the exact same gesture means "a jerk," and in Greece and Turkey it conveys an insulting or vulgar sexual invitation.

*Implied main idea:*

_____

_____

# MAIN IDEAS: Test E-1

**A.** Circle the letter of the correct topic of each paragraph. Then circle the letter of the main idea—the author's primary point about the topic.

1. Plain white vinegar can be used in place of many household products—to the benefit of both the environment and your wallet. For example, placing a few shallow bowls of vinegar in a smoky room will freshen it just as well as—if not better than—aerosol-spray room deodorizers will. Vinegar is a natural freshener and will not release polluting chemicals into the air, as spray deodorizers may. Vinegar is also an effective fabric softener—just toss one cup into the final rinse cycle of your washing machine (or add a dash to the rinse water, if you're hand-washing). Unlike commercial fabric softeners, vinegar contains no dyes or perfumes that may chemically pollute. Last, vinegar can be used in place of store-bought glass cleaners when three tablespoons are mixed with one quart of warm water.

   *Topic:*    a. Household Products      c. Plain White Vinegar
               b. Commercial Fabric Softeners    d. A Glass Cleaner

   *Main idea:* a. Household products come in a large variety and a wide range of prices.
               b. Commercial fabric softeners contain dyes and perfumes.
               c. Plain white vinegar is an inexpensive and environmentally safe substitute for some household products.
               d. Unlike commercial products such as aerosol-sprays and fabric softeners, plain white vinegar is environmentally safe.

2. Swiss bank accounts are no longer the safe places they once were for Americans hoping to evade U.S. laws. The Swiss have agreed to reveal information about the accounts of Americans accused of stock swindles. And, although tax evasion by out-of-country clients is not a crime according to Swiss law, the Swiss will now release information about the bank accounts of American mobsters charged with not paying their taxes.

   *Topic:*    a. Safe Places      c. U.S. Laws
               b. Swiss Bank Accounts    d. American Mobsters

   *Main idea:* a. America mobsters seek safe places in which to hide the money they earned illegally.
               b. Swiss bank accounts are not the safe places they once were for Americans hoping to escape U.S. laws.
               c. According to American law, tax evasion is a crime.
               d. The Swiss will now reveal information about the bank accounts of Americans accused of stock swindles.

*(Continues on next page)*

**B.** Each of the following groups of items includes one main idea (topic sentence) and two supporting details. In the spaces provided, label each item with one of the following:

**MI** (for *Main Idea*)
**SD** (for *Supporting Detail*)

### Group 1

_____ a. Growth factors have healed eye wounds that previously would have required surgery.

_____ b. Scientists have discovered human substances called growth factors, chemicals that may revolutionize medicine.

_____ c. Researchers feel growth factors may turn out to cure sterility in men and Alzheimer's disease.

### Group 2

_____ a. Couples who knew each other only slightly but fell instantly in love found that their feelings for each other grew weaker instead of stronger.

_____ b. The couples who considered themselves happily married reported that they were not powerfully attracted to their partners when they first met, but that they gradually found each other more attractive as they grew to know and understand each other.

_____ c. Love at first sight is a poor basis for a happy marriage, according to a study of one thousand married and divorced couples.

# MAIN IDEAS: Test E-2

Topic sentences appear at various locations within the following paragraphs. Identify each topic sentence by writing its sentence number in the space provided. In the one case where the paragraph has a topic sentence both *near* the beginning and *at* the end, write in both sentence numbers.

1.  [1]Queen Isabella of Spain, who died in 1504, boasted that she'd had only two baths in her life—at birth and before her marriage. [2]In colonial America, leaders frowned on bathing, because it involved nudity, which, they feared, could lead to loose morals. [3]Indeed, laws in Virginia and Pennsylvania either limited or outright banned bathing—and, for a time in Philadelphia, anyone who bathed more than once a month faced jail. [4]Furthermore, some of the early Christian churches discouraged sudsing up because of its association with the depravity common in the Roman baths. [5]Clearly, the notion that "cleanliness is next to godliness" has not always been a popular one.

    *Topic sentence(s):* _____

2.  [1]Propaganda is information that is methodically spread in order to persuade audiences to adopt a certain opinion. [2]Advertising is an ever-present form of propaganda in our lives. [3]Four common propaganda techniques are frequently observed in the advertising we see and hear every day. [4]One technique, the testimonial, involves a well-known person appearing on behalf of the product being sold. [5]Advertisers assume that if we like Cher and admire her looks, we'll feel positive about a fitness club that she endorses. [6]Another common propaganda technique, the bandwagon, makes us want to be "one of the gang." [7]"Everybody's switching to..." "Don't be left out..." or "All across America, people are discovering..." are phrases that signal a bandwagon approach. [8]The plain folks propaganda technique is especially popular on TV these days. [9]In plain folks commercials, we see and hear "regular" consumers talk about their experience using a certain phone company, headache remedy or brand of coffee. [10]A final common propaganda technique, the transfer, encourages us to link two unrelated objects in our mind. [11]When a powerful cougar prowls around a shiny new car, for example, advertisers hope we will transfer our sense of the animal's speed, strength, and beauty to our vision of their product. [12]These four propaganda devices are put to work in ads every day on TV and radio and in newspapers and magazines.

    *Topic sentence(s):* _____

*(Continues on next page)*

3.  [1]Sociologists have several basic methods of doing research. [2]First is the experiment, which is useful for clearly defined questions in which varying factors can be controlled. [3]Sociologists also use the survey, which is useful for gaining facts about a particular group; in order to be valid, the survey must be random. [4]Direct observation is helpful for in-depth studies of social processes, but to useful, such observation must be made by a skilled researcher. [5]Finally, existing information can be studied as the basis for new conclusions.

    *Topic sentence(s):* _____

4.  [1]Frozen foods are commonly thought to be inferior to fresh or even canned versions. [2]The fact is, however, that frozen foods can be superior in several ways. [3]Because vitamins are usually destroyed by the passage of time, fresh or canned fruits and vegetables can lose much of their nutrients from the farm to the dinner table. [4]But foods that are frozen have their vitamins "locked in" at their just-picked peak (as some ads rightfully claim), so there is very little, if any, vitamin loss. [5]Also, prepared frozen dinners provide portion control, something that home-cooked meals generally do not. [6]Finally, the nutrition labeling on prepared frozen foods is often far more complete than that on canned ones—and fresh foods almost invariably lack any kind of nutritional labeling. [7]This nutrition information can be extremely helpful to those watching their intake of cholesterol, sodium, calories, fat and so forth.

    *Topic sentence(s):* _____

5.  [1]Stories of the mythical Camelot depict a world of dashing knights in shining armor and beautiful damsels in distress. [2]In actuality, that world probably consisted of smelly men in rusty tin suits and damsels in a certain kind of distress—the distress of being constantly pregnant and of having absolutely no rights in a male-dominated society. [3]Those same stories often glorified war with brave men fighting to the death for king and country. [4]Actually, most battle fatalities were direct results of medieval medicine. [5]Letting the "bad blood" out of a sick person was a common medical procedure, and basic cleanliness was not. [6]Other stories of the fabled Camelot housed royalty in glittering palaces, clothed them in silks, and shrouded them in mystery and awe. [7]But what is awesome about living in a cold, stone, rat-infested fortress with poor ventilation? [8]As for silks, war-indebted kings could rarely afford such commodities from foreign lands. [9]Wool from home usually did the trick. [10]And there's certainly nothing mysterious about the discomfort caused by coarse woolen undergarments or the health problems caused by the infrequent, if any, washings of such clothing. [11]It seems that through the years the harsh realities of life in the Middle Ages have become overlooked, and we prefer to create our own fantastic, if unrealistic, scenarios of history.

    *Topic sentence(s):* _____

# MAIN IDEAS: Test E-3

**A.** Topic sentences appear at different locations within the following two paragraphs. Identify each topic sentence by writing the sentence number in the space provided.

1. [1]What do words mean? [2]Many words have two kinds of meaning: the dictionary meaning of a word is called its denotation; any additional meanings it suggests are its connotations. [3]For example, the dictionary defines "communism" as an economic system based on community ownership of property. [4]That is its denotation. [5]But for many Americans, "communism" also carries a sharp emotional connotation: prison camps, forced labor, and firing squads. [6]Politicians and advertisers tend to use words more for their emotional connotations than for their actual meanings, or denotations.

   *Topic sentence:* _____

2. [1]The American ideal of a lush green lawn is borrowed from England, where the cool misty climate makes it easy to grow grass. [2]In America, however, lawns are an energy-intensive, wasteful, and nonproductive form of landscaping. [3]To begin with, achieving a picture-perfect lawn requires gallons of expensive fertilizer and hazardous pesticides that pollute ground water and run off into lakes and rivers. [4]In addition, lawn owners often exterminate the insects, moles, and gophers that play a part in the balance of nature. [5]Equally destructive is the constant watering lawns require, often where water is a limited resource. [6]Finally, the lawn must be mowed on a regular basis to give it that green carpet effect, requiring endless output of human and mechanical energy. [7]After all the labor and expense, the final result is a flat carpet that lacks interesting features, wildlife, or edible produce.

   *Topic sentence:* _____

**B.** Circle the letter of the sentence that best expresses the implied main idea of each of the following two paragraphs.

3. One reason tabloids publish untrue stories about celebrities, even though they know the celebrities might sue, is free advertising. If there is a lawsuit, it will make the news, and the tabloid gains the publicity. Furthermore, in a lawsuit the burden of proof is on the celebrity, not the paper. Such lawsuits are also both expensive and time-consuming; a court delay, for example, can prevent a movie star from beginning work on a new project. and the chances of collecting a significant amount of damages are slim. Finally, tabloids publish untrue stories for the obvious reason: whether it is true or not, people love celebrity gossip—and it sells papers.

*(Continues on next page)*

*Implied main idea:*
a. Tabloids publish untrue stories about celebrities.
b. Tabloids publish untrue stories about celebrities because celebrities will think twice about suing.
c. There are a few reasons why tabloids publish untrue stories about celebrities even though the celebrities might sue.
d. Even if celebrities sue tabloids over untrue stores, they are unlikely to collect a lot of money for damages.

4.    In the late 1980s, concern about the deadly effects of illegal drugs became a top national issue. Politicians loudly proclaimed a "war on drugs," and TV news shows carried regular reports about the fatal toll of drugs, especially "crack" cocaine. These drugs do have a terrible effect on individuals and society, but the facts about them are somewhat different from their popular image. Each year, about two thousand people die from heroin overdoses, and about three thousand die from cocaine-related causes. At the same time, 50,000 people die every year because of alcohol—including thousands of innocent victims of drunk drivers. Additionally, a third of a million people die every year from cancers due to smoking cigarettes.

*Implied main idea:*
a. In the late 1980s, politicians proclaimed a "war on drugs."
b. Our "war on drugs" ignores the two deadliest (though legal) drugs of all, alcohol and tobacco.
c. Thousands of people die each year from heroin overdoses and cocaine-related causes.
d. More people die each year from alcohol-related causes than from cocaine-related causes.

C. Write out the implied main idea of paragraph 5.

5.    Scientists have wondered for years how an insect with a brain the size of a pinhead can migrate almost two thousand miles from various points in North America to winter in California and Mexico. To complicate the mystery, due to the monarch's short life span, the butterfly who migrates in the fall is a few generations removed from the one who did it the year before. Therefore, it makes the journey home without the benefit of memory. One more puzzling aspect of this insect has intrigued scientists throughout their studies: out of all the butterflies in the world, the monarch is the only type that migrates.

*Implied main idea:*

_____

_____

# 3

# Supporting Details

You know from the previous chapter that the main idea is the umbrella statement covering all of the other material in a paragraph—examples, reasons, facts, and other specific details. All of those specific details are also called *supporting details*—they are the necessary information that backs up and explains the main idea.

## MAJOR AND MINOR DETAILS

There are two kinds of supporting details—major and minor. Taken together, the main idea and its major supporting details form the basic framework of paragraphs. The major details are the primary points that support the main idea. Paragraphs usually contain minor details as well. While the major details explain and develop the main idea, they, in turn, are expanded upon by the minor supporting details.

You've already learned that a paragraph's main idea is more general than its supporting details. Similarly, major supporting details are more general than minor supporting details. An important reading skill is the ability to distinguish the major details from the minor ones.

To get a better idea of the role of major and minor supporting details, consider the following main idea from a popular science article:

### Main Idea

The sex lives of insects are full of horrible events.

This sentence immediately brings to mind such a question as, "Just what is meant by horrible events?" This is where supporting details come in: they clarify and explain. Turn to the next page to see the same main idea with a major supporting detail:

## Main Idea and Major Detail

The sex lives of insects are full of horrible events. In many cases, only the female partner leaves a sexual encounter alive.

Now we have a better idea of what the main idea really means. Often, however, the major details themselves are further explained, and that's where the minor support comes in. A major detail introduces a new point, and minor details develop that point. Here is the same paragraph with several minor details that provide more information about the major detail:

## Main Idea and Major and Minor Details

The sex lives of insects are full of horrible events. In many cases, only the female partner leaves a sexual encounter alive. The female praying mantis, for example, occasionally bites her mate's head off during sex. In the case of a certain species of fly, the female follows mating by sucking the body content of the male out through his mouth. Yet another example is seen in the queen ant and her mate, both of whom have wings. When they have finished their encounter high in the air, the male's wings fall off and he drops dead.

See if you can separate major from minor support in the following paragraph. It begins with the main idea and continues with several major and minor details. (To round off the paragraph, the main idea is restated at the end.) Try to locate and put a check in front of the *three* details that give major supporting information about the main idea.

As you read, keep an eye out for certain words that show the writer is adding a new point. Examples of such addition words are *first, next, another, in addition,* and *finally.*

### Service Stations No More

Gas stations still provide gas, but often they no longer provide service. For one thing, attendants at many stations no longer pump gas. Motorists pull up to a combination convenience store and gas island where the attendant with clean hands is comfortably enclosed in a glass booth with a trap for taking money. Drivers must get out of their cars to pay for and pump their own gas, which has the bonus of perfuming their hands and clothes with a hint of gas. In addition, even at stations with "pump jockeys," workers have completely forgotten other services that once went hand in hand with pumping gas. They no longer know how to ask, "Check your oil or water?" Drivers must plead with attendants to wash windshields. And the last attendant who checked tire pressure must have died at least ten years ago. Finally, many gas stations no longer have mechanics on the premises. Limping down the highway in a backfiring car for emergency help at the friendly service station is a thing of the past. Car owners cannot even assume that their neighborhood station offers simple maintenance services. The skillful mechanic who can replace a belt or fix a tire in a few minutes has been replaced by a bored teenager in a jumpsuit who doesn't know a carburetor from a charge card. Today's gas stations are fuel stops, but too often that is all they are.

Now see if you checked correctly the three major supporting details. You'll find them after the main idea in the following outline of the paragraph:

**Main idea:** Many gas stations no longer provide service.

**Major supporting details:**

1. Attendants at many stations no longer pump gas.
2. Even at stations with "pump jockeys," workers have forgotten other services.
3. Many gas stations no longer have mechanics on the premises.

A more complete outline, showing minor details as well, would be as follows:

**Main idea:** Many gas stations no longer provide service.

**Major and minor supporting details:**

1. Attendants at many stations no longer pump gas.
   a. Stations are often combined with convenience stores, at which attendants only take money.
   b. Drivers must get out of their cars to pay for and pump gas.
2. Even at stations with "pump jockeys," workers have forgotten other services.
   a. Attendants do not ask to check oil and water.
   b. Attendants do not wash windshields.
   c. Attendants do not check tire pressure.
3. Many gas stations no longer have mechanics on the premises.
   a. The neighborhood station can no longer be counted on to help in emergencies.
   b. Stations may not even offer simple maintenance services.
   c. Skillful mechanics have been replaced by attendants who are ignorant about cars.

Notice how the complete outline about gas stations goes from the general to the specific. The more general statements are clarified and developed by the points beneath them. At a glance, you can see that the major supporting details introduce new points and that the minor details expand on those points. The outline, by its very nature, divides the paragraph into main idea, major supporting details, and minor supporting details.

One excellent way, then, to gain experience in identifying major supporting details is to outline a selection. In doing so, you make clear the relationships between the basic parts of a piece. Recognizing such relationships is an important part of effective study.

## HOW TO LOCATE MAJOR DETAILS

By now you may see that to locate major details, you must (1) find the main idea and (2) decide on the points that are *primary support* for that main idea. Practice these steps by reading the paragraph below. Identify and underline the main idea. Then ask yourself, "What are the chief points the author uses to back up the main idea?" Finally, fill in the main idea and major details in the outline that follows. The rest of the details in the passage will be minor details.

¹Two influences in particular help create teenage underachievers in school. ²Many such underachievers have experienced poor relationships with their parents. ³For example, parents may be poor role models, may reject their children, interact inconsistently with them, or neglect to urge them to be independent. ⁴Not surprisingly, the parents of underachievers often are anxious and unhappy with themselves as parents. ⁵Another influence on underachieving teens is the school itself, which may simply be too boring for the interests and needs of students. ⁶The fault may lie with teachers, curriculum, or both.

**Main idea:** _____

_____

1. _____

_____

2. _____

_____

By the time you finished the paragraph, you probably realized that the first sentence presents the main idea: "Two influences in particular help create teenage underachievers in school." The rest of the paragraph then develops that idea by introducing and discussing the two influences. Those influences are introduced in sentences 2 (poor relationships with parents) and 5 (the school). Sentences 2 and 5, then, contain the major supporting details—both essential to the author's explanation.

The other sentences (3, 4, and 6) go on to develop those major points— they are the minor supporting details. Minor supporting details may be important to a thorough understanding, but they can be eliminated without removing the author's primary points. Note how the following version of the paragraph—without the minor details—still makes sense.

> [1]Two influences in particular help create teenage underachievers in school. [2]Many such underachievers have experienced poor relationships with their parents. [5]Another influence on underachieving teens is the school itself, which may simply be too boring for the interests and needs of students.

Note that an addition word *(Another)* introduces the second major detail.

## A Note on Maps

Many students find it helpful to organize material in a very visual way. They create a *map*, or diagram, to show the relationship between the main parts of a selection. A map of the above paragraph might look like this:

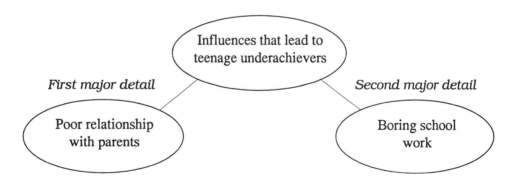

## ➤ *Practice 1*

Major and minor supporting details are mixed together in the two groups that follow. The details in each group support a given main idea. Separate the major, more general details from the minor ones by filling in the outline or map. Some details have been filled in for you.

### Group 1

*Note:* Check (✓) each item after you use it. Doing so will help you see which items you have left.

**Main idea:** There are several reasons for the failure of the neighborhood clothing store.

- Two competitors within two blocks ✓
- Relied on word of mouth
- High expenses ✓
- Poor advertising
- Faced a side street ✓
- Unexpected rise in wholesale prices
- No display ad in Yellow Pages
- Bad location
- High salaries for workers

**Major detail:** 1. _____

Minor details:      a. *Two competitors within two blocks*

     b. *Faced a side street*

**Major detail:** 2. _____

Minor details:      a. _____

     b. _____

**Major detail:** 3. *High expenses* _____

Minor details:      a. _____

     b. _____

### Group 2

*Note:* Check (✓) each item after you use it. Doing so will help you see which items you have left.

**Main idea:** Certain substitutions can lower the amount of fat in your diet .

- Ground turkey breast instead of ground beef
- Substitutes for high-fat dairy products ✓
- Boiled ham instead of bacon
- Reduced-calorie margarine instead of butter ✓
- Skim milk instead of whole milk
- Substitutes for fats
- Broth or wine instead of oil for light "frying" ✓
- Yogurt instead of sour cream
- Substitutes for high-fat meats

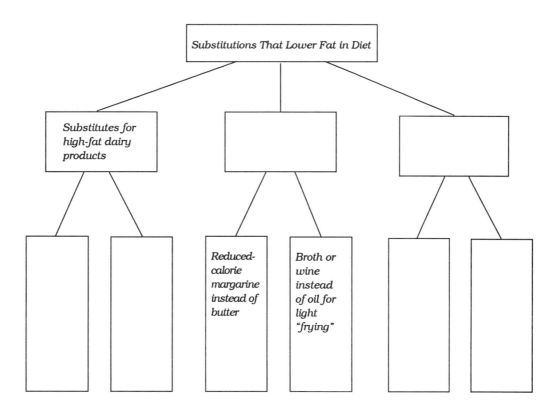

## ➢ *Practice 2*

Both major and minor details are used to support the main idea in each of the paragraphs that follow. Separate the major, more general details from the minor ones by filling in the outline or map in each case.

1.    Not all addictions are to drugs or alcohol. Some people are addicted to sports. Their lives in winter are spent watching, playing, and talking about football and hockey. In the summer their lives revolve around baseball, golf, and tennis. Other people are television addicts. As soon as they walk in the door of their home or apartment, they flip on the television to start getting their "fix." They seem to schedule much of their lives around their favorite shows, of which there are many. Love addicts are perhaps the most obsessive of all. Such people cannot function in their everyday lives if they don't have a boyfriend or a girlfriend, and their moods are only as good as the status of their relationship. Such people are unable to break off damaging personal relationships, and they will return again and again to a partner who misuses and abuses them.

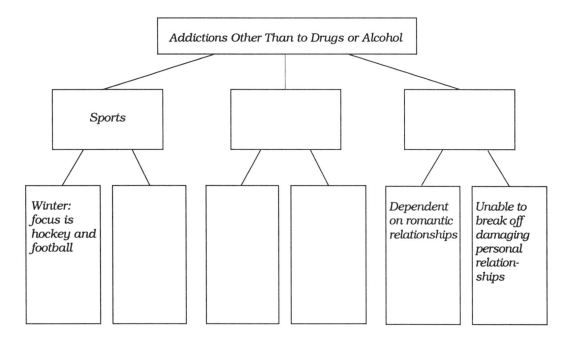

2.    Animals open up their mouths for several important reasons besides hunger. One is to warn an intruder away from the animal's territory. Lizards and fish threaten other animals by opening their mouths, and bears and wolves show their teeth before attacking. Another reason animals "open wide" is to quiet aggression. The lion, for example, yawns to distract other lions that might be ready for a fight. Other animals, including the crocodile, open their mouths

when they need their teeth cleaned. Little birds will come in and eat leftover food off the crocodile's teeth—acting like live toothbrushes. Finally, an open mouth may be used to signal an interest in the opposite sex. Wide-open beaks are an important part of the penguin's courtship dance.

**Main idea:** _____

_____

1. _____

   Examples: _____

   _____

2. _____

   Example: _____

3. _____

   Example: _____

4. _____

   Example: _____

## Asking Questions

We have seen that one way to identify major details is to find the main idea and ask, "What are the chief points the author uses to back up the main idea?" Another way to locate major details is to turn the main idea into a question that begins with a question word: *who, what, where, when, why,* or *how.* For the passage earlier in this chapter on underachievers, we could have asked, "*What* are the two influences that help create teenage underachievers?"

See if you can turn the main idea of the paragraph below into a basic question about the passage. Then try to answer that question by finding the major supporting details of the paragraph. After filling in the blank spaces, read the comments that follow the paragraph.

Sexual abuse of the young—a tragedy that victimizes one in every four girls and one in every ten boys under age 18—can often be prevented. When children are very young, they should be taught that they have a right to the privacy of their own bodies. In addition, parents should teach children to recognize potential abusers and how to say *no* to adults. Having been trained to be obedient, children often hesitate to expose people who tell them to "keep our special secret," especially if those persons are friends or relatives. (As many as 85 percent of sexually abused children are victims of someone they know and trust.) Similarly, parents should encourage children to trust their instincts to run away from elders that make them feel uneasy.

Question formed out of the main idea:_____

_____

Supporting details that answer the question:

1. _____

2. _____

3. _____

The first sentence of this passage states that sexual abuse of the young can often be prevented. That probably made you think of the question: "How can sexual abuse of the young be prevented?" As you read on, you see that the passage describes three ways that sexual abuse can be prevented. The fact that the paragraph answers your question confirms that you have found the main idea (stated in the first sentence). And by converting the main idea into a question, you have made yourself alert to the major supporting details of a passage. Those major details are: 1) Young children should be taught they have a right to the privacy of their own bodies, 2) parents should teach children to recognize potential abusers and how to say *no* to adults, and 3) parents should encourage children to run away from from elders that make them feel uneasy.

## ➤ *Practice 3*

To find the major details in the following paragraphs, you will ask and answer questions about the main idea. Note that both paragraphs have been taken from the previous chapter.

1.   Complete and then answer the question formed from the main idea of the following paragraph.

Serious depression, as opposed to the fleeting kind we all feel at times, has several warning signs. Some or all may be present within the affected individual. One symptom of depression is a change in sleep patterns—either sleeplessness or sleeping too much. Another sign is abnormal eating patterns, either eating too much or loss of appetite. Finally, a general feeling of hopelessness may signal depression. People feel indifferent to their families and jobs and may begin to think that life is not worth living.

What are the warning signs of _____?

a. _____

b. _____

c. _____

2.   Write out and then answer a question formed from the main idea of the following paragraph.

Every thirty-seven seconds, a car is stolen somewhere in the United States. Although this statistic is frightening, it is possible for drivers to prevent car theft if they take a few simple precautions. When they leave their cars, they should lock all valuables in the trunk or glove compartment to avoid tempting a thief to break in. Parking in the middle of the block on a busy, well-lighted street will also deter would-be thieves. The most obvious precaution, of course, is always to lock the car and take the keys—even if the driver is stopping for just a minute. One out of every five stolen cars was left unlocked with the keys in the ignition.

What question does the passage answer? _____

_____

a. _____

b. _____

c. _____

## READING CAREFULLY

You have seen that major details support the main idea and that minor details expand on the major ones. The minor and major details thus work together to clarify the main idea. For example, let's consider again the paragraph about incompetent bosses from the previous chapter. The main idea is underlined, and the major details are boldfaced. The rest are minor details.

<u>Many bosses share two weaknesses</u>. First, **they are often poor communicators**. They tell people what to do and how and when to do it, without explaining the reasons for their rules, and they do not welcome feedback or questions. In addition, **many bosses are not well-rounded people**. Their jobs tend to be their lives, and they expect everybody who works for them to think and act the way they do. These bosses frown upon hearing that a family matter will keep an employee from working late, and they come out of their office looking irritated if there is too much talk or laughter during a coffee break.

Clearly, both the major and minor details are helpful for the reader to really understand the main idea. The general ideas that many bosses are often poor communicators and are not well-rounded people are clarified by the minor details. This illustrates that a careful reading of *both* major and minor details can be important for good comprehension.

Try using your recognition of major and minor details to help you carefully read the passage below. After a close reading, answer the questions that follow.

Symbols, common to all societies, take many forms. What people wear, for one thing, often has symbolic meaning. Queens, priests, the police, and medicine men wear costumes that are symbols of their occupations. A wedding band signifies that one is married, and special buttons, ribbons, and tattoos can represent various group memberships. In fact, objects of any kind may be symbols. Flags are symbols of countries, states, ships, and organizations. Trophies stand for excellence and special achievement, whether in the acting profession or for something as familiar as a baseball or bowling championship. And on our streets, red and green lights have specific meanings. However, the most common symbols of all in human society are words, which have their meanings only because people agree on what they stand for.

1.   To find the major details of the paragraph, which question would be helpful?
     a.  What are examples of things people wear that have symbolic meaning?
     b.  What forms do symbols take?
     c.  What are the most common symbols in human society?

2.   The major details of the paragraph are
     a.  what people wear, objects of any kind, words.
     b.  queens, priests, the police, and medicine men.
     c.  countries, states, ships, and organizations.

3.   *Fill in the blank*: The most common symbols are _____

4.   *Fill in the blank*: An example in the paragraph of a symbol worn by people is

     _____

5.   Green lights (meaning "go") are an example of which major detail?

     _____

The answer to question 1 is *b*. The answer to question 2 is *a*. The answer to 3 is *words*. Any one of the following can be the answer to question 4: costumes that are symbols of their occupations, a wedding band, special buttons, ribbons, or tattoos. The answer to 5 is *objects of any kind.*

## ➤*Practice 4*

Answer the questions that follow the paragraphs.

A.   When we call someone *pig* or *swine*, we do not mean it as a compliment. But pigs do not deserve to be used as a symbol for an insult. They are probably not as dirty as they are made out to be. According to one pig keeper, swine are very clean when allowed to live in a clean environment. He feels pigs are usually dirty simply because their keepers don't clean their pens. In any case, no one has proven that the pig that wallows in mud prefers that to a cool bath. Furthermore, pigs are smarter than most people think. Many farmers, for example, have observed that pigs frequently undo complicated bolts on gates in search of adventure or romance. So the next time you call someone a pig, perhaps he or she ought to be someone you wish to praise.

1. In general, the major details of this passage are
    a. reasons why pigs are dirty.
    b. ways in which pigs are "better" than people think.
    c. ways to insult or compliment people.

2. Specifically, the major details are
    a. Pigs are probably not as dirty as people think; pigs are smarter than most people think.
    b. Pigs may be dirty because their pens are dirty; it hasn't been proved that pigs prefer mud to a cool bath; pigs have been seen undoing complicated bolts.
    c. People use *pig* and *swine* as insults; *pig* and *swine* should be considered praise.

3. One pig keeper feels that pigs will stay clean if they are
    a. given baths.
    b. praised.
    c. kept in a clean environment.

4. What example is given to show that pigs are smarter than they are often thought to be? _____

5. The answer to question 4 is
    a. the main idea.
    b. a major detail.
    c. a minor detail.

B. Persons suffering from mental illness have been treated inhumanely for much of history. Some societies simply shipped their unbalanced citizens out of the country. So-called "ships of fools" would sail to uninhabited lands where the mentally ill passengers were left to fend for themselves. In other times and places, the mentally ill were thought to be witches or possessed by the devil. They were subject to torture, exorcism and even execution. Still other societies thought the mentally ill were deliberate wrong-doers who could be punished into health. These societies followed the lead of Celsus, a first-century Roman scholar, who recommended that victims of mental illness be punished "by hunger, chains, and fetters."

6. In general, the major details of this passage are
    a. causes of mental illness.
    b. places where people were mentally ill.
    c. inhumane ways of treating the mentally ill.

7. *Complete the summary of the first major detail:* Some societies got rid of their mentally ill by _____

   _____.

8. *Complete the summary of the second major detail:* The mentally ill were sometimes treated as though they were_____

   _____.

9. *Fill in the blank:* People who thought the mentally ill behaved badly on purpose felt that mental illness should be treated by _____

   _____.

10. The information in the last sentence of the passage is
    a. the main idea.
    b. a major detail.
    c. a minor detail.

## ➤ Review

To review what you've learned in this chapter, answer each of these questions about supporting details.

1. *Fill in the blanks:* Major supporting details are more (*general, specific*) _____ than main ideas. Minor supporting details are more (*general, specific*) _____ than major details.

2. *Circle the letter of each of the three answers that apply:* Supporting details can be
   a. reasons           d. main ideas
   b. topics            e. facts
   c. examples          f. central points

3. Label each part of the outline form below with one of the following:
   • Main Idea
   • Major Supporting Detail
   • Minor Supporting Detail

   _____

   1. _____

      a. _____

      b. _____

   2. _____

# SUPPORTING DETAILS: Test A-1

**A.** Complete the outline by filling in each blank with one item from the list below. Begin by finding and filling in the main idea, and then go on to the missing supporting details.

*Note:* Check (✓) each item after you use it. Doing so will help you see which items you have left.

- It is a myth that regular margarine is less fattening than butter. ✓
- Margarine and butter have the same number of calories.
- It is a false idea that honey is healthier than sugar.
- Some of our beliefs about food are false notions, or myths.
- Although vitamin A is necessary to the functioning of the eye, it cannot improve vision problems. ✓
- The nutrients in honey are in too small amounts to be significant. ✓
- Many other foods contain as much vitamin A as carrots.
- Honey *is* sugar.
- Margarine differs from butter in the type of fat it contains, not in how much fat it contains.
- It is a myth that one must eat carrots to improve eyesight and vision problems. ✓

**Main idea:** _____

**Major detail:** 1. *It is a myth that regular margarine is less fattening than butter.*

**Minor details:**     a. _____

               b. _____

               _____

**Major detail:** 2. _____

**Minor details:**     a. *The nutrients in honey are in too small amounts to be significant.*

               b. _____

**Major detail:** 3. *It is a myth that one must eat carrots to improve eyesight and*

               *vision problems.*

**Minor details:**     a. *Although vitamin A is necessary to the functioning of the eye, it*

               *cannot improve vision problems.*

               b. _____

*(Continues on next page)*

**B.** Prepare a map of the paragraph by finishing the main heading and filling in the three major details. Use single words or brief phrases, not full sentences.

Note that the topic sentence is boldfaced.

Everyone is familiar with steam heat, gas heat, and solar heat. But how about corn heat? Inventor Carroll Buckner has devised a stove that runs on raw kernels of corn. **Buckner claims the stove has several advantages.** First, it's economical. He claims his invention can heat a house in the winter for about thirty dollars a month, assuming that corn is two dollars a bushel. Also, whereas the emissions from wood-burning stoves can harm the environment, a corn-burning stove, says Buckner, doesn't pollute the air. Finally, the stove would help the economy. Specifically, by creating a demand for corn, the stove would provide a new market for America's troubled farmers.

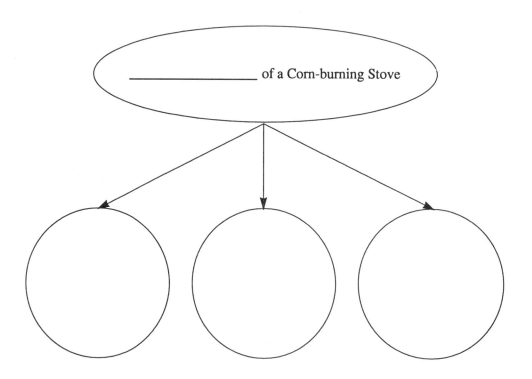

_____ of a Corn-burning Stove

## SUPPORTING DETAILS: Test A-2

A. Below each of the following passages is a question raised by the main idea of the passage. Answer the question by circling the letter of the major supporting details.

Most teens who smoke are familiar with the health hazards of smoking, yet because of certain factors, many of them drift into the habit anyway. A teenager with one parent who smokes is twice as likely to smoke as one with nonsmoking parents. Also, young people are more likely to smoke if their friends do. The chances are nine out of ten that a teenager whose best friend smokes will also start to smoke. In addition, teens who mature late are more likely to smoke than others, apparently because they hope that smoking will make them look more adult.

1. What are the factors that increase the likelihood that teenagers will smoke?
   a. Nonsmoking parents; a best friend that smokes; looking more adult.
   b. Parents who smoke; friends who smoke; late maturation.
   c. Having one parent; having a best friend; late maturation.

You are part of a network of family and friends that can give you advice, emotional support, and practical help. However, this network operates most effectively when you use it well. First, be sure you are willing to help others at least as much as they help you. People are going to be much more ready to give of themselves if you have built up a history of giving to them as well. When you do need advice or help, try to ask for only one thing at a time rather than overwhelming someone with too many requests. Most people are ready to lend a hand, but they may understandably balk if too much is expected. After all, they need time to deal with the daily needs and conflicts of their own lives. Finally, you should be willing to accept the advice and offers of help you do get. There is little benefit to brushing them off and giving excuses for not doing anything about the problems in your life.

2. What are the ways to make sure your personal support network works well?
   a. Be part of a network of family and friends that give advice, emotional support, and practical help.
   b. Belong to a network of family and friends; use the network well.
   c. Be willing to help network members; try to ask for one thing at a time; be willing to accept the advice and help offered.

*(Continues on next page)*

**B.** Complete the question formed from the main idea of the following paragraph. Then write the answers to the question—the three major details—on lines a, b, and c.

There are three principal kinds of animal diets. In a carnivorous diet, animals feed on other animals. Most fish are carnivorous. So too are owls, snakes, and wolves. On an herbivorous diet, animals subsist on plant food. Cattle, Japanese beetles, seed-eating birds, and plant lice are among the many herbivores. With the omnivorous diet, animals have a mixed diet. They feed on both vegetable and animal matter, dead or alive. Many kinds of worms, crabs, lobsters, insects, bears and raccoons are omnivorous. Humans are also omnivores.

3-6. What are the three _____

      a. _____

      b. _____

      c. _____

**C.** Write out the question formed from the main idea of the following paragraph. Then write the missing answers to the question—three of the four major details—on lines a, b, and d.

Snoring is the number one complaint in marriages all around the world. The honks, hoots, and snorts created by snorers annoy their mates and deprive them of sleep. Fortunately, there are some means of preventing snoring. First, the snorer should avoid breathing through his mouth. Mouth-breathing can be discouraged if the snorer sleeps on his side with his forearm under his chin—effectively pressing his mouth shut. Secondly, the snorer should increase the humidity in his bedroom. A humidifier or even a pot of water in the room may help. In addition, snoring may disappear if an overweight snorer loses some pounds. And finally, a snorer should avoid drinking alcohol in the evening.

7-10. What question does the passage answer? _____

_____

      a. _____

      b. _____

      c. If overweight, lose some pounds.

      d. _____

# SUPPORTING DETAILS: TEST A-3

Read each paragraph below, and answer the questions that follow.

A. [1]Many people pass through several stages in reacting to their unemployment. [2]At first they undergo a sequence of shock, relief, and relaxation. [3]In many cases they had anticipated that they were about to lose their jobs, so when the dismissal comes, they may feel a sense of relief that at last the suspense is over. [4]On the whole they remain confident and hopeful that they will find a new job when they are ready. [5]During this time, they maintain normal relationships with their family and friends. [6]The first stage lasts for about a month or two. [7]The second stage centers on a strong effort to find a new job. [8]If workers have been upset or angry about losing their jobs, the feeling tends to evaporate as they gather their resources and concentrate on finding a new job. [9]This stage may last for up to four months. [10]But if another job is not found during this time, people move into the third stage, which lasts about six weeks. [11]Their self-esteem begins to crumble, and they experience high levels of self-doubt and anxiety.

1. In general, the supporting details of this paragraph are
   a. unemployed people.
   b. stages of reaction to unemployment.
   c. relationships of the unemployed with family and friends.
   d. reactions to finding a new job.

2. The sentence with the main idea is
   a. sentence 1.
   b. sentence 2.
   c. sentence 3.
   d. sentence 11.

3. Specifically, the supporting details of this paragraph are
   a. shock, relief, and relaxation.
   b. normal relationships with family and friends and abnormal relationships with family and friends.
   c. anticipating the loss of a job and searching for another job.
   d. shock, relief, and then relaxation; concerted efforts to find a new job; great anxiety and a loss of self-esteem.

4. According to the passage, why might people feel a sense of relief at losing their job?
   a. They want to collect unemployment insurance.
   b. The suspense of waiting to lose their job ends.
   c. A new and better job is already lined up.
   d. They can then concentrate on finding a new job.

*(Continues on next page)*

5. The answer to question 4 can be found in
   a. sentence 1.
   b. sentence 2.
   c. sentence 3.
   d. sentence 11.

6. An unemployed person is likely to experience great self-doubt in
   a. the first stage.
   b. the second stage.
   c. the third stage.
   d. all stages.

B.  When a Japanese person is embarrassed, he will not usually frown and look away as a Westerner might. Instead, he will probably laugh. When a Navajo Indian is angry, he will not be likely to raise his voice. He is more likely to speak extra quietly. And when a native of the Andaman Islands wants to show his happiness when a relative visits, he will not smile and embrace the visitor. Instead, he will sit in the visitor's lap and cry. All these examples demonstrate the fact that displays of emotion and their meaning vary greatly from culture to culture.

7. The last sentence of this paragraph provides
   a. the main idea.
   b. a major detail.
   c. a minor detail.

8. In general, the major supporting details of this paragraph are
   a. reasons.
   b. statistics.
   c. examples.
   d. stages.

9. How many major supporting details are in this paragraph?
   a. One
   b. Two
   c. Three
   d. Four

10. When a Navajo Indian is angry, he is likely to
    a. yell loudly.
    b. laugh.
    c. sit in someone's lap and cry.
    d. speak quietly.

## SUPPORTING DETAILS: Test B-1

**A.** Complete the outline by filling in each blank with one item from the list below. Begin by finding and filling in the main idea, and then go on to the missing supporting details.

*Note:* Check (✓) each item after you use it. Doing so will help you see which items you have left.

- Surprise quizzes ✓
- A great deal of writing ✓
- Three major tests ✓
- Freshman English is a demanding course. ✓
- Frequent test situations ✓
- Term paper ✓
- Three novels ✓
- Short stories in an anthology ✓
- Extensive reading load ✓
- Frequent in-class writing assignments ✓
- A few written summaries of articles ✓
- Magazine and newspaper articles ✓
- Comprehensive final exam ✓

**Main idea:** _Freshman English is a demanding Course._

**Major detail:** 1. _Frequent test situations._

**Minor details:**  a. *Surprise quizzes*

b. *Three major tests*

c. _Comprehensive final exam._

**Major detail:** 2. *Extensive reading load*

**Minor details:**  a. *Magazine and newspaper articles*

b. _Three novels_

c. *Short stories in an anthology*

**Major detail:** 3. _A great deal of writing_

**Minor details:**  a. *Term paper*

b. _Frequent in-class writing assignments_

c. *A few written summaries of articles*

*(Continues on next page)*

**B.** Complete the map based on the following paragraph. Note that the topic sentence is boldfaced.

When a female elephant gives birth, she is often helped by another female from the herd. This "friend" may actually help deliver the baby with her trunk and often washes the newborn. The females take turns "babysitting" the young of the herd while the other mothers eat. In addition, elephants care for one another when they are ill—they have been known to take food and water to sick herdmates for many weeks. Finally, elephants also tend to the dying. They will often surround a dying elephant, trying to lift it back on its feet; and if it dies, they will stay sadly with the body for some time and even attempt to bury it. **Because of these and other behaviors, the elephant has earned the reputation as one of the most intelligent animals.**

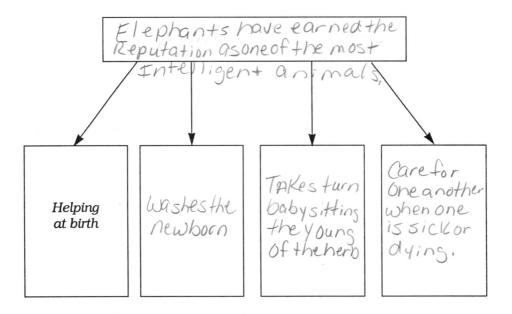

Elephants have earned the
Reputation as one of the most
Intelligent animals.

| Helping at birth | Washes the newborn | Takes turn babysitting the young of the herd | Care for one another when one is sick or dying. |

# SUPPORTING DETAILS: Test B-2

**A.** Below each of the following passages is a question raised by the main idea of the passage. Answer the question by circling the letter of the major supporting details.

Burn injuries are classified in three categories, according to their severity. First-degree burns are burns that leave a painful red mark but do not break the skin, and thus they do not often become infected. Burns that are classified as second-degree burn through the skin, which develops blisters. Second-degree burns are often extremely painful, and, since the skin has been broken, they may become infected. In a third-degree burn, both the outer layer and lower layer of skin are burned. There may be little pain because nerve endings have been destroyed. Because so much of the skin's protection has been lost, the possibility of serious, possibly fatal infection is great with a third-degree burn.

1. What are the three categories of burn injuries?
   a. Painful red mark; blisters; and burning of outer and lower layer of skin.
   b. Rare infections; occasional infections; frequent serious infections.
   c. First-degree burns; second-degree burns; and third-degree burns.

There are three basic rules for getting results from complaining. The first rule is to go to the top, such as the president of a company. Chief executives usually are more sensitive about customer satisfaction and the company's reputation than other employees. The second rule is to believe that you deserve fair treatment. Your self-confidence will project itself and favorably influence the person who takes your complaint. The third rule is to have notes which enable you to present the facts of your case logically and concisely. No one wants to hear or read a long and unorganized account of what happened to you.

2. What are three basic rules for getting results from complaining?
   a. Go to the president of a company; influence the person who takes your complaint; take notes.
   b. Go to the top of the company, such as the president; remember that nobody wants to hear or read a long, unorganized account of your case.
   c. Go to the top of the company; believe you deserve fair treatment; have concise, organized notes on your case.

*(Continues on next page)*

**B.** Complete the question formed from the main idea of the following paragraph. Then write the answers to the question—the three major details—on lines a, b, and c.

> You can plan your exercise program in ways that will help you stick to it. Most importantly, set a regular time for exercise. If you know that exercise is something you always do before breakfast, it will become a regular feature of your day that you won't constantly be tempted to skip. It's also important to be comfortable as you exercise. Decide what clothing feels good to you—shorts and a T-shirt, a bathing suit, or long underwear—and make sure that clothing is available when you need it. Finally, start your program at a reasonable pace. Nothing is more discouraging than pulling a muscle the first week trying to go too fast.

3-6. In what ways can you plan an exercise program to _in ways to help you stick to it._

   a. _Set a regular time for exercise._
   b. _Decide what clothing feels good to you._
   c. _Start your program at a reasonable pace._

**C.** Write out the question formed from the main idea of the following paragraph. Then write the answers—the three major details—on lines a, b, and c.

> According to pollster Louis Harris, there are three popular reasons for getting married. The most popular reason is for love, cited by 83 percent of both men and women as good grounds for getting married. The next most popular reason for getting married is "to be with a particular person," which was stated by 55 percent of the population. Finally, according to 44 percent, "to have children" is another compelling reason to get married.

7-10. What question does the passage answer? _Reason to get married._

   a. _Most popular reason is for love._
   b. _To be with a particular person._
   c. _To have childern._

# SUPPORTING DETAILS: Test B-3

Read each paragraph below, and answer the questions that follow.

A.   [1]Many people who do sit-ups may not be getting the full benefit of the exercise because they're doing them incorrectly. [2]Here are three common sit-up errors—and what should be done instead. [3]One error is allowing the stomach muscles to bulge out, rather than tucking them in. [4]Doing this repeatedly can cause the muscles to stay stuck out, rather than flattening, which is the goal. [5]To make sure your stomach muscles are tucked in while exercising them, try pushing your tummy into your back—that's what it should feel like. [6]Another error is not breathing while doing sit-ups. [7]That's because a lot of people instinctively hold their breath during physical exertion—but they don't get the oxygen necessary to fuel an effective workout. [8]The proper (and easiest) way to breathe during sit-ups is to inhale during the easy part (lowering your back) and then to exhale during the hard part (lifting yourself up). [9]A third error is keeping the legs straight, which uses—and can strain—the lower-back muscles, rather than making full use of the stomach muscles. [10]For safer, more effective sit-ups, keep those knees bent.

1. In general, the major details of this paragraph are
   a. common exercise errors and how to correct them.
   b. common sit-up errors and how to correct them.
   c. the proper ways to breathe during sit-ups.
   d. ways to avoid straining the lower-back muscles during sit-ups.

2. The first major detail is
   a. instead of allowing stomach muscles to bulge, tuck them in.
   b. three common sit-up errors.
   c. instinctively not breathing while doing sit-ups.
   d. not getting the full benefit of doing sit-ups.

3. The second major detail is
   a. instead of keeping the legs straight during sit-ups, keep knees bent.
   b. make sure your stomach muscles are tucked in while exercising them.
   c. allowing the stomach muscles to bulge can cause them to stay stuck out.
   d. instead of not breathing during sit-ups, inhale while lowering the back and exhale while lifting up.

4. The major details of the paragraph are introduced with the addition words
   a. *three, one, and.*
   b. *another, and, then.*
   c. *one, another, third.*

*(Continues on next page)*

5. To avoid using and straining the lower-back muscles while doing sit-ups,
   a. keep your knees bent.
   b. tuck your stomach muscles in.
   c. exhale while lifting yourself up.
   d. keep your legs straight.

**B.**    [1]Chimpanzees, skillful tool-users, use several objects found in their environment as tools. [2]First of all, they use sticks. [3]They have been seen inserting carefully trimmed sticks into termite mounds and then withdrawing the sticks and eating the termites that cling to them; they also are known to use sticks to steal honey from beehives. [4]In addition, chimps use leaves in a variety of ingenious ways. [5]For example, they have been seen rolling leaves into cones to use as drinking cups, dampening them and using them to clean their bodies, and chewing them until they can serve as sponges. [6]Finally, chimpanzees have been observed using stones to crack open nuts.

6. In general, the major details of this paragraph are
   a. chimpanzee behaviors.
   b. various animal tools.
   c. the ways chimpanzees use sticks to accomplish tasks.
   d. objects from the environment used as tools by chimpanzees.

7. How many major details are in this paragraph?
   a. Two
   b. Three
   c. Four
   d. Five

8. Sentence 1 provides
   a. the main idea.
   b. a major detail.
   c. a minor detail.

9. Sentence 2 provides
   a. the main idea.
   b. a major detail.
   c. minor details.

10. Sentence 5 provides
    a. the main idea.
    b. a major detail.
    c. minor details.

## SUPPORTING DETAILS: Test C-1

**A.** Complete the outline by filling in each blank with one item from the list below. Begin by finding and filling in the main idea, and then go on to the missing supporting details.

*Note:* Check (✓) each item after you use it. Doing so will help you see which items you have left.

- Ads appeal to the desire to be physically attractive. ✓
- Cosmetic ads always use very attractive people.
- Numerous foods are described as low-fat.
- Television ads make emotional appeals.
- Ads appeal to worries about being socially unacceptable.
- Ads emphasize concerns about bad breath. ✓
- Sex appeal is used to promote such products as cars and food. ✓
- Body odor is shown as something to be very embarrassed about.
- Ads appeal to concerns for a healthy diet.
- Many foods are associated with athletic activities. ✓

**Main idea:** _____

**Major detail:** **1.** *Ads appeal to the desire to be physically attractive.* _____

**Minor details:** a. _____

b. *Sex appeal is used to promote such products as cars and food.*

**Major detail:** **2.** _____

**Minor details:** a. *Ads emphasize concerns about bad breath.* _____

b. _____

_____

**Major detail:** **3.** _____

**Minor details:** a. _____

b. *Many foods are associated with athletic activities.*

*(Continues on next page)*

**B.** Complete the map of the following paragraph. Note that the topic sentence is boldfaced.

> **Sociologists have identified four basic types of religious organization.** A "church" is a well-established religious group that claims to be the only true religion. The Catholic Church, for example, holds that all other religions are mistaken. A "denomination" is a well-established religious group that accepts other groups as equally true. Most Protestant groups, for example, accept other Protestants on equal terms. They are thus regarded as denominations. A "cult" is a group that is at odds with the rest of society, but that accepts other religions as valid. "New Age" religious movements that believe in reincarnation or witchcraft fall into this category. Finally, a "sect" is a group that is at odds with society, and also claims to be the only true path to God. The People's Temple, whose members committed mass suicide in 1979, was a notorious example of a sect.

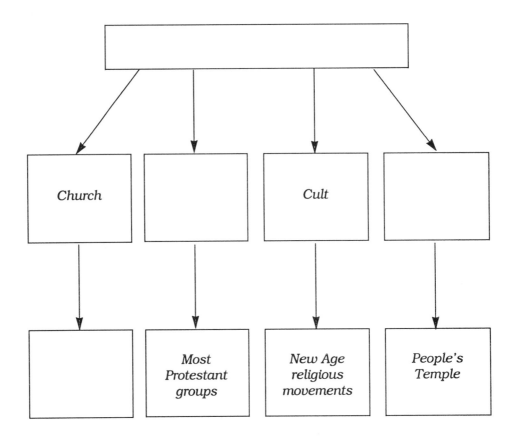

# SUPPORTING DETAILS: Test C-2

A. Below each of the following passages is a question raised by the main idea of the passage. Answer the question by circling the letter of the major supporting details.

A new puppy will be a member of the family for a long time, so you should choose one carefully. Many people, however, make their selections impulsively because puppies are so cute. You can best resist this temptation by doing some reading even before you begin shopping for your pet, so that you can know ahead of time which breeds suit your family's lifestyle. For example, if no one has time to walk the dog, don't pick a breed that needs a lot of exercise. Also, look for a curious pup when shopping, since curiosity is a sign of intelligence. One way to find a pet with a healthy dose of curiosity is to clap your hands and see which puppies act most interested.

1. What should people look for in choosing a puppy?
   a. Cuteness; a breed that doesn't need a lot of exercise; good health.
   b. A member of the family; a breed that suits your family's lifestyle.
   c. A breed that suits your family's lifestyle; curiosity.

You can influence the the resale value of a car when you purchase it and while you use it. The most important element in pricing a used auto is the depreciation rate. This figure is found in consumer manuals for cars of the same model and age. By learning depreciation rates, you can buy a car that depreciates less than others. Since mileage is the next important consideration, you should try to stick to the average 12,000 miles per year in a car you hope to sell eventually. Used-car buyers naturally are also concerned about the mechanical condition of a car, so it pays to do regular maintenance. Finally, the appearance of the car's body and interior affect its value, so it's important to avoid rust and dents and to keep the inside clean.

2. What can be done when purchasing and using a car to influence its resale value?
   a. Price a used auto; learn depreciation rates; read the mileage; note the mechanical condition.
   b. Buy a car with a low depreciation rate; stick to average mileage; do regular mechanical maintenance; maintain the car's appearance.
   c. Read consumer manuals for cars of the same model and age; buy a car with an average of 12,000 miles per year; note the mechanical condition of a car.

*(Continues on next page)*

**B.** Complete the question formed from the main idea of the following paragraph. Then write the answers to the question—the three major details—on lines a, b, and c.

Many people dream of being celebrities, but they might change their minds if they considered all the disadvantages there are to being famous. For one thing, celebrities have to look perfect all the time. There's always a photographer ready to take an unflattering picture of a famous person looking dumpy in old clothes. Celebrities also sacrifice their private lives. Their personal struggles, divorces, or family tragedies all end up as front-page news. Most frighteningly, celebrities are in constant danger of the wrong kind of attention. Threatening letters and even physical attacks from crazy fans are things the celebrity must contend with.

3-6.    What disadvantages _____

      a. _____

      b. _____

      c. _____

**C.** Write out the question formed from the main idea of the following paragraph. Then write the answers—the three major details—on lines a, b, and c.

Parents are often heard to say that their children were "different from the moment they were born—Jimmy was always such a good baby, and Susie was always so fussy!" Researchers who have studied large numbers of children from birth through elementary school agree that many children do seem to fit into one of three categories from the beginning of their lives. The first category is "easy children." These youngsters are generally cheerful and cooperative, and they quickly adapt to new situations. Next comes the "slow-to-warm-up" children. This group consists of children who look at life in a more negative fashion, taking time to adjust to new people and circumstances. Finally there are the "difficult" children. Intense reactions, little regularity in habits, and being easily upset by change are the characteristics of this group.

7-10.    What question does the passage answer? _____

_____

      a. _____

      b. _____

      c. _____

# SUPPORTING DETAILS: Test C-3

Read each paragraph below, and answer the questions that follow.

A.  [1]Adult children who move back home can avoid family conflicts by following some helpful tips. [2]First, they should contribute what they can—and it doesn't necessarily have to be in terms of money: Being productive family members will help them earn their keep. [3]This can involve tutoring or coaching younger sisters or brothers, or helping Mom and Dad with household chores and errands. [4]Second, these "returnees" should not expect their parents to rescue them from difficulties. [5]As adults, they are responsible for getting out of their own scrapes—and for trying to avoid them in the first place. [6]Last, they must respect their parents' lifestyles and own needs for independence. [7]It is unrealistic to expect parents' lives to revolve around the needs of a grown child, as they may have when the child was younger.

1.  In general, the major details of this paragraph are
    a.  ways that adult children living at home can contribute.
    b.  tips to help adult children living at home avoid family conflicts.
    c.  responsibilities of adult children for getting out of their own scrapes and for trying to avoid them in the first place.
    d.  ways to tutor or coach young siblings or to help parents with household chores.

2.  Specifically, the major details are
    a.  tutoring or coaching younger sisters or brothers; helping with household chores and errands; respecting their parents' lifestyles.
    b.  adult children who move back home; younger sisters and brothers; parents.
    c.  contribute what they can; be responsible for their own difficulties; respect their parents' lifestyles and needs for independence.
    d.  getting out of their own scrapes; avoiding them in the first place; not expecting parents' lives to revolve around the needs of a grown child.

3.  Sentence 1 provides
    a.  the main idea.
    b.  a major detail.
    c.  a minor detail.

4.  Sentence 2 provides
    a.  the main idea.
    b.  a major detail.
    c.  a minor detail.

*(Continues on next page)*

5. Sentence 4 provides
   a. the main idea.
   b. a major detail.
   c. a minor detail.

B.   The climate becomes colder when the amount of dust at high altitudes in the atmosphere increases. There are several ways that dust may get into the atmosphere. Volcanic eruptions can add so much dust that sunlight is scattered back to outer space. Chimneys, especially industrial smokestacks, also throw large amounts of dust into the atmosphere. The burning of tropical forests to clear land for farming is another way the amount of airborne dust is increased. Finally, should a nuclear war ever occur, it might add so much dust to the atmosphere that it could cause a new ice age—a nuclear winter in which the climate becomes so cold that no new crops can be grown.

6. In general, the major details of this paragraph are
   a. reasons why dust in the atmosphere makes the climate colder.
   b. ways that dust may get into the atmosphere.
   c. natural causes of dust getting into the atmosphere.
   d. ways that industry puts dust into the atmosphere.

7. How many major details are in this paragraph?
   a. One
   b. Two
   c. Three
   d. Four

8. One source of dust in the atmosphere is
   a. sunlight.
   b. farming.
   c. chimneys.
   d. cold weather.

9. An enormous amount of dust in the atmosphere could lead to
   a. warmer weather.
   b. burning of tropical forests.
   c. volcanic eruptions.
   d. a new ice age.

10. The last major detail is introduced with the addition word
    a. *several.*
    b. *add.*
    c. *finally.*
    d. *also.*

## SUPPORTING DETAILS: Test D-1

A. Complete the outline by filling in each blank with one item from the list below. Begin by finding and filling in the main idea, and then go on to the missing supporting details.

*Note:* Check (✓) each item after you use it. Doing so will help you see which items you have left.

- Social adjustment is troublesome. ✓
- Feelings of guilt and resentment may persist between the former husband and wife. ✓
- Starting to date again can be nerve-wracking. ✓
- Emotional difficulties among the original family members are common. ✓
- Divorce has serious negative consequences. ✓
- Married friends may exclude singles from social plans. ✓
- Financial adjustments are necessary. ✓
- Children may be confused, hurt, and even blame themselves. ✓
- Alimony, child support, and property dispersal must be dealt with. ✓
- High lawyers' fees can be a burden. ✓

**Main idea:** _Divorce has serious negative consequences_

**Major detail:** 1. _Social adjustment is troublesome_

**Minor details:**
a. *Starting to date again can be nerve-wracking.*
b. _Married friends may exclude singles from social plans._

**Major detail:** 2. *Emotional difficulties among the original family members are common.*

**Minor details:**
a. *Feelings of guilt and resentment may persist between the former husband and wife.*
b. _Children may be confused, hurt, and even blame themselves_

**Major detail:** 3. _Finanical adjustments are necessary._

**Minor details:**
a. *Alimony, child support, and property dispersal must be dealt with.*
b. _High lawyers fee can be a burden_

*(Continues on next page)*

B. Complete the map of the following paragraph by filling in the main heading and the missing major supporting details. Note that the topic sentence is boldfaced.

> **Through the years, experts have suggested various purposes for imprisonment in our country.** Prior to 1800 it was widely assumed that the punishment of deviants is necessary if the community is to feel morally satisfied. In recent years there has been a renewed interest in punishment—not for the sake of vengeance, but to restore a sense of moral order. During the last century and a half, the concept of rehabilitation has dominated penal philosophy. In this view, crime resembles "disease," something foreign and abnormal to most people. It is presumed that individuals are not to blame for the disease, and that we should focus on curing them. The notion of deterrence rests on assumptions about human nature that are difficult to prove. Even so, studies suggest that the certainty of apprehension and punishment does tend to lower crime rates. Finally, some argue that neither rehabilitation or deterrence really works, so that it is useless to send people to prison with these goals in mind. Instead, imprisonment should be used as selective confinement, reducing crime rates by keeping "hard-core" criminals off the streets. One study of young men in Philadelphia showed that 6 percent of the men were responsible for over half the crimes committed by the entire group.

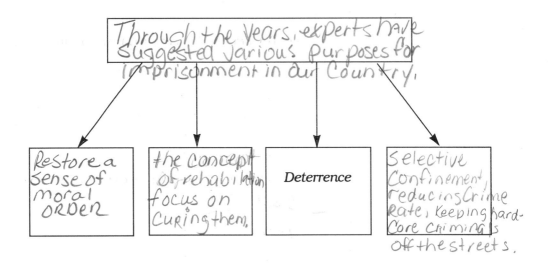

## SUPPORTING DETAILS: Test D-2

A. Below each of the following passages is a question raised by the main idea of the passage. Answer the question by circling the letter of the major supporting details.

Psychologists use several theories to explain different sides of human behavior. Best-known is the psychoanalytic theory, which holds that people are driven largely by needs and desires that they are not aware of—the so-called "subconscious" mind. Another theory, behaviorism, suggests that people's actions are based largely on past experiences of reward and punishment. We do things that brought us pleasant results in the past and avoid things that brought unpleasant results. Yet another theory, "gestalt" psychology, emphasizes the role of overall patterns in our thinking. For example, we find it much easier to remember a tune than a series of unconnected musical notes.

1. What are the theories which psychologists use to explain different sides of human behavior?
   a. People's actions; overall human patterns in thinking.
   b. The "subconscious" mind; past experiences of reward and punishment; the ability to remember a tune better than a series of unconnected musical notes.
   c. The psychoanalytic theory; behaviorism; gestalt psychology.

Millions of Americans still smoke in spite of increasing evidence that tobacco smoke kills. There are several reasons for this—complicated reasons which differ from one person to the next. One of the primary reasons is that smoking is highly addictive, some say as addictive as heroin. Smokers trying to quit may suffer from withdrawal symptoms which they cannot overcome. A second reason for continued smoking is that it becomes a social habit. These habits are hard to break and become even more difficult if others in the same social group continue to smoke. A third reason for many to continue smoking is that they just don't believe reports that smoking is dangerous. They see tobacco advertisements with attractive people doing interesting and exciting things. They listen to tobacco companies deny the evidence that cigarettes are harmful, and they read that the government continues to subsidize tobacco farmers. Faced with contradictory information, they choose to believe that smoking will not hurt them.

2. What are the reasons that millions of Americans still smoke despite the evidence that smoking is harmful?
   a. Smoking is addictive; it's a hard-to-break social habit; smokers choose to believe smoking is safe.
   b. Smoking is addictive; trying to quit may result in withdrawal symptoms; smoking is a hard-to-break social habit; tobacco companies deny that cigarettes are harmful.
   c. Smoking is addictive; tobacco ads make smoking look attractive; people choose to believe that smoking is harmless.

*(Continues on next page)*

**B.** Complete the question formed from the main idea of the following paragraph. Then write the answers to the question—the three major details—on lines a, b, and c.

> Some people are total bores; they make us yawn and our eyes glaze over when we are forced to associate with them. There are a few characteristics which are telltale signs of the chronic bore. The first is talking too much; bores always try to dominate the conversation. The second is repeating the same stories over and over, even when reminded that their listeners have heard those stories before. Their most irritating habit, however, is trying to make their personal experiences relate to every topic of conversation, no matter how irrelevant.

3-6.    What characteristics are _____

_____

a.  _____

b.  _____

c.  _____

**C.** Write out the question formed from the main idea of the following paragraph. Then write the answers—the three major details—on lines a, b, and c.

> Does popcorn beat peanuts? Yes, says an Ontario manufacturing firm that has substituted air-popped popcorn for the standard Styrofoam "peanuts" packing material. The firm has found three ways in which popcorn is preferable to "peanuts" as package filler. First, popcorn is biodegradable, making it more environmentally friendly than Styrofoam "peanuts," which will live on in waste-disposal systems for vast lengths of time. Second, when stored unpopped, corn takes up only a fraction of the space of "peanuts." Finally, the cost of popcorn is roughly one-fourth that of foam peanuts.

7-10.    What question does the passage answer? _____

_____

a.  _____

b.  _____

c.  _____

## SUPPORTING DETAILS: Test D-3

Read each paragraph below, and answer the questions that follow.

A.  [1]Studies done in the '30s in New Guinea by social scientist Margaret Mead show that all cultures do not share our views of the differences between the sexes. [2]The mountain people called the Arapesh, for example, do not think men and women are different in temperament. [3]They expect both sexes to be equally gentle, home-loving, and what we would call "maternal" in their relations with others. [4]The neighboring Mundugumor people, by contrast, are as fierce as the Arapesh are gentle. [5]Men and women are equally "macho," paying less attention to their children than to plotting for power and position. [6]A third tribe, the Tchambuli, do believe the sexes are different in temperament, but their sex roles are the reverse of ours. [7]Tchambuli women are the practical, hard-headed providers, while the men of the tribe spend their days beautifying themselves and looking for approval from the women.

1.  In general, the major supporting details of this paragraph are
    a.  differences between the sexes.
    b.  examples of differing cultural views of the sexes.
    c.  studies done by Margaret Mead.
    d.  a series of stereotypes about Western culture.

2.  How many major details are in this paragraph?
    a.  Two
    b.  Three
    c.  Four
    d.  Five

3.  The Arapesh do not think that men and women are
    a.  equally gentle.
    b.  "maternal."
    c.  alike in temperament.
    d.  different in temperament.

4.  _____ TRUE OR FALSE? Regardless of a culture's view, the women are always the ones most concerned with looking good for the opposite sex.

5.  The Arapesh and the Mundugumor peoples
    a.  consider men and women to be alike in temperament.
    b.  consider men and women to be equally gentle.
    c.  consider men and women to be equally fierce.
    d.  consider men and women to be very different from each other.

6.  The people whose sex roles are the reverse of ours are the
    a.  Arapesh.
    b.  Mundugumor.
    c.  Tchambuli.

*(Continues on next page)*

**B.** ¹Women in childbirth are often offered medication to relieve pain. ²However, that medication can have long-lasting unwanted effects. ³Newborns whose mothers have received drugs are generally sleepier and less responsive for the first hours and even days of life than babies of unmedicated women. ⁴Even after the effects of the medication wear off, mothers who received drugs often report that they feel less loving and positive about their babies. ⁵It appears that whether a woman first experiences her baby as alert or as sluggish affects her long-term feelings for the infant.

7. In general, the major details of this paragraph are
   a. medications.
   b. unwanted effects.
   c. ways women feel about their babies.
   d. long-term feelings.

8. Specifically, the major details of this paragraph are
   a. mothers who received drugs for pain during childbirth; less responsive newborns.
   b. babies are sleepier and less responsive; mothers have less positive feelings for their infants.
   c. medications; mothers in childbirth; newborns.
   d. being offered medication to relieve pain; whether a woman first experiences her baby as alert or as sluggish.

9. Sentence 2 provides
   a. the main idea.
   b. a major detail.
   c. a minor detail.

10. Sentence 3 provides
    a. the main idea.
    b. a major detail.
    c. a minor detail.

## SUPPORTING DETAILS: Test E-1

A. Complete the outline by filling in each blank with one item from the list below. Begin by finding and filling in the main idea, and then go on to the missing supporting details.

*Note:* Check (✓) each item after you use it. Doing so will help you see which items you have left.

- The race of offenders affects their treatment.
- Women are less likely to receive the death penalty than men. ✓
- Nonwhites are awarded parole and probation less often than whites. ✓
- More lenient sentences are given to the elderly. ✓
- The sex of offenders influences the severity of their sentences.
- Blacks are executed more often for capital crimes.
- Several factors have been found to influence the justice system's treatment of criminals.
- Young offenders are given special treatment.
- There is more reluctance to sending a mother to prison than a father.
- The age of offenders is considered in sentencing. ✓

**Main idea:** _____

_____

**Major detail:** **1.** _____

Minor details:     a. *Women are less likely to receive the death penalty than men.*

    b. _____

_____

**Major detail:** **2.** _____

Minor details:     a. *Nonwhites are awarded parole and probation less often*

    *than whites.*

    b. _____

**Major detail:** **3.** *The age of offenders is considered in sentencing.*

Minor details:     a. _____

    b. *More lenient sentences are given to the elderly.*

*(Continues on next page)*

**B.** Complete the map of the following paragraph by filling in the heading (the general idea of the map) and the missing major supporting details. Note that the topic sentence is boldfaced.

To a greater or lesser extent, all of us have learned aggressive responses. We are each a potential aggressor. **A number of conditions have been found to provoke our acts of aggression.** For one thing, pain heightens aggressiveness. Any decidedly aversive event, whether a dashed expectation, a personal insult, or a physical pain, can incite an emotional outburst. Among environmental irritants, the most-studied is heat. Studies found that, compared to students who answered questionnaires in a room with a normal temperature, those who did so in an uncomfortably hot room (over 90° F) reported feeling more tired and aggressive and expressed more hostility toward a stranger they were asked to rate. Attacks by another are especially conducive to aggression. Experiments confirm that attacks breed retaliatory attacks, especially when the victim perceives the attack as intentional. Finally, crowding—the subjective feeling of not having enough space—can be stressful. The stress experienced by animals allowed to overpopulate a confined environment produces heightened aggressiveness. And it is undeniably true that dense urban areas suffer higher rates of crime and emotional distress.

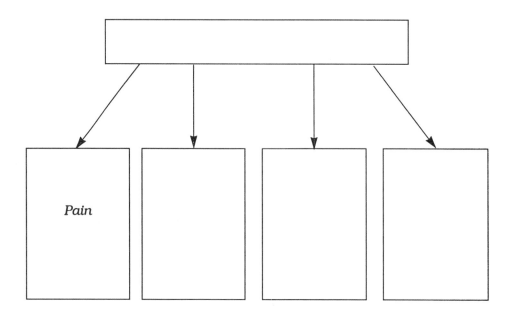

Pain

# SUPPORTING DETAILS: Test E-2

A. Below each of the following passages is a question raised by the main idea of the passage. Answer the question by circling the letter of the major supporting details.

Various types of communication exist. Intrapersonal communication describes a person talking to himself or herself. In interpersonal communication, two or three people who are near each other talk with one another. Group communication takes place when groups of people communicate with one another in a face-to-face encounter. In mass communication, communicators use a mass medium to communicate over some distances to large audiences.

1. What types of communication exist?
   a. One person; two or three people; groups of people; mass communicators.
   b. Communication face to face; communication over some distances to large audiences over a mass medium.
   c. Intrapersonal communication; interpersonal communication; group communication; mass communication.

Queen Isabella of Spain, who died in 1504, boasted that she'd had only two baths in her life—at birth and before her marriage. In colonial America, leaders frowned on bathing because it involved nudity, which, they feared, could lead to loose morals. Indeed, laws in Virginia and Pennsylvania either limited or outright banned bathing—and, for a time in Philadelphia, anyone who bathed more than once a month faced jail. Furthermore, some of the early Christian churches discouraged sudsing up because of its association with the depravity common in the Roman baths. Clearly, the notion that "cleanliness is next to godliness" has not always been a popular one.

2. What examples show that cleanliness has not always been so popular?
   a. Queen Isabella of Spain had only two baths; colonial American leaders frowned on bathing; some early Christian churches discouraged washing.
   b. Queen Isabella of Spain had only two baths; laws in Virginia and Pennsylvania either limited or banned bathing; even a jail sentence could be imposed.
   c. Queen Isabella of Spain had only two baths; once anyone who bathed more than once a month in Philadelphia faced jail; immoral behavior was common in the Roman baths.

*(Continues on next page)*

**B.** Complete the question formed from the main idea of the following paragraph. Then write the answers to the question—the three major details—on lines a, b, and c.

> Music, according to William Congreve, the 17th-century English playwright, "hath charms to sooth a savage breast." Congreve might be surprised to learn that music not only soothes emotions, it is therapeutic. In Poland, for instance, researchers found that music is an effective antidote to headaches. And at a Midwestern university, doctors have shown that music in the delivery room shortens labor. Also, Canadian doctors discovered that classical music is such a good painkiller for cancer patients that some no longer have to take painkilling drugs.

3-6.    What are some ways in which music _____

_____

a. _____

b. _____

c. _____

**C.** Write out the question formed from the main idea of the following paragraph. Then write the answers—the three major details—on lines a, b, and c.

> Although the debate continues over how important heredity is versus environment, scientists have learned that a number of human characteristics clearly have genetic factors. Physical traits are most strongly determined by heredity. For instance, height, obesity, and patterns of tooth decay are just a few of the traits that have been found to be determined by our genes. Intellectual traits are also strongly influenced by genes. To illustrate, research indicates that scores on intelligence tests and memory have a strong hereditary basis. In addition, personality factors and emotional disorders are greatly influenced by heredity. Shyness, special talents and interests, and schizophrenia are all influenced by genetic transmission.

7-10.    What question does the passage answer? _____

_____

a. _____

b. _____

c. _____

# SUPPORTING DETAILS: Test E-3

Read each paragraph below, and answer the questions that follow.

A.  [1]Everything that we notice—see, smell, hear or touch—forms a brief mental impression called a sensory memory. [2]Information is stored in this sensory memory for only a few tenths of a second before it disappears forever. [3]Information that is retained for slightly longer must enter what's called the short-term memory. [4]This form of memory can store about seven items for about 30 seconds—about enough information to dial a telephone number. [5]In order to be remembered for a long period, information must pass into the long-term memory. [6]No one knows just how much information can be stored in a person's long-term memory, but the capacity seems enormous. [7]The three types of human memory allow a person to discard unnecessary information and retain more important information for as long as it is valuable.

1. In general, the major supporting details of this paragraph are
   a. everything that we notice.
   b. information that we remember.
   c. the types of human memory.
   d. problems of human memory.

2. Specifically, the major supporting details of this paragraph are
   a. seeing, smelling, hearing, and touching.
   b. sensory memory, short-term memory, long-term memory.
   c. what is remembered and what is forgotten.
   d. keeping information and discarding information.

3. Sentences 1 and 2 provide
   a. a lead-in to the main idea.
   b. the main idea.
   c. a major supporting detail.

4. Sentence 7 provides
   a. the main idea.
   b. a major supporting detail.
   c. a minor supporting detail.

5. A sensory memory
   a. is a brief mental impression.
   b. lasts for about 30 seconds.
   c. lasts for a long period.
   d. usually makes its way into the long-term memory.

*(Continues on next page)*

6. To be available for more than 30 seconds, a memory must pass into a person's
   a. sensory memory.
   b. short-term memory.
   c. long-term memory.

**B.**   ¹Advertising's main goal is, of course, to sell products, but advertising also has other effects. ²By increasing the demand for products, advertising encourages economic growth. ³There is some evidence that by helping to maintain competition among businesses, advertising leads to lower prices for consumer goods. ⁴A case can even be made for advertising as a source of information. ⁵New products are often introduced in ads, which frequently demonstrate how the products are used and provide information on special features and prices. ⁶This information is intended to sell products, but it can also result in better-informed consumers.

7. In general, the major details of this paragraph are
   a. forms of advertising.
   b. the ways in which advertising increases the demand for products.
   c. advertising's effects in addition to selling products.
   d. how new products are often introduced.

8. Sentence 1 provides
   a. the main idea.
   b. a major detail.
   c. a minor detail.

9. Sentence 2 provides
   a. the main idea.
   b. a major detail.
   c. a minor detail.

10. Specifically, the major details of this paragraph are
    a. advertising sells products, maintains competition among businesses, and introduces new products.
    b. advertising encourages economic growth, leads to lower prices for consumer goods, and provides useful consumer information.
    c. products, competition, consumer goods, and information on special features and prices.
    d. advertising, competition, and better-informed consumers.

# 4

# Transitions

Consider the following sentences:

> "I dislike my job. The pay is good," said Burt.

> Lori enjoys working in her yard. She likes growing vegetables.

> "Open your books to page 22," the teacher said. "Hand in your papers."

Does Burt dislike his job because the pay is good? Is growing vegetables all Lori does in her yard? And does the teacher expect students to open their books and hand in their papers at the same time? We're not sure because the above sentences are unclear. To clarify them, transitions are needed. *Transitions* are words and phrases that show the relationships between ideas. They are like signposts that direct travelers. To show how transitions guide us, here are those same sentences, but this time with transitional words included:

> "I dislike my job, *even though* the pay is good," said Burt.

> Lori enjoys working in her yard. *For example*, she likes growing vegetables.

> "Open your books to page 22," the teacher said, "*after* you hand in your papers."

Now we know that Burt dislikes his job despite the good pay and that cultivating vegetables is just one of the yard projects Lori enjoys. We also now know that the teacher wants the papers handed in *before* books are opened. Transitions have smoothed the way from one idea to the other. In Latin, *trans* means "across," so transitions live up to their name—they carry the reader "across" from one thought to another.

There are a number of ways in which transitions connect ideas and show relationships. Here is a list of the major types of transitions.

1  Words that show addition
2  Words that show time
3  Words that show contrast
4  Words that show comparison
5  Words that show illustration
6  Words that show cause and effect

Each of these kinds of transitions will be explained in the pages that follow.

## 1  WORDS THAT SHOW ADDITION

Put a check beside the item that is easier to read and understand:

_____  People are renting more videotaped movies. Renting costs less than ever before. Videotaped movies are popular because they are now readily available everywhere.

_____  One reason people are renting more videotaped movies is that renting costs less than ever before. Videotaped movies are also popular because they are now readily available everywhere.

The words *one* and *also* in the second item make the relationship between the sentences more clear. The author is listing reasons why renting videotaped movies is so popular. The first reason is that the cost is lower than ever. A second reason is that the movies are so readily available. *One*, *also* and words like them are known as addition words.

**Addition words** tell you that the writer is presenting one or more ideas that continue along the same line of thought as a previous idea. They introduce ideas that *add to* a thought already mentioned. Here are some common addition words:

| one | in addition | first of all | furthermore |
| also | moreover | second | last of all |
| another | next | third | finally |

**Examples:**

My friend Ellen is so safety-conscious that she had her wooden front door replaced with a steel one. *Also*, she had iron bars inserted on all her apartment windows.

By recycling, our township has saved thousands of dollars in landfill expenses. *Furthermore*, we have made money by selling recycled glass, paper, and metal.

There are several places you can enjoy with your family without spending much money. *First*, the hands-on science museum downtown asks only for a donation. *Secondly*, there is the zoo, which is free on Sundays.

## ➤ *Practice 1*

Complete each sentence with a suitable transition from the box on the preceding page. Try to use a variety of transitions.

1. As soon as the weather turned warm, ants invaded our kitchen. A few _____ visited the bathrooms.

2. There are several ways to use old jeans. _____, you can use them for patching other jeans.

3. One million stray dogs live in the New York City metropolitan area. _____, there are more than 500,000 stray cats in the same area.

4. "_____, and most important," said my adviser, "you've got to complete that term paper or you won't graduate on time."

5. Janice told me she can't go out with me on Friday night. First of all, she has to wash her hair. Second, she's expecting a phone call. And _____, she thinks she's going to have a headache.

## 2 WORDS THAT SHOW TIME

Put a check beside the sentence that is easier to read and understand:

_____ The two neighboring families got along well. They are not on speaking terms.

_____ Previously, the two neighboring families got along well. Now they are not on speaking terms.

The words *previously* and *now* in the second item clarify the relationship between the sentences. *Before* the families got along well, and *now* they don't speak to each other. *Previously* and *now* and words like them are time words.

These transitions indicate a **time relationship**. They tell us *when* something happened in relation to something else happening. Here are some common time words:

| first | next | as | while |
|-------|------|----|-------|
| then | before | now | during |
| often | after | until | immediately |
| since | soon | previously | frequently |

**Examples:**

*First* I skim the pages of the television guide to see what movies will be on. *Then* I circle the ones I want to record on the VCR.

*As* I got ready to go home, my boss asked me to sweep the stockroom floor.

*During* World War II, meat was rationed.

## Helpful Points About Transitions

Here are two points to keep in mind about transitions.

1. Some transition words have the same meaning. For example, *also, moreover,* and *furthermore* all mean "in addition." Authors typically use a variety of transitions to avoid repetition.

2. In some cases the same word can serve as two different types of transition, depending on how it is used. For example, the word *first* may be used as an addition word to show that the author is beginning a train of thought, as in the following sentence:

    My mother has some strange kitchen habits. *First*, she loves to cook with the radio on full blast. Moreover, . . . .

   *First* may also may be used to signal a time sequence, as in this sentence:

    Our English class turned into a shambles this morning. *First*, the radiator began squeaking. Then, . . . .

## ➤ *Practice 2*

Complete each sentence with a suitable transition from the above box. Try to use a variety of transitions.

1. _____ my cousin took a long shower, there was no hot water left for anyone else in the house.

2. To make chicken stock, begin by putting a pot of water on the stove to boil. _____ drop in a chicken and some diced celery and onions.

3. Dan waited impatiently all day for the Monday night football game to begin on TV, but _____ the first half, he fell asleep.

4. Recent advances in medicine make it possible to treat babies even _____ they are born.

5. Some students listen to their stereo, eat snacks, and talk on the phone _____ doing their homework.

## 3 WORDS THAT SHOW CONTRAST

Put a check beside the sentence that is easier to read and understand:

_____ Even though roller coasters scare Wanda terribly, she loves riding on them.

_____ Roller coasters scare Wanda terribly. She loves riding on them.

In the second item, the two sentences seem to contradict each other. We want to ask, "Does Wanda like roller coasters or doesn't she?" In the first item, the phrase *even though* makes clear the relationship between the two ideas: In spite of the fact that roller coasters scare her, Wanda still loves riding on them. *Even though* and words like them are contrast words.

**Contrast words** show that two things *differ* in one or more ways. Here are some common contrast words:

| | | | |
|---|---|---|---|
| but | in contrast | conversely | on the other hand |
| however | instead | nevertheless | on the contrary |
| yet | still | even though | in spite of |
| although | despite | | |

**Examples:**

Some people think they have to exercise every day to stay in shape. *However*, three workouts a week are all they need to do.

Some people look upon eating as something to be done quickly, so they can get on to better things. *In contrast*, other people think eating is one of the better things.

Professional writers don't wait for inspiration. *On the contrary*, they stick to a strict schedule of writing.

➤ *Practice 3*

Complete each sentence with a suitable transition from the box on the preceding page. Try to use a variety of transitions.

1. _____ the diner was a pleasant place to eat, it still went out of business.

2. We use seventeen muscles when we smile; _____, we have to use forty-three muscles to frown.

3. At first we were planning on spending our vacation at a campground, _____ now we've decided just to relax at home.

4. Paula was not satisfied with her paper _____ the fact that she had already written five drafts.

5. Keeping his independence is important to Michael. _____, he likes to consult his parents before he makes certain decisions.

## 4  WORDS THAT SHOW COMPARISON

Put a check beside the sentence that is easier to read and understand:

_____ Driving a car is a skill that we learn through practice. Writing a paper is a skill that we learn through hands-on experience.

_____ Driving a car is a skill that we learn through practice. In like manner, writing a paper is a skill that we learn through hands-on experience.

The first item makes us wonder, "What has learning to drive a car got to do with writing a paper?" The phrase *in like manner* makes it clear that the author intends to *compare* learning to write a paper with learning to drive a car. *In like manner* and words like them are comparison words.

These **comparison words** signal that the author is pointing out a similarity between two subjects. They tell us that the second idea is *like* the first one in some way. Here are some common comparison words:

| | | | |
|---|---|---|---|
| like | just as | in like manner | as well |
| as | likewise | in a similar fashion | equally |
| just like | similarly | in the same way | |

**Examples:**

When buying milk, my mother always takes a bottle from the back of the shelf. *Similarly,* when my father buys a newspaper, he usually grabs one from the middle of the pile.

If movie makers have a big hit, they tend to repeat the winning idea in their next movie, *just like* certain authors who keep writing the same type of story over and over.

When individuals communicate, they are more likely to solve their problems. *In a similar fashion*, countries can best solve their problems through communication.

## ➤ *Practice 4*

Complete each sentence with a suitable transition from the preceding page. Try to use a variety of transitions.

1.  Lighting a cigarette in a darkened theater will not win you any friends.
    _____, talking out loud with your movie partner will soon make people scowl in your direction.

2.  There are so many gopher holes in our back yard that it looks _____ a miniature golf course.

3.  Spicy foods make me very thirsty. Believe it or not, ice cream affects me _____.

4.  Japanese women once blackened their teeth to improve their appearance. _____, some Indian women stained their teeth red.

5.  _____ rats become hostile when they are made to live in a crowded cage, humans become more aggressive in crowded conditions.

## 5   WORDS THAT SHOW ILLUSTRATION

Put a check beside the sentence that is easier to read and understand:

_____ I've become very absent-minded. Last week, for instance, I went to work on my day off.

_____ I've become very absent-minded. Last week I went to work on my day off.

The second item makes us think the author's claim to be absent-minded may be totally based on what happened on his or her day off. The words *for instance* in the first item make it clear that what happened on that day off is just one *example* of the absent-mindedness. *For instance* and other words like them are illustration words.

These **illustration words** indicate that an author will provide one or more examples to develop and clarify a given idea. They tell us that the second idea is *an example* of the first. Here are some common illustration words:

| for example | to illustrate | once |
| for instance | such as | including |

**Examples:**

My grandmother doesn't hear well anymore. *For instance*, whenever I say, "Hi, Granny," she answers, "Fine, just fine."

There are various ways you can save money, *such as* bringing lunch to work and automatically putting aside a small portion of your check each week.

My cousin Dave will do anything on a dare. *Once* he showed up for a family dinner wearing only swimming trunks and a snorkeling mask.

## ➤ Practice 5

Complete each sentence with a suitable transition from the above box. Try to use a variety of transitions.

1.  People have chosen to end their lives in a variety of unusual ways. _____, in ancient China people committed suicide by eating a pound of salt.

2.  My mother believes in various superstitions, _____ the idea that if you drop a fork, it means company's coming.

3.  Ladies and gentlemen, I can spell any word in the dictionary backwards. _____, I will now write the Pledge of Allegiance backwards on this chalkboard.

4.  Animals were once tried for crimes. _____, in 1740 a cow convicted of witchcraft was hanged by the neck until dead.

5.  There are soap opera fans that take the shows much too seriously. _____, some viewers actually send threats to soap opera "villains."

## 6   WORDS THAT SHOW CAUSE AND EFFECT

Put a check beside the sentence that is easier to read and understand:

_____  The varnish wore off our wooden patio table. Fungus has begun to grow on it.

_____  Because the varnish wore off our wooden patio table, fungus has begun to grow on it.

In the first item, it seems the author is simply listing two things that have happened to the patio table. The word *because* in the second item makes the relationship between the two ideas clear—the protective varnish wore off, *so* the fungus was able to grow. *Because* and words like it are cause-and-effect words.

These **cause-and-effect words** signal that the author is explaining why something happened or will happen. Here are some common cause-and-effect words:

| | | | |
|---|---|---|---|
| thus | because | because of | if ... then |
| as a result | result in | consequently | since |
| therefore | leads to | accordingly | so |

**Examples:**

My sister became a vegetarian *because* she doesn't want to eat anything that had a mother.

*If* it gets too humid out, then our wooden doors swell up and become hard to open and shut.

My boss's correspondence had built up while he was on vacation. *As a result*, I've been typing letters for the last two days.

## ➤ Practice 6

Complete each sentence with a suitable transition from the above box. Try to use a variety of transitions.

1.  _____ property taxes in the city have gone sky high, many corporations are moving to the suburbs.

2.  Lisa's résumé is impressive; _____, she has already had several job interviews.

3.  _____ my family is full of great Italian cooks, canned ravioli tastes like cardboard to me.

4.  Some zoo animals have not learned how to be good parents. _____, baby animals are sometimes brought up in zoo nurseries and even in private homes.

5.  Car dealers like to sell a certain number of cars in any given month. They are _____ more likely to hold sales near the end of a month.

## ➤ Review

To review what you've learned in this chapter, complete each of the following sentences about transitions.

1.  Transitions are words that signal the *(main ideas in, relationships between, importance of)* _____ ideas.

2.  A(n) _____ transition means that the writer is adding to an idea or ideas already mentioned.

3.  A(n) _____ transition signals that two things are alike in some way.

4.  The transition *after* signals a(n) _____ relationship.

5.  The transition *therefore* signals a(n) _____ relationship.

## TRANSITIONS: Test A-1

**A.** Fill in each blank with the appropriate transition from the box. Use each transition once.

| | | |
|---|---|---|
| just as | before | for instance |
| also | because | yet |

1. Elephants, the largest of all land mammals, are fascinating creatures. An adult weighs about 12,000 pounds, _____ its eyes are almost exactly the size of a human's.

2. When Carla went back to work, she began teaching Harry how to cook. "_____ you chop an onion," she said to him patiently, "you must peel it."

3. When I was home with the flu yesterday, I thought I would miss a math test. But _____ our teacher was absent too, the test was postponed.

4. Not only does Joanne do all her own sewing; she _____ designs many of the clothes she makes.

5. _____ humans keep cows for milk, some ants keep aphids for the sweet honeydew they produce.

6. Fast-food restaurants used to sell only relatively high-fat, high-calorie foods. In recent years, however, most such restaurants have improved their menus. _____, some of them now have salad bars. McDonald's even sells low-fat burgers these days.

*(Continues on next page)*

B. Fill in each blank with the appropriate transition from the box. Use each transition once. Read the passage carefully to see which transition logically fits in each answer space.

| | | |
|---|---|---|
| although | for instance | also |
| like | | |

The duck-billed platypus (pronounced *plat' ah pus*) of Australia is surely one of the strangest of creatures. (7)_____, despite the fact that the platypus is a mammal, it lays eggs, (8)_____ a bird. (9)_____, it has webbed feet like a duck, and it walks on its knuckles to avoid damaging the webbing. Other strange features of the platypus come in handy when it dives underwater. The animal's eye and ear openings are automatically covered by folds of skin. (10)_____ it is then deaf and blind, the platypus finds its way underwater by feeling around with its sensitive duck-like bill.

# TRANSITIONS: Test A-2

A. Circle the letter of the answer that describes the relationship indicated by the italicized transition.

1. First the pinch hitter selected a bat from the rack. *Then* he took a few practice swings.

   The relationship between the first and second sentences is one of
   a. contrast.          b. time.          c. cause and effect.

2. The Golden Rule teaches us that we should treat others *in the same way* that we would want to be treated ourselves.

   The sentence expresses a relationship of
   a. comparison.          b. contrast.          c. illustration.

3. *If* the company doesn't make a profit by the end of this year, *then* some employees will have to be laid off.

   The sentence expresses a relationship of
   a. illustration.          b. cause and effect.          c. contrast.

4. Our neighborhood kids had some great Halloween costumes this year. *For instance*, I had one trick-or-treater dressed as a crayon and another as a chocolate kiss.

   The relationship of the second sentence to the first is one of
   a. addition.          b. comparison.          c. illustration.

5. Many people do not know how to respond when someone they know is dying. Hospice workers, *however*, are experienced in giving comfort to dying people.

   The relationship of the second sentence to the first is one of
   a. contrast.          b. comparison.          c. illustration.

6. It's impossible to do everything perfectly, and *moreover*, it's ridiculous to try.

   The relationship of the second part of the sentence to the first part is one of
   a. contrast.          b. illustration.          c. addition.

*(Continues on next page)*

B. Fill in each blank with the appropriate transition from the box. Use each transition once. Read the passage carefully to see which transition logically fits in each answer space.

| | | |
|---|---|---|
| previously<br>for example | but | therefore |

Some measures intended to control crime have backfired. In California, (7)_____, a "Victim's Bill of Rights" was passed a few years ago. This law broadened the type of evidence that could be presented in court. The idea was to keep criminals from being freed due to so-called "legal technicalities." (8)_____ defense attorneys soon learned that they, too, could use this law. In rape trials, especially, the new law could be used to shift part of the blame onto the victim—to present evidence, (9)_____ not permitted in court, that the victim was reckless or sexually "loose." A law intended to protect crime victims (10)_____ turned out to have just the opposite effect.

# TRANSITIONS: Test A-3

A. This part of the test will check your ability to recognize the relationships (signaled by transitions) within and between sentences. Read each passage and answer the questions that follow.

### Passage 1

[1]A long sausage in a bun received the name "hot dog" in 1906. [2]The new name came about as the result of a cartoonist's poor spelling ability. [3]A sausage vendor, Harry Stevens, sold what he called "dachshund sausages" (named after the short-legged dog) at New York City baseball games. [4]During one of those games, newspaper cartoonist Tad Dorgan was in the audience. [5]He sketched a cartoon of a live dachshund, smeared with mustard and folded into a bun. [6]Not knowing how to spell "dachshund," however, he settled on "dog," giving the cartoon the caption "Get your hot dogs!" [7]Once the cartoon was published in newspapers, readers began demanding their own "hot dogs."

1. Sentence 2 expresses a relationship of
   a. time.                    c. cause and effect.
   b. illustration.            d. contrast.

2. The relationship of the first part of sentence 4 to the rest of the sentence is one of
   a. comparison.              c. addition.
   b. time.                    d. contrast.

### Passage 2

[1]Today, beach towns are popular tourist resorts. [2]But until a couple of hundred years ago, the seacoast was a place of danger. [3]People stayed away from the coast because they feared capture by pirates or slave-raiders. [4]Today's mountain resorts were once also places of fear. [5]The Donner party of pioneers starved, froze, and resorted to cannibalism, not far from the present-day vacation spots around Lake Tahoe, California. [6]In fact, many of the places we might like to go to in order to "get away" on vacation were once feared and avoided. [7]Have you ever daydreamed of being stranded on a tropical desert island? [8]That was once no daydream, but a terrible punishment for sailors found guilty of mutiny.

3. The relationship of sentence 2 to sentence 1 is one of
   a. addition.                c. comparison.
   b. contrast.                d. illustration.

4. Sentence 3 expresses a relationship of
   a. addition.                c. comparison.
   b. contrast.                d. cause and effect.

(Continues on next page)

**B.** The following six transitions have been removed from the textbook passage below. Read the passage carefully to see which transition logically fits in each answer space. Then write in each transition.

*Note:* You may find it helpful to check (✓) each transition after you insert it into the passage.

| while | if | then |
|-------|----|----|
| often | however | similar |

We (5)_____ wait for others to model a behavior before acting ourselves. This is frequently the case when the behavior involves helping someone else. By taking the lead, (6)_____, we can become models for others. Try the following experiment. Ask a friend to drop a large handful of loose papers in the middle of a busy sidewalk, pretending that it is an accident. Observe from afar how many people stop to help your friend pick up the papers. (7)_____ try the same thing a second time, using the same or a(n) (8)_____ location at an equally busy hour. But this time you should help pick up the papers, all the (9)_____ pretending to be a stranger. You will probably find that when you help, others are more likely to help, too. This is a useful principle to remember to get people involved in a bottle-recycling drive or a neighborhood cleanup. (10)_____ you start it, then others are likely to follow.

## TRANSITIONS: Test B-1

A. Fill in each blank with the appropriate transition from the box. Use each transition once.

| | | |
|---|---|---|
| furthermore | since | on the other hand |
| for instance | equally | until |

1. I'd love to spend my Christmas bonus on presents for my family and my girlfriend. _____, it would probably be more sensible to use it to pay some bills.

2. Clothing styles are often thought to reflect other aspects of society. One man, _____, uses the length of skirts to predict stock market moves.

3. Tina's father is an overly cautious parent. He wants to know where she is every minute, and he won't let her drive his car _____ she is 20.

4. Thanksgiving is my favorite holiday because my whole family gets together then. _____, we have all my favorite foods for dinner, including Aunt Lena's sweet-potato bread.

5. My daughter says that right now, nursing and teaching are _____ attractive to her. They both offer the opportunity to help others and to make a good salary.

6. I store old tax returns, boxes of photos, and folding chairs in my bedroom closet. And _____ the closet is so crowded, I keep my shoes under my bed and some of my sweaters in the linen closet.

*(Continues on next page)*

B. Fill in each blank with the appropriate transition from the box. Use each transition once. Read the passage carefully to see which transition logically fits in each answer space.

| | | |
|---|---|---|
| consequently | in spite of | first of all |
| like | | |

I really hate shopping for clothing. (7)_____, my small budget doesn't allow me to buy anything expensive. (8)_____, it takes me a lot of walking around just to find something I like that is both moderately priced and that I really want to wear. Another thing I dislike about shopping is having to try on so many clothes, most of which make me look (9)_____ a misshapen pear (except, of course, for the clothes that I can't even get into). "There have to be better things we are meant to do with our lives," I mutter, "than shop for clothes." (10)_____ my annoyance at the process, I persist; I want to get it over with and not have to think about it again for a long time. After an afternoon of walking in and out of stores in the mall, scrubbing the kitchen floor and cleaning the oven begin to sound good to me.

# TRANSITIONS: Test B-2

**A.** Circle the letter of the answer that describes the relationship indicated by the italicized transition.

1. My sister is late for everything. *Once* she arrived at a friend's wedding just as the bride said, "I do."

    The relationship of the second sentence to the first is one of
    a. contrast.              b. illustration.              c. addition.

2. Koala bears are related to kangaroos, not bears. *Likewise,* panda "bears" are related to raccoons.

    The relationship of the second sentence to the first is one of
    a. comparison.              b. contrast.              c. cause and effect.

3. "I would have liked the cigarette lighter you gave me except for two things," said Janet. "First of all, I don't like silver. *Secondly,* I don't smoke."

    The relationship of the last sentence to the one before it is one of
    a. illustration.              b. time.              c. addition.

4. *Because* she shops carefully, Jackie dresses well on a low budget.

    The relationship between the first and second parts of the sentence is one of
    a. addition.              b. cause and effect.              c. comparison.

5. Nate is convinced that Helen dislikes him. *However,* she likes him very much, but is too shy to let him know.

    The relationship of the second sentence to the first is one of
    a. comparison.              b. illustration.              c. contrast.

6. Jake raked our entire yard on Saturday and put all the leaves at the curb. *Then* the wind picked up and not only blew most of the leaves back in the yard, it blew our neighbors leaves there too.

    The relationship between the events in the two sentences is one of
    a. illustration.              b. time.              c. comparison.

*(Continues on next page)*

**B.** Fill in each blank with the appropriate transition from the box. Use each transition once. Be sure to read the passage carefully to see which transition logically fits in each answer space.

| | | |
|---|---|---|
| in addition | as a result of | despite |
| previously | | |

The movie *Out of Africa* was popular when it was released a few years ago. It introduced its attractive heroine, Isak Dinesen, to many people who had (7)_____ known nothing about her. (8)_____ seeing the movie, many were inspired to read the two books Dinesen had written about her life in Kenya: *Shadows on the Grass* and *Out of Africa*. Dinesen's life in Africa was tragic in many ways. The coffee farm she founded failed, and her unfaithful husband gave her venereal disease. (9)_____, her lover died in an airplane crash. (10)_____ those tragedies, she had wonderful memories of Kenya that she transformed into unforgettable stories.

# TRANSITIONS: Test B-3

A. This part of the test will check your ability to recognize the relationships (signaled by transitions) within and between sentences. Read each passage and answer the questions that follow.

## Passage 1

[1]On beaches in most parts of the U.S., it is illegal for women to appear "topless" and routine for men to do so. [2]However, at one time men too were forbidden to expose their upper halves. [3]As recently as 1934, eight men were arrested for topless bathing at Coney Island in New York. [4]They were each fined $1 and warned to wear more modest shoulder-to-thigh swimming suits. [5]"All of you fellows may be Adonises," said the judge, referring to a mythical young man of great beauty, "but there are many people who object to seeing so much of the human body exposed."

1. The relationship of sentence 2 to sentence 1 is one of
   a. addition.          c. comparison.
   b. contrast.          d. cause and effect.

2. The relationship between the two parts of the quotation in sentence 5 is one of
   a. comparison.        c. illustration.
   b. time.              d. contrast.

## Passage 2

[1]In 1850 an old pear tree stood at the corner of Third Avenue and East Thirteenth Street in New York City. [2]It still bore fruit, although it had been planted more than two hundred years before by Peter Stuyvesant when he came from Holland to what was then New Amsterdam. [3]The tree was finally removed after it was destroyed in a carriage accident in 1867. [4]In that period, the streets were made of cobblestones, which were hard to walk on, but pathways made of smooth, flat stones were provided for pedestrians at street corners. [5]Today one of the buildings that stood near the corner in the 1860s remains, but most of the buildings, like the old tree, are gone. [6]Likewise, the cobblestones have been replaced by smooth asphalt streets, and an electric traffic light stands today where the pear tree once stood.

3. The word or words signaling the relationship of sentence 4 to sentence 3 are
   a. *In that period.*      c. *were made of.*
   b. *but.*                 d. *on.*

4. The relationship of sentence 6 to sentence 5 is one of
   a  illustration.          c. contrast.
   b. cause and effect.      d. comparison.

*(Continues on next page)*

B. The following six transitions have been removed from the passage below. Read the passage carefully to see which transition logically fits in each answer space. Then write in each transition.

*Note:* You may find it helpful to check (✓) each transition after you insert it into the passage.

| also | for example | however |
|------|-------------|---------|
| because of | such as | while |

Many people have been known to watch (5)_____ someone else is being harmed without trying to help at all. An altruistic person, (6)_____, would try to help when he or she sees a problem. (7)_____, an altruistic person who walks by a parked car with its lights on may try to turn them off. Altruism can (8)_____ motivate people to give money and time to worthy causes. Extreme altruists—(9)_____ the people who leap in front of a train to save a child's life—will even give their lives for others. In short, altruistic actions can range from the trivial to the heroic.

But some people feel there is really no such thing as altruism; they feel that a so-called altruistic action is basically motivated by discomfort at seeing someone else's suffering. Help is given, they say, only (10)_____ the giver's distress, not the receiver's.

## TRANSITIONS: Test C-1

**A.** Fill in each blank with the appropriate transition from the box. Use each transition once.

| | | |
|---|---|---|
| however | just as | also |
| after | for example | consequently |

1. The average square inch of human skin includes 19 million cells. It _____ contains 625 sweat glands, 60 hairs, and 19 feet of blood vessels.

2. All states require that children be buckled into car seats when riding. _____, the number of children killed in auto accidents has dropped.

3. Some thieves read the newspapers to find out good times to rob houses. _____, after reading the obituaries, such thieves may "clean out" a home while the family is at a loved one's funeral.

4. Abraham Lincoln began to grow a beard only _____ being elected to the presidency. An 11-year-old girl told him that with a beard he "would look a great deal better, for your face is so thin."

5. Whenever something bad happens to me, my grandmother tries to help me through it. When I was depressed after breaking up with my boyfriend, she told me, "_____ we must go through the storm before seeing the rainbow, we often must experience sorrow before joy."

6. Freedom of religion is what drew many to the New World. _____, not all who sought such freedom were anxious to grant it to others. For example, the Puritans persecuted the Quakers because of their beliefs.

*(Continues on next page)*

**B.** Fill in each blank with the appropriate transition from the box. Use each transition once. Read the passage carefully to see which transition logically fits in each answer space.

| | | |
|---|---|---|
| such as<br>in spite of | on the contrary | during |

In the early days of industrialized America, many children worked full-time in factories and even mines. (7)_____ their small size and youth, children would often work up to fourteen hours a day. Work conditions were often brutal, with children subjected to horrors (8)_____ being chained to their beds at night and to their factory machines (9)_____ the day. Childhood was not seen as a time of protection and privilege for these children; (10)_____, the children were viewed merely as smallish adults. Eventually, laws were passed that gave juveniles special protection.

# TRANSITIONS: Test C-2

A. Circle the letter of the answer that describes the relationship indicated by the italicized transition.

1. *Despite* a common belief to the contrary, Nero did not fiddle while Rome burned; the fiddle had not yet been invented.

   The relationship signaled by the transition is one of
   a. time.　　　　　　b. comparison.　　　　　c. contrast.

2. Many common household cleaners, *including* ammonia and chlorine bleach, can cause serious injury if they are misused.

   The relationship signaled by the transition is one of
   a. illustration.　　　　b. addition.　　　　　c. contrast.

3. *Since* the Morans are always late, we didn't rush to get to the restaurant on time.

   The relationship of the first half of the sentence to the second half is one of
   a. comparison.　　　　b. cause and effect.　　c. illustration.

4. There are three basic rules to writing headlines. *First of all*, the headline should emphasize the main point of the story.

   The relationship signaled by the transition is one of
   a. addition.　　　　　b. cause and effect.　　c. contrast.

5. Martha works two jobs all week. *During* the weekend she tries to catch up on her housework and sleep.

   The relationship signaled by the transition is one of
   a. comparison.　　　　b. time.　　　　　　c. illustration.

6. The Larsens' beach house, *like* many others around it, is made of unfinished wood that has turned silvery-gray in the salty air.

   The relationship signaled by the transition is one of
   a. contrast.　　　　　b. cause and effect.　　c. comparison.

*(Continues on next page)*

B. Fill in each blank with the appropriate transition from the box. Use each transition once. Be sure to read the passage carefully to see which transition logically fits in each answer space.

| | | |
|---|---|---|
| however<br>like | for instance | also |

Clothing is not only a means of keeping warm and decently covered: it's (7)_____ a means of communication. We affect others' perceptions of us by the way we dress. If we are trying to establish ourselves as part of a group, we adopt the dress style of that group. That's why an applicant for an executive position shows up for the interview dressed (8)_____ an executive: dark suit, conservative shoes, subdued jewelry. (9)_____, if we're trying to put distance between ourselves and a group, we dress in a way that expresses that distance. (10)_____, a person who shows up for a formal wedding in jeans, a T-shirt and dirty sneakers communicates his or her feeling of hostility to the rest of the crowd.

# TRANSITIONS: Test C-3

**A.** This part of the test will check your ability to recognize the relationships (signaled by transitions) within and between sentences. Read each passage and answer the questions that follow.

*Passage 1*

[1]High school seniors are expected to make crucial decisions about their future careers, yet many of them are still unrealistic about what they plan to do. [2]They seem to have little knowledge of what their chosen careers involve or how much training they require. [3]For instance, a study of more than 6,000 high school seniors in Texas showed that only about half were planning to get the appropriate amount of education for the careers they had chosen. [4]The rest were planning too many or too few years of training. [5]A more disturbing finding is that most of the students did not seem to be choosing careers that matched their interests.

1. The relationship between the two parts of sentence 1 is one of
   a. addition.                  c. illustration.
   b. contrast.                  d. cause and effect.

2. The relationship of sentence 3 to sentence 2 is one of
   a. addition.                  c. illustration.
   b. contrast.                  d. time.

*Passage 2*

[1]As a result of the reorganization of many railway systems, about 3,000 miles of track are being abandoned each year. [2]Rather than let this flat, cleared land area go to waste, these abandoned rail lines are being converted into auto-free paths called rail-trails. [3]For city dwellers penned in by traffic and concrete, the trails are offering new outdoor hiking opportunities. [4]For those confined to wheelchairs, they are providing attractive, auto-free paved trails. [5]Finally, for the nostalgic, rail-trails can be a interesting way to hike from town to town, much as our ancestors did. [6]Thus the rail beds are preserved for possible future use, while at the same time they provide recreation in the present.

3. The relationship between the two parts of sentence 1 is one of
   a. contrast.                  c. cause and effect.
   b. comparison.                d. illustration.

4. The relationship of sentence 5 to previous sentences is one of
   a. addition.                  c. contrast.
   b. time.                      d. cause and effect.

*(Continues on next page)*

**B.** The following six transitions have been removed from the passage below. Read the passage carefully to see which transition logically fits in each answer space. Then write in each transition.

*Note:* You may find it helpful to check (✓) each transition after you insert it into the passage.

| result in | like | finally |
| including | next | but |

In some ways, the American criminal-justice system is (5)_____ a "wedding cake" with four layers, representing different kinds of cases. In the top layer are notorious criminal cases that get heavy news coverage. Our image of the justice system—of elaborate trials, highly paid defense lawyers, endless appeals—is formed by these cases, (6)_____ they are only a small fraction of the total. The (7)_____ layer down is made up of other serious felonies—murders, rapes, robberies—that don't get as much news coverage. Most of these cases are "plea-bargained," but usually result in prison terms. In the next layer are "less serious" felonies, (8)_____ car theft, that may not result in prison terms. (9)_____, the lowest and largest layer is made up of the huge number of misdemeanors such as traffic violations. These cases are handled in a routine way, and seldom (10)_____ jail terms.

## TRANSITIONS: Test D-1

A. Fill in each blank with the appropriate transition from the box. Use each transition once.

| | | |
|---|---|---|
| but | next | in the same way |
| also | to illustrate | leads to |

1. When I'm nervous I tend to jump to conclusions. _____, this morning I yelled at my daughter for using my fountain pen and not returning it, and then I found it at the bottom of my briefcase.

2. Other boys like to collect normal things, like baseball cards, but my little brother Dwayne collects dead bugs. He _____ collects loose chunks of sidewalk (which he insists on calling moon rocks).

3. My problem with the history final was not that I hadn't studied. I really knew the material well, _____ I had stayed up so late studying that I was too tired to think clearly during the test.

4. Fear often _____ self-destructive behavior. For instance, fear of hearing bad news keeps people from having health checkups that can prevent bad news.

5. In 1835 Halley's comet appeared and Mark Twain was born. Twain predicted that he'd die when Halley's comet showed up again. And he did die in 1910, the year of the comet's _____ appearance.

6. Variety may be the spice of life, but certain things should continue to be done _____ from year to year. What would Christmas be like, for instance, if the angel my brother made in kindergarten was no longer at the top of the tree or if radio stations no longer played Christmas carols?

*(Continues on next page)*

**B.** Fill in each blank with the appropriate transition from the box. Use each transition once. Be sure to read the passage carefully to see which transition logically fits in each answer space.

| | | |
|---|---|---|
| for instance | in a similar fashion | another |
| at the same time | | |

According to historians, some young leaders-to-be were being trained to rule their countries' armies (7)_____ that they played. (8)_____, the young king of Rome "played" war on a chessboard full of pure gold soldiers. The soldiers were a gift from the emperor Napoleon. (9)_____ young leader, Czar Peter III of Russia, watched as his toy soldiers, dressed in full military uniforms, "changed the guard" in front of a miniature castle. (10)_____, Great Britain's famous wartime leader Sir Winston Churchill used his model British soldiers to conduct realistic ceremonies and to beat his brother's toy "enemy" soldiers.

## TRANSITIONS: Test D-2

A. Circle the letter of the answer that describes the relationship indicated by the italicized transition.

1. Honeybees attack just to protect their hives. *Therefore*, if you run away from the hive when attacked, the bees will eventually lose interest in you.

   The relationship between the two sentences is one of
   a. cause and effect.    b. time.    c. contrast.

2. We started our day at the county fair by attending a woodworking demonstration. *Next* we watched a tractor-pulling contest.

   The relationship of the second sentence to the first is one of
   a. illustration.    b. time.    c. cause and effect.

3. Poverty is associated with special health problems. *For example*, poor people are more likely to die of heart disease than the wealthy.

   The relationship of the second sentence to the first is one of
   a. contrast.    b. comparison.    c. illustration.

4. *In spite of* the sub-zero weather and forecasts of heavy snow, Roger insists on running his usual five miles today.

   The relationship between the two parts of the sentence is one of
   a. time.    b. comparison.    c. contrast.

5. The Leaning Tower of Pisa is an instantly recognized symbol of Italy *just as* the Pyramids are a symbol of Egypt.

   The relationship between the two parts of the sentence is one of
   a. contrast.    b. comparison.    c. illustration.

6. I have a limited interest in people whose main topic of conversation is themselves. *Another* group I avoid is people who never allow facts to interfere with their opinions.

   The relationship signaled by the transition is one of
   a. addition.    b. illustration.    c. cause and effect.

*(Continues on next page)*

**B.** Fill in each blank with the appropriate transition from the box. Use each transition once. Be sure to read the passage carefully to see which transition logically fits in each answer space.

| | | |
|---|---|---|
| also | consequently | because |
| for example | | |

Plants can be surprisingly destructive. (7)_____, root systems can push bricks apart, lift concrete, and eventually topple buildings. Plants that find niches on the surfaces of buildings are (8)_____ amazingly destructive. (9)_____ they must extract needed nutrients, they gradually dissolve the surfaces on which they grow. Roofing tiles, plaster, and even glass cannot resist the plants. Invading plants can relatively quickly turn an abandoned factory site into a field and then into woodland. Especially in tropical areas, dense vegetation completely overwhelms abandoned cities; (10)_____, they can be lost for centuries.

# TRANSITIONS: Test D-3

A. This part of the test will check your ability to recognize the relationships (signaled by transitions) within and between sentences. Read each passage and answer the questions that follow.

### Passage 1

[1]Many of today's children learn that Cinderella wore glass slippers, but the popular heroine didn't always have breakable shoes. [2]Her old and international story was accidentally slightly changed in that regard by the French writer Charles Perrault, who popularized it with his version, published in 1697. [3]Perrault referred to Cinderella's slippers as being made of "verre," the French word for glass. [4]However, the old French versions which were his sources, used the word "vair"—white squirrel fur. [5]In other words, generations of children have had the pleasure of the dramatic image of glass shoes because of a mistranslation.

1. The word that signals the relationship between the two parts of sentence 1 is
   a. *many.*
   b. *but.*
   c. *today's.*
   d. *always.*

2. The relationship of sentence 4 to sentence 3 is one of
   a. addition.
   b. illustration.
   c. comparison.
   d. contrast.

### Passage 2

[1]Scientists have learned that the way we view exercise strongly influences our performance. [2]Research on Russian weightlifters, for example, demonstrated that if they were told the weights were heavy, they perceived an exercise to be more difficult. [3]If they were told the weights were light, then they considered the exercise easier. [4]Similarly, one Russian weightlifter broke a record that had eluded him after his trainer told him the weights he was lifting were not as heavy as they in fact were. [5]In another study, when people exercising on a stationary bicycle were told they were going uphill, their heart rates increased noticeably.

3. The relationship between the two parts of sentence 3 is one of
   a. contrast.
   b. comparison.
   c. illustration.
   d. cause and effect.

4. The relationship of sentence 4 to sentence 3 is one of
   a. addition.
   b. time.
   c. comparison.
   d. illustration.

*(Continues on next page)*

B. The following six transitions have been removed from the textbook passage below. Read the passage carefully to see which transition logically fits in each answer space. Then write in each transition.

*Note:* You may find it helpful to check (✓) each transition after you insert it into the passage.

| | | |
|---|---|---|
| also | for example | because |
| in contrast | similarly | during |

(5)_____ to preindustrial societies, modern societies make it much easier for people to get divorced. Today, geographic mobility allows people who get divorced to do so in relative privacy. (6)_____ or following a divorce, many couples do not have to face all of their relatives and old friends or even one another. . . .

Female employment and small families (7)_____ make divorce more likely in modern societies. A major impact of the massive entry of women into the labor force has been to decrease the dependence of wives on their husbands for economic support. This change has had many beneficial effects. (8)_____, a woman need no longer cling to a brutal or drunken husband merely because she has nowhere else to turn. But it also encourages some women to give up on a relationship more quickly. (9)_____, husbands have greater economic freedom to divorce wives who work, (10)_____ working wives are seldom granted a great deal of alimony. The conditions that have enabled people to seek marriages based on romance have also enabled them to continue that search if a marriage fails to satisfy.

# TRANSITIONS: Test E-1

**A.** Fill in each blank with the appropriate transition from the box. Use each transition once.

| | | |
|---|---|---|
| but | another | equally |
| before | because | including |

1. _____ there are no clocks in gambling casinos, gamblers can easily lose all sense of time. That is clearly what the casino management wants to happen. The longer people stay at the tables or in front of the slot machines, the better.

2. Journalistic standards have changed. _____ the 1988 presidential election, journalists didn't generally report on politicians' sex lives. Now almost every aspect of a candidate's life is examined in the media.

3. My father had wanted to go to college, _____ being drafted during World War II made him change his plans. Now that he's retired, he's finally going to take some college courses.

4. The restaurant's food is excellent, and its great service is _____ good.

5. Most of the elephant species that have existed are extinct, _____ a hippo-like animal considered to be the first elephant in the world. It had no trunk and was only about two feet high.

6. There have been many fictional "captains." One is Captain Marvel, the red-suited comic-strip superhero. _____ is Captain Nemo, captain of the submarine in Jules Verne's *Twenty Thousand Leagues Under the Sea*.

*(Continues on next page)*

**B.** Fill in each blank with the appropriate transition from the box. Use each transition once. Be sure to read the passage carefully to see which transition logically fits in each answer space.

| finally second | so | such as |

Better-educated people are healthier. Why should this be so? First, people with more education tend to come from families with more money, (7)_____ they can afford to eat better, get better preventive health care, and get better medical treatment. (8)_____, one thing learned in school may be sensible work and living habits: More affluent and better-educated people exercise more and eat fewer high-cholesterol foods. Then, formal schooling may increase self-confidence and decrease stress, which is often a factor in causing or making worse diseases (9)_____ hypertension, heat ailments, stroke, and ulcers. (10)_____, it's possible that people who are sophisticated enough to see the value of a good education are also aware of the importance of a healthy way of life.

# TRANSITIONS: Test E-2

**A.** Circle the letter of the answer that describes the relationship indicated by the italicized transition.

1. The "Blue" Danube River isn't blue, and, *likewise*, the Nile River isn't Nile green. In fact, both are muddy brown.

    The relationship between the two parts of the first sentence is one of
    a. contrast.          b. comparison.          c. cause and effect.

2. At night, the city streets are often dangerous and cold. *Therefore,* many homeless women sleep in the hallways of train stations and other public buildings.

    The relationship between the two sentences is one of
    a. contrast.          b. cause and effect.          c. addition.

3. Many new parents have difficulty adjusting to being "tied down." *Conversely,* parents of college-age children feel a welcome sense of freedom.

    The relationship between the two sentences is one of
    a. comparison.          b. illustration.          c. contrast.

4. Emotions have a physical basis—in our hormone system. They are *also* grounded in our experience.

    The relationship of the second sentence to the first is one of
    a. addition.          b. illustration.          c. time.

5. As a child, I frequently had dreams in which I fell through seemingly endless space—*until* I woke up.

    The relationship of the last part of the sentence to the rest of the sentence is one of
    a. time.          b. addition.          c. comparison.

6. Norma is driven to organize her environment. *For instance,* she keeps her personal correspondence organized in file cabinets and her clothing organized according to color.

    The relationship of the second sentence to the first is one of
    a. time.          b. addition.          c. illustration.

*(Continues on next page)*

B. Fill in each blank with the appropriate transition from the box. Use each transition once. Be sure to read the passage carefully to see which transition logically fits in each answer space.

| | | |
|---|---|---|
| thus | then | such as |
| first | | |

At a recent conference on space automation, a social physicist suggested that the planet Mars be used for a giant scientific experiment. Millions of tons of blue-green algae, (7)_____ seaweed and pond scum, would (8)_____ be genetically altered here on Earth to survive the temperatures and radiation levels on Mars. (9)_____ they would be transported by space shuttle and "seeded" into the Martian atmosphere. These organisms would then digest the carbon dioxide on Mars, changing it into oxygen, and (10)_____ within a few thousand years humans would be able to live on the red planet. Critics of the plan question the ethics of "polluting" other planets with our life forms.

# TRANSITIONS: Test E-3

A. This part of the test will check your ability to recognize the relationships (signaled by transitions) within and between sentences. Read each passage and answer the questions that follow.

*Passage 1*

[1]Some of the staples of Italian-American cooking are not native to Italy. [2]For example, veal Parmesan, an American favorite, is not eaten in Italy. [3]It was invented when immigrants adapted the Italian recipe for eggplant Parmesan for use with the abundant meat available in the U.S. [4]Spaghetti and meatballs is another American dish unknown in Italy, as is pizza with everything on it. [5]Italian pizza is topped with one or two ingredients, and it is not sliced before it is served.

1. The relationship of sentence 2 to sentence 1 is one of
   a. time.
   b. contrast.
   c. illustration.
   d. comparison.

2. The relationship of sentence 4 to the previous two sentences is one of
   a. addition.
   b. time.
   c. contrast.
   d. cause and effect.

*Passage 2*

[1]When a crowd is watching as someone threatens to jump from a building, its behavior seems determined by the time of day. [2]In daylight, the crowd is usually quite quiet, but under the cover of darkness, many individual members will shout encouragement to the person to kill himself. [3]A similar reaction was seen when women college students took part in an experiment where they were asked to press a button to shock other volunteers. [4]When the button-pushing women were visible to the victims, they administered only brief shocks, but when they were allowed to wear gowns and masks that hid their identities, they shocked the volunteers twice as much. [5]Clearly the feeling of being anonymous causes people to engage in anti-social behavior.

3. The relationship of sentence 3 to sentence 2 is one of
   a. cause and effect.
   b. time.
   c. contrast.
   d. comparison.

4. Sentence 4 expresses relationships of contrast and
   a. addition.
   b. time.
   c. illustration.
   d. cause and effect.

*(Continues on next page)*

B. The following six transitions have been removed from the textbook passage below. Read the passage carefully to see which transition logically fits in each answer space. Then write in each transition.

*Note:* You may find it helpful to check (✓) each transition after you insert it into the passage.

| | | |
|---|---|---|
| however | just as · | led |
| for example | also | until |

(5)_____ the 1960s, individual patients were almost always the focus of psychotherapy. Even today, it is the most common therapy form. (6)_____ a medical patient has a tumor, hernia, or heart attack, so too, an individual has a phobia, psychosis, or anxiety attack. Certain therapists, (7)_____, began to suspect that mental illness might better be thought of as a family affair. The problems observed in one individual might simply be the tip of the iceberg, with deeper systematic problems occuring at a subterranean level. Just as a poisoned water supply could make one family member obviously sick and not strongly affect others, so too, a sickness in the whole family system might be observed in just one child. (8)_____, one student wrote about the dynamics in her family that (9)_____ her to have severe anxiety attacks:

> Until I went to see a family counselor with my mother, I was not aware that I had been assuming three different roles in my household other than the role of daughter. The counselor told me that I am (10)_____ parent, wife, and husband. She said that I am living in the dilemma of a typical alcoholic family.

# 5

# Patterns of Organization

To help readers understand their main points, authors try to present supporting details in a clearly organized way. Details might be arranged in any of several common patterns. Sometimes authors may build a paragraph or longer passage exclusively on one pattern; often, the patterns are mixed. By recognizing the patterns, you will be better able to understand and remember what you read.

## THE FIVE BASIC PATTERNS OF ORGANIZATION

Here are the most commonly used patterns of organization:

1 Time Order
2 List of Items
3 Comparison and/or Contrast
4 Cause and Effect
5 Definition and Example

All five of the patterns are based on relationships you learned about in the last chapter. All five, then, involve transition words that you should now recognize. The time order pattern, for example, is marked by transitions that show time (*first, then, next, after,* and so on). The list on the next page shows some of the transitions used with each pattern:

| Pattern | Transitions Used |
|---|---|
| Time order | Words that show time (*first, then, next, after . . .*) |
| List of Items | Words that show addition (*also, another, moreover, finally . . .*) |
| Comparison/Contrast | Words that show comparison or contrast (*like, just as, however, in contrast . . .*) |
| Cause and Effect | Words that show cause and effect (*because, as a result, since, leads to . . .*) |
| Definition and Example· | Words that show illustration (*for example, to illustrate, such as . . .*) |

The following pages provide explanations and examples of each pattern.

## 1   TIME ORDER

Arrange the following group of sentences into an order that makes sense. Put a *1* in front of the sentence that should come first, a *2* in front of the sentence that comes next, and a *3* in front of the sentence that should be last. The result will be a short paragraph.

\_\_\_\_\_  By 1959, the number of TV sets in the country had risen to 50 million.

\_\_\_\_\_  After eight years, there were a million TV sets in the U.S.

\_\_\_\_\_  Interest in television grew rapidly after the major radio networks, NBC and CBS, began broadcasting television programs in July of 1941.

Authors usually present events in the order in which they happen, resulting in a pattern of organization known as *time order*. Clues to the pattern of the above sentences are dates and a transition (*after*) that shows time. The sentences should read as follows:

> Interest in television grew rapidly after the major radio networks, NBC and CBS, began broadcasting television programs in July of 1941. After eight years, there were a million TV sets in the U.S. By 1959, the number of TV sets in the country had risen to 50 million.

As a student, you will see time order used frequently. Textbooks in all fields describe events and processes, such as the events leading to the Boston Tea Party, the important incidents in Abraham Lincoln's life, the steps involved as for a bill to travel through Congress, or the process of photosynthesis.

The following transition words often signal that a paragraph or selection is organized according to *time order*:

*Time Transitions*

| | | | |
|---|---|---|---|
| first | next | as | while |
| second | before | now | during |
| then | after | until | when |
| since | soon | later | finally |

Other signals for this pattern are dates, times, and such words as *stages, series, steps,* and *process.*

The two most common kinds of time order involve a *series of events or stages* and a *series of steps (directions).* Each is discussed below.

### Series of Events or Stages

Following is a paragraph that is organized according to time order. Complete the outline of the paragraph by listing the missing stages in the order in which they happen.

Children master language in predictable stages. At about six months, babies start to babble, which means they repeat simple sounds, such as "ma-ma-me-me." About three or four months later, they can repeat sounds that others make. During this stage, parents and babies often babble alternately almost as if they are carrying on little conversations. These interchanges are rich in emotional meaning, although the sounds themselves are meaningless. At the next stage, toddlers learn the meanings of many words, but they are not yet able to talk themselves. A toddler might understand a sentence such as "Bring me your sock" but be unable to say any of the words. Eventually, the child begins to talk in single words and in two-word sentences.

**Main idea:** *Children master language in predictable stages.*

1. _____

   _____

2. *Three or four months later, babies can repeat sounds and carry*

   *on little "conversations."*

3. _____

   _____

4. _____

   _____

You should have added these points to the outline: (1) At about six months, babies begin to repeat simple sounds. (3) Toddlers understand many words, but cannot talk. (4) Eventually a child talks in single words and two-word sentences.

## ➤ *Practice 1a*

The following passage describes a sequence of events. Outline the paragraph by filling in the main idea and major details.

> The 1960s were a time of profound turmoil and change in America. The first thunderclap occurred in 1964, with the bullets that assassinated President John Kennedy and depressed the spirit of the country. Then in 1965, urban riots brought to the foreground the simmering issue of racial equality. A minor summer incident involving police in Watts, a black section of Los Angeles, set off five days of looting and rioting that left thirty-four people dead. Over a hundred major urban riots, all centered in black ghettos in cities like Newark and Detroit, were to follow. And by 1968, anti-war protests against the increasing American presence in Vietnam began to spread across the country. They centered on college campuses, and soon almost every major campus in the United States was torn by rallies, teach-ins, and riots.

**Main idea:** _____

1. _____

2. _____

3. _____

## Series of Steps (Directions)

Below is an example of a paragraph in which steps in a process are organized according to time order. Complete the outline of the paragraph that follows by listing the missing steps in the correct sequence.

> Here is a way to relax that is easy and can even be done in just a few minutes. First, lie down with your arms at your sides and your fingers open. When you are comfortable, close your eyes and put all distracting thoughts out of your mind. Next, tighten all the muscles of your body at once. Push your toes together, tighten your buttocks and abdomen, clench your fists, and squeeze your eyes shut. Hold this position for about seven seconds. Then, let everything relax, and feel the tension flow out of your body. After that, take a deep breath through your mouth and hold it for twenty seconds; then let it out slowly, and breathe slowly and easily, as you do when you are sleeping. Finally, think of a pleasant scene. Concentrate on this scene as you feel your whole body becoming calm and relaxed.

**Main idea:** *To relax quickly, follow an easy five-step relaxation*

*technique.*

1. _____

_____

2. _____

_____

3. *Tighten all muscles, and then relax.* _____

4. _____

_____

5. _____

_____

You should have added these steps: (1) Lie down, arms at your sides and fingers open. (2) When comfortable, close your eyes and clear your mind. (4) Take a deep breath through your mouth, hold it for twenty seconds, let it out, and breathe slowly and easily. (5) Concentrate on a pleasant scene as you feel yourself relax.

## ➤ Practice 1b

The following passage gives directions that involve several steps that must be done in order. Complete the outline below the paragraph.

> There are several steps to remembering your dreams. To begin with, you must make up your mind to do so, for consciously deciding that you want to remember increases the likelihood that it will happen. Then put a pen and a notebook near your bed, so that you can write down what you remember as soon as you wake up. When possible, turn off your alarm before you go to sleep so that you can wake up gradually, which will increase the likelihood of remembering your dreams. Finally, when you wake up in the morning and remember a dream, write it down immediately, even before getting out of bed.

**Main idea:** _____

1. *Make up your mind to remember your dreams.* _____

2. _____

3. _____

4. _____

## 2  LIST OF ITEMS

Arrange the following group of sentences into an order that makes sense. Put a *1* in front of the sentence that should come first, a *2* in front of the sentence that comes next, and a *3* in front of the sentence that should be last. The result will be a short paragraph.

_____ Also check a puppy's personality by watching how it plays with other puppies.

_____ There are some important points to keep in mind when choosing a puppy.

_____ First of all, look for signs of good health, including clear and bright eyes and firm pink gums.

This paragraph begins with the main idea: "There are some important points to keep in mind when choosing a puppy." The next two sentences go on to list two of those points, resulting in the pattern of organization known as a *list of items*. The transitions *first of all* and *also* introduce the points being listed and indicate their order: "First of all, look for signs of good health, including clear and bright eyes and firm pink gums. Also, check a puppy's personality by watching how it plays with other puppies."

A *list of items* refers to a series of details (such as examples, reasons, or facts) that support a point. The items have no time order, so they are listed in the order the author prefers. The transitions used in lists of items tell us that another supporting detail is being added to one or more already mentioned. Following are some transitions that show addition and that often signal a listing pattern of organization:

*Addition Transitions*

| | | | |
|---|---|---|---|
| and | in addition | first of all | furthermore |
| also | moreover | first | last of all |
| another | next | second | finally |

## A List of Items Paragraph

In the passage below, the main point has been italicized. See if you can count the number of items in the author's list and also identify the type of item being listed. Note that transitions will help you find the items. After doing this exercise, read the explanation that follows.

> *Poverty has changed in significant ways in the last thirty years.* For one thing, poverty today is increasingly an urban phenomenon. At one time, most of America's poor lived in small towns and rural areas. Today, poverty has risen in urban areas, as many industries have moved out of central cities. Second, poverty has been increasingly feminized. Over half

of the poor families in the country are headed by women. Single, deserted, or divorced mothers (and their children) are five times as likely to be poor as two-parent families. Last, although the great majority of the poor are white, racial minorities are overrepresented in the ranks of poverty. Blacks are three times as likely as white to be poor, and Hispanics twice as likely.

Number of items listed: _____

What type of item is listed? _____

_____

This paragraph consists of a main idea, stated in the topic sentence (the first sentence), followed by a list of three items, all supporting the main idea. The type of item listed in the paragraph is *changes in poverty* (urban, feminized, overrepresentation of racial minorities). Notice that the items might have been listed in any order without affecting the main idea of the paragraph.

## ➤ *Practice 2*

The following passages use a listing pattern. Underline each main idea. Then count the number of items used to support the main idea. Finally, answer the questions that follow each passage.

1.  Parents should seriously consider their children's requests for a pet, for there are definite advantages to owning a pet. First, if parents set down rules and stick to them, a child can learn responsibility by taking charge of feeding and, in the case of dogs, walking a pet. Also, while caring for any pets, such as tropical fish or hamsters, children learn about the animals' characteristics and habits. And finally, the unconditional love most pets express for their owners is another advantage; children benefit from the warmth and love their pets provide.

    How many items are listed? _____

    What type of item is listed? _____

2.  There are several ways to be an active listener. A common way to show that you are listening and interested is to ask questions about what the other person is saying. You can also rephrase what the other person has said to be sure you have understood. For example, you might say something like, "So what you're saying is . . . ." Yet another way to show your interest is to watch for clues to feelings in the other person's tone of voice or posture. That allows you to comment on or ask about the emotional reactions you notice, which shows that you care about that person's feelings.

How many items are listed? _____

What type of item is listed? _____

_____

## 3    COMPARISON AND/OR CONTRAST

Arrange the following group of sentences into an order that makes sense. Put a *1* in front of the sentence that should come first, a *2* in front of the sentence that comes next, and a *3* in front of the sentence that should be last. The result will be a short paragraph.

_____    Buffalo and Monte Carlo are about the same distance from the equator.

_____    Buffalo, New York, and the European resort town of Monte Carlo, Monaco, are strangely alike and different, geographically speaking.

_____    Yet Buffalo is known for its long brutal winters and very hot summers, and Monte Carlo is famous for its mild climate.

The first sentence of this paragraph is the general one, the one with the main idea: "Buffalo, New York, and the European resort town of Monte Carlo, Monaco, are strangely alike and different, geographically speaking." The words *alike* and *different* suggest a comparison and/or contrast pattern of organization. The comparison word *same* and the contrast word *yet* in the other two sentences show that the cities are indeed being compared *and* contrasted: "Buffalo and Monte Carlo are about the same distance from the equator. Yet Buffalo is known for its long brutal winters and very hot summers, and Monte Carlo is famous for its mild climate."

The *comparison-contrast* pattern shows how two things are alike or how they are different, or both. When things are *compared*, their similarities are pointed out; when they are *contrasted*, their differences are discussed. (Buffalo and Monte Carlo are similar in their distance from the equator; they are different in their climates.)

In our daily lives we compare and contrast things all the time, whether we are aware of it or not. For example, a simple decision such as whether to make a hamburger or a Swiss cheese sandwich for lunch requires us to compare and contrast the two choices. We may consider them both because of their similarities—they both taste good and are filling. We may, however, choose one over the other because of how they differ—a hamburger requires cooking while a cheese sandwich can be slapped together in about thirty seconds. If we are in a rush, we will probably choose the sandwich. If not, we may decide to have a hot meal and cook a hamburger instead.

Here are some common transitions showing comparison and contrast:

*Comparison Transitions*

| like | just like | just as | alike |
|------|-----------|---------|-------|
| likewise | equally | resembles | also |
| similarly | similarities | same | similar |

*Contrast Transitions*

| however | on the other hand | different |
|---------|-------------------|-----------|
| in contrast | as opposed to | differently |
| instead | unlike | differs from |

## A Comparison/Contrast Paragraph

In the following paragraph, the main idea is stated in the first sentence. As is often the case, the main idea indicates a paragraph's pattern of organization. In this case, the transition *differently* is a hint that the paragraph may be organized in a comparison-contrast pattern. Read the paragraph, and answer the questions below. Then read the explanation that follows.

> In middle age, men and women often view life very differently, especially among couples who have led traditional lives. By middle age, the husband is often comfortable in his position at work and has given up any dreams of advancing further. He may then become more family oriented. In contrast, once the children are grown, the wife may find herself free to explore interests and develop abilities she has had no time for in the previous fifteen or twenty years. Unlike her husband, she may be more interested in non-family activities than ever.

1. Is this paragraph comparing, contrasting, or both?

   _____

2. What two things are being compared and/or contrasted? _____

   _____

3. Which three comparison or contrast transition words are used in the paragraph?

   _____

This paragraph is only contrasting, not comparing—it discusses only differences, not similarities. The two things being contrasted are the views of traditional middle-aged men and women. The transition words that show contrast are *differently, in contrast,* and *unlike.*

## ➤ *Practice 3*

The following passages use the pattern of *comparison* or *contrast*. Read each passage and answer the questions which follow.

A.   Although mysteries and science fiction may seem like very different kinds of writing, the two forms share some basic similarities. First of all, both are action-oriented, emphasizing plot at the expense of character development. Possibly for this reason, both types of literature have been scorned by critics as being "mere entertainment" rather than "literature." But this attack is unjustified, for both mysteries and science fiction share a concern with moral issues. Science fiction often raises the question of whether or not scientific advances are beneficial to humanity. And a mystery story rarely ends without the guilty person being brought to justice.

Check the pattern which is used in this paragraph:

_____ Comparison

_____ Contrast

What two things are being compared or contrasted?

1. _____          2. _____

B.   The conflict over secrecy between the federal government and journalists arises from the different roles they play in society. The government has the job of conducting foreign policy. To do so effectively, government officials sometimes prefer to distort or withhold information. Journalists, however, see their role as digging up and giving information to the public. If they always sought government permission before publishing information, they would be able to print or broadcast only what the government wanted to appear in the media.

Check the pattern which is used in this paragraph:

_____ Comparison

_____ Contrast

What two things are being compared or contrasted?

1. _____          2. _____

## 4   CAUSE AND EFFECT

Arrange the following group of sentences into an order that makes sense. Put a *1* in front of the sentence that should come first, a *2* in front of the sentence that comes next, and a *3* in front of the sentence that should be last. The result will be a short paragraph.

_____ The need for the specialized knowledge of industry leads to a system of formal education.

_____ A society's change from an agricultural base to an industrial one results in the growth of formal education and a weaker family.

_____ And because formal education replaces the instruction of older family members, the family's authority is weakened.

As the words *leads to, results in,* and *because* suggest, this paragraph is organized in a *cause and effect* pattern. The paragraph begins with the general idea: "A society's change from an agricultural base to an industrial one results in the growth of formal education and a weaker family." Next comes a more detailed explanation: "The need for the specialized knowledge of industry leads to a system of formal education. And because formal education replaces the instruction of older family members, the family's authority is weakened."

Information that falls into a *cause-effect* pattern addresses itself to the questions "Why does an event happen?" and "What are the results of an event?" In other words, this pattern answers the question "What are the *causes* and/or *effects* of an event?"

Authors usually don't just tell what happened; they try to tell about events in a way that explains both *what* happened and *why.* A textbook section on the sinking of the ship the *Titanic,* for example, would be incomplete if it did not include the cause of the disaster—going at a high speed, the ship collided with an iceberg. Or if the banks of the Mississippi River are flooded, a newspaper will not simply report about the flooding. An article on this event would also tell why the flooding happened—heavy rains caused the river to overflow. An important part of any effort to understand events and processes includes learning about cause-effect relationships.

Explanations of causes and effects very often use transitions such as the following:

*Cause-and-Effect Transitions*

| | | | |
|---|---|---|---|
| thus | because | because of | causes |
| as a result | result in | result | effects |
| therefore | since | consequently | leads to |

## A Cause and Effect Paragraph

Read the paragraph on the next page and see if you can answer the questions about cause and effect. Then read the explanation to see how you did.

Drinking alcohol can lead to different states of consciousness. Although the changes vary from person to person, some broad generalizations are possible. One or two drinks usually result in feelings of warmth, relaxation, and decreased inhibitions. Such limited drinking can be enjoyed by many people without serious drawbacks. Slightly heavier drinking often causes people to believe they can do things better than they really can. For example, after a few drinks a person may believe he is speaking eloquently when, in fact, his speech is slurred or even unintelligible. Or someone may believe she can drive perfectly well when her reactions and judgment have actually been weakened by alcohol.

1.   What are the two *causes* described in this paragraph?

a. _____

b. _____

2.   What are the two kinds of *effects*?

a. _____

b. _____

3.   What three cause-effect signal words or phrases are used?

_____

While this paragraph discusses drinking alcohol as a cause in general, it divides drinking into two categories—"one or two drinks" and "slightly heavier drinking." The first cause, then, is "one or two drinks"; its effect can be "feelings of warmth, relaxation, and decreased inhibitions." The second cause is "slightly heavier drinking"; its effect may be to make drinkers "believe they can do things better than they really can." The cause-effect signals here are *lead to, result in,* and *causes.*

## ➤ *Practice 4*

The three activities that follow (A, B, and C) will give you a sharper sense of cause-and-effect relationships.

**A.**   The following sentences describe a cause-and-effect relationship. For each sentence, identify both the cause and the effect.

1. The orange crop in Florida is poor this year because of a late spring freeze.

Cause:_____

Effect:_____

2. Mr. Coleman's bankruptcy was the result of his compulsive gambling.

Cause:_____

Effect:_____

3. Last winter I twisted my ankle by slipping and falling on a patch of ice.

Cause:_____

Effect:_____

4. Linda's new boss did not appreciate her excellent work habits, so Linda began to do her work carelessly.

Cause:_____

Effect:_____

**B.** The following sentences all list either two causes leading to the same effect or two effects resulting from a single cause. Identify causes and effects in each sentence. Here is an example of how to do this activity.

**Example**

High winds and hailstones as big as golf balls resulted in $10,000 worth of property damage.

High winds: *cause*
Hailstones: *cause*
Property damage: *effect*

5. Uncontrolled high blood pressure can lead to a stroke or a heart attack.

Uncontrolled high blood pressure: _____

Stroke: _____

Heart attack: _____

6. Because the defense lawyer's objection was valid, the judge threw out the evidence and dismissed the case.

Valid objection: _____

Thrown-out evidence: _____

Dismissed case: _____

7. After ammunition and food supplies had run low, the general surrendered.

Ammunition was low: _____

Food supplies were low: _____

The general surrendered: _____

8. Tonia's grades have improved since she put herself on a study schedule and stopped going out on weeknights.

Tonia's better grades: _____

A study schedule: _____

Not going out on weeknights: _____

C. Each of the following passages lists either several causes leading to the same effect or several effects resulting from a single cause. In the spaces provided, identify the causes and effects in each paragraph.

9. Even the best listeners cannot possibly listen carefully to everything that they hear. Among the reasons for this is the overload of messages most of us encounter each day. Besides the numerous hours we spend hearing other people speak, we may spend several more hours listening to the radio or television. It isn't possible to avoid having our attention wander at least part of all this time. Preoccupation with our personal concerns is another reason we don't always listen carefully. A romance gone sour or a good grade on a test may take prominence in our mind even as someone is speaking to us. In addition, the simple fact that we are at times surrounded by noise interferes with listening. For example, many voices at a noisy party or the sound of traffic may simply make it difficult for us to hear everything that is being said.

Inability to listen carefully all the time: _____

Message overload: _____

Preoccupation with personal concerns: _____

Surrounding noise: _____

10. Research over the last decade or so has shown that meditation can have positive effects on drug users and people with certain health problems. Studies have demonstrated that when people who take drugs become meditators, they either cut back on drug use or stop using drugs altogether. In one study of a group that practiced meditation, for example, the number of marijuana users fell from 78 percent to 12 percent after twenty-one months of meditation. Meditation has also been shown to lower blood pressure and regulate the heartbeat, both of which may be of considerable help to those with cardiovascular problems. And because meditation is a highly effective relaxation technique, it can also prove useful to those with stress-related diseases.

Meditation: _____

Decrease or elimination of drug use: _____

Cardiovascular improvements: _____

Stress relief: _____

## 5   DEFINITION AND EXAMPLE

Arrange the following group of sentences into an order that makes sense. Put a *1* in front of the sentence that should come first, a *2* in front of the sentence that comes next, and a *3* in front of the sentence that should be last. The result will be a short paragraph.

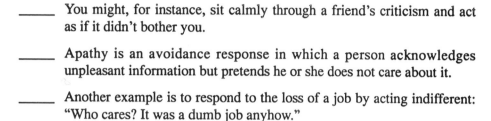

_____ You might, for instance, sit calmly through a friend's criticism and act as if it didn't bother you.

_____ Apathy is an avoidance response in which a person acknowledges unpleasant information but pretends he or she does not care about it.

_____ Another example is to respond to the loss of a job by acting indifferent: "Who cares? It was a dumb job anyhow."

This paragraph begins with a definition: "Apathy is an avoidance response in which a person acknowledges unpleasant information but pretends he or she does not care about it." The second sentence clarifies the special meaning of apathy here with an example: "You might, for instance, sit calmly through a friend's criticism and act as if it didn't bother you." The third sentence then provides a second example: "Another example is to respond to the loss of a job by acting indifferent: 'Who cares? It was a dumb job anyhow.'" The second and third sentences include the illustration transitions *for instance* and *example*. As you can see, the *definition and example* pattern of organization includes just what its name suggests: a definition and one or more examples.

To communicate successfully, an author must help readers understand the words and ideas that are being expressed. If a word is likely to be new to readers, the author may take time to include a *definition* before going on. Then, to clarify the definition, which might be too general to be easily understood, the author may present explanatory details, including one or more *examples*. Examples help readers better understand what is meant and strengthen support for the ideas they illustrate.

Textbooks often contain definitions and examples. They introduce students to new words and provide examples of how those words are used to make them clearer and more familiar. Typically, the definition appears first, followed by one or more examples. But sometimes the examples are given first and then the definition. And note that definitions may be given without examples, and examples are frequently used to illustrate general statements other than definitions.

Examples are often introduced by transitions like the following:

*ιple Transitions*

| for example | to illustrate | one |
| for instance | such as | specifically |
| as an illustration | to be specific | including |

## A Definition and Example Paragraph

The following paragraph defines a word, explains it a bit, and then gives an example of it. After reading the paragraph, see if you can answer the questions that follow.

> [1]Acrophobia is an intense, unreasonable fear of high places. [2]People with acrophobia exhibit physical symptoms in response to being at great heights. [3]One sufferer from extreme acrophobia, Sally Maxwell, is unable to go above the third floor of any building without feeling enormous anxiety. [4]Her acrophobia began one evening when she was working alone in her office on the eighth floor of a large building. [5]Suddenly she was struck with terror by the idea that she might jump or fall out the open window. [6]She crouched behind a steel filing cabinet, trembling, unable to move. [7]When she finally gathered her belongings and left the building, she was sweating, her breathing was rapid, and her heart was pounding. [8]Yet she had no rational explanation for her fears.

What word is being defined? _____

What is the definition? _____

_____

Which sentence explains more about the word? _____

In which sentence does the example begin? _____

The word "acrophobia" is defined in the first sentence—"an intense, unreasonable fear of high places." The second sentence explains a bit more about acrophobia. The story about Sally Maxwell, which begins in the third sentence, provides an example of how acrophobia affects one sufferer; by including it, the author makes the new term more clear by helping readers better visualize what it means.

## ➤ *Practice 5*

The following passages include a definition and one or more specific examples, each marked by a transition. In the spaces provided, write the number of the definition sentence and the number of the sentence where each example begins.

A.   [1]A boycott is an organized refusal by a group of people to deal with another person or group to achieve a specific goal. [2]An illustration is the famous boycott that began in 1955 when Mrs. Rosa Parks of Montgomery, Alabama, refused to obey a local ordinance requiring black people to sit at the back of city busses. [3]Mrs. Parks was arrested, and that sparked off a boycott of the Montgomery bus system by blacks. [4]The boycott was organized and led by Dr. Martin Luther King, Jr. [5]Rather than continue to lose revenue needed to run the bus system, the city repealed the ordinance.

Definition _____   Example _____

B.   [1]Although most people would agree that lying to gain unfair advantage over an unknowing victim is wrong, another kind of mistruth—the "white lie"—isn't so easy to dismiss as completely unethical. [2]White lies are untruths that are unmalicious, or even helpful, to the person to whom they are told. [3]Over half of all white lies are justified as a way to prevent embarrassment. [4]Such lying is often given the approving label "tact." [5]Sometimes a face-saving lie saves face for the recipient, such as when you pretend to remember someone at a party in order to save them from the embarrassment of being forgotten. [6]Other white lies are told to prevent a large conflict. [7]You might, for instance, say you're not upset at a friend's teasing in order to prevent the hassle that would result if you expressed your annoyance.

Definition _____   Example 1 _____   Example 2 _____

## Topic Sentences and Patterns of Organization

A paragraph's topic sentence often indicates its pattern of organization. For example, the topic sentence of a paragraph you worked on earlier is: *There are several steps to remembering your dreams*. This sentence probably made you suspect that the paragraph goes on to list those steps. If so, the paragraph would be organized according to time order (a series of steps).When a paragraph turns out to include the information you expect (as it does in that case), then you know you have found the correct pattern.

Another good example is the paragraph you read earlier on drinking alcohol. The topic sentence of that paragraph is: *Drinking alcohol can lead to different states of consciousness*. The words *lead to* suggest that this paragraph may be about causes and effects. And, in fact, the paragraph *is* about two causes ("one or two drinks" and "slightly heavier drinking") and their effects.

So if you are having trouble recognizing a paragraph's pattern of organization, you may find it helpful to think about its topic sentence. Try, for instance, to guess the pattern of the paragraph with this topic sentence:

While there are thousands of self-help groups, they all fall into three basic classifications.

The statement that self-help groups "fall into three basic classifications" is a strong indication that the paragraph will list those classifications. The topic sentence helps us guess that the paragraph may be a list of three items—that is, the three classifications.

## ➤ Practice 6

Circle the letter of the pattern of organization that each topic sentence suggests.

1. Cleaning up a playground can have surprising results.

   a. Definition and example    b. Cause and effect    c. Comparison/contrast

2. Although Abby and Susan are twins, you could not find two more different girls.

   a. Time order          b. Cause and effect          c. Comparison/contrast

3. Once upon a time, there was an evil princess.

   a. Time order          b. List of items          c. Definition and example

4. Bicycles can be equipped with many extra safety features.

   a. Definition and example          b. Cause and effect          c. List of items

5. An *antonym* is a word that means the opposite of another word.

   a. Time order          b. Cause and effect          c. Definition and example

## ➤ Review

To review what you've learned in this chapter, complete each of the following sentences about patterns of organization.

1. A paragraph's pattern of organization is the pattern in which its (*supporting details, main idea, causes and effects*) _____ _____ is or are organized.

2. The pattern in which a series of details are presented in any order the author considers best is called a _____.

3. The pattern in which the details discuss how two or more things are alike or different is a pattern of _____.

4. When a passage provides a series of directions for the reader to follow, it uses a _____ order.

5. When textbook authors provide a definition of a term, they are also likely to provide one or more _____ to help make that definition clear.

# PATTERNS OF ORGANIZATION: Test A-1

**A.** 1-4. Arrange the scrambled sentences below into a logical paragraph by numbering them *1*, *2*, *3*, and *4* in an order that makes sense. Then circle the letter of the primary pattern of organization used.

Note that transitions will help you by clarifying the relationships between sentences.

___3___ Opossums may also try to bluff their way out of a tight spot by hissing and baring their teeth. (If you've ever seen an opossum's teeth, then you know how effective simply showing them can be.)

___1___ The opossum can react to danger in one of several ways, depending on the variety of opossum and the situation.

___2___ First, some opossums use the skunk's method of defense—they spray an unpleasant odor.

___4___ Finally, the best-known of opossum defenses is to "play dead" by entering into a coma-like state brought on by fear.

5. The primary pattern of organization is
   a. time order.
   b. list of items.
   c. comparison.
   d. definition and example.

*(Continues on next page)*

**B.** Label each item with the letter of its main pattern of organization. Use each letter once.

| | |
|---|---|
| **a** Time order | **d** Cause and effect |
| **b** List of items | **e** Definition and example |
| **c** Comparison and/or contrast | |

_____d_____ 6. Exercise causes calories to burn up and flab to become more firm. As a result, exercise is a very useful part of any weight-reducing effort.

_____A_____ 7. Libraries lend more than books. First of all, many offer borrowers music on records and tapes. In addition, some lend films and art work. It's even possible at some libraries to borrow equipment such as VCRs and movie projectors.

_____e_____ 8. Phobias are intense, irrational fears that are out of proportion to the actual danger in a situation. For instance, people with the fear of open places *(agoraphobia)* are often reluctant to leave their homes.

_____b_____ 9. On the afternoon of July 20, 1968, the lunar module, the *Eagle*, landed on the moon with astronauts Neil Armstrong and Edwin Aldrin. Six and a half hours after landing, the hatch of the *Eagle* was opened, and Armstrong began to descend a ladder to the surface of the moon.

_____C_____ 10. Some lawns seem to stay green with very little work, like my neighbor's lawn. Others, like the grass in my own back and front yards, require various fertilizers and lots of water to look only bad (instead of terrible).

# PATTERNS OF ORGANIZATION: Test A-2

For each paragraph, write the number of the topic sentence in the space provided. Then circle the letter of the main pattern of organization.

A.   [1]Boys who mature early physically have a decided advantage over their more slowly maturing peers. [2]Early maturers become heroes in sports and leaders in both formal and informal activities. [3]Other boys look up to them; girls have crushes on them. [4]Even adults tend to trust them. [5]They are more self-confident and independent than other boys. [6]In contrast, their less mature male peers, with their high-pitched voices and underdeveloped physiques, feel inadequate. [7]They are weaker at sports and more awkward with girls.

  1.  Topic sentence: _____

  2.  Main pattern of organization:
      a.  Time order
      b.  Comparison and/or contrast
      c.  Definition and example

B.   [1]Artificial intelligence (AI) is a term that describes computer programs that solve problems by "thinking" the way people do. [2]Most of these programs are based on sets of rules similar to logical thinking. [3]One AI program, for instance, was designed to diagnose infectious diseases. [4]It is about as efficient as most doctors. [5]In some fields, such as geology, AI programs have solved problems far more quickly than people could.

  3.  Topic sentence: _____

  4.  Main pattern of organization:
      a.  Time order
      b.  Cause and effect
      c.  Definition and example

C.   [1]Not all pit bulls are naturally vicious. [2]Those pit bulls that are savagely aggressive have been trained to be so in various ways. [3]Some owners, for example, try to make their dogs more aggressive by forcing them to run on treadmills until they are exhausted. [4]Other training methods incude putting collars of barbed wire on the dogs, feeding them live kittens or small dogs, and feeding them gunpowder or hot sauce. [5]In addition, some owners strengthen their pit bulls' jaws, already strong, by swinging the dog from a rope while its teeth are clutching a tire.

  5.  Topic sentence: _____

  6.  Main pattern of organization:
      a.  List of items
      b.  Contrast
      c.  Definition and example

*(Continues on next page)*

D.    [1]Martin Luther King, Jr., did not always arise with the sun. [2]But on Monday, December 5, 1955, the excited young minister could not sleep. [3]Impatiently he paced the house, waiting for the first bus of the day to reach its stop near his front porch. [4]The vehicle was usually crowded with black domestics on their way to the kitchens and yards of the white employers of Montgomery, Alabama; it would be a good test of the boycott he and others had urged local blacks to undertake. [5]King had prepared himself for disappointment and hoped to be cheered by partial success. [6]But the first bus was empty, and the second, and the third. [7]The elated pastor undertook a wider investigation in his car. [8]This was the beginning of a very important day in the civil rights movement.

7. Topic sentence: _____

8. Main pattern of organization:
   a. Time order
   b. List of items
   c. Cause and effect

E.    [1]Most teenagers who smoke are familiar with the health hazards of smoking, yet for various reasons they drift into the habit anyway. [2]A teenager with one parent who smokes is twice as likely to smoke as one with nonsmoking parents. [3]Also, young people are more likely to smoke if their friends do. [4]The chances are nine out of ten that a teenager whose best friend smokes will also start to smoke. [5]In addition, teens who mature late are more likely to smoke than others, apparently because they hope that smoking will make them look more adult.

9. Topic sentence: _____

10. Main pattern of organization:
    a. Time order
    b. Definition and example
    c. List of items

## PATTERNS OF ORGANIZATION: Test A-3

Read each paragraph and answer the questions or follow the directions provided.

A.  Non-traditional job schedules are becoming more common in many American industries. One popular option is job sharing. This concept allows two employees, often working mothers, to split the hours and benefits of a full-time job. Flextime is another alternative job arrangement. Employees working on flextime can arrive and leave as they choose, as long as they put in the required number of hours per day. Another newcomer on the job scene is the compressed workweek. Employees on this schedule work longer shifts than usual, but fewer days per week.

1.  The main pattern of organization of the paragraph is
    a.  comparison and/or contrast.
    b.  list of items.
    c.  definition and example.

2-5. Outline the paragraph by writing out briefly the main idea and the major supporting details.

**Main idea:**_____

_____

**Supporting details:**

1. _____
2. _____
3. _____

*(Continues on next page)*

**B.** Successful garage sales are planned well in advance. About a month before the sale, find out whether the town or city you live in requires you to get a permit to hold your sale. Next, gather and prepare all the items you want to sell, sprucing them up whenever possible by washing or repairing them. Then print and post notices of your sale. Last of all, arrange your merchandise on card or picnic tables, along with price labels for each item, and get ready to collect your well-earned profits.

6. The main pattern of organization of the paragraph is
   a. time order.
   b. comparison and/or contrast.
   c. list of items.

7-10. Complete the diagram of the paragraph.

> **Implied main idea:** There are several steps to preparing for a successful garage sale.

**Steps in a Garage Sale**

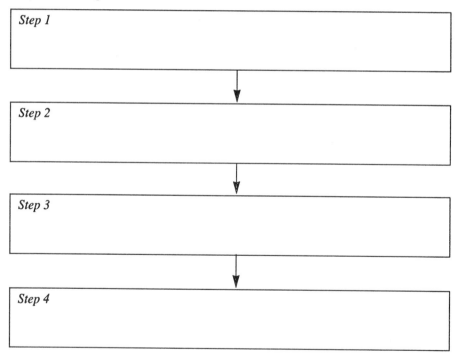

# PATTERNS OF ORGANIZATION: Test B-1

A. 1-4. Arrange the scrambled sentences below into a logical paragraph by numbering them *1, 2, 3,* and *4* in an order that makes sense. Then circle the letter of the primary pattern of organization used.

Note that transitions will help you by clarifying the relationships between sentences.

_____ Also, high tuitions affect the amount of time available for studying; because loans and scholarships are hard to get, many students have to put in numerous hours at work in order to afford school.

_____ For one thing, it undoubtedly prevents some students from attending college in the first place.

_____ Finally, those who do manage to get loans know that they must begin their careers with large debts.

_____ The high cost of college today causes problems for many students in more ways than one.

5. The primary pattern of organization is
   a. contrast.
   b. comparison.
   c. cause and effect.
   d. definition and example.

*(Continues on next page)*

**B.** Label each item with the letter of its main pattern of organization. Use each letter once.

| | |
|---|---|
| **a** Time order | **d** Cause and effect |
| **b** List of items | **e** Definition and example |
| **c** Comparison and/or contrast | |

_____ 6. The construction of federally subsidized highways and the shortage of housing in central cities led to the movement to the suburbs.

_____ 7. To begin word processing, first turn on the computer. Next, insert the master editing disk into Drive A. Then put a blank, formatted disk into Drive B and get ready to write.

_____ 8. A good study space is well-lighted and well-supplied with paper, pens, and study aids. In addition, it is quiet and free from distractions such as television or stereo. Finally, it includes a comfortable chair and desk space.

_____ 9. A forensic psychologist is a psychologist who interprets professional information for courtroom purposes. At the trial of John Hinckley, Jr., for instance, several forensic psychologists testified about whether or not Hinckley was mentally competent enough to be considered legally responsible for his attempt to assassinate then President Ronald Reagan.

_____ 10. Most birds are born in either of two very different states. Some are born weak, blind, and usually naked. About all they can do for themselves is open their mouths for food. Other newborn baby birds are born bright-eyed and covered with down. As soon as their down is dry, they are able to peck at things and run after their parents.

# PATTERNS OF ORGANIZATION: Test B-2

For each paragraph, write the number of the topic sentence in the space provided. Then circle the letter of the main pattern of organization.

A.   [1]People are different from other primates, but not as different as they might like to think. [2]It's true that that there are significant contrasts in size and proportion between humans and other primates. [3]And, of course, humans are by far the more intelligent. [4]Nevertheless, to use chimpanzees as an example, both they and humans have the same muscles and bones, located in almost the same places and working in nearly the same ways. [5]The internal organs of both animals are also very much alike, as are their blood and other body fluids. [6]Seen under a microscope, even their genes are strikingly similar.

1.   Topic sentence: _____

2.   Main pattern of organization:
     a.   Cause and effect
     b.   List of items
     c.   Comparison and/or contrast

B.   [1]There are often more than two sides to a question, and offering only two choices when more actually exist is called an Either-Or Fallacy. [2]For example, the statement "Either you are with us or against us" assumes that there is no middle ground. [3]Or consider the following conclusion: People opposed to total freedom of speech are really in favor of censorship. [4]This argument ignores the fact that a person could believe in free speech as well as in laws that prohibit slander or that punish someone for yelling "Fire!" in a crowded theater.

3.   Topic sentence: _____

4.   Main pattern of organization:
     a.   Time order
     b.   Cause and effect
     c.   Definition and example

C.   [1]Are you having trouble getting rid of a cold, the flu, or a nagging sore throat? [2]Studies at the University of Oklahoma Dental School have shown that your old toothbrush may carry the germs that are causing your illness. [3]The studies have found that people who change their toothbrushes about every two weeks recover from common winter ills faster than people who use their toothbrushes for a month or more. [4]Old toothbrushes can culture the germs that can cause colds, influenza, pneumonia, strep throat, diarrhea, and sinus disease. [5]Another study found that disease germs can live in an unused toothbrush for as long as a week. [6]They can start to thrive again every time you brush your teeth.

*(Continues on next page)*

5. Topic sentence: _____

6. Main pattern of organization:
   a. Time order
   b. Cause and effect
   c. Definition and example

**D.** [1]Often when children move back home, unpleasant tensions and disagreements arise. [2]However, adult children who move back home can avoid family conflicts by following these tips. [3]First, they should contribute what they can—and it need not be in terms of money: Being productive family members will help them earn their keep. [4]This can involve tutoring or coaching younger sisters or brothers, or helping Mom and Dad with chores and errands. [5]Second, these "returnees" should not expect their parents to rescue them from difficulties. [6]As adults, they are responsible for getting out of their own scrapes—and for trying to avoid them in the first place. [7]Last, they must respect their parents' lifestyles and own needs for independence. [8]It is unrealistic to expect parents' lives to revolve around the needs of a grown child, in the manner they may have when the child was younger.

7. Topic sentence: _____

8. Main pattern of organization:
   a. Cause and effect
   b. Comparison and/or contrast
   c. List of items

**E.** [1]In January of 1954, Ernest and Mary Hemingway left Nairobi on a vacation trip on which they flew over grazing elephants, hippos bathing in the lakes, and huge flocks of feeding flamingos. [2]As they were circling a spectacular waterfall, a flock of ibises flew in front of the plane. [3]When the pilot dived to avoid the birds, he struck an abandoned telegraph wire that crossed the gorge. [4]In the crash that followed, Ernest sprained his shoulder; Mary was only slightly injured. [5]Luckily, a boat came down the river the next morning, and its crew rescued them. [6]By that evening, they were on board a small plane bound for Entebbe. [7]The plane lifted from the plowed field that served as a runway, then crashed and burst into flames. [8]Ernest escaped by breaking through a window with his head and injured shoulder, and Mary got out through another window. [9]Twice in two days they had crashed and come out alive, but Ernest had injured his head, his backbone, and a kidney; after this, even writing a letter was difficult for him.

9. Topic sentence: _____

10. Main pattern of organization:
    a. Time order
    b. List of items
    c. Contrast

# PATTERNS OF ORGANIZATION: Test B-3

Read each paragraph and answer the questions or follow the directions provided.

A. Middle-aged adults are returning to school in increasing numbers. Some want to learn to do their jobs better. College courses can help them improve their job skills and keep up in their fields. Others return to school because more credits may mean a raise or promotion. Teachers, for instance, get raises for reaching certain levels of education. Also, some adults return to the classroom because of interest in a new field, such as telecommunication or computer programming. Finally, others want to study subjects for the sake of learning, such as foreign languages, history, or literature. Such classes help adults spend their time in more productive and interesting ways and deepen their understanding of themselves and their world.

1. The organizational patterns of the paragraph are list of items and
   a. time order.
   b. definition and example.
   c. cause and effect.

2-5. Complete the outline of the paragraph by writing in the four major supporting details.

   **Main idea:** There are several reasons why middle-aged adults are returning to school.

   **Supporting details:**

   1. _____

   2. _____

   3. _____

   4. _____

*(Continues on next page)*

**B.**   The process by which children learn their sex roles contains three main elements. One is conditioning through rewards and punishments. For example, boys who play with model airplanes and girls who play with dolls will usually be encouraged by their parents. On the other hand, boys who prefer dolls and girls who prefer airplanes will often be criticized or even punished. Another element is imitation. Young children will usually imitate adults who they think are like themselves. This means that boys will usually imitate their fathers and girls their mothers. The third and perhaps the most important element is self-definition. Children quickly learn that all people are either male or female and define themselves as belonging to one sex rather than the other. They then use this self-definition to choose their future interests and to develop their personalities and social roles.

6. The main pattern of organization of the paragraph is
   a. time order.
   b. list of items.
   c. comparison.

7-10. Fill in the diagram of the paragraph.

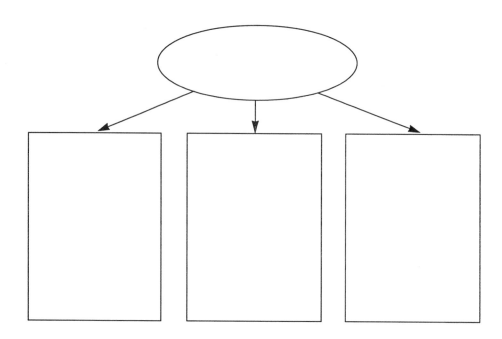

## PATTERNS OF ORGANIZATION: Test C-1

A. 1-4. Arrange the scrambled sentences below into a logical paragraph by numbering them *1, 2, 3,* and *4* in an order that makes sense. Then circle the letter of the primary pattern of organization used.

Note that transitions will help you by clarifying the relationships between sentences.

_2_ But the original Italian story is the gruesome tale of the Princess Talia, who falls into a deep magical sleep in the woods, where she is raped by a nobleman and, later on, gives birth to twins, whom the nobleman's wife tries to have killed and cooked for dinner.

_3_ It is often said that fairy tales, with their heavy doses of terror and violence, are too scary for young children.

_1_ The story of Sleeping Beauty that today's children know, for example, involves a princess who is put to sleep by a wicked witch and then awakened by the kiss of her true love.

_4_ But today's versions of fairy tales are actually less frightening than the original stories.

5. The primary pattern of organization is
   a. list of items.
   b. comparison and/or contrast.
   c. cause and effect.
   d. definition and example.

*(Continues on next page)*

**B.** Label each item with the letter of its main pattern of organization. Use each letter once.

| a Time order | d Cause and effect |
|---|---|
| b List of items | e Definition and example |
| c Comparison and/or contrast | |

_____ 6. There are many good low- or non-fat foods that are high in protein. Lean meat, fish, poultry, and dried beans and peas all fit the bill. Skim milk and non-fat yogurt are fat-free high-protein foods.

_____ 7. Two-way listening is what occurs when a listener gives some feedback to a speaker on what he or she has been saying. One type of such feedback is questioning the speaker to clarify a point.

_____ 8. A new labor contract along with a rise in the price of paper forced the price of the daily edition of the newspaper to increase from twenty-five to thirty cents.

_____ 9. To make an unforgettable sandwich, spread a thick layer of peanut butter on two slices of bread. Then separate two or three Oreo cookies and place the halves onto the peanut butter on one of the slices of bread. Next, place the other piece of bread over the cookies (peanut-butter side down, of course), and eat.

_____ 10. Both Lamarck and Darwin made scientific observations. However, Lamarck built his hypothesis on what scientists consider unsound thinking. Darwin, on the other hand, offered convincing evidence for his theory of evolution.

# PATTERNS OF ORGANIZATION: Test C-2

For each paragraph, write the number of the topic sentence in the space provided. Then circle the letter of the main pattern of organization.

A. [1]The use of fire by prehistoric people probably affected wildlife both intentionally and unintentionally. [2]In all likelihood, early people used fire to drive game toward waiting hunters. [3]Later, new plant growth in the burned areas would attract more wild animals. [4]In addition, accidental fires must have also occurred frequently. [5]Because prehistoric people had trouble starting fires, they kept burning embers on hand. [6]The result must have been widespread accidental fires, especially in dry areas. [7]Certainly, these fires also would have greatly altered the habitat for wildlife.

   1. Topic sentence: _____

   2. Main pattern of organization:
      a. Time order
      b. Cause and effect
      c. Comparison and/or contrast

B. [1]Alaska's road to statehood involved a series of "owners." [2]The original people to live in the huge state of Alaska were Eskimos, Aleuts (natives of the Aleutian Islands, which lie off of Alaska), and Indians. [3]In 1731, a Russian explorer landed on the Alaskan coast. [4]Russia claimed the land as her own, and in the years that followed, many Russians were involved in exploring the coast and trading with the Alaskan natives. [5]The United States held discussions with Russia about purchasing Alaska as early as 1859, but the deal was put off by the American Civil War. [6]In 1867, the U.S. purchased the Alaskan territory for $7.2 million. [7]The territory became the 49th state in 1959.

   3. Topic sentence: _____

   4. Main pattern of organization:
      a. Time order
      b. List of items
      c. Comparison/contrast

C. [1]Habituation is the term for a common behavior pattern: the more we are exposed to something, the less aware we become of it and, therefore, the less we respond to it. [2]During the Vietnam War, reports from the combat zone appeared every night on television. [3]Viewers soon became so used to the news stories that scenes of violence and body counts no longer horrified them. [4]The war became just another television program.

   5. Topic sentence: _____

*(Continues on next page)*

6. Main pattern of organization:
   a. List of items
   b. Definition and example
   c. Comparison/contrast

D.   [1]The names of many people, real and fictional, have become permanent parts of the language. [2]General Ambrose Everett Burnside, for one, is remembered because of his long side whiskers. [3]The Civil War-era general lent his name, with its syllables reversed, to the word *sideburns*. [4]Another character whose name has been adopted into the language is that of Atlas, a giant from Greek mythology who supported the heavens on his shoulders. [5]An early collection of maps had a picture of Atlas holding up the world, and *atlas* has come to mean any book of maps. [6]Still another name-turned-word is that of Sir Robert Peel, the founder of the London (England) Metropolitan Police. [7]London policemen are still called *bobbies* in honor of Sir Robert.

7. Topic sentence: _____

8. Main pattern of organization:
   a. Time order
   b. List of items
   c. Comparison/contrast

E.   [1]A psychology professor introduced the same male guest lecturer to two different classes. [2]The first class was told to expect a rather cold, dull, uninteresting person. [3]The second class was told to expect a warm, intelligent, friendly lecturer. [4]The lecturer presented identical information in the same manner to both groups. [5]The first group found his lecture boring and did not ask questions; the second group found him warm and stimulating and asked many questions. [6]This experiment has been replicated successfully many times. [7]The outcome of these experiments suggest that telling someone what to perceive in another person will influence what is experienced.

9. Topic sentence: _____

10. The main pattern of organization of this discussion of a cause-effect relationship is
    a. time order.
    b. definition and example.
    c. comparison/contrast.

## PATTERNS OF ORGANIZATION: Test C-3

Read each paragraph and answer the questions or follow the directions provided.

**A.** Criticism is a valuable means of helping ourselves and others achieve personal growth. But because it is often done carelessly or cruelly, criticism has a bad reputation. Here are some guidelines for offering criticism constructively. First, wait until the person asks for feedback on his performance or actions. Unasked-for criticism is not usually valuable. Second, describe the person's behavior as specifically as possible before you criticize it. Instead of just saying, "You were awful," tell the person exactly what you observed. And finally, try to balance your criticism with positive statements. Look for significant points in the other person's performance that you can honestly praise.

1. The main pattern of organization of the paragraph is
   a. list of items.
   b. cause and effect.
   c. definition and example.

2-5. Complete the outline of the paragraph.

**Main idea:**_____

_____

**Supporting details:**

1. _____
2. _____
3. _____

*(Continues on next page)*

**B.**   Why do people daydream? One cause of daydreaming is routine or boring jobs that are tolerable only when workers imagine themselves doing something else. Deprivation also leads to daydreaming. During World War II, conscientious objectors who volunteered to go on semi-starvation diets for six months focused their daydreams on food. Some even hung enticing pictures of foods on their walls to give themselves something to daydream about. Another reason people daydream is to discharge hostile feelings. For example, if an angry student imagines dropping his instructor out of a classroom window, it might help him to laugh at and dismiss his annoyance with her. Some people also daydream as a way to plan for the future so that by the time they face the situations they imagine, they will know what to say and how to act.

6. The implied main idea of the paragraph is:
   a. Many people daydream.
   b. There are several reasons for daydreaming.
   c. Daydreaming may help people cope with deprivation and hostility.

7. The paragraph's main pattern of organization is
   a. time order.
   b. contrast.
   c. cause and effect.

8-10. Complete the map of the major details of the paragraph.

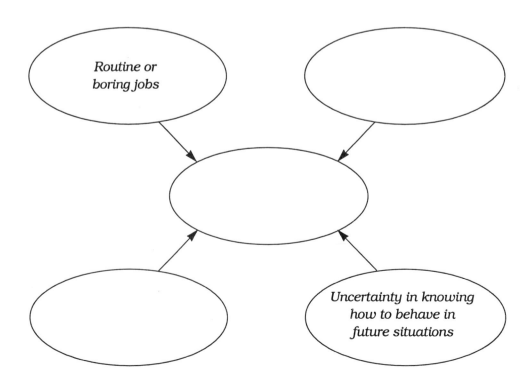

Routine or boring jobs

Uncertainty in knowing how to behave in future situations

# PATTERNS OF ORGANIZATION: Test D-1

A. 1-4. Arrange the scrambled sentences below into a logical paragraph by numbering them *1*, *2*, *3*, and *4* in an order that makes sense. Then circle the letter of the primary pattern of organization used.

Note that transitions will help you by clarifying the relationships between sentences.

_____ When you have chosen your apartment, have a lawyer or other person knowledgeable about leases examine your lease before you sign it.

_____ When you're looking for an apartment, begin by making a list of promising openings. Check the classified ads and two or three real estate offices for apartments within your price range and desired locale.

_____ As you inspect each apartment, make sure that faucets, toilets, stoves, and electrical wiring and outlets are functioning efficiently and safely.

_____ After you have made a solid list, visit at least five of the most promising openings.

5. The primary pattern of organization is
   a. time order.
   b. list of items.
   c. cause and effect.
   d. definition and example.

*(Continues on next page)*

**B.** Label each item with the letter of its main pattern of organization. Use each letter once.

| | |
|---|---|
| **a** Time order | **d** Cause and effect |
| **b** List of items | **e** Definition and example |
| **c** Comparison and/or contrast | |

_____ 6. Today's telephones offer various convenient features. Computerized dialing is one popular feature; another is automatic redialing of a telephone which is busy or unanswered.

_____ 7. Television news stories resemble newspaper articles in being timely and appealing to a wide audience. However, television news coverage tends to be more superficial, emphasizing the visual aspects of a story rather than important background issues.

_____ 8. Many drivers take to the roads in July and August, when families traditionally go on vacation. As a result, oil companies sometimes raise the price of gasoline during the summer months.

_____ 9. Even before he meets the three witches, Macbeth has dreamed of becoming king of Scotland. Then the witches predict he will be king; finally, his wife convinces him to murder King Duncan and take over the country.

_____ 10. In a mystery story, the term "red herring" refers to a false or misleading clue inserted into the story to deceive the reader. One famous red herring is Sherlock Holmes' farewell note to Dr. Watson in "The Final Problem," which leads the reader to believe Holmes has fallen to his death.

# PATTERNS OF ORGANIZATION: Test D-2

For each paragraph, write the number of the topic sentence in the space provided. Then circle the letter of the main pattern of organization.

A.  ¹Mass hysteria is a type of group behavior that involves a widely held and contagious anxiety, usually as a result of a false belief. ²The reaction in part of the country to the radio broadcast of *The War of the Worlds* is one example. ³A dramatization of Martians landing on Earth was so realistic that people began to panic and flee before the realization set in that they were reacting to a radio play. ⁴The medieval witch hunts are another good example of mass hysteria. ⁵They were based on the belief that witches were the cause of many problems in late medieval society, including natural disasters and illness. ⁶Those accused of being witches (mainly old women) were tortured until they confessed or they died. ⁷As many as 500,000 people were burned to death by the clergy between the fifteenth and seventeenth centuries.

1. Topic sentence: _____

2. Main pattern of organization:
   a. List of items
   b. Comparison
   c. Definition and example

B.  ¹The word "museum" makes people think of dinosaur skeletons, Egyptian mummies, and ancient cave drawings. ²But there are less well-known museums available to entertain and educate people of all interests. ³One such unusual museum is Mont Hollertz Chevyland USA in Elm Creek, Nebraska. ⁴More than eighty Chevrolet automobiles, all restored and in running condition, are displayed there. ⁵Then there's the Liberace Museum in Las Vegas. ⁶Many possessions of the flashy pianist-showman are on exhibit there. ⁷They include customized cars, a jeweled miniature piano presented to Liberace by the Queen of England, and Liberace's $60,000 copy of King George V's coronation robe. ⁸Yet another in the number of off-beat museums is the Red Light Museum in Washington, D.C. ⁹This museum serves to house mementoes of the world's oldest profession, prostitution. ¹⁰A nineteenth-century sex manual, a racy Victorian-era slide show, and erotic postcards are among the exhibits there.

3. Topic sentence: _____

4. Main pattern of organization:
   a. List of items
   b. Comparison and/or contrast
   c. Definition and example

C.  ¹Though natural-fiber purists may turn up their noses at it, polyester-and-cotton-blend clothing has advantages over all-cotton garments. ²For one thing, polyester, which is man-made, costs less than cotton, which grows naturally, but is expensive

*(Continues on next page)*

to process. ³Therefore, cotton/polyester clothing is more economical than pure cotton garments. ⁴Also, the polyester content of cotton clothing helps the garments retain their shape after repeated washings. ⁵That's because this synthetic does not share cotton's tendency to shrink or stretch after immersion. ⁶But perhaps polyester's most endearing quality is its "no-wrinkle policy." ⁷Unlike pure cotton, polyester blends require little or no ironing—hooray!

5. Topic sentence: _____

6. Main pattern of organization:
   a. Time order
   b. Comparison and/or contrast
   c. Definition and example

**D.**　¹Many social scientists agree that a person's birth order—that is, whether he or she is the oldest, middle, or youngest child—has a significant influence on the development of his or her personality. ²First-born children, for example, are likely to be more trusting of authority figures than later-born children. ³This is probably because of having extra amounts of interaction with their parents early in life. ⁴It has also been shown that men who were first born are apt to conform easily to social pressures. ⁵And finally, first-born children of both sexes seem eager to attain power. ⁶This could explain the high number of prominent people, including politicians, artists and entertainers, who were the first-born in their families.

7. Topic sentence: _____

8. Main pattern of organization:
   a. Time order
   b. Cause and effect
   c Definition and example

**E.**　¹We have progressed steadily toward outer space ever since the first supersonic jet flights of the late 1950s. ²The pilots who broke the sound barrier in the X-l and X-15 planes often flew into the highest reaches of our atmosphere and almost achieved weightlessness. ³Following these flights, satellites began to be put into orbit, first by the Soviet Union and then by the United States. ⁴The next step was a series of manned flights in tiny space capsules launched into orbit by massive booster rockets. ⁵From the first Mercury flights to the Apollo flights that eventually landed on the moon, this stage marked humankind's efforts to reach our nearest neighbor—our moon. ⁶During the 1970s, the Pioneer and Viking programs sent unmanned probes to the planets in our solar system and even beyond. ⁷One interstellar probe has been flung out of our solar system into the space between the stars and should, theoretically, go on exploring forever.

9. Topic sentence: _____

10. Main pattern of organization:
    a. Time order
    b. Comparison and/or contrast
    c. Cause and effect

## PATTERNS OF ORGANIZATION: Test D-3

Read each paragraph and answer the questions or follow the directions provided.

A. Psychologists use several theories to explain different sides of human behavior. Best known is the psychoanalytic theory, which holds that people are driven largely by needs and desires that they are not aware of—the so-called "subconscious" mind. Another theory, behaviorism, suggests that people's actions are based largely on past experiences of reward and punishment. We do things that brought us pleasant results in the past and avoid things that brought unpleasant results. Yet another theory, "gestalt" psychology, emphasizes the role of overall patterns in our thinking. For example, we find it much easier to remember a tune than a series of unconnected musical notes.

1. The main pattern of organization of the paragraph is
   a. time order.
   b. list of items.
   c. comparison.

2-5. Complete the outline of the paragraph.

**Main idea:**_____

_____

**Supporting details:**

1. _____

   _____

2. _____

   _____

3. _____

   _____

*(Continues on next page)*

**B.**    For a variety of reasons, millions of Americans still smoke in spite of increasing evidence that tobacco smoke kills. One of the primary reasons is that smoking is highly addictive—some say as addictive as heroin. Smokers trying to quit may suffer from withdrawal symptoms which they cannot overcome. A second reason for continued smoking is that it becomes a social habit. For example, some smokers don't feel comfortable at a party without a cigarette. These habits are hard to break and become even more difficult if others in the same social group continue to smoke. A third reason for many to continue smoking is that they just don't believe reports that smoking is dangerous. They see tobacco advertisements with attractive people doing interesting and exciting things. They listen to tobacco companies deny the evidence that cigarettes are harmful, and they read that the government continues to subsidize tobacco farmers. Faced with contradictory information, they choose to believe that smoking will not hurt them.

6.  The paragraph is mainly organized into a
    a.  series of events.
    b.  list of reasons for a particular effect.
    c.  several examples that are contrasted.

7-10.  Complete the following map of the paragraph.

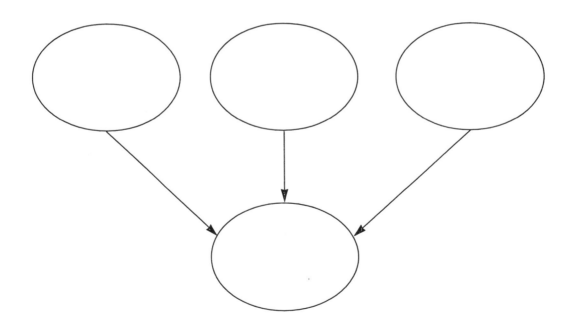

## PATTERNS OF ORGANIZATION: Test E-1

A. 1-4. Arrange the scrambled sentences below into a logical paragraph by numbering them *1, 2, 3,* and *4* in an order that makes sense. Then circle the letter of the primary pattern of organization used.

Note that transitions will help you by clarifying the relationships between sentences.

_____ Americans, for example, use an enormous variety of artifacts, from paper clips to spaceships.

_____ Artifacts are those objects made and used by a society, which may have invented the object or borrowed the idea from others.

_____ On the other hand, in technologically advanced societies, there are numerous artifacts.

_____ In those societies whose technologies are relatively undeveloped, there are few artifacts—a few tools, cooking utensils, and so on.

5. The combined pattern of organization is
   a. time order and cause/effect.
   b. list of items and comparison.
   c. definition/example and list of items.
   d. definition/example and contrast.

*(Continues on next page)*

B. Label each item with the letter of its main pattern of organization. Use each letter once.

| | |
|---|---|
| **a** Time order | **d** Cause and effect |
| **b** List of items | **e** Definition and example |
| **c** Comparison and/or contrast | |

_____ 6. Earth's atmosphere consists of five layers: the troposphere, the stratosphere, the mesosphere, the ionosphere, and the exosphere.

_____ 7. To train a puppy, first buy some small dog biscuits or other small dog treats. Then teach the puppy one short command, such as "Sit!" —speaking the word loudly and firmly until he or she obeys. When you get a correct response, give the dog a treat and praise him or her loudly.

_____ 8. Climate is the average weather experienced in a given geographic area. Areas fall into climate categories according to their year-round temperature and rainfall. An oppressively hot and humid region, for instance, would be said to have a tropical climate.

_____ 9. The main difference between washable wallcoverings and scrubbable wallcoverings is durability. While both products are washable, scrubbable wallcoverings can be cleaned more vigorously.

_____ 10. Children's names can have far-reaching effects on them, according to scientists. Researchers have found, for example, that a child's self-image may be influenced by the stereotypes associated with names. Thus a child named Gertrude may feel ugly, and a Percy may think of himself as weak.

# PATTERNS OF ORGANIZATION: Test E-2

For each paragraph, write the number of the topic sentence in the space provided. Then circle the letter of the main pattern of organization.

A.  [1]After resting for 1500 years, Italy's Mount Vesuvius woke up to do enormous damage. [2]When the volcano erupted in the early afternoon of August 24, 79 A.D., the residents of Pompeii, four miles away, could see and hear the explosion, which sent a black cloud into the sky. [3]However, it wasn't until a second and greater explosion soon followed that the city directly suffered the effects of the volcanic eruption. [4]Within a day, Pompeii and its inhabitants were buried under 30 to 50 feet of stones and ash, and the nearby city of Herculaneum was buried soon after in a river of mud and ash.

1. Topic sentence: _____

2. Main pattern of organization:
   a. Time order
   b. List of items
   c. Definition and example

B.  [1]An eidetic memory is the ability to recall every detail of a memory as clearly as if one were looking at a photograph. [2]An interesting example is the law student with eidetic memory who was accused of cheating on an examination because his test paper contained exactly the words in his textbook. [3]To prove his innocence, he studied an unfamiliar passage for five minutes and then wrote down more than 400 words from it without making a mistake.

3. Topic sentence: _____

4. Main pattern of organization:
   a. List of items
   b. Comparison and/or contrast
   c. Definition and example

C.  [1]Sociologists have identified several common reasons why people join religious cults. [2]Many cult members come from homes filled with conflict; seeking to escape that conflict, they are drawn to the apparent security and acceptance offered by the cult. [3]Another reason people join a cult is that they may be overwhelmed by the demands of adult life. [4]The cult, with its strict rules and rigid discipline, relieves them from many personal decisions. [5]Finally, many cult members are highly idealistic persons—they are gratified by the feeling that by joining the cult, they are committing their lives to the establishment of a better world.

5. Topic sentence: _____

6. Main pattern of organization:
   a. Definition and example
   b. Comparison
   c. List of items

*(Continues on next page)*

**D.**   [1]While management styles vary, there are certain factors that separate the good administrator from the poor one. [2]A good manager anticipates problems and prepares for them, but a poor manager is often taken by surprise. [3]The effective administrator recognizes repeated problems and makes changes to eliminate them; the less effective boss deals with one crisis at a time, never seeing the connections between them. [4]In addition, a good boss delegates work to others, while the poor one prefers to take on one extra task after another rather than train employees to do the work right. [5]The effective administrator is also flexible enough to adapt to changing situations. [6]In contrast, the poor one often clings to the old rules whether or not they apply.

7. Topic sentence: _____

8. Main pattern of organization:
   a. Contrast
   b. Cause and effect
   c. Definition and example

**E.**   [1]Physical-fitness fans, note well. [2]Researchers say that long, hard exercise may increase the body's production of a hormone that depresses the immune system. [3]A research team discovered that more than 13 percent of the 2,300 runners who competed in a major marathon came down with a cold or the flu within a week after the event. [4]Of those who trained, but didn't compete in the marathon, only two percent got colds or flu. [5]The researchers claim it was not simply the stress of the competitive event that felled the marathoners: In the two months before the race, those who trained more than 60 miles per week got twice as many colds and flu as those who trained fewer than 20 miles per week. [6]It was discovered that the harder-training group had a much higher increase of the hormone cortisol in their bodies after their workouts than those who did lighter training. [7]Cortisol is valuable for people who do long, hard exercise, because it fights inflammation—but it also depresses the natural killer cells that destroy viruses, say the researchers.

9. Topic sentence: _____

10. Main pattern of organization:
    a. Time order
    b. Cause and effect
    c. Definition and example

## PATTERNS OF ORGANIZATION: Test E-3

Read each paragraph and answer the questions or follow the directions provided.

A.  Sociologists have several basic methods of doing research. First is the experiment, which is useful for clearly defined questions in which varying factors can be controlled. Sociologists also use the survey, which is useful for gaining facts about a particular group; in order to be valid, the survey must be random. Direct observation is helpful for in-depth studies of social processes, but to be useful, such observation must be made by a skilled researcher. Finally, existing information can be studied as the basis for new conclusions.

1.  The main pattern of organization of the paragraph is
    a.  time order.
    b.  list of items.
    c.  definition and example.

2-6.  Complete the outline of the paragraph. Begin with the main idea, and then fill in the major supporting details.

   **Main idea:**_____

   _____

   **Supporting details:**

   1.  _____
   2.  _____
   3.  _____
   4.  _____

*(Continues on next page)*

B.   Role conflict refers to the condition in which the different roles an individual is expected to play make incompatible demands. A working mother provides an example. In meeting the requirements of a full-time job, she automatically violates the expectation that a mother will put her children's needs before everything else. In meeting the cultural demands of motherhood (staying home if the child is sick, attending school plays) she automatically violates the requirements of a nine-to-five job. A priest provides another example. He is expected to treat confessions as strictly confidential. But a priest, like any other citizen, has responsibilities toward the community. What should he do if a parishioner confesses that he has commited several rapes and cannot control his behavior? In living up to one role expectation (confidentiality), the priest violates another (community responsibility). The key point here is that the difficulties the individuals in these positions experience—the feelings of conflict, inadequacy, and anguish—are not of their own making. They are built into their roles.

7.   The main pattern of organization of the passage is
   a.  cause and effect.
   b.  list of items.
   c.  definition and example.

8-10.   Complete the map of the passage.

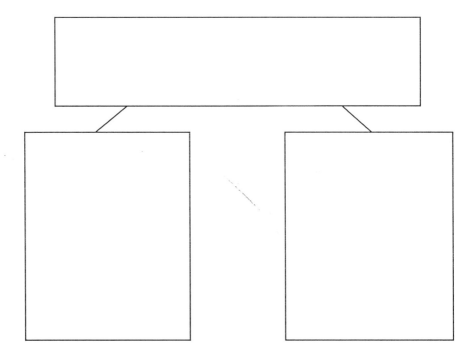

# 6

# Fact and Opinion

On the television police drama *Dragnet*, whenever witnesses began to speak emotionally or to give their own theories, the hero, Sgt. Joe Friday, would ask for "just the facts." He wanted neutral, unbiased information—the kind that can be proven true or false—rather than a witness's interpretation of what happened.

The kind of information Sgt. Friday preferred, however, isn't easy to come by. When most speakers and writers communicate, they include their opinions of a subject. What they say is therefore at least partly biased.

While bias is often unavoidable, many writers do try to remain as objective as possible. News articles and scientific reports are examples of writing in which authors try to be as factual as they can. However, opinions are central to other types of materials, such as editorials, political speeches, and advertisements. Writers of these materials try to convince readers who have different viewpoints to change their minds.

Both facts and opinions can be valuable to readers, but knowing the difference between the two is important in evaluating what is read. Thus, like Sgt. Friday, skilled readers must be able to distinguish *fact* from *opinion*.

Sorting out facts from opinions is something you do already, perhaps without even realizing it. For example, imagine a friend saying, "I saw a science-fiction movie last night about aliens invading Earth. The special effects were great; the aliens looked like reptiles—they had green skin and forked tongues. The acting was terrible, though." Hearing this description, you would probably realize your friend's comments are a mixture of fact and opinion.

# FACT

A *fact* is a statement that can be proven true through objective evidence. This evidence may be physical proof or the spoken or written testimony of witnesses. In the friend's comments about the movie, the facts are that it was about aliens invading Earth and that the aliens had green skin and forked tongues. If you wanted to, you could check the truth of these statements by questioning other witnesses or watching the movie yourself.

Following are some more facts—they can be checked for accuracy and thus proven true.

> *Fact:* The Quad Tower is the tallest building in this city.
> (A researcher could go out and, through inspection, confirm that the building is the tallest.)

> *Fact:* Albert Einstein willed his violin to his grandson.
> (This statement can be checked in historical publications or with Einstein's estate.)

> *Fact:* The 1990 Cincinnati Reds won the World Series in four games.
> (Anyone can check sports records to confirm this.)

# OPINION

An *opinion* is a statement that cannot be objectively proven true or false. Opinions usually express the beliefs, feelings, or judgments that a person has about a subject. Your friend, for instance, said that the movie's special effects were great and that the acting was terrible. These statements may be reasonable ones with which other people would agree, but they cannot be objectively proven. They are opinions. You might see the movie and reach very different conclusions.

Here are some more opinions:

> *Opinion:* The Quad Tower is the ugliest building in the city.
> (There's no way to prove this statement because two people can look at the same building and come to different conclusions about its beauty. "Ugly" is a *value word*, a word we use to express a value judgment. Value words are signals that an opinion is being expressed. By their very nature, these words represent opinions, not facts.)

> *Opinion:* Einstein should have willed his violin to a museum.
> (Who says? Not his grandson. This is an opinion.)

*Opinion:* The 1990 Cincinnati Reds were the best team in the history of baseball.

(Whether something is "best" is always debatable. "Best" is another value word.)

## Writing Facts and Opinions

To get a better sense of fact and opinion, take a few minutes to write three facts about yourself and then to write three of your opinions. Here, for example, are three facts about me and three of my opinions.

Facts about me:

- I am six feet tall.
- I do my writing on a Macintosh computer.
- I have two sisters and one wife.

Three of my opinions:

- Schools, including colleges, should require students to do a great deal of reading.
- Macintosh computers are superior to IBM computers.
- In its first five seasons, *L. A. Law* was the best dramatic series ever shown on television.

Now write your facts and opinions in the space below:

Facts about you:

- _____
  _____
- _____
  _____
- _____
  _____

Three of your opinions:

- _____
  _____
- _____
  _____
- _____
  _____

## More About Fact and Opinion

To sharpen your understanding of fact and opinion, read the following statements and decide whether each is fact or opinion. Put an **F** (for "fact") or an **O** (for "opinion") beside each statement.

_____ 1. My brother Gary is very handsome.

_____ 2. Last night, a tree outside our house was struck by lightning.

_____ 3. Installing a new sink is an easy job for the do-it-yourselfer.

_____ 4. Richard Nixon was the worst president our country ever had.

_____ 5. Certain birds bury their eggs on the slopes of a dying volcano, where heat from volcanic steam incubates the eggs.

_____ 6. Ellen believes in astrology.

_____ 7. Ostriches do not hide their heads in the sand.

_____ 8. The economy, in fact, is in the worst shape it's been in for years.

_____ 9. The Grimm brothers collected their fairy tales from other collections and from storytellers.

_____ 10. The pop star Madonna is a bad influence on our son.

Now read carefully the following explanations of the ten items.

1. This is an opinion. You may like the way your brother looks (maybe because he looks so much like you), but other people might not find him so attractive. The word *handsome* is another value word.

2. This is a statement of fact. You and your family might have seen or heard the lightning strike, or you could go outside later and see the type of damage done to the tree.

3. This is an opinion. The word *easy* suggests a judgment is being made and can mean quite different things to different people.

4. This is an opinion. Not everyone would evaluate Richard Nixon's performance in this way. Here the value word *worst* shows us that a judgment is being expressed.

5. This is a statement of fact. People have observed and recorded this aspect of the life of these birds; it's not a matter of opinion.

6. This is a fact. Ellen's belief is an opinion, but the fact that she has that belief can be confirmed—we can ask her.

7. This is a fact (contrary to popular belief) which can be checked through observation and reports of observations.

8. This is an opinion. Just because someone says something is a fact doesn't make it so. Different people will judge economic factors differently.

9. This is a fact. It can be confirmed through the Grimms' writings and through research on the background of their stories.

10. This is an opinion—it all depends on what someone considers "bad."

## ➤ *Practice 1*

Here are short reviews taken from a newspaper movie guide. Some reviews present only factual reports; others contain opinions about the movie as well. Identify the factual reviews with an **F** and the reviews that include both a factual report and an opinion with an **F + O**.

_____ 1. **Room Service, '38.** The Marx Brothers, Lucille Ball. A penniless theatrical producer and his aides fake the measles to keep from being kicked out of a hotel.

_____ 2. **Born Free, '66.** Virginia McKenna, Bill Travers. Touching story of a pet lioness who must be trained to live in the wilds of Kenya. Good family viewing.

_____ 3. **Pretty Woman, '90.** Richard Gere, Julia Roberts. A corporate raider pays a hooker to be his escort for a business week in Beverly Hills.

_____ 4. **Chinatown, '74.** Jack Nicholson, Faye Dunaway. One of the few undisputed classics of the '70s, a near-perfect thriller. Nicholson is great as the half-boiled private eye, Dunaway is suitably mysterious as "The Woman," and the score is hypnotic.

_____ 5. **Killer Klowns From Outer Space, '88.** Grant Cramer, Suzanne Snyder. Teens flee from large clowns who shoot people with popcorn.

_____ 6. **Cocoon, '85.** Don Ameche, Wilford Brimley. Residents of a Florida retirement home find a fountain of youth in an abandoned swimming pool supercharged with an alien life force.

_____ 7. **The Little Mermaid, '88.** A mermaid princess falls in love with an earthly prince. From the Hans Christian Anderson tale. Animated.

_____ 8. **9 to 5, '80.** Jane Fonda, Lily Tomlin, Dolly Parton. Some inspired early scenes in this satire about oppressed secretaries, but it comes apart about halfway through. You'll know when.

\_\_\_\_\_ 9. **Crazy People, '90.** Dudley Moore, Daryl Hannah. An adman lands in a mental asylum and turns the inmates into copywriters.

\_\_\_\_\_ 10. **Whose Life Is It Anyway? '81.** Richard Dreyfuss, John Cassavetes. Dreyfuss is superb as a paralyzed sculptor who wants to die. His comic gifts keep this adaptation of Brian Clark's Broadway play from being unrelievedly sad.

## Other Points About Fact and Opinion

There are several added points to keep in mind when separating fact from opinion.

**1**     Statements of fact may be found to be untrue.

Suppose you went to the science-fiction movie your friend spoke of and discovered the aliens actually had blue rather than green skin. (Perhaps your friend is color-blind.) His statement would then be an error, not a fact. It is not unusual for evidence to show that a "fact" is not really true. It was once considered to be a fact that the world was flat, for example, but that "fact" turned out to be an error.

**2**     Opinions may be masked as facts.

People sometimes present their opinions as facts, as shown in practice sentence 8 on page 226. Here are two more examples:

In point of fact, neither candidate for the mayor's office is well-qualified.

The truth of the matter is that frozen foods taste as good as fresh foods.

Despite the words to the contrary, the above are not statements of fact but statements of opinion.

**3**     Remember that value words often represent opinions. Here are examples of value words:

*Value Words*

| best | great | beautiful |
|------|-------|-----------|
| worst | terrible | bad |
| better | lovely | good |
| worse | disgusting | wonderful |

Value words often express judgments—they are generally subjective, not objective. While factual statements report on observed reality, subjective statements interpret reality. For example, the observation that it is raining outside is an objective one. The statement that the weather is bad, however, is subjective, an interpretation of reality. (Some people consider rain to be good weather.)

4    Finally, remember that much of what we read and hear is a mixture of fact and opinion.

Recognizing facts and opinions is important because much information that sounds factual is really opinion. A political candidate, for example, may say, "My record is *outstanding*." Voters would be wise to wonder what the value word *outstanding* means to this candidate. Or an advertisement may claim that a particular automobile is "the most economical car on the road today," a statement that at first seems factual. But what is meant by *economical*? If the car offers the most miles per gallon but the worst record for expensive repairs, you might not agree that it's economical.

## ➤ *Practice 2*

Some of the statements below are facts, and some are opinions. Label facts with an **F** and opinions with an **O**. Remember that facts can be proven, but opinions give personal views.

_____  1. Novels by Dean R. Koontz include *Cold Fire, Watchers,* and *The Bad Place.*

_____  2. *Watchers,* by Dean R. Koontz, is a terrifying story that is bound to keep you awake at night.

_____  3. A Colorado farmer wrote the car maker Henry Ford asking to exchange six mounted moose heads for a new car.

_____  4. Henry Ford was wrong when he claimed that laziness and idleness cause most of the world's troubles.

_____  5. Letting a faucet drip continually is the best way to prevent frozen water pipes.

_____  6. Permanent precautions against frozen pipes include wrapping them in fiberglass insulation or heat tape.

_____  7. Too many drugs are prescribed for people suffering from depression.

_____  8. Depression is most common among persons between the ages of twenty-five and forty-four.

_____  9. More Bibles have been printed than any other book in history.

_____  10. The Roman Catholic concept of God is more correct than the Protestant or the Jewish view.

## ➤ *Practice 3*

Some of the statements below are facts, and some are opinions; in addition, three include fact and opinion. Label facts with an **F**, opinions with an **O**, and statements of fact *and* opinion with an **F + O**.

_____ 1. German shepherds are the scariest dogs alive.

_____ 2. The dog that bites people the most often, according to one twenty-seven-year study, is the German shepherd.

_____ 3. German shepherds, which always make poor pets, are used in police work and as guide dogs for the blind.

_____ 4. Because many studies have concluded that smoking is a health hazard, cigarettes should be banned.

_____ 5. Nothing smells as bad as a smoke-filled room.

_____ 6. Smoking is a major cause of lung cancer.

_____ 7. Executives of corporations that pollute the environment should be jailed.

_____ 8. Waste chemicals from some companies have gotten into community water supplies.

_____ 9. Canada and the United States negotiated on how to control acid rain, the biggest pollution problem of all.

_____ 10. In point of fact, pollution is the greatest danger humankind faces today.

## Facts and Opinions in Passages

People tend to accept what they read as fact, but much of what we read is actually opinion. Keeping an eye out for opinion will help you to think for yourself and to question what you read.

Two sentences in the following passage are facts, two are opinions, and one combines fact and opinion. Read the passage, and identify facts with an **F**, opinions with an **O**, and the statement of fact *and* opinion with an **F + O**.

[1]There were several queens of Egypt by the name of Cleopatra, including the one who ruled in the days of Antony and Caesar. [2]She is one of the most interesting figures in Egyptian history. [3]History records that she was born in 69 B.C. and killed herself almost forty years later. [4]The story of how she killed herself is very easy to believe. [5]Reports say she killed herself with an asp, the Egyptian cobra—a symbol of Egyptian royalty, so there could have been no better way for the queen to end her life.

1. _____ 2. _____ 3. _____ 4. _____ 5. _____

Sentence 1 contains facts set down in historical records. Sentence 2 expresses an opinion—some may feel Cleopatra is not one of the most interesting figures in Egyptian history. Sentence 3 contains more facts of history. Sentence 4 contains an opinion—how easy something is to believe will differ from person to person. The last sentence is a mixture of fact and opinion: The beginning parts of the sentence are facts, but what the best way would have been for Cleopatra to end her life is certainly a matter of opinion.

## ➤ *Practice 4*

The following passage contains five sentences. Two sentences are facts, two are opinions, and one combines fact and opinion. Identify the facts with an **F**, the opinions with an **O**, and the statement of fact *and* opinion with an **F + O**.

[1]Plants that people call weeds are often undeserving of such a negative name. [2]Ralph Waldo Emerson had the right idea—he once described a weed as "a plant whose virtues have not yet been discovered." [3]Clearly, weeds aren't always so bad. [4]For example, they can replenish depleted top soil with minerals. [5]Also, some plants that are called weeds are edible and contain vitamins.

1. _____ 2. _____ 3. _____ 4. _____ 5. _____

## ➤ *Review*

To review what you've learned in this chapter, complete each of the following sentences about facts and opinions.

1.  A *(fact, opinion)* _____ can be proven true through objective evidence.

2.  *(Facts, Opinions)* _____ often include words that express judgments.

3.  An example of a comparison that expresses a personal judgment is *(taller, more attractive)* _____ .

4.  Readers would probably expect a(n) *(editorial, political speech, news report, film review)* _____ to be totally factual.

# FACT AND OPINION: Test A-1

**A.** Six of the statements below are facts, and six are opinions. Identify statements of fact with an **F** and statements of opinion with an **O**.

_____ 1. The equator is 24,901.55 miles long.

_____ 2. In 1924, the Model T Ford could be purchased for $290.

_____ 3. The Model T was the most significant invention of the first half of this century.

_____ 4. By the end of this century, electric cars and small family helicopters will be in common use.

_____ 5. The core of a pencil is made out of graphite and clay, not lead.

_____ 6. A bouquet of red roses is the best possible Mother's Day gift.

_____ 7. Roses have been found in dry bouquets in ancient Egyptian tombs.

_____ 8. Masses of flowers all in one color are more attractive than plantings of two or more colors.

_____ 9. Jay Leno became official host of *The Tonight Show* in 1992.

_____ 10. Leno is the greatest talk-show host of them all.

_____ 11. Marijuana affects the heart, raising the blood pressure and heart rate as much as 50 percent after only one joint.

_____ 12. The most important fact about any job is whether you like the people you work with.

*(Continues on next page)*

**B.** Here are short reviews taken from a newspaper movie guide. Some reviews provide only factual reports; others contain opinions about the movie as well. Identify the factual reviews with an **F**; identify reviews that also contain opinion with an **F + O**.

_____ 1. **Streets, '90.** Christina Applegate, David Mendenhall. A teenage prostitute and a runaway rich kid flee a motorcycle patrol officer who is a homicidal killer.

_____ 2. **The Soldier, '82.** Ken Wahl, Klaus Kinski. A stupid CIA adventure about terrorists.

_____ 3. **The Competition, '80.** Richard Dreyfuss, Amy Irving. Underrated romantic comedy-drama about two classical pianists who fall in love while competing for a top musical prize.

_____ 4. **Glory, '89.** Matthew Broderick, Denzel Washington. White Col. Robert Gould Shaw trains and leads the Civil War's first black regiment. Washington's performance won him an Oscar.

_____ 5. **Witness for the Prosecution, '58.** Tyrone Power, Marlene Dietrich. Agatha Christie's nail-biter about a London murder trial, directed by the matchless Billy Wilder. Superb acting by Power as the accused and Dietrich as his wife.

**C.** The following paragraph contains three sentences. One is a fact, one is an opinion, and one sentence combines fact and opinion. Identify the fact with an **F**, the opinion with an **O**, and the combination of fact and opinion with an **F + O**.

[1]Nothing is more irritating than the bite of a mosquito. [2]The itch results from an allergic reaction to the mosquito's saliva, which enters the bite wound as the insect sucks out blood. [3]Strangely enough, only female mosquitos bite.

1. _____          2. _____          3. _____

# FACT AND OPINION: Test A-2

A. Some of the items below are facts, and some are opinions; in addition, *three* combine both fact *and* opinion. Identify facts with an **F**, opinions with an **O**, and combinations of fact and opinion with an **F + O**.

_____ 1. My son once left half a sandwich under his bed for over a week.

_____ 2. My son is a delightful companion to everyone who knows him.

_____ 3. My son is majoring in education, but he should have chosen law.

_____ 4. New York City is not the capital of New York State.

_____ 5. New York City, where visitors can see Broadway plays, museums, and the Statue of Liberty, is the perfect place for a summer vacation.

_____ 6. The Empire State Building is easily the most memorable of all the sights in New York.

_____ 7. Elephants, the largest of all land animals, live as long as seventy to eighty years.

_____ 8. Researchers have found that elephants react nervously to rabbits and dachshunds, but not to mice.

_____ 9. Maybe the lively scampering of the rabbits and dachshunds is what makes elephants nervous.

_____ 10. Because they use their trunks both to clean themselves and to eat, elephants are the most fascinating animals in the zoo.

*(Continues on next page)*

**B.** Each passage below contains five sentences. Two sentences express facts, two express opinions, and one combines fact *and* opinion. Identify facts with an **F**, opinions with an **O**, and combinations of fact and opinion with an **F + O**.

1.    [1]There are few more annoying problems than hiccups, which can last for hours or even days. [2]According to one doctor who has studied them, hiccups are usually caused by eating or drinking too quickly. [3]People do some pretty strange things to remedy this ridiculous problem. [4]Some common remedies include holding your breath, eating a teaspoon of sugar, and putting a paper bag over your head. [5]Undoubtedly, that last one is the strangest one of all.

   1. _____        2. _____        3. _____        4. _____        5. _____

2.    [1]The first bathing suits for women were created in the mid-1800s. [2]Invented by a man, they were ridiculous-looking, high-necked costumes that included knee-length skirts, elbow-length sleeves, black stockings, and shoes. [3]Once such suits became wet, they could weigh as much as the bather, and in fact, they actually caused drowning on more than one occasion. [4]It is incredible that women ever agreed to wear such clothing. [5]Only a man could have invented something quite so impractical.

   1. _____        2. _____        3. _____        4. _____        5. _____

# FACT AND OPINION: Test A-3

**A.** Read the following textbook excerpts and identify facts with an **F**, opinions with an **O**, and combinations of fact *and* opinion with an **F + O**.

_____ 1. Your attitude about college work is even more crucial than any reading or study skill.

_____ 2. Most newborns sleep two-thirds of the time, on the average of sixteen hours a day.

_____ 3. Some tycoons built their fortunes by ruthlessly destroying the competition. A classic example was John D. Rockefeller. He organized Standard Oil in 1870.

_____ 4. Many instructors working with older adults are insensitive to their students' feelings of discouragement.

_____ 5. Studies show that in the United States the amount of touching usually decreases with age. Sixth graders touch each other less than do first graders. Parents touch their older children less often than their younger ones.

_____ 6. Amelia Bloomer (1818-1894) published the first newspaper issued expressly for women. She called it *The Lily*.

*(Continues on next page)*

**B.** After reading the following textbook passage, identify each of the listed excerpts as either fact (**F**) or opinion (**O**).

> The Shaker religious communities were founded by Ann Lee, an Englishwomen who came to America in 1774. "Mother Ann" believed that Christ would come to earth again as a woman and that she was that woman. With a handful of followers she founded a community near Albany, New York. The group grew rapidly. After her death in 1784 her movement continued to expand. By the 1830s her followers had established about 20 successful communities.
>
> The Shakers practiced celibacy. Believing the Second Coming was at hand, they saw no reason to add to the human race. Each group lived in a Family House. The sexes were strictly separated. Property was held in common but controlled by elders. Because the Shakers put so much stress upon equality and voluntary acceptance of rules, members did not feel oppressed by those rules.
>
> The Shaker religion was joyful and intense. Much group singing and dancing provided the members with emotional release from their tightly controlled lives. An industrious, skillful people, they made a special virtue of simplicity. Some of their furniture is among the most classically beautiful ever designed in America.

_____ 7. The Shaker religious communities were founded by Ann Lee, an Englishwomen who came to America in 1774.

_____ 8. "Mother Ann" believed that Christ would come to earth again as a woman and that she was that woman.

_____ 9. Each group lived in a Family House.

_____ 10. Some of their furniture is among the most classically beautiful ever designed in America.

# FACT AND OPINION: Test B-1

A. Six of the statements below are facts, and six are opinions. Identify statements of fact with an **F** and statements of opinion with an **O**.

_____ 1. It would be nice to have more than 24 hours in a day.

_____ 2. Earth makes a complete rotation on its axis every 23 hours, 56 minutes and 4.09 seconds.

_____ 3. Persian cats are the most beautiful of all felines.

_____ 4. A cat once fell from a building's twentieth floor and suffered only a pelvic fracture.

_____ 5. Joining the armed forces is the best way to learn a job skill.

_____ 6. The voting age in America is 18.

_____ 7. If 18-year-olds are old enough to serve in the military, they're old enough to vote.

_____ 8. At the turn of the century, only one of ten married women held a paying job.

_____ 9. For self-fulfillment, any mother in today's world should hold down an outside job as well as care for her children.

_____ 10. *Bartlett's Familiar Quotations* reprints more quotations—769—on the word "love" than on any other word except "man."

_____ 11. *True Grit* was John Wayne's finest movie.

_____ 12. President and Mrs. George Washington once placed ads in the newspaper as they searched for a cook and a coachman.

*(Continues on next page)*

**B.** Here are short reviews taken from a newspaper movie guide. Some reviews provide only factual reports; others contain opinions about the movie as well. Identify the factual reviews with an **F**; identify reviews that also contain an opinion with an **F + O**.

_____ 1. **Tango & Cash, '89.** Sylvester Stallone, Kurt Russell. Framed and sent to prison, two rival Los Angeles police officers must work together to clear themselves.

_____ 2. **The Morning After, '86.** Jane Fonda, Jeff Bridges. A boozing actress wakes up next to a stabbed man and drives around Los Angeles with a stranger trying to figure out what happened.

_____ 3. **The Boston Strangler, '68.** Tony Curtis, Henry Fonda. Curtis is really quite good as Beantown's most famous mass-murderer, a psychotic woman-killer who makes murderous house-calls. A psychological drama, not a slasher movie.

_____ 4. **Good Guys Wear Black, '79.** Chuck Norris, Anne Archer. Norris is a U.S. secret agent. Includes the stunt where he crashes feet-first through the windshield of a speeding car.

_____ 5. **Treasure Island, '50.** Bobby Driscoll, Robert Newton. Walt Disney changes the ending of Stevenson's novel, and everything is prettier, of course. Great fun, nonetheless, and Driscoll is terrific as young Jim Hawkins.

**C.** The following paragraph contains three sentences. One is a fact, one is an opinion, and one sentence combines fact and opinion. Identify the fact with an **F**, the opinion with an **O**, and the combination of fact and opinion with an **F + O**.

[1]The flashing of fireflies is one of the most delightful sights of a summer night. [2]These charming little insects blink their lights as part of the mating ritual. [3]Although many different varieties of firefly may be blinking in one area, males and females of the same type find one another through the pattern of flashes.

1. _____                2. _____                3. _____

# FACT AND OPINION: Test B-2

A. Some of the items below are facts, and some are opinions; in addition, *three* combine both fact *and* opinion. Identify facts with an **F**, opinions with an **O**, and combinations of fact and opinion with an **F + O**.

_____ 1. Rice grows in a warm, wet climate.

_____ 2. Rice is far better with stir-fried vegetables than noodles are.

_____ 3. Brown rice provides more B vitamins than white rice does.

_____ 4. White rice is the result of milling that removes much of the grain's nutrients; thus one should eat only brown rice.

_____ 5. Comic strips are not suitable reading for adults.

_____ 6. In 1907, the *San Francisco Chronicle* began publishing the first daily comic strip—"Mr. Mutt," later named "Mutt and Jeff."

_____ 7. It's very amusing to note that before Popeye the Sailor became a children's cartoon, he was a freely-swearing character in an adult comic strip.

_____ 8. Boxing, an overly violent sport, should finally be outlawed.

_____ 9. Basketball was invented in 1891 when a YMCA instructor created a game using two peach baskets and a soccer ball.

_____ 10. Baseball players have been known to do some really ridiculous things; for example, some players break in a new glove by rubbing it with shaving cream.

*(Continues on next page)*

B. Each passage below contains five sentences. Some sentences express facts, and some express opinions. In addition, each paragraph includes one sentence that combines fact *and* opinion. Identify facts with an **F**, opinions with an **O**, and the combinations of fact and opinion with an **F + O**.

1. [1]Legally, a check doesn't have to come from a checkbook; it can be written on any material. [2]For instance, a man in Iowa painted a check for $30 on a door and delivered it to a neighbor to whom he owed the money. [3]An Englishman named Albert Haddock paid his taxes in the strangest possible way: he painted a check on the side of a cow. [4]Although such unconventional checks are legal, the law allows the persons being paid to refuse to accept them. [5]The government ought to outlaw such unconventional checks altogether.

   1. _____    2. _____    3. _____    4. _____    5. _____

2. [1]The TV series *The Little House on the Prairie* was based on a series of books by Laura Ingalls Wilder. [2]Wilder's nine books, beginning with *Little House in the Big Woods*, tell about the author's life as part of a pioneer family in the American West. [3]The books give the finest firsthand picture of pioneer life ever written for children. [4]Wilder, who did not begin writing the stories until she was almost 60, had a really amazing memory for the details of her childhood. [5]Every school and public library should own several copies of Wilder's books.

   1. _____    2. _____    3. _____    4. _____    5. _____

# FACT AND OPINION: Test B-3

A. Read the following textbook excerpts and identify facts with an **F**, opinions with an **O**, and combinations of fact *and* opinion with an **F + O**.

_____ 1. Apple trees generally do not begin to bloom and bear fruit until they are five to eight years old.

_____ 2. Farm life in the 1890s was harsh and dull.

_____ 3. *Walden* is Henry David Thoreau's moving and beautifully written account of the two years he lived alone on the shores of Walden Pond.

_____ 4. In the United States, the majority of children under 18 years old live in a household with their mother and father.

_____ 5. Many years ago, J. P. Foley defined *abnormal* as "a deviation from the statistical norms of a particular cultural group." There are good points and bad points about Foley's definition.

B. Read the following textbook passage, and then identify each of the listed statements from the passage as either a fact (**F**) or an opinion (**O**).

The Shawnee chief Tecumseh made a bold and imaginative effort to bind the tribes east of the Mississippi into a great confederation. Traveling from the Wisconsin country to the Floridas, he persuaded tribe after tribe to join him. "Let the white race perish," Tecumseh declared. "They seize your land; they corrupt your women . . . Back whence they came, upon a trail of blood, they must be driven!"

Tecumseh was joined in his campaign by his brother Tenskwatawa, known as the Prophet. Instead of aping white customs, the Prophet said, Indians must give up all white ways. They must reinvigorate their own culture. Ceding lands to the whites must stop because the Great Spirit intended that the land be used by all.

The Prophet, a fanatic, saw visions and claimed to be able to control the movement of the heavenly bodies. Tecumseh, however, possessed true genius. A powerful orator and a great organizer, he had deep insight into the needs of his people. General Harrison himself said of Tecumseh: "He is one of those uncommon geniuses which spring up occasionally to produce revolution and overturn the established order of things." The two brothers made an outstanding team—by 1811 thousands of Indians were organizing to drive the whites off their lands.

*(Continues on next page)*

_____ 6. Traveling from the Wisconsin country to the Floridas, he persuaded tribe after tribe to join him.

_____ 7. Tecumseh was joined in his campaign by his brother Tenskwatawa, known as the Prophet.

_____ 8. Tecumseh . . . possessed true genius.

_____ 9. The two brothers made an outstanding team . . .

_____ 10. . . . by 1811 thousands of Indians were organizing to drive the whites off their lands.

# FACT AND OPINION: Test C-1

A. Six of the statements below are facts, and six are opinions. Identify statements of fact with an **F** and statements of opinion with an **O**.

_____ 1. The first television commercial, for a Bulova wristwatch, was broadcast in 1941.

_____ 2. Watching sports events in person is better than watching them on TV.

_____ 3. Children should not be allowed to watch more than one hour of television a day.

_____ 4. Cigarette advertising was banned on TV on January 1, 1971.

_____ 5. There is simply no excuse for being late.

_____ 6. Any student who walked into our biology class after the bell rang was marked late.

_____ 7. Fish is no good without tartar sauce.

_____ 8. In 1855, the U.S. Army purchased camels to be used in the exploration of the Southwestern deserts.

_____ 9. Science has done more to improve humanity than all the world's philosophers combined.

_____ 10. Bessie Smith, known as the "Empress of the Blues," was killed in a car accident in 1937.

_____ 11. A week after the stock-market crash, Columbia released Smith's recording of "Nobody Knows You When You're Down and Out."

_____ 12. Nobody, not even Anita Baker, can sing that song better than Smith did.

*(Continues on next page)*

**B.** Here are short reviews taken from a newspaper movie guide. Some reviews provide only factual reports; others contain opinions about the movie as well. Identify the factual reviews with an **F**; identify reviews that also contain an opinion with an **F + O**.

_____ 1. **Little Darlings, '80.** Tatum O'Neal, Kristy McNichol. Two sexually curious girls go to summer camp and make a bet: whoever loses her virginity first, wins. Sounds vulgar, but with affecting performances, especially McNichol's.

_____ 2. **Funny Farm, '88.** Chevy Chase, Madolyn Smith. A sportswriter and his wife move to a cottage in the country.

_____ 3. **My Mom's a Werewolf, '89.** Susan Blakely, John Saxon. Bitten on the toe by a pet-shop owner, a woman turns into a werewolf.

_____ 4. **Norma Rae, '79.** Sally Field, Ron Leibman. Field is great in her Oscar-winning role as the simple, courageous textile worker who organizes a union.

_____ 5. **Every Which Way but Loose, '78.** Clint Eastwood, Sondra Locke. A movie only an Eastwood fan could love. A yokel with a pet chimp falls in love with a bar-band crooner, who may or may not be married.

**C.** The following paragraph contains three sentences. One is a fact, one is an opinion, and one sentence combines fact and opinion. Identify the fact with an **F**, the opinion with an **O**, and the combination of fact and opinion with an **F + O**.

[1]People who think of Alaska as an unattractive frozen wasteland are just plain wrong. [2]Alaska is a land of various wildlife, varying climates, and hundreds of forms of plant life. [3]In fact, the highest mountains in North America are in Alaska, where they have a starring role in some unforgettable scenery.

1. _____          2. _____          3. _____

# FACT AND OPINION: Test C-2

A. Some of the items below are facts, and some are opinions; in addition, *three* combine both fact *and* opinion. Identify facts with an **F**, opinions with an **O**, and combinations of fact and opinion with an **F + O**.

_____ 1. Most high school graduates should work for a year before attending college.

_____ 2. Nine U.S. presidents, including Washington and Lincoln, did not go to college.

_____ 3. Law enforcement officials agree that security systems deter thieves from stealing car radios.

_____ 4. Given the fact that car theft costs Americans millions of dollars a year, all cars should be manufactured with built-in security systems.

_____ 5. Auto manufacturers are working with electronic experts to create an anti-theft radio, one that is useless when removed from the car.

_____ 6. CNN covers the news more intelligently than the three non-cable networks do.

_____ 7. Certain large news magazines (including *Time,* the best of the group) publish national and international editions every week.

_____ 8. The book *Alice's Adventures in Wonderland* was written by Charles Lutwidge Dodgson under the pen name Lewis Carroll.

_____ 9. *Alice's Adventures in Wonderland* is one of the more charming children's books.

_____ 10. Dodgson got the famous illustrator John Tenniel to illustrate *Alice's Adventures in Wonderland.* Other artists have illustrated the book since, but none has surpassed Tenniel's enchanting drawings.

*(Continues on next page)*

**B.** Each passage below contains five sentences. Some sentences express facts, and some express opinions. In addition, each paragraph includes one sentence that combines fact *and* opinion. Identify facts with an **F**, opinions with an **O**, and combinations of fact and opinion with an **F + O**.

1.   [1]Mickey Mouse was originally drawn by Walt Disney's old friend Ubbe Iwerks. [2]Without Iwerks, Mickey Mouse would have remained a minor, forgotten character, and Disney would never have come into his own. [3]Iwerks worked for the Disney studio from 1924 to 1930 and then again from 1940 until his death in 1971. [4]During these years he worked on various animated films, including *Song of the South* (1946) and *Mary Poppins* (1964). [5]The teamwork of Disney and Iwerks was the single most important step in the success of the Disney studio, which continued to produce widely praised animated feature films.

   1. \_\_\_\_\_     2. \_\_\_\_\_     3. \_\_\_\_\_     4. \_\_\_\_\_     5. \_\_\_\_\_

2.   [1]School administrators should either improve our children's unhealthy lunch menus or be replaced. [2]There is little value in teaching academics to children only to hurt their minds and bodies with junk food at lunch time. [3]A survey of schools throughout the country shows that school lunch menus include high-sodium, high-fat, and low-fiber foods. [4]In addition, some school districts allow sugary and high-fat foods to be sold in vending machines, which proves that school administrators really care too little about our children. [5]The first step towards improving our children's health should be to abolish vending machines from the schools.

   1. \_\_\_\_\_     2. \_\_\_\_\_     3. \_\_\_\_\_     4. \_\_\_\_\_     5. \_\_\_\_\_

# FACT AND OPINION: Test C-3

**A.** Read the following textbook excerpts and identify facts with an **F**, opinions with an **O**, and combinations of fact *and* opinion with an **F + O**.

_____ 1. The selections throughout the book are lively and appealing.

_____ 2. The Parthenon was built in Athens in the fifth century B.C. and dedicated to the goddess Athena. It remains an example of near-perfect architectural design.

_____ 3. Infertility rates have been rising over the past twenty years: 10 to 15 percent of couples who want a baby cannot conceive.

_____ 4. *The Kid* (1921), one of Charlie Chaplin's greatest films, starred Chaplin and a four-year-old named Jackie Coogan.

_____ 5. Nixon, responding to charges that he had paid almost no income taxes during his presidency, published his 1969-1972 returns. They showed that he had paid only $1,600 in two years during which his income had exceeded half a million dollars.

**B.** Read the following textbook passage, and then identify each of the listed excerpts from the passage as either fact (**F**), opinion (**O**), or both fact and opinion (**F + O**). (Two of the excerpts are both fact and opinion.)

> Frederick Douglass, a former slave who had escaped from Maryland, was one of the most remarkable Americans of his generation. While a bondsman he had received a full portion of beatings and other indignities. But he had been allowed to learn to read and write and to learn a trade. (Such opportunities were denied to the vast majority of slaves.) Settling in Boston, he became an agent of the Massachusetts Anti-Slavery Society and a featured speaker at its public meetings.
>
> Douglass was a majestically handsome man who radiated determination and indignation. In 1845 he published his *Narrative of the Life of Frederick Douglass*, one of the most gripping accounts of a slave's life ever written. Douglass insisted that emancipation alone would not provide the slaves with freedom. He demanded full equality, social and economic and well as political. Few white northerners accepted his reasoning. But fewer still who heard him or read his works could afterward maintain that all blacks were dull-witted or resigned to inferior status.

*(Continues on next page)*

_____ 6. Frederick Douglass, a former slave who had escaped from Maryland, was one of the most remarkable Americans of his generation.

_____ 7. But he had been allowed to learn to read and write and to learn a trade.

_____ 8. Settling in Boston, he became an agent of the Massachusetts Anti-Slavery Society and a featured speaker at its public meetings.

_____ 9. Douglass was a majestically handsome man who radiated determination and indignation.

_____ 10. In 1845 he published his *Narrative of the Life of Frederick Douglass*, one of the most gripping accounts of a slave's life ever written.

# FACT AND OPINION: Test D-1

A. Six of the statements below are facts, and six are opinions. Identify statements of fact with an **F** and statements of opinion with an **O**.

_____ 1. The first words spoken by Thomas Edison into his invention, the phonograph, were, "Mary had a little lamb."

_____ 2. Edison's first patented invention was a voting machine.

_____ 3. Edison was the world's greatest inventor.

_____ 4. Cicadas, commonly called seventeen-year locusts, hibernate in the ground for seventeen years at a time.

_____ 5. Clearly, cicadas are one of nature's strangest insects.

_____ 6. In Cleveland, two robbers once stole $25 from a convenience store after scaring off the cashier with a cicada.

_____ 7. Snakes are far scarier than cicadas.

_____ 8. Honey is better in tea than sugar, but sugar is better in coffee.

_____ 9. Honey can cause a dangerous disease called botulism in children under one year of age.

_____ 10. The school's research funds ought to be going into medical studies, not into digging up ancient cities.

_____ 11. Archeologists study historic cultures by analyzing their objects and buildings.

_____ 12. Modern builders should not be allowed to construct buildings on sites where historic objects are found.

*(Continues on next page)*

**B.** Here are short reviews taken from a newspaper movie guide. Some reviews provide only factual reports; others contain opinions about the movie as well. Identify the factual reviews with an **F**; identify reviews that also contain an opinion with an **F + O**.

_____ 1. **Christine, '83.** Keith Gordon, John Stockwell. Clever, funny thriller about a haunted car that has a marked effect on the personality of its owner.

_____ 2. **Loose Cannons, '90.** Gene Hackman, Dan Aykroyd. A detective works a murder case with his partner who has multiple personalities.

_____ 3. **Clownhouse, '89.** Nathan Forrest Winters, Brian McHugh. Three brothers are trapped in an old house with three escaped killers wearing clown suits.

_____ 4. **Charlotte's Web, '73.** Hanna-Barbera's strictly conventional animation doesn't diminish the charm of E. B. White's classic children's story about a spider and her piglet friend.

_____ 5. **Friday the 13th, Part VIII: Jason Takes Manhattan, '89.** Jensen Daggett, Scott Reeves. Hockey-masked slasher Jason follows a Crystal Lake teen and her friends on a cruise to New York.

**C.** The following paragraph contains three sentences. One is a fact, one is an opinion, and one sentence combines fact and opinion. Identify the fact with an **F**, the opinion with an **O**, and the combination of fact and opinion with an **F + O**.

$^1$Canned food was introduced in 1810, but the can opener was not invented until 1858. $^2$It is ridiculous but true that for almost fifty years, the military troops and explorers who used canned foods had to rely on bayonets, hammers and chisels, and even rifle fire to open them. $^3$It's unbelievable that no one invented the can opener sooner.

1. _____        2. _____        3. _____

# FACT AND OPINION: Test D-2

A. Some of the items below are facts, and some are opinions; in addition, *three* combine both fact *and* opinion. Identify facts with an **F**, opinions with an **O**, and combinations of fact and opinion with an **F + O**.

_____ 1. Adults shouldn't consume dairy products.

_____ 2. Goat's milk is more easily digested by some who are allergic to cow's milk, and goat's milk tastes better, too.

_____ 3. Archaeologists have concluded that cattle were first domesticated in Greece around 6000 B.C.

_____ 4. The mule can kick backwards with both feet without losing its balance.

_____ 5. In the Middle Ages it was commonly believed that the seat of man's intelligence was his heart.

_____ 6. The Middle Ages was the worst time to be alive; for example, in the mid-fourteenth century, the bubonic plague killed millions of people.

_____ 7. During the Middle Ages it was mainly the clergy that could read and write; most other people—including royalty—did not have these skills.

_____ 8. Rubber is a wonderful elastic substance at first made only from the sap of certain tropical plants and now often made synthetically.

_____ 9. Joseph Priestley, an eighteenth century scientist, named the substance *rubber* because it could rub away pencil marks.

_____10. Priestley's contributions in the field of rubber were far less important than the work of Charles Goodyear.

*(Continues on next page)*

**B.** Each passage below contains five sentences. Some sentences express facts, and some express opinions. In addition, each paragraph includes one statement of fact *and* opinion. Identify facts with an **F**, opinions with an **O**, and the combination of fact and opinion with an **F + O**.

1. ¹Americans have become much too concerned about success and about owning things. ²According to a recent study, as many as 80 percent of job résumés contain false or misleading information. ³Also, studies show that Americans use as much as 50 percent of their paycheck to pay back consumer loans. ⁴For their wardrobes alone, consumers each year pay out millions of dollars, dollars that should have ended up in such worthy projects as health research and in housing for the homeless. ⁵It's time for Americans to become less selfish and to contribute more to the community.

   1. _____     2. _____     3. _____     4. _____     5. _____

2. ¹A common definition of retirement includes the idea of leaving the labor force, but that notion of retirement is too narrow. ²After retiring, it is much better to remain involved in the work world part-time. ³Some companies have recently supported this type of involvement for the retired by hiring two or three older part-timers in place of one full-time employee. ⁴The Travelers Corporation, for example, has employed six hundred retired employees for three hundred shared jobs. ⁵Other retirees have continued to work part-time by volunteering for organizations such as hospitals and museums.

   1. _____     2. _____     3. _____     4. _____     5. _____

# FACT AND OPINION: Test D-3

**A.** Read the following textbook excerpts and identify facts with an **F**, opinions with an **O**, and combinations of fact *and* opinion with an **F + O**.

_____ 1. The maze is a tool sometimes used by psychologists as they measure animals' learning ability.

_____ 2. The most difficult problem for single fathers is balancing the demands of work and child care.

_____ 3. By far the most important indirect effect of industrialization occurred in the South, which soon began to produce cotton for the new textile factories of Great Britain and New England.

_____ 4. All seed-producing plants have roots which grow downward in the young seedling even as the stem grows upward.

_____ 5. Beethoven came on the scene at a favorable moment in history.

**B.** The passages below are from a textbook and a newspaper editorial page. Identify each of the listed excerpts from the passages as either a fact (**F**), an opinion (**O**), or fact *and* opinion (**F + O**). (Only one of the listed excerpts combines fact and opinion.)

**Textbook passage:**

Psychologist Neil Jacobson has developed a marital treatment plan that aims at teaching couples how to deal with conflict in more positive and constructive ways. That is, he teaches couples how to do less blaming and criticizing and how to be more supportive, cooperative, and resourceful. In the early part of the treatment, the couples practice discussing their problems, whatever these may be, during the treatment hour. As they talk, the therapist coaches and corrects them, showing them how to listen carefully, make clear criticisms, avoid name-calling, generate solutions, and so forth. Later the couple is assigned to engage in and tape two problem-solving sessions per week at home. The tapes are then analyzed by the couple and the therapist together during the treatment hour. . . .

This is a hopeful new approach, very appealing in terms of practicality.

_____ 6. In the early part of the treatment, the couples practice discussing their problems, whatever these may be, during the treatment hour.

_____ 7. This is a hopeful new approach, very appealing in terms of practicality.

*(Continues on next page)*

**From a newspaper editorial page:**

Even casual observers of school reform know that one of the most frequently heard topics revolves around the length of the school year. . . .

We hear endlessly about the 240-plus days put in by Japanese students and, by implication, we assume that most of the rest of the world is a lot closer to their standard than to ours.

Actually, the great majority of the world's countries are closer to our standard than to that of the Japanese. Almost all of them have more than our 180 days but most do not have many more. The international median is 190 days. Of some 27 countries and provinces, only six exceed 200 days. . . .

All of this suggests a couple of things. First, the length of the school *day* may be a bigger issue than the length of the school *year* since students in other countries tend to spend more hours in the classroom than American students. Second, the broader issue of the quality of time in school is probably much more significant than the issue of the quantity of time.

_____  8. The international median is 190 days. Of some 27 countries and provinces, only six exceed 200 days.

_____  9. First, the length of the school *day* may be a bigger issue than the length of the school *year* since students in other countries tend to spend more hours in the classroom than American students.

_____  10. Second, the broader issue of the quality of time in school is probably much more significant than the issue of the quantity of time.

# FACT AND OPINION: Test E-1

A. Six of the statements below are facts, and six are opinions. Identify statements of fact with an **F** and statements of opinion with an **O**.

_____ 1. The tarantula spider can live for as long as two years without food.

_____ 2. Yuma, Arizona, is a wonderful place to live.

_____ 3. Yuma, on average, receives more sunshine than any other city in the country.

_____ 4. Couples should know each other for at least a year before getting married.

_____ 5. For various reasons, some spouses take separate vacations.

_____ 6. In point of fact, it is always better for spouses to vacation together.

_____ 7. It's never too early to teach children to have good manners and to share in some small way in the household chores.

_____ 8. Choking on food kills more people each year than airplane accidents, electrical shock, or lightning.

_____ 9. The very least that everyone should know about first-aid procedures is how to perform the Heimlich maneuver.

_____ 10. Although Marie Curie had won a Nobel Prize, she was denied membership in the French Academy because she was a woman.

_____ 11. The French Academy made a mistake in not giving membership to Marie Curie.

_____ 12. Baltimore's traffic lights were designed with the color-blind in mind—green lights have a vertical shape, and red ones are horizontal.

(Continues on next page)

**B.** Here are short reviews taken from a newspaper movie guide. Some reviews provide only factual reports; others contain opinions about the movie as well. Identify the factual reviews with an **F**; identify reviews that also contain an opinion with an **F + O.**

_____ 1. **The Incredible Mr. Limpet, '64.** Don Knotts, Carole Cook. Timid bookkeeper is transformed into a fish and helps the U.S. track Nazi subs during World War II.

_____ 2. **California Suite, '78.** Alan Alda, Jane Fonda. Choppy parade of Neil Simon one-liners is enlivened by Maggie Smith, who won a best-supporting-actress Oscar.

_____ 3. **The Frozen Dead, '67.** Dana Andrews, Anna Palk. A scientist uses a girl's disembodied head to re-animate Nazis frozen 20 years before.

_____ 4. **Never on Sunday, '60.** Melina Mercouri, Jules Dassin. Pleasantly corny romance about a vain man who tries to "civilize" a naughty prostitute.

_____ 5. **Divorce, American Style, '67.** Dick Van Dyke, Debbie Reynolds. Some funny, funny moments in this satire of the American institution of divorce with a hilarious supporting performance from Jason Robards as a divorced man scheming to get his ex remarried.

**C.** The following paragraph contains three sentences. One is a fact, one is an opinion, and one sentence combines fact and opinion. Identify the fact with an **F**, the opinion with an **O**, and the combination of fact and opinion with an **F + O.**

[1]The Lincoln Memorial is surely America's best loved public monument. [2]Designed by Henry Beacon, it was dedicated on Memorial Day, 1922, more than 50 years after a memorial to Lincoln was first proposed. [3]Most people probably learn to love the monument through seeing its picture, which is on the penny and the five-dollar bill.

1. _____          2. _____          3. _____

# FACT AND OPINION: Test E-2

A. Some of the items below are facts, and some are opinions; in addition, *three* include both fact *and* opinion. Identify facts with an **F**, opinions with an **O**, and statements of fact and opinion with an **F + O**.

_____ 1. No natural disaster is quite as terrifying as a volcano exploding.

_____ 2. A volcanic explosion took place in Indonesia in 1815, and the following summer in the eastern United States, temperatures were more than ten degrees cooler than usual.

_____ 3. It's unfortunate that people drink so many sugary soft drinks in this country.

_____ 4. One of the more delicious of the soft drinks, Coca-Cola, was first intended to cure various ills, including headaches.

_____ 5. In the late 1890s, when Coke was first sold, it included a small amount of cocaine, which was then legal.

_____ 6. The globefish keeps itself from being eaten by gulping so much water that it becomes too large to be swallowed by its enemies.

_____ 7. Another very weird creature is the desert snail—it sometimes sleeps for as long as three or four years.

_____ 8. Some insects can live for as long as a year after their heads are cut off.

_____ 9. Here's a disgusting fact: By the time the average person is 70, he or she will have shed about 40 pounds of dead skin.

_____ 10. Changes in temperature can alter the height of the Eiffel Tower (usually 984 feet tall) by as much as six inches.

*(Continues on next page)*

**B.** Each passage below contains five sentences. Some sentences express facts, and some express opinions. In addition, each paragraph includes one combination of fact *and* opinion. Identify facts with an **F**, opinions with an **O**, and combinations of fact and opinion with an **F + O**.

1. [1]Red is the most common color for barns throughout the United States. [2]It's fortunate that red is such a good color for barns because the early farmers who established the tradition didn't have a selection of paint colors to choose from. [3]Pioneer farmers painted their barns with a mixture of skim milk, linseed oil, lime, and iron oxide, with the iron oxide furnishing the red color to the mixture. [4]Since outdoor paints are now available in a variety of colors, today's farmers paint their barns red out of choice, not necessity. [5]Everyone of taste would certainly agree that the countryside would be less beautiful if it were dotted with, for example, jet-black, purple or ultramarine barns.

    1. _____      2. _____      3. _____      4. _____      5. _____

2. [1]A Canadian chemist believes that a rare genetic disorder explains the legend of vampires, the scariest of supernatural creatures. [2]He says that "vampires" were the victims of porphyria, a hereditary disease that affects the blood. [3]The symptoms of porphyria include extreme sensitivity to light as well as a tightening of the lips and gums that could make the teeth look long and fang-like. [4]The only remedy for porphyria in the Middle Ages was for the victim to drink blood, which helped to replace a substance missing in the porphyria victim's own blood. [5]This disorder suggests that there is probably also a scientific explanation for all of the other so-called "monsters" of old legends.

    1. _____      2. _____      3. _____      4. _____      5. _____

# FACT AND OPINION: Test E-3

**A.** Read the following textbook excerpts and identify facts with an **F**, opinions with an **O**, and combinations of fact *and* opinion with an **F + O**.

_____ 1. Alcohol was discovered and drunk during the Stone Age; its use precedes the fashioning of metal instruments.

_____ 2. No reform movement of any era was more significant, more ambiguous, or more provocative of later historical investigation than the drive to abolish slavery.

_____ 3. Alfred Stieglitz published 54 volumes of *Camera Work* between 1903 and 1917, giving us the finest record ever made of the art of photography.

_____ 4. The world's literature is greatly enriched by *The Arabian Nights*, a series of stories supposedly told by Scheherazade in order to so fascinate her husband that he would not carry out his stated intent of murdering her.

_____ 5. As a general Washington was not a brilliant strategist like Napoleon.

**B.** The passages below are from an almanac and *Time* magazine. After reading each passage, identify each listed excerpt from the passage as either fact (**F**), opinion (**O**), or both fact *and* opinion (**F + O**). (Only one statement is both fact and opinion.)

### From *The People's Almanac #2:*

After four miscarriages, Lady Bird finally gave birth to two daughters, Lynda Bird and Luci Baines. Thus the entire family (including the dog, Little Beagle Johnson) had the initials L.B.J. With their parents constantly busy, Lynda and Luci were raised largely by hired help. As Luci commented candidly about her father: "Eventually, I learned to love him as a person, not as a father—because he seldom had time to be a father." Nevertheless, LBJ took great pride in his children, and in 1968 he announced, "I'm the luckiest man alive. None of my girls drinks or smokes or takes dope and they both married fine men."

*(Continues on next page)*

During the White House years, Lady Bird established herself as the most influential First Lady in history, barring only Eleanor Roosevelt. She campaigned effectively for her husband aboard her own "Lady Bird Special" and helped win approval for "the Lady Bird Bill," a significant piece of highway beautification legislation that eliminated thousands of billboards and junk heaps.

_____ 6. After four miscarriages, Lady Bird finally gave birth to two daughters, Lynda Bird and Luci Baines.

_____ 7. Thus the entire family (including the dog, Little Beagle Johnson) had the initials L.B.J.

_____ 8. During the White House years, Lady Bird established herself as the most influential First Lady in history, barring only Eleanor Roosevelt. She campaigned effectively for her husband aboard her own "Lady Bird Special" and helped win approval for "the Lady Bird Bill," a significant piece of highway beautification legislation that eliminated thousands of billboards and junk heaps.

**From an essay in *Time*:**

In April scientists reported that ozone damage is far worse than previously thought. Ozone depletion not only causes skin cancer and eye cataracts; it also destroys plankton, the beginning of the food chain atop which we humans sit. . . .

Ozone depletion and the greenhouse effect are human disasters. They happen to occur in the environment. But they are urgent because they directly threaten man. A sane environmentalism, the only kind of environmentalism that will win universal public support, begins by unashamedly declaring that nature is here to serve man.

_____ 9. Ozone depletion not only causes skin cancer and eye cataracts; it also destroys plankton, the beginning of the food chain atop which we humans sit.

_____ 10. A sane environmentalism, the only kind of environmentalism that will win universal public support, begins by unashamedly declaring that nature is here to serve man.

# 7

# Inferences

You have probably heard the expression "to read between the lines." When you "read between the lines," you pick up ideas that are not directly stated in what you are reading. These implied ideas are often important for a full understanding of what an author means. Discovering the ideas in writing that are not stated directly is called *making inferences*, or *drawing conclusions*.

## INFERENCES IN EVERYDAY LIFE

Consider first how often you make inferences in everyday life. For example, suppose you are sitting in a coffee shop at lunchtime. A woman sits down at the next table. Here is what you observe:

- She is wearing an expensive-looking suit, a silk blouse, gold jewelry, and a gold band on the third finger of her left hand.
- The woman opens a brief case and takes out some manila folders; she begins to study them.
- You notice that she also has a child's crayon drawing in the briefcase.

As you sit in the coffee shop, you may make several inferences about this woman:

- She's on her lunch break.
- She works in an office, perhaps as a lawyer or an executive.
- She is married and has a young child.

How did you arrive at these inferences? First of all, you used your experience and general knowledge of people. Secondly, you made informed guesses based on the facts you observed. Of course, your inferences might not all prove true. For example, the woman could own her own business, or the child's drawing might have been done by her nephew or niece. You cannot prove or disprove your guesses without asking the woman directly, but your inferences may well be correct.

Take a moment now and jot down what you might infer if you saw each of the following:

1.   A high school has uniformed security guards patrolling the halls.

Your inference: _____

2.   A dog cringes when someone tries to pet him.

Your inference: _____

The inferences you probably made are that, in the first situation, the high school has had some very disturbing discipline and/or crime problems and, in the second situation, the dog has previously been mishandled.

Take a moment now to look at the following *New Yorker* cartoon.

*"Dad, can you read?"*

Drawing by Peter Steiner; © 1990 The New Yorker Magazine, Inc.

Now put a check by the two inferences that are most logically based on the information given in the cartoon.

____ 1. The father has a problem with his vision.
____ 2. The little boy is doing his homework.
____ 3. The man must watch a great deal of television.
____ 4. The father cannot read.
____ 5. The father prefers a good novel to watching TV.

Here is an explanation of each item:

1. This inference is well supported by the cartoon. The father is wearing glasses, and he is sitting very close to the TV set.
2. This is not a logical inference. The cartoonist would have given us more clues if he wanted us to think that the boy was reading a school book.
3. This is a logical inference. The boy's question and the father's activity in the picture lead us to believe that the boy never sees his father reading, only watching TV.
4. This inference is not well supported. The father doesn't seem to read much, but that doesn't mean he cannot; in fact, the magazine on the television suggests that he can read.
5. This is not a logical inference. The boy's question tells us that he never sees his father reading.

## ➢ *Practice 1*

Put a check by the inference *most logically based* on the information provided. Look first at the example.

**Example**

A student always sits in the back of the classroom.

\_\_\_ a. The student dislikes the course.

\_\_\_ b. The student is unprepared for class.

✓ c. The student feels uncomfortable in the front of the room.

\_\_\_ d. The student is farsighted.

The correct answer is *c*. Based on the information we are given, we can conclude only that the student—for some reason—does not like sitting in the front. We are not given enough information to know why the student feels this way.

1. A pencil has teeth marks on it.

    \_\_\_ a. The person who used the pencil was nervous.

    \_\_\_ b. The pencil was chewed up by a toddler or pet.

    \_\_\_ c. Someone or something chewed the pencil.

    \_\_\_ d. The pencil belongs to someone who is trying to quit smoking.

2. A person is in the lobby of a hospital in a wheelchair.

    \_\_\_ a. The person is paralyzed.

    \_\_\_ b. The person would like someone to push him or her.

    \_\_\_ c. The person is disabled in some way.

    \_\_\_ d. The person is about to be admitted to the hospital.

3.  A car has bumper stickers that read, "I Brake for Animals," "Save the Whales," and "Have You Thanked a Green Plant Today?"

    ___ a. A driver of the car supports environmental issues.

    ___ b. A driver of the car is an environmental scientist.

    ___ c. A driver of the car has pets.

    ___ d. The owner of the car is a college student.

4.  The street is wet, but the sidewalks are dry.

    ___ a. An unusual rain fell only on the street.

    ___ b. It rained everywhere, but someone dried the sidewalks.

    ___ c. A street-cleaning vehicle sprayed the street.

    ___ d. Children with water guns must have played on the street.

5.  Inside of a car with an out-of-town license are several maps, suitcases, and bags of snacks.

    ___ a. The driver of the car is on vacation.

    ___ b. The driver of the car is on a business trip.

    ___ c. The driver of the car has children.

    ___ d. The driver of the car is on a trip of some kind.

## INFERENCES IN READING

In reading, too, we make logical leaps from the information given in a straightforward way to ideas that are not stated directly. As the scholar S. I. Hayakawa has said, inferences are "statements about the unknown made on the basis of the known." To draw inferences, we use all the clues provided by the writer, our own experience, and logic.

In this book, you have already practiced making inferences in the chapter on vocabulary. There you had to use context clues within sentences to infer the meanings of words. Also, in the chapter on main ideas, you had to "read between the lines" in order to find implied main ideas. The intent of this chapter is to broaden your ability to make inferences about what you read.

Read the following passage and then check the three inferences that can logically be drawn from it.

> A famous psychology experiment conducted by Dr. John B. Watson demonstrates that people, like animals, can be conditioned—trained to respond in a particular way to certain stimulations. Watson gave an eleven-month-old baby named Albert a soft, furry white rat. Each time Albert tried to stroke the rat, Dr. Watson hit a metal bar with a hammer. Before long, Albert was not only afraid of white rats but also of white rabbits, white dogs, and white fur coats. He even screamed at the sight of a Santa Claus mask.

_____ 1. Dr. Watson did not like small children.

_____ 2. Before the experiment, Albert was not afraid of white rats.

_____ 3. Albert had been familiar with rats before the experiment.

_____ 4. If he had seen a black fur coat, Albert would have screamed.

_____ 5. Albert connected the loud noise of the hammer striking the metal bar with the white rat.

_____ 6. Albert was afraid of loud noises from the beginning.

Here is an explanation of each item:

1. This is not a logical inference. While the passage may make us wonder about Watson's attitude toward babies, it doesn't give enough information for us logically to infer that he did not like small children.

2. This is a logical inference. Because Albert tried to pet the rat, it is fair to assume that he wasn't frightened of the animal.

3. This is not a logical inference. The passage gives no clues about Albert having previous experience with rats.

4. This is not a logical inference. The passage makes no mention of Albert's response to any color but white.

5. This is a logical inference. Because the loud noise appears to have changed Albert's attitude toward the rat, we can assume he associated the noise with the rat.

6. This is a logical inference. Since the noise is what made Albert afraid of the rat, we have to infer that he was afraid of the noise. In addition, experience tells us that babies are likely to be frightened of unexpected loud noises.

The following activities will improve your ability to make inferences as you read.

## ➤ *Practice 2*

Read the following passage. Then circle the letter of the most logical answer to each question, based on the facts given in the passage.

A corporate president recently made a visit to a nearby Indian reservation as part of his firm's public relations program. "We realize that we have not hired any Indians in the five years our company has been located in this area," he told the assembled tribesmen, "but we are looking into the matter very carefully." "Hora, hora," said some of the Indians. "We would like to eventually hire 5 percent of our total work force from this reservation," he said. "Hora, hora," shouted more of the Indians. Encouraged by their enthusiasm, the president closed his short address by telling them that he hoped his firm would be able to take some hiring action within the next couple of years. "Hora, hora, hora," cried the total group. With a feeling of satisfaction the president left the hall and was taken on a tour of the reservation. Stopping in a field to admire some of the horses grazing there, the president asked if he could walk up closer to the animals. "Certainly," said his Indian driver, "but be careful not to step in the hora."

1. To get the main point of this passage, the reader must infer
   a. the location of the reservation.
   b. what kind of company the president headed.
   c. the meaning of the word "hora."

2. From the president's speech, we can infer that
   a. his firm had a great interest in hiring the Indians.
   b. his firm had little interest in hiring the Indians.
   c. his firm had a stated policy never to hire Indians.

3. From the passage, we can infer that
   a. the Indians believed the president's speech.
   b. the Indians did not believe the president's speech.
   c. the Indians were confused by the president's speech.

4. From the passage, we can infer that the president
   a. thought the Indians deserved to be hired.
   b. thought his company should not hire the Indians.
   c. misinterpreted the Indians' reaction to his speech.

5. From the passage, we can infer that the main reason the president spoke to the Indians about jobs was that
   a. they needed the jobs.
   b. he thought promising jobs to the Indians would make his company look good.
   c. he thought hiring the Indians would be good for his company.

## ➤ Practice 3

Read the following passage and check the three inferences that are most logically based on the given facts.

The *Chicago Tribune* once wrote that Henry Ford was an ignoramus. Ford sued, challenging the paper to "prove it." During the trial, Ford was asked dozens of simple, general information questions: "When was the Civil War?" "Name the presidents of the United States." And so on. Ford, who had little formal education, could answer very few. Finally, exasperated, he said, "I don't know the answers to those questions, but I could find a man in five minutes who does. I use my brain to think, not store up a lot of useless facts."

___  1. Henry Ford was probably angered by the article in the *Chicago Tribune*.

___  2. Ford frequently sued people.

___  3. Ford won the case in court.

___  4. The *Tribune* won the case in court.

___  5. Ford would have been more successful had he had a formal education.

___  6. Ford believed that knowing where to find a fact is good enough.

___  7. Ford regretted not having a more formal education.

___  8. Ford believed that knowing how to think is more important than knowing facts.

## INFERENCES IN LITERATURE

Inference is very important in reading literature. While writers of factual material usually state directly what they mean, creative writers often *show* what they mean. It is up to the reader to infer the point of what the creative writer has to say. For instance, a non-fiction writer might write the following:

Marian was angry at her father.

But the novelist might write:

Marian's eyes narrowed when her father spoke to her. She cut him off in mid-sentence with the words, "I don't have time to argue with you."

The author has *shown* us the anger with specific detail rather than simply stating the fact of the anger. To understand imaginative writing, then, you must often use your inference skills—just as you do in everyday life.

Applying inferences skills can increase your appreciation of such literary forms as novels, short stories, plays, essays, autobiographies, and poetry. Poetry, especially, by its nature implies much of its meaning. Implications are often made through comparisons. For example, Emily Dickinson begins one of her poems:

Hope is the thing with feathers
That perches in the soul
And sings the tune without the words,
And never stops at all.

Dickinson compares hope here with a singing bird. This implies, among other things, that hope is a sweet and welcome thing.

On the next page is the passage that starts the autobiography *Growing Up* by the *New York Times*' columnist Russell Baker. Read it, and then do the activity that follows.

At the age of eighty my mother had her last bad fall, and after that her mind wandered free through time. Some days she went to weddings and funerals that had taken place half a century earlier. On others she presided over family dinners cooked on Sunday afternoons for children who were now gray with age. Through all this she lay in bed but moved across time, traveling among the dead decades with a speed and ease beyond the gift of physical science.

"Where's Russell?" she asked one day when I came to visit at the nursing home.

"I'm Russell," I said.

She gazed at this improbably overgrown figure out of an inconceivable future and promptly dismissed it.

"Russell's only this big," she said, holding her hand, palm down, two feet from the floor. That day she was a young country wife with chickens in the backyard and a view of hazy blue Virginia mountains behind the apple orchard, and I was a stranger old enough to be her father.

Early one morning she phoned me in New York. "Are you coming to my funeral today?" she asked.

It was an awkward question with which to be awakened. "What are you talking about, for God's sake?" was the best reply I could manage.

"I'm being buried today," she declared briskly, as though announcing an important social event.

"I'll phone you back," I said and hung up, and when I did phone back she was all right, although she wasn't all right, of course, and we all knew she wasn't.

She had always been a small woman—short, light-boned, delicately structured—but now, under the white hospital sheet, she was becoming tiny. I thought of a doll with huge, fierce eyes. There had always been a fierceness in her. It showed in that angry, challenging thrust of the chin when she issued an opinion, and a great one she had always been for issuing opinions.

"I tell people exactly what's on my mind," she has been fond of boasting. "I tell them what I think, whether they like it or not." Often they had not liked it. She could be sarcastic to people in whom she detected evidence of the ignoramus or the fool.

"It's not always good policy to tell people exactly what's on your mind," I used to caution her.

"If they don't like it, that's too bad," was her customary reply, "because that's the way I am."

And so she was. A formidable woman. Determined to speak her mind, determined to have her way, determined to bend those who opposed her. In that time when I had known her best, my mother had hurled herself at life with chin thrust forward, eyes blazing, and an energy that made her seem always on the run.

She ran after squawking chickens, an axe in her hand, determined on a beheading that would put dinner in the pot. She ran when she made the beds, ran when she set the table. One Thanksgiving she burned herself badly when, running up from the cellar oven with the ceremonial turkey, she tripped on the stairs and tumbled back down, ending at the bottom in the debris of giblets, hot gravy and battered turkey. Life was combat, and victory was not to the lazy, the timid the slugabed, the drugstore cowboy, the libertine, the mushmouth afraid to tell people exactly what was on his mind whether people liked it or not. She ran.

Now put a check by the six inferences most solidly based on the words and images in the passage. Refer to the passage as needed when making your choices.

\_\_\_\_ 1. Baker's mother knew she was remembering past events.

\_\_\_\_ 2. Baker's mother thought she was actually living at the time of some memories.

\_\_\_\_ 3. The author's mother's last bad fall must have affected her mind.

\_\_\_\_ 4. Baker's mother predicted the day of her own funeral.

\_\_\_\_ 5. Once she imagined that her funeral would take place that day.

\_\_\_\_ 6. In describing the incident in which his mother said, "I'm being buried today," Baker uses the term "all right" with two different meanings.

\_\_\_\_ 7. Baker's mother had been a calm woman with a patient, encouraging manner.

\_\_\_\_ 8. She was an energetic, blunt person.

\_\_\_\_ 9. Baker chose to describe his mother more sentimentally than realistically.

\_\_\_ 10. His mother's travels "among the dead decades" caused Baker himself to remember earlier days.

Here are explanations for each of the ten inferences.

1-2. Because Baker's mother expected the real Russell to be only two feet high, we know that she was unaware of where she was and that she was mentally experiencing earlier times in her life. Thus inference 1 is not well supported, but inference 2 is solidly based on the given details.

  3. The first sentence of the passage connects Baker's mother's fall with her mind wandering "free through time." Therefore the details of the passage also support inference 3.

4-5. Baker doesn't state that his mother's funeral took place on the day she said it would. This tells us that she did not predict the day of her funeral, but that she only imagined it was about to happen. You thus should have checked 5, but not 4.

  6. Since the two uses of the term "all right" seem contradictory ("she was all right, although she wasn't all right"), we can assume that Baker intends them to have different meanings. Thus the statement is a well-supported inference.

In writing "when I did phone back she was all right," Baker refers to his mother having overcome the false belief that she was being buried that day. But when he states "she wasn't all right, of course, and we all knew she wasn't," Baker refers to his mother's general poor physical and mental condition, which she had not overcome.

7-8. The author's description of his mother as someone who had been "always on the run" tells us she was more energetic than calm. And because he describes her as someone with "fierceness in her" who "always told people exactly what was on her mind," sometimes sarcastically, we can conclude that she was more blunt than patient and encouraging. Thus inference 7 is not well supported, but inference 8 is.

9. This inference is not supported by the passage. In discussing a senile parent, some writers might be tempted to dwell on their warmest, sweetest memories. Since Baker describes his mother as a blunt and impatient person who was often disliked, we can conclude that he has avoided sentimentality.

10. This inference is strongly based on the details of the passage. Baker remembers, for instance, how determined and energetic a person his mother was, running after chickens with an axe and once tumbling down the basement stairs after running up with the Thanksgiving turkey.

## ➤ Practice 4

Below is the beginning of Philip Roth's novel *Goodbye, Columbus*. Read the passage, and then circle the letter of the most logical answer to each question, based on the facts given in the passage.

*myopic*: better able to see things near at hand than things far away

The first time I saw Brenda she asked me to hold her glasses. Then she stepped out to the edge of the diving board and looked foggily into the pool; it could have been drained, myopic Brenda would never have known it. She dove beautifully, and a moment later she was swimming back to the side of the pool, her head of short-clipped auburn hair held up, straight ahead of her, as though it were a rose on a long stem. She glided to the edge and then was beside me. "Thank you," she said, her eyes watery though not from the water. She extended a hand for her glasses but did not put them on until she turned and headed away. I watched her move off. Her hands suddenly appeared behind her. She caught the bottom of her suit between thumb and index finger and flicked what flesh had been showing back where it belonged. My blood jumped.

That night, before dinner, I called her.

"Who are you calling?" my Aunt Gladys asked.

"Some girl I met today."

"Doris introduced you?"

"Doris wouldn't introduce me to the guy who drains the pool, Aunt Gladys."

"Don't criticize all the time. A cousin's a cousin. How did you meet her?"

"I didn't really meet her. I saw her."

"Who is she?"

"Her last name is Patimkin."

"Patimkin I don't know," Aunt Gladys said, as if she knew anybody who belonged to the Green Lane Country Club. "You're going to call her you don't know her?"

"Yes," I explained. "I'll introduce myself."

"Casanova," she said, and went back to preparing my uncle's dinner. None of us ate together; my Aunt Gladys ate a five o'clock, my cousin Susan at five-thirty, me at six, and my uncle at six-thirty. There is nothing to explain this beyond the fact that my aunt is crazy.

"Where's the suburban phone book?" I asked after pulling out all the books tucked under the telephone table.

"What?"

"The suburban phone book. I want to call Short Hills."

"That skinny book? What, I gotta clutter my house with that, I never use it?"

"Where is it?"

"Under the dresser where the leg came off."

"For God's sake," I said.

"Call information better. You'll go yanking around there, you'll mess up my drawers. Don't bother me, you see your uncle'll be home soon. I haven't even fed you yet."

"Aunt Gladys, suppose tonight we all eat together. It's hot, it'll be easier for you."

"Sure, I should serve four different meals at once. You eat pot roast, Susan with the cottage cheese, Max has steak. Friday night is his steak night, I wouldn't deny him. And I'm having a little cold chicken. I should jump up and down twenty different times? What am I, a work-horse?"

"Why don't we all have steak, or cold chicken—"

"Twenty years I'm running a house. Go call your girl friend."

1. Brenda may not have put on her glasses until she turned away because she was
   a. confused.
   b. forgetful.
   c. vain.

2. When the narrator says his blood jumped, he is referring to his
   a. distaste for Brenda's behavior.
   b. surprise.
   c. sexual interest.

3. From the comparison of Brenda's head to "a rose on a long stem," we can infer that
   a. the narrator is interested in flowers.
   b. the narrator admires Brenda.
   c. Brenda is a florist.

4. We can conclude that Doris
   a. is related to the narrator.
   b. is a good friend of the narrator.
   c. once dated the narrator.

5. Aunt Gladys's nephew probably wants to call Brenda
   a. to arrange to introduce her to Doris.
   b. to watch her swim again.
   c. to ask her out on a date.

6. Aunt Gladys thinks
   a. her nephew should only call girls he has been formally introduced to.
   b. her nephew is being overly forward by calling Brenda Patimkin.
   c. both of the above.

7. Aunt Gladys appears to be
   a. a quiet, easygoing woman.
   b. a blunt, stubborn, and unreasonable woman.
   c. a mean, revengeful, and insane woman.

8. Brenda lives
   a. in the city.
   b. in the suburbs.
   c. at the country club.

9. We can conclude that the members of Aunt Gladys's family
   a. dislike each other.
   b. have different tastes in foods.
   c. have different working hours and so cannot eat together.

10. The narrator's attitude toward his "crazy" aunt is one of
    a. anger and hate.
    b. disappointment and shame.
    c. tolerance and affection.

## ➤ Review

To review what you've learned in this chapter, complete each of the following sentences about inferences.

1. An inference is a conclusion that is (*directly stated, suggested*) _____ by the author.

2. When making inferences, it is (*a mistake, useful*) _____ to use our own experience as well as the author's clues.

3. When making inferences, it is (*a mistake, useful*) _____ to use our sense of logic as well as the author's clues.

4. Drawing inferences is a key skill in reading literature because writers of fiction do not so much (*tell, show*) _____ us what they mean as (*tell, show*) _____ us with specific details.

## INFERENCES: Test A-1

A. Read each passage below. Then check the *two* statements after each passage which are most logically supported by the information given.

1. Frank Sinatra is well-known for his effect upon women in the audience. His reputation as a singer who made the girls swoon, however, began in 1942 at a low point in his career. Then publicity agent George Evans had an idea to make the singer more popular. Evans hired twelve young girls and paid them to jump, scream, moan, and faint when Sinatra sang. He also passed out hundreds of free tickets to the show. The night of the concert, when Sinatra started singing, the twelve hired girls obediently went to pieces. Their example was so contagious that thirty girls in the audience fainted. The next day, newspapers were full of pictures of girls being carried out of the theater after Sinatra sang. The singer's reputation was made.

____ a. Girls were screaming and fainting at concerts long before the Beatles came on the scene.

____ b. Young men did not enjoy Sinatra's singing.

____ c. George Evans was the most important single influence on Frank Sinatra's career.

____ d. Publicity stunts can strongly influence a show business career.

____ e. Frank Sinatra had no success as a singer until 1942.

2. In the early 1980s, daytime soap operas were known for their many characters engaged in casual sex. Movies such as *Risky Business* played the prostitution business for laughs. Any number of TV series featured two people meeting at a party or bar, then waking up in bed the following day. By 1987, however, that had changed. Several TV movies were made about AIDS and its impact on society. *Days of Our Lives*, a soap opera known for its steamy story lines, chronicled a young man's trip to the pharmacy to buy condoms. One of its lead characters, previously a faithless swinger, was in a loving but chaste relationship with one woman. The producer of *Risky Business* told the *Los Angeles Times* that the same movie "could not and should not be made in 1987."

____ a. The AIDS epidemic was widely recognized in the early 1980s.

____ b. Concern about AIDS had grown between the early 1980s and 1987.

____ c. Television and movie trends reflect sexual attitudes in general society.

____ d. Daytime soap operas usually depict sexual relationships only within marriage.

____ e. The producer of *Risky Business* regretted making the film in the early 1980s.

*(Continues on next page)*

**B.** After reading the passage below, check the *six* statements which are most logically supported by the information given.

Our heartbeat, sleeping habits, brain activity, body temperature, and much more operate in certain rhythms or cycles. Scientists called chronobiologists try to understand how our "internal clocks" operate to regulate such cycles. One experiment conducted by chronobiologists involved placing a 27-year-old woman in an underground cave for 130 days. She was cut off from any way to measure the passage of time—there was no natural light in the cave, nor any clocks. The temperature was a constant 69 degrees. When the woman was brought out of the cave at the end of the four-month period, her sleep cycle had changed dramatically. She would stay awake 20 to 25 hours, then sleep about ten hours. Her menstrual cycle had stopped. She believed she had been in the cave for only two months.

_____ 1. Chronobiologists are apparently biologists who specialize in human rhythms and cycles.

_____ 2. The experiment suggests that the human "internal clock" is influenced by such external cues as light and temperature changes.

_____ 3. The woman in the experiment never returned to the condition she was in before the experiment.

_____ 4. The woman spent four months in total darkness.

_____ 5. In the absence of a clock or the natural light and darkness of a day, it can be hard to judge how much time has passed.

_____ 6. Experiments can reveal much about human behavior that is not otherwise readily apparent.

_____ 7. Some of the effects on the woman in the experiment probably resulted from having no exercise for 130 days.

_____ 8. The researchers probably considered 69 degrees to be a pretty comfortable temperature for humans.

_____ 9. The rhythm of the human body is usually not influenced by the natural rhythm of a day on Earth.

_____ 10. The woman in the experiment probably planned for numerous activities to keep her busy and interested while she was in the cave.

## INFERENCES: Test A-2

A. Following is a well-known poem by the American poet Carl Sandburg. Read the poem, and then circle the letters of the inferences which are most logically supported by the information given.

*Austerlitz, Waterloo, Gettysburg, Ypres, Verdun:* battlefields where many died

### Grass

Pile the bodies high at Austerlitz and Waterloo.
Shovel them under and let me work—
    I am the grass; I cover all.

And pile them high at Gettysburg
And pile them high at Ypres and Verdun.
Shovel them under and let me work.
Two years, ten years, and passengers ask the conductor:
    What place is this?
    Where are we now?

    I am the grass.
    Let me work.

1. The poem refers to bodies of
   a. the living.
   b. all those who have died.
   c. those who have died in wars.

2. The words "pile them high" suggest that
   a. the deaths were not in vain.
   b. there are many bodies to pile up.
   c. the bodies must all be recovered.

3. The supposed speaker of the poem is
   a. a train passenger.
   b. the grass.
   c. a conductor.

4. The poet implies that
   a. time passes too slowly.
   b. no matter how much time passes, time cannot hide the horrors of war.
   c. even the horrors of war are forgotten in time.

5. The poet implies that
   a. nature's work outlasts man's.
   b. man and nature are equal partners.
   c. man's work will outlast anything nature does.    *(Continues on next page)*

**B.** Read the following passage, and then check the *five* statements which are most logically supported by the information given.

> Your sister has a new boyfriend. The first time you meet him, he corners you and talks to you for an hour about football, a subject in which you have no interest at all. You come away with the impression that he is an inconsiderate bore. The next two times you see him, however, he says not a word about football; instead, he participates in the general conversation and makes some witty and intelligent remarks. What is your impression of him now? Do you find him likable and interesting on the basis of the last two encounters? Do you average out the early minus and the later plus and come out with a neutral zero? Neither is likely—what is likely is that you still think of him as an inconsiderate bore. For psychological research suggests that first impressions, as our mothers and fathers told us, are quite lasting.

____ 1. First impressions are usually negative.

____ 2. It's a bad idea to discuss football when you first meet someone.

____ 3. It is useful to make good first impressions.

____ 4. To make a good impression, it helps to notice what interests the other person.

____ 5. A "neutral zero" impression of someone would be negative.

____ 6. A "neutral zero" impression of someone would be neither positive nor negative.

____ 7. It's not so difficult to remain objective about others.

____ 8. It's not so easy to be objective about others.

____ 9. Second impressions can be even more powerful than first impressions.

____ 10. We have to work to be objective in judging others.

# INFERENCES: Test A-3

After reading each selection, circle the letter of the best answer to each question.

A.　Early one January morning in 1800, villagers in Aveyron, southern France, captured a remarkable creature. He was an 11- or 12-year-old boy who appeared to be wild. The boy was naked in the winter weather and pocked with scars. Villagers thronged to see this wild boy, who continually tried to escape. How long he had been lost or abandoned or why, no one knew. He took no notice of anyone who talked to him. Observers guessed that he was deaf and mute. They assumed he had lived most of his young life without human contact, subsisting on roots, acorns, and raw potatoes.

　　The "savage boy" quickly became a celebrity and was taken to Paris. There he was observed by those who thought that life in the wild might be superior to civilization. But as a "noble savage," the boy proved to be a sore disappointment to the Parisians. They found him "a disgusting, slovenly boy, affected with spasmodic . . . convulsive motions . . . biting and scratching those who contradicted him, expressing no kind of affection for those who attended upon him." The boy was soon diagnosed as an "idiot" and placed in an institute for deaf-mutes.

1. Some people believed that a "wild child" would
   a. have grown up with a human family.
   b. have a perfect nature, unspoiled by civilization.
   c. wear clothing.
   d. express little affection for those who took care of him.

2. From this passage, we can conclude that children who grow up in the wild
   a. cannot hear.
   b. have no fears.
   c. have no emotions.
   d. do not develop normally.

3. A possible reason for the wild boy not taking "notice of anyone who talked to him" is that
   a. he was too stubborn to listen.
   b. people were saying unpleasant things to him.
   c. French words had no meaning for him.
   d. he was always too hungry.

B.　Drinking or drug use accounts for more than half of U.S. traffic deaths every year. More people die on our highways annually than were killed in the Vietnam War. It's time to learn a lesson from other countries around the world and borrow the harsh penalties some of them impose on people convicted of drunk driving. In Turkey, for example, drunk drivers are taken 20 miles out of town and forced to walk back under police escort. In Norway, the drunk spends three weeks in jail at hard labor and loses his license for a year. In Russia, the drunk driver loses his license for life. In South Africa, the drunk is given either a 10-year prison term or a fine of $10,000, and sometimes both. And in Bulgaria, a second drunk driving conviction carries the death penalty.

*(Continues on next page)*

4. From the passage, we can conclude that
   a. there are more drunks in Norway than in Turkey.
   b. different cultures deal with crime very differently.
   c. Bulgaria executes more people found guilty of various crimes than any other country.
   d. drunk drivers are rarely punished in the United States.

5. From the passage, we can conclude that the author feels
   a. the U.S. should use all the drunk driving penalties in Turkey, Norway, the Soviet Union, South Africa, and Bulgaria.
   b. even war is better than drunk driving.
   c. harsher penalties would cut down on drunk driving in this country.
   d. Bulgaria has the best approach for dealing with drunk drivers.

C.   The so-called greenhouse effect, which may be heating up Earth's atmosphere, was originally observed on the planet Venus. Its thick atmosphere traps so much heat from the Sun that Venus's surface basked in a temperature of 800 degrees. This is just one example of the ways in which looking at the other planets can help us to understand Earth. A theory suggests that the dinosaurs might have been killed off by a comet that struck Earth millions of years ago. The impact produced a huge cloud that covered Earth's surface and blocked off sunlight—and its beneficial effects on plants and animals—for months or years. This theory was first inspired by study of giant dust storms on the planet Mars.

6. The passage implies that the study of other planets is
   a. rare.
   b. very difficult.
   c. sometimes informative.
   d. expensive.

7. From the passage we can conclude that scientists
   a. now know why the dinosaurs became extinct.
   b. aren't sure why the dinosaurs became extinct.
   c. don't care why the dinosaurs became extinct.
   d. will one day know for sure why the dinosaurs became extinct.

8. From the passage, we can conclude that a huge cloud is thought to be capable of killing off the dinosaurs because
   a. the cloud would have made it too dark out for the dinosaurs to hunt.
   b. the cloud could have contained poison.
   c. the dinosaurs may well have been allergic to many of the particles in the huge cloud.
   d. by blocking sunlight for so long, the cloud would have killed many of the plants and animals eaten by dinosaurs.

# INFERENCES: Test B-1

A. Read each passage below. Then check the *two* statements after each passage which are most logically supported by the information given.

1.  Many experts say that pink has a special charm. A California probation department that used to have trouble quieting violent juvenile offenders now puts them in bubble-gum-pink cells. Within a few minutes the offenders stop screaming and banging and often even fall asleep. Also, in a college experiment, a group of children were put in small enclosures of various colors. All of the pens became covered with graffiti—except one that was painted pink.

    ___ a. Pink paint is resistant to graffiti.

    ___ b. Some colors affect people.

    ___ c. Most probation departments now use pink cells.

    ___ d. Pink seems to calm people down.

    ___ e. Pink is most children's favorite color.

2.  How does one succeed in business in a foreign country? A famous consultant for the UN advises, "When in Rome, do as the Romans do." Carry lots of business cards in Japan, and make sure they're translated into Japanese, since they are considered an important picture of who you are in the company. Bow whenever you are bowed to, and rise only after your partner does. Don't do business on the fourth of the month, since the number four also means death in Japanese. It's okay to eat and leave promptly at business dinners in China, since short speeches are given throughout the meal rather than a long one at the end. However, being prompt is rude in the Mideast, so you should arrive late and sit close enough to the other person to feel his breath so you will not appear unfriendly. Holding hands with your business associate is even better. But be careful not to show the soles of your feet while you are seated, as it is considered unclean and offensive to your host.

    ___ a. To succeed in business in a foreign country, one should learn about that country's culture.

    ___ b. It is rude to be prompt in Japan.

    ___ c. The UN consultant feels that it's best to do business in Rome.

    ___ d. The Japanese probably also prefer not to do business on the thirteenth of each month.

    ___ e. Some behavior considered natural is really culturally based.

*(Continues on next page)*

**B.** Read the passage below, taken from a *Ms.* magazine essay titled "Being a Boy" by Julius Lester. Check the *six* statements most logically supported by the information given.

> *pummeling:* beating        *assertion:* claim        *adept:* very skilled
> *decathlon:* an athletic competition with ten track-and-field events

As boys go, I wasn't much. I mean, I tried to be a boy and spent many childhood hours pummeling my hardly formed ego with failure at cowboys and Indians, baseball, football, lying, and sneaking out of the house. When our neighborhood gang raided a neighbor's pear tree, I was the only one who got sick from the stolen fruit. I also failed at setting fire to our garage, an art at which any five-year-old boy should be adept. I was, however, the neighborhood champion at getting beat up. "That Julius can take it, man," the boys used to say, almost in admiration, after I emerged from another battle, tears brimming in my eyes but refusing to fall.

My efforts at being a boy earned me a pair of scarred knees that are a record of a childhood spent falling from bicycles, trees, the tops of fences, and porch steps; of tripping as I ran (generally from a fight), walked, or simply tried to remain upright on windy days. I tried to believe my parents when they told me I was a boy, but I could find no objective proof for such an assertion. Each morning during the summer as I cuddled up in the quiet corner with a book, my mother would push me out the back door and into the yard. And throughout the day as my blood was let as if I were a patient of 17th-century medicine, I thought of the girls sitting in the shade of porches, playing with their dolls, toy refrigerators and stoves.

There was the life, I thought! No constant pressure to prove oneself. No necessity always to be competing. While I humiliated myself on football and baseball fields, the girls stood on the sidelines laughing at me, because they didn't have to do anything except be girls. The rising of each sun brought me to the starting line of yet another day's Olympic decathlon, with no hope of ever winning even a bronze medal.

Through no fault of my own I reached adolescence. While the pressure to prove myself on the athletic field lessened, the overall situation got worse—because now I had to prove myself with girls. Just how I was supposed to go about doing this was beyond me, especially because, at the age of 14, I was four foot nine and weighed seventy-eight pounds. (I think there may have been one 10-year-old girl in the neighborhood smaller than I.) Nonetheless, duty called, and off I went.

____ 1. The author was never part of the neighborhood gang.

____ 2. Being small can be a disadvantage to a boy.

____ 3. When he was young, the author liked to read.

____ 4. As a boy, the author wasn't strong, but he was brave.

____ 5. The author's mother sometimes physically abused him.

____ 6. Despite his humiliations, the author kept trying to prove himself as a male.

____ 7. Life would be easier for some people if society allowed for more individual differences.

____ 8. The author finally began to play "girls' games."

____ 9. The author eventually became more skilled on the athletic field.

____ 10. The author's athletic humiliations were replaced by dating difficulties.

## INFERENCES: Test B-2

**A.** Below is a poem by Matthew Prior (who lived in England from 1664–1721). Read the poem, and then check the *five* inferences most solidly based on it.

*affliction:* a condition of pain, suffering, or anxiety

### A Reasonable Affliction

On his death-bed poor Lubin lies
    His spouse is in despair;
With frequent cries, and mutual sighs,
    They both express their care.

"A different cause," says Parson Sly,
    "The same effect may give:
Poor Lubin fears that he may die;
    His wife, that he may live."

____ 1. Lubin is deathly ill.

____ 2. His wife is also deathly ill.

____ 3. Lubin and his wife are very religious.

____ 4. The poet recognizes that most marriages are bad ones.

____ 5. The poet recognizes that spouses aren't always devoted to each other.

____ 6. The reader's view of Lubin and his wife changes greatly in the second stanza.

____ 7. Lubin is not a rich man.

____ 8. Lubin's wife hopes to inherit his great wealth.

____ 9. When Parson Sly speaks of "a different cause," he refers to the different reasons why Lubin is crying and his wife is crying.

____ 10. The word *affliction* (in the title) refers to two different problems, Lubin's and his wife's.

*(Continues on next page)*

**B.** Read the following passage from an essay titled "In Depth, but Shallowly" by humorist Dave Barry. Then check the *five* statements which are most logically supported by the information given.

> If you want to take your mind off the troubles of the real world, you should watch local TV news. I know of no better way to escape reality, except perhaps heavy drinking.
>
> Local TV news programs have given a whole new definition to the word *news*. To most people, *news* means *information about events that affect a lot of people*. On local TV news shows, *news* means *anything that you can take a picture of, especially if a local TV News Personality can stand in front of it*. This is why they are so fond of car accidents, burning buildings, and crowds: these are good for standing in front of. On the other hand, local TV news shows tend to avoid stories about things that local TV News Personalities cannot stand in front of, such as budgets and taxes and the economy. If you want to get a local TV news show to do a story on the budget, your best bet is to involve it in a car crash.

\_\_\_\_ 1. Barry respects the way local TV newspeople cover important issues.

\_\_\_\_ 2. He feels the news should help viewers escape the harsh realities of life.

\_\_\_\_ 3. He feels local TV newscasts should do a better job of covering local issues.

\_\_\_\_ 4. He believes the economy is more newsworthy than a car accident.

\_\_\_\_ 5. Barry's main point is that there are too many accidents and fires in this country.

\_\_\_\_ 6. Barry's main point is that local TV newspeople ignore important stories because they are visually uninteresting.

\_\_\_\_ 7. Barry's main point is that local TV newspeople believe car accidents and burning buildings are more important public issues than local economics.

\_\_\_\_ 8. Barry feels that the economy is an important topic for local news shows.

\_\_\_\_ 9. He probably dislikes TV in general.

\_\_\_ 10. Barry thinks it is unlikely that a local TV news show will do many stories on the budget.

## INFERENCES: Test B-3

After reading each passage, circle the letter of the best answer to each question.

**A.**  Situation comedies, soap operas, action-adventure shows, and character dramas have all been familiar parts of the TV landscape for years. In the 1980s, however, a new breed of show was developed. *Hill Street Blues* was the pioneer of this innovative type of programming. Although the action centered around a rundown inner-city police station, *Blues* was not a typical car-chasing, shoot-'em-up police show. Its characters were closely examined, on the job and off, with their frailties as well as their virtues exposed. Continuing plot lines ran through the shows, tying them together from week to week and even season to season. A single episode might run the range of emotions from hilarity to tragedy. Since the introduction of *Hill Street Blues*, other shows such as *L. A. Law* and *Northern Exposure* have continued the development of this breed of show.

1. The passage suggests
   a. *Hill Street Blues* was not a particularly successful show.
   b. *Hill Street Blues* influenced the format of other shows.
   c. *Hill Street Blues* never had car chases or shootings.
   d. all of the above.

2. The passage suggests that
   a. characters in the *Hill Street Blues* type of show are funnier than those in situation comedies.
   b. the *Hill Street Blues* type of show will soon go out of fashion.
   c. police shows are likely to be more successful than soap operas and situation comedies.
   d. shows like *Hill Street Blues* and *L. A. Law* combine elements from a number of previously popular types of shows.

3. The author suggests that action-centered police shows typically
   a. had no car-chasing.
   b. were a new breed of show.
   c. did not examine characters' lives closely.
   d. were likely to run the range of emotions from hilarity to tragedy.

**B.**  Beginning in the 1920s, Emanuel Haldeman-Julius became a millionaire by choosing books that had not sold well, giving them new titles, and reprinting them. A novel first called *The Golden Fleece* was reprinted by the Kansas publisher as *The Quest for a Blonde Mistress*. Yearly sales jumped from 600 to 50,000. Similarly, a play by Victor Hugo, *The King Amuses Himself*, was reissued as *The Lustful King Enjoys Himself*, and sales increased by more than 400 percent.

4. Haldeman-Julius counted on people preferring books about
   a. royalty.
   b. blondes.
   c. sex.
   d. quests.

*(Continues on next page)*

285

5. Haldeman-Julius was apparently skilled
   a. as a literary critic.
   b. in marketing.
   c. as an author.
   d. all of the above.

C.   When Pennsylvania state treasurer R. Budd Dwyer called a news conference for Jan. 22, 1987, reporters believed they would hear Dwyer, who had recently been convicted on bribery charges, announce his resignation. Instead, Dwyer defended his innocence and bitterly criticized the press and his accusers. Noticing some TV crews packing up to leave, he encouraged them to stay, saying, "You're not going to want to miss this." Dwyer then pulled a .357 Magnum from an envelope and shot himself dead as the cameras rolled. TV stations had to come to a decision quickly as to how much, if any, of the incident they would show. A few stations, citing their obligation to provide the whole story, broadcast the entire bloody scene, even though it was during a day when many children were home from school due to a heavy snow. Most cut away after showing Dwyer with the gun barrel in his mouth. Still others judged the scene too shocking and merely described what happened, without broadcasting any pictures.

6. A sensational news story like the Dwyer suicide
   a. must have been staged by the media.
   b. raises ethical questions for the media.
   c. is expensive for the media.
   d. is a typical media event.

7. From the passage, we can assume that Mr. Dwyer
   a. had actually intended to resign from his state position at the news conference.
   b. decided at the last minute to kill himself.
   c. really felt he was guilty.
   d. never intended to resign, but planned on shooting himself.

8. We might conclude that
   a. Mr. Dwyer was probably depressed.
   b. Mr. Dwyer wanted his death to shock people.
   c. Mr. Dwyer believed the media was partly responsible for his conviction.
   d. all of the above.

# INFERENCES: Test C-1

**A.** Read each passage below. Then check the *two* statements after each passage which are most logically supported by the information given.

1. Theft in the workplace is estimated to cost between $30 and $40 billion per year—that is in cash, goods and property. The causes for this loss include employee pilferage, check fraud, embezzlement, burglary, vandalism and shoplifting. It is further estimated that another $230 billion is stolen from businesses through "time theft." Time thieves are employees who take phony sick days, get someone else to punch in their cards on the time clock and conduct private business in the workplace.

   ___ a. The author feels that time theft is not as bad as property theft.

   ___ b. The greatest losses to businesses come through time theft, not property theft.

   ___ c. More money is lost to businesses through check fraud than through embezzlement.

   ___ d. Theft in the workplace is worse in the U.S. than in most other countries.

   ___ e. Employees steal more from companies than strangers do.

2. George Washington's honesty is a trait that has been well-publicized. The famous story of how little George chopped down his father's favorite cherry tree, then bravely admitted to the deed has an honored place in American presidential history. The cherry tree story was first recorded in 1806 by Parson Mason Locke Weems, a Maryland preacher and storyteller. Unfortunately, Parson Weems was none too honest himself, and it appears that he invented the story of George and the cherry tree. There is no record of the cherry tree incident anywhere until it appears in Weems' book. The parson, it seems, thought it acceptable to teach the virtue of honesty through a made-up story. We can judge Weems' own truthfulness by the fact that he describes himself in the book as "formerly rector of Mount Vernon Parish." Such a parish never existed.

   ___ a. The passage suggests that George Washington was not so honest after all.

   ___ b. We can conclude that Parson Weems knew George Washington well.

   ___ c. Widely accepted stories about history are not necessarily true.

   ___ d. Parson Weems wrote about a virtue he didn't have himself.

   ___ e. George Washington's father probably had no cherry trees.

*(Continues on next page)*

**B.** After reading the passage below, check the *six* statements which are most logically supported by the information given.

> Maria Lopez gets up early six days a week to open up the small *bodega* (store) she runs in Saucillo, a village in the state of Chihuahua in northern Mexico. Señora Lopez stocks a limited number of items for her customers. She sells some products that require refrigeration, such as milk, eggs, meats, and vegetables, as well as staples like flour, salt, sugar, and canned goods.
>
> Most of Maria's customers work in a nearby oil refinery or are farmers. To help feed their families, many grow some of their own food and raise animals. Maria calls nearly all her customers by their first names and always attends their christenings, weddings, and funerals. She saves the freshest produce and best cuts of meat for her favorite customers and even keeps up with their diets.
>
> Tony Lopez, Maria's third cousin, manages a large Kroger supermarket on the west side of San Antonio, Texas. . .Tony tries to spend at least an hour a day on the shopping floor chatting with customers and employees. But most of his time is taken up meeting with route salespeople for various grocery distributors and checking with Kroger's regional buyers.
>
> Keeping such a mammoth store fully stocked requires careful planning, buying, and coordinating. Each morning, a computer printout from Kroger's regional office in San Antonio tells Tony the previous day's sales. It also provides a great deal more information: how many quarts of milk, crates of grapefruit, boxes of Tide (in each size), and packages of Green Giant frozen peas were sold.

_____ 1. While Maria Lopez and Tony Lopez get their information in different ways, both are well-informed about their customers' needs and tastes.

_____ 2. The cousins probably get together often to discuss the similarities and differences in their work.

_____ 3. Maria Lopez is more a part of her customers' lives than Tony Lopez is of his.

_____ 4. Despite the differences in their stores, Maria and Tony probably earn very similar incomes.

_____ 5. We can assume that a smaller percentage of Tony's customers raise some of their own food than the percentage of Maria's customers that do.

_____ 6. A computerized analysis of stock would be as useful for Maria's work as it is to Tony's.

_____ 7. A large, diversified grocery store would probably not make enough money in a town like Saucillo to survive.

_____ 8. The differences between Maria's store and Tony's store are closely tied to the differences between the communities they serve.

_____ 9. Since Tony has a much larger and more modern store to work in, he must enjoy his work a lot more than Maria does.

_____ 10. The Kroger customers expect less of a personal relationship with their store's manager than the *bodega*'s customers do.

# INFERENCES: Test C-2

A. Following are two poems. "The Example" is by W. H. Davies (1870-1940), who was born in England and spent six years in the U.S., living the life of a hobo. "I Stood Upon a High Place" is by the U.S. writer Stephen Crane (1871-1900). Read each poem, and then circle the letters of the inferences which are most logically supported by the information given.

### The Example

Here's an example from　　　　　Now let my bed be hard,
　A butterfly;　　　　　　　　　　No care take I;
That on a rough, hard rock　　　I'll make my joy like this
　Happy can lie;　　　　　　　　Small butterfly,
Friendless and all alone　　　　Whose happy heart has power
On this unsweetened stone.　　To make a stone a flower.

1. The words "Whose happy heart has power / To make a stone a flower" mean that
   a. the butterfly is magical and can turn a stone into a flower.
   b. the butterly had the power of finding stones that resemble flowers.
   c. since the butterfly lacked a flower, it happily accepted the available substitute—the stone.

2. When he says "Now let my bed be hard, / No care take I" the speaker implies that
   a. he does not want his life to be like a hard rock.
   b. he wants to sleep on a hard rock.
   c. his life is hard, but he can enjoy it.

3. The poet has used the butterfly as an example of
   a. physical beauty.
   b. magical power.
   c. making the best of things.

### I Stood Upon a High Place

I stood upon a high place,
And saw, below, many devils
Running, leaping,
And carousing in sin.
One looked up, grinning,
And said, "Comrade! Brother!"

4. In saying he "stood upon a high place," the speaker suggests that he felt
   a. more righteous than the devils he saw.
   b. jealous of the playful devils.
   c. beneath the devils he saw.

*(Continues on next page)*

5. In saying "Comrade! Brother!" the devil means to imply that
   a. the speaker is an angel.
   b. the speaker is friendly.
   c. the speaker is also a sinner.

**B.** Read the following passage, and then check the *five* statements which are most logically supported by the information given.

Some behavioral psychologists have suggested that the personality could be precisely molded by training. However, research now indicates that a child's temperament is probably predetermined, at least to some extent. That is not to say that parents cannot guide and advise their children and help them to achieve a sense of self-worth. But trying to force a child to fit a particular model would probably be counterproductive. Setting limits for an aggressive child or gently urging a shy one to try new experiences could help youngsters to realize their full potential.

Psychotherapist Alan Loy McGinnis advises against attempts to radically redesign the personality. Rather, he quotes the Hasidic Rabbi Zusya to illustrate the wisdom of trying to develop what is uniquely oneself. Zusya said that when he reached the kingdom of God, he knew he would not be asked, "Why weren't you Moses? Why weren't you David?" but "Why weren't you Zusya? Why weren't you fully you?"

____ 1. Apparently there's not much we can learn about human nature from research.

____ 2. The passage suggests that with guidance, a very shy child can become extremely outgoing.

____ 3. In the past, behavioral psychologists have believed that the personality could be significantly changed.

____ 4. Personality is determined by a child's environment, not his genes.

____ 5. Genetic makeup has a great deal to do with personality.

____ 6. The author suggests that personality is determined only by genetic makeup.

____ 7. Rabbi Zusya probably believed that everyone has a unique contribution to make to society.

____ 8. The author would probably agree with the idea that anyone can be a great artist, politician, or religious leader.

____ 9. The passage suggests that it's better not to judge yourself in comparison to others.

____ 10. The passage suggests that it is wise to be accepting of your child's fundamental temperament and interests.

## INFERENCES: Test C-3

**A.** After reading this textbook selection, circle the letter of the best answer to each question.

Pepsi-Cola has been warring against arch-rival Coca-Cola for more than half a century. Back in the 1930s, Pepsi announced that it was cutting the price of its largest serving, then a dime, and offered consumers "twice as much for a nickel, too." So began the soft-drink industry's first price war.

For decades thereafter, Pepsi-Cola continued to be a distant number two to Coke. In the early 1960s, for example, Coke enjoyed a sales lead over Pepsi of more than 2 to 1. However, in 1963 Pepsi began a marketing campaign that has survived in various forms to this day. It announced the birth of "The Pepsi Generation." "Lifestyle advertising" was launched and aimed at younger viewers.

"We made a decision in the 1960s," recalls Alan Pottasch, Pepsi-Cola USA's senior vice president of creative services, "to stop talking about the product and to start talking about the user." Adopting a long-term positioning strategy, Pepsi was fighting not only to improve the brand's market share but to improve its "share of mind." As Pottasch notes, "the word Coke had practically become generic." Pepsi marketers decided that they should position their product with the next generation of consumers, who had not yet become firmly attached to Coca-Cola. Rather than getting Coke loyalists to switch brands, Pepsi hoped to win over an uncommitted and desirable target market.

1. The passage suggests that Pepsi-Cola and Coca-Cola
   a. have numerous cola rivals.
   b. are the two best-selling cola drinks in the U.S.
   c. attract customers solely on the basis of taste.

2. The Pepsi-Cola Company did not expect its "Pepsi Generation" campaign to
   a. quickly equal or surpass Coca-Cola sales.
   b. ever succeed in making Pepsi the number one selling cola.
   c. last for more than a few years.

3. Pepsi considered a "desirable target market" to be
   a. Coke loyalists.
   b. younger viewers.
   c. people who considered the word *Coke* generic.

*(Continues on next page)*

**B.** Below is the beginning of an essay titled "The Plot Against People" by *New York Times* columnist Russell Baker. After reading the passage, check the *five* statements which are most logically supported by the information given.

*inanimate:* lifeless          *idle:* not busy
*classified:* grouped       *cunning:* slyness

Inanimate objects are classified scientifically into three major categories—those that break down, those that get lost, and those that don't work.

The goal of all inanimate objects is to resist man and ultimately to defeat him, and the three major classifications are based on the method each object uses to achieve its purpose. As a general rule, any object capable of breaking down at the moment when it is most needed will do so. The automobile is typical of the category.

With the cunning peculiar to its breed, the automobile never breaks down while entering a filling station which has a large staff of idle mechanics. It waits until it reaches a downtown intersection in the middle of the rush hour, or until it is fully loaded with family and luggage on the Ohio Turnpike. Thus it creates maximum inconvenience, frustration, and irritability. . . .

Many inanimate objects, of course, find it extremely difficult to break down. Pliers, for example, and gloves and keys are almost totally incapable of breaking down. Therefore, they have had to evolve a different technique for resisting man.

They get lost. Science has still not solved the mystery of how they do it, and no man has ever caught one of them in the act.

_____ 1. We can conclude that the author does not own an automobile anymore.

_____ 2. The author writes about "inanimate objects," but describes them as having some characteristics of living beings.

_____ 3. The author has probably had frustrating experiences with things that broke down, got lost, and didn't work.

_____ 4. The author expects his readers to have had frustrating experiences with things breaking down, getting lost, and not working.

_____ 5. The essay appears to be about all types of "inanimate objects," both manmade and objects found in nature.

_____ 6. The passage's humor partly stems from the author's exaggerations.

_____ 7. The passage has probably already discussed objects that don't work.

_____ 8. The passage's humor partly stems from the truth behind the author's points.

_____ 9. When the author refers to science and scientific classification, he expects to be taken seriously.

_____ 10. In real life, the author tends to lose things more often than others do.

# INFERENCES: Test D-1

**A.** Read each passage below. Then check the *two* statements after each passage which are most logically supported by the information given.

1. Many of us use alarm clocks to help us wake up, and we're not overly concerned that the alarm noise will awaken any other sleepers. But in Japan's railroad companies, 40 or 50 locomotive operators sleep in a big dormitory while on call for work. However, they have to get up at differing times for their shifts, and alarm clocks would awake most of them at once. So the railroad companies have installed timed mechanical shaking devices in the beds of the operators to awaken each at his proper hour. In addition to providing a shaking motion to the bed, these devices also inflate an air bag under each operator to help propel him out of bed. All of this is done noiselessly, unless, of course, the indignant operators protest out loud!

   ____ a. Alarm clocks are rare in Japan.

   ____ b. The locomotive operators in the dormitory are not likely to oversleep.

   ____ c. The locomotive operators' beds are not very comfortable to sleep on.

   ____ d. Very few Japanese want to work as locomotive operators.

   ____ e. There's more than one way to achieve a goal.

2. Most people would like to think that they choose their friends on the basis of personal characteristics. A classic study of a housing complex for married students at the Massachusetts Institute of Technology (MIT) suggests that proximity—nearness and availability—can be a decisive factor. Researchers asked couples to list their friends in the complex. They found that residents were far more likely to list the couple in the next apartment than one that lived two doors away, and more likely to visit with a couple two doors away than with one three or four doors away. A distance of thirty feet or a short elevator ride made the difference between friends and strangers! More recent studies have confirmed the importance of proximity. One possible explanation is that whenever people encounter strangers, they feel tense. The more they see a person, the more they come to think of that person as predictable and safe, and hence the more likely they are to strike up a conversation that leads to friendship. This would explain why the most popular couples in the MIT housing complex were those who lived at the bottom of the stairs near the garbage cans that everyone used.

   ____ a. Most people probably think their personal preferences determine whom they choose for friends.

   ____ b. In fact, our personal preferences have no effect on who our friends are.

   ____ c. A person who lives in a big country is more likely to be have more friends than someone who lives in a small country.

   ____ d. Someone living in an apartment house is likely to have more friends than someone who lives on a farm.

   ____ e. A garbage collector is likely to have more friends than a mailperson.

*(Continues on next page)*

**B.** Read the passage below, taken from an essay titled "Darkness at Noon" by Harold Krents, an attorney who was born blind. Then check the *six* statements which are most logically supported by the information given.

*narcissistic:* self-admiring
*cum laude:* with honor

Blind from birth, I have never had the opportunity to see myself and have been completely dependent on the image I create in the eye of the observer. To date it has not been narcissistic.

There are those who assume that since I can't see, I obviously also cannot hear. Very often people will converse with me at the top of their lungs, enunciating each word very carefully. Conversely, people will also often whisper, assuming that since my eyes don't work, my ears don't either.

For example, when I go to the airport and ask the ticket agent for assistance to the plane, he or she will invariably pick up the phone, call a ground hostess and whisper: "Hi, Jane, we've got a 76 here." I have concluded that the word "blind" is not used for one of two reasons: Either they fear that if the dread word is spoken, the ticket agent's retina will immediately detach, or they are reluctant to inform me of my condition of which I may not have been previously aware.

On the other hand, others know that of course I can hear, but believe that I can't talk. Often, therefore, when my wife and I go out to dinner, a waiter or waitress will ask Kit if "*he* would like a drink" to which I respond that "indeed *he* would.". . .

The toughest misconception of all is the view that because I can't see, I can't work. I was turned down by over forty law firms because of my blindness, even though my qualifications included a *cum laude* degree from Harvard College and a good ranking in my Harvard Law School class.

\_\_\_ 1. It would offend Krents if people were to use the word "blind" in reference to him.

\_\_\_ 2. The airline's code for a blind passenger was "76."

\_\_\_ 3. It is better to whisper to blind people than to speak to them loudly.

\_\_\_ 4. Krents prefers that people speak to him in a normal tone of voice.

\_\_\_ 5. Sighted persons are sometimes uncomfortable directing conversation toward a blind person.

\_\_\_ 6. Krents' wife is not blind.

\_\_\_ 7. Blindness seems to harm a person's intelligence.

\_\_\_ 8. Some employers are biased against blind workers.

\_\_\_ 9. Harvard is apparently biased against blind students.

\_\_\_ 10. Krents is outspoken about his blindness.

## INFERENCES: Test D-2

A. Following is a well-known poem, "Ozymandias" (pronounced ŏ-zĭ-măn´-dē-əs), by the English poet Percy Shelley. Read the poem, and then circle the letters of the inferences which are most logically supported by the information given.

*vast:* large  
*visage:* face  
*sneer:* scornful smile  

*pedestal:* bottom support  
*colossal:* huge  
*boundless:* endless  

### Ozymandias

I met a traveler from an antique land,  
Who said: Two vast and trunkless legs of stone  
Stand in the desert. Near them, on the sand,  
Half sunk, a shattered visage lies, whose frown,  
And wrinkled lip, and sneer of cold command,  
Tell that its sculptor well those passions read,  
Which yet survive, stamped on these lifeless things,  
The hand that mocked them, and the heart that fed:  
And on the pedestal these words appear:  
"My name is Ozymandias, King of Kings:  
Look on my works, ye Mighty, and despair!"  
Nothing beside remains. Round the decay  
Of that colossal wreck, boundless and bare  
The lone and level sands stretch far away.

1. The place the traveler described was
   a. an old, yet active desert city.
   b. a barren spot in the desert where a culture once thrived.
   c. a land where travelers can find numerous antiques for sale.

2. At that place was
   a. a broken statue.
   b. a painting.
   c. a sculptor.

3. The features on the face were those of
   a. a respectful, obedient citizen.
   b. a judgmental, unfriendly leader.
   c. a wise and compassionate leader.

4. The words on the pedestal show that the person represented by the statue
   a. was a king.
   b. felt few people had achieved more than he had.
   c. both of the above.

*(Continues on next page)*

295

5. One of the poet's main points is that human vanity and pride
   a. were greater many years ago than they are today.
   b. stand up to the test of time.
   c. are ridiculous in the face of time and change.

**B.** Read the following passage, and then check the *five* statements which are most logically supported by the information given.

> Not long ago, smoldering cigarette butts caused almost 400,000 acres of the mighty Yellowstone National Park in Montana to go up in smoke. Its natural beauty was feared lost forever. But even as experts were declaring the blackened ground sterilized of any life, tiny shoots of grass were pushing up through the cinders. Within weeks, wind, rain, and the actions of birds seeded large areas of wildflowers that attracted colonies of insects. Following the insects were hungry birds, including the industrious nutcrackers, which carried in whitebark pinecones from far away to bury in the ground. The fire melted the lodgepole pinecones, scattering seeds for reforestation and providing food for squirrels and chipmunks. And treetop dwellers like the fish osprey found new nesting territory opened up by the burning of the forest canopy.

\_\_\_\_ 1. Most forest fires are caused by carelessness.

\_\_\_\_ 2. Experts can be wrong.

\_\_\_\_ 3. The fire was not at all destructive.

\_\_\_\_ 4. The blackened ground was sterilized of any life.

\_\_\_\_ 5. Nature has ways of seeding empty spaces.

\_\_\_\_ 6. Wildflowers provide food for insects.

\_\_\_\_ 7. Pinecones have more than one function in nature.

\_\_\_\_ 8. The fish osprey had never before lived in Yellowstone National Park.

\_\_\_\_ 9. Soon the parklands will look exactly as they used to.

\_\_\_ 10. The parkland's rebirth was due to the interaction of the fire, animals, plants, and weather.

# INFERENCES: Test D-3

After reading each selection, circle the letter of the best answer to each question.

*urban sprawl:* the spreading out of cities     *unprecedented:* new
*provincialism:* narrowness in thought     *exasperated*: greatly irritated

A. By making automobiles available to the masses, the growing industry changed the face of America. The spreading web of paved roads fueled urban sprawl, real estate booms in California and Florida, and a new roadside culture. Thousands of "auto camps" opened to provide tourists with tents and crude toilets. "Auto clubs" like the Tin Can Tourists Association (named for the tin can tied to the radiator cap of a member's car) sprang up to aid travelers. Automobile travel broke down provincialism and advanced standardized dialects and manners. By 1930 almost two farm families in three had cars. When asked why her family had bought a Model T when they had no indoor plumbing, a farm woman replied, "You can't go to town in a bathtub." Across the country the automobile gave the young unprecedented freedom from parental authority. After hearing 30 cases of "sex crimes" (19 of which occurred in cars), an exasperated juvenile court judge in Indiana declared that the automobile was "a house of prostitution on wheels."

1. The availability of automobiles
   a. reduced the number of farmers.
   b. lowered people's standards for cleanliness.
   c. weakened people's manners.
   d. made it less necessary for people to live in densely populated areas.

2. The more interaction there is between different groups of people,
   a. the more a roadside culture is likely to form.
   b. the more alike their speech is likely to become.
   c. the more urban sprawl there will be.
   d. the less urban sprawl there will be.

3. The real estate booms in California and Florida must have been made possible by
   a. the profits from automobile sales.
   b. the widespread development of paved roads.
   c. a growing interest in farm life.
   d. standardized dialects.

4. To the young, freedom from parental authority meant
   a. more sexual activity.
   b. better manners.
   c. joining an auto club.
   d. all of the above.

*(Continues on next page)*

5. The automobile industry
   a. must have quickly become an important source of employment in the U.S.
   b. brought consumers to a variety of businesses.
   c. in some cases weakened ties between immediate family members.
   d. all of the above.

**B.**    Oscar Stohr and Jack Yufe are identical twins who were separated as babies after their parents' divorce. Oscar was reared as a strict Catholic by his maternal grandmother in the Sudetenland of Czechoslovakia. As a member of the Hitler youth movement in Nazi Germany, he learned to hate Jews. By contrast, his brother Jack was reared in Trinidad by the twins' Jewish father. Jack joined an Israeli settlement at age 17 and later served in the Israeli army. During World War II, he felt loyal to the British, reflecting his years in Trinidad, and hated the Nazis.

The brothers met briefly in 1954, but Jack was warned by a translator not to tell Oscar that he was Jewish. In 1979, at age 47, the twins were reunited by social scientists interested in studying the degree to which environmental forces shape human behavior. Since Oscar and Jack were born with the same genes, any later differences in personality must result from their dissimilar upbringings.

Researchers found that, while physically alike, the twins differ in many important aspects. Jack is a workaholic; Oscar enjoys leisure-time activities. Whereas Oscar is a traditionalist who is domineering toward women, Jack is a political liberal who is much more accepting of feminism. Finally, Jack is extremely proud of being Jewish, while Oscar never mentions his Jewish heritage.

6. We can assume that Trinidad
   a. was once Oscar's home.
   b. had British ties.
   c. is still Jack's home.
   d. had an Israeli kibbutz.

7. During World War II,
   a. Oscar must have been loyal to the Nazi cause.
   b. Oscar must have known his brother was anti-Nazi.
   c. the brothers must have fought against each other in opposing armies.
   d. all of the above was probably true.

8. The passage suggests that
   a. Oscar and Jack's mother kept in touch with them.
   b. the twins' parents had different religions.
   c. Oscar is unaware of his Jewish heritage.
   d. Jack and Oscar eventually became good friends.

# INFERENCES: Test E-1

**A.** Read each passage below. Then check the *two* statements after each passage which are most logically supported by the information given.

1. Getting rid of the eyesores in a neighborhood does more than simply beautify; it can improve the economic and social life of an area. Recently a neighborhood in Philadelphia decided to improve its appearance by planting a community garden and installing trash cans. As a result, neighbors spent more time together outdoors. Thus graffiti writers and more serious offenders were discouraged from frequenting the area. The cleaner streets and safer atmosphere also attracted more customers to local businesses.

___ a. The passage suggests that local businesses paid for the community garden and trash cans.

___ b. Residents of an area can greatly influence the quality of their own neighborhood.

___ c. The trash cans in the Philadelphia neighborhood kept graffiti writers away.

___ d. Most neighborhoods are in need of a community garden.

___ e. Graffiti writers prefer to be active when no one is watching.

2. When the Spanish conqueror Pizarro transferred the capital of Peru from a site in the mountains 11,000 feet above sea level to lowland Lima, it wasn't just for a change of scenery. The Spanish conquerors observed early that domestic animals taken to the mountains failed to reproduce. And for over 50 years after the Spanish brought their wives and settled the Andes, no Spanish children were born in any of the higher altitudes. The Indians, however, described by Spanish priests as healthy and vigorous, were fertile in the same climate. The difference was that over the 9,000 years that the Indians had lived in the Andes, they had developed enlarged lungs, a high red-cell count, and lower blood pressure, all of which enabled them to live normal lives at high altitudes.

___ a. The Indians had invited the Spanish to govern Peru.

___ b. The Spaniards were used to living in the mountains.

___ c. Enlarged lungs make better use of the oxygen in the thin air of higher altitudes.

___ d. A people's genetic makeup can be gradually changed by the environment.

___ e. The Indians who lived in the mountains had no domestic animals.

*(Continues on next page)*

B. After reading the passage below, check the *six* statements which are most logically supported by the information given.

If you have ever seen pictures of a Ku Klux Klan rally, you would probably agree that one of their striking characteristics is the white, hooded robes worn by the Klan members. No one's individual features can be discerned in such a costume. Klansmen blend into a mass of undifferentiated similarity.

We would expect the Klan to explain its robes in terms of a uniform that sets members apart from nonmembers. Social psychologists see another purpose such clothing serves: the anonymity of the costume produces a psychological state known as deindividuation. In deindividuation, self-awareness is reduced. The fear of negative evaluation by others is diminished. The individual is consequently more apt to engage in impulsive, antisocial, and nonnormatively sanctioned behaviors. Deindividuation is also a potential cause of aggression, and this fact has been shown in a number of experiments.

\_\_\_\_   1. When they believe they cannot be identified, many people are more likely to cause harm to others.

\_\_\_\_   2. We can conclude that social psychologists are against uniforms.

\_\_\_\_   3. The passage suggests that uniforms are always worn in order to make people more impulsive, antisocial, and aggressive.

\_\_\_\_   4. A person acting as part of a group feels less responsibility for his actions than he would if he acted alone.

\_\_\_\_   5. The fear of negative evaluation makes people more likely to be aggressive.

\_\_\_\_   6. Uniform robes with hoods that cover people's faces provide more deindividuation than they would without hoods.

\_\_\_\_   7. Social psychologists are psychologists who study human behavior in social groups.

\_\_\_\_   8. A person is as likely to be aggressive when wearing everyday clothing as when a member of a uniformed group.

\_\_\_\_   9. When soldiers are drilled and trained to act as part of a unit, they are taking part in a process that involves deindividuation.

\_\_\_\_ 10. Klansmen are more likely to be aggressive when wearing their robes than when dressed in everyday clothing.

## INFERENCES: Test E-2

A. Following is Edward Arlington Robinson's well-known poem about a wealthy man named Richard Cory. Read the poem, and then check the *five* statements which are most logically supported by the information given.

*Clean favored:* privileged to be clean (since he did no manual work).
*imperially:* in a superior way (since the rich had a superior, more healthy diet than the poor)
*quietly arrayed:* not dressed in a showy manner

### Richard Cory

Whenever Richard Cory went down town,
We people on the pavement looked at him;
He was a gentleman from sole to crown,
Clean favored, and imperially slim.

And he was always quietly arrayed,
And he was always human when he talked;
But still he fluttered pulses when he said
"Good-morning," and he glittered when he walked.

And he was rich—yes, richer than a king,
And admirably schooled in every grace;
In fine, we thought that he was everything
To make us wish that we were in his place.

So on we worked, and waited for the light,
And went without the meat, and cursed the bread;
And Richard Cory, one calm summer night,
Went home and put a bullet through his head.

____ 1. Richard Cory treated the poor disrespectfully.
____ 2. Richard Cory had many personal friends.
____ 3. The speaker is poor.
____ 4. Richard Cory was admired.
____ 5. Richard Cory was married.
____ 6. The poor people in town envied Richard Cory.
____ 7. Richard Cory had an unhappy love affair.
____ 8. Richard Cory was not as fortunate as he seemed.
____ 9. The poor preferred bread to meat.
____ 10. Money does not buy happiness.

*(Continues on next page)*

**B.** Read the following passage from *The Language of Clothes* by writer and educator Alison Lurie, and then check the *five* statements which are most logically supported by the information given.

*banal:* not interesting or attractive

In the past, sexual modesty was often proposed as the purpose of dress. The Bible tells us that this was the original reason for wearing clothes: Adam and Eve, once they realized that they were naked, "sewed fig leaves together, and made themselves aprons." Historically, however, shame seems to have played very little part in the development of costume. In ancient Egypt, Crete and Greece the naked body was not considered immodest; slaves and athletes habitually went without clothing, while people of high rank wore garments that were cut and draped so as to show a good deal when in motion.

Some modern writers believe that the deliberate concealment of certain parts of the body originated not as a way of discouraging sexual interest, but as a clever device for arousing it. According to this view, clothes are the physical equivalent of remarks like "I've got a secret"; they are a tease, a come-on. It is certainly true that parts of the human form considered sexually arousing are often covered in such a way as to exaggerate and draw attention to them. People done up in shiny colored wrappings and bows affect us just as a birthday present does: we're curious, turned on; we want to undo the package. . . .

Many visitors to nudist camps report that the sight of all that uncovered flesh brings fatigue and a sense of being slightly unwell. Later, after one gets used to it as the ancients were, it seems merely banal.

____ 1. The author spends a good deal of time studying the Bible.

____ 2. Every culture has agreed on the purpose of dress.

____ 3. Sexual modesty is one trait that means the same to all cultures.

____ 4. In ancient Egypt, Crete, and Greece, people showed more of their bodies than we do.

____ 5. In ancient Egypt, Crete, and Greece, athletes were slaves.

____ 6. Clothing and sexuality are related.

____ 7. The passage suggests that nudity in nudist camps generally leads to loose sexual behavior.

____ 8. In a society without clothing, the naked body is not particularly thrilling.

____ 9. We might conclude from the passage that a tight dress can be more sexy to some than a topless bathing suit.

____ 10. Behavior we consider basic may not be basic to other cultures.

## INFERENCES: Test E-3

After reading each passage, circle the letter of the best answer to each question.

A.  In the mid-1970s the networks tried to break down traditional viewing habits by introducing a new format, the mini-series. The idea was to get people hooked on the series in the first episode—usually broadcast on Sunday night—so they would tune in again the next several evenings. Mini-series have proven very popular, and they are often scheduled during "sweep periods," when TV stations are monitored to determine audience sizes. (Sweeps are usually conducted three times a year—November, February and May—and are used to set advertising rates. High ratings means higher ad rates for the local stations and networks.)

   The mini-series concept actually came from public broadcasting, which began showing BBC-produced serials such as *The Forsyte Saga* in 1969 and *Upstairs Downstairs*.

1. Since mini-series usually begin on Sunday nights, we can conclude that
   a. the first episode usually lasts an hour.
   b. mini-series appeal to the most religious Americans.
   c. many Americans watch TV on Sunday nights.
   d. there are usually fewer TV ads on Sunday nights.

2. Advertisers probably like mini-series because
   a. they are educational.
   b. they are more wholesome than many other TV shows.
   c. their popularity means many people will see the show's ads.
   d. the networks might charge less for ads during mini-series.

3. From the passage, we can conclude that public broadcasting
   a. broadcasts ads during its mini-series.
   b. influenced the networks.
   c. has "sweep periods."
   d. would not begin its serials on Sunday nights.

B.  In colonial America, anyone could become a physician merely by adopting the label. There were no medical schools or medical societies to license or regulate what was a free-for-all trade. Sometimes clergymen tried to provide medical care to their parishioners, and care of a sort was offered by all kinds of laypeople as well. Documents of the time record a doctor who sold "tea, sugar, olives, grapes, anchovies, raisins, and prunes" along with medicinals, and also tell of a woman who "Acts here in the Double Capacity of a Doctoress and Coffee Woman." Training for medical practice, such as it was, was given by apprenticeship.

4. In comparison to today, a medical practice in colonial America
   a. must have been harder to establish.
   b. must have been more expensive to establish.
   c. probably required more study.
   d. was less likely to be full-time.

*(Continues on next page)*

5. Considering the medical training of that time, we might conclude
   a. most doctors did medical research.
   b. people were lucky to get good medical care.
   c. very few people would have been considered qualified to be medical apprentices.
   d. all of the above.

C.   Calvin Klein and Gloria Vanderbilt are both jeans designers whose products were widely purchased by teens and preteens in the early 1980s. These jeans were considered a high-fashion item, and manufacturers knew that their popularity might not last. Market studies show that parents are willing to purchase high-fashion items for their youngsters during reasonably good economic times. However, let general economic activity decline by as much as 1 percent, and one can anticipate that the sales of high-fashion items will decline about 15 percent. To compensate for this possible decline, the manufacturers of Vanderbilt and Klein jeans charged approximately 25 to 30 percent more for a pair of jeans than more conservative, mass-producing manufacturers. Of course, an additional risk was also incurred. Prospective customers could have refused to pay the amount demanded for the jeans, preferring instead to buy less expensive ones produced and labeled for K-Mart, Penney's, or Wards. In this instance, however, designer jeans did prove highly successful. Parents were willing to spend the extra cash for a Klein or Vanderbilt label.

6. The passage clearly implies that designer jeans are priced higher in order to
   a. better compete with jeans from K-Mart, Penney's, and Wards.
   b. cover the decline in sales that would result if the economy weakened.
   c. pay for the high-fashion labels.
   d. all of the above.

7. The passage suggests that
   a. high-fashion jeans are more risky to make and sell than "mass-produced" jeans.
   b. high-fashion jeans can be more profitable than "mass-produced" jeans.
   c. sales of "mass-produced" jeans suffer less than high-fashion jeans do when the economy weakens.
   d. all of the above.

8. In the early 1980s, the country's economy must have been
   a. relatively strong.
   b. at its all-time peak.
   c. about to change.
   d. quite weak.

# 8

# Purpose
# and Tone

An important part of reading critically is realizing that behind everything you read is an author. This author is a person who has a reason for writing a given piece and who works from a personal point of view. To fully understand and evaluate what you read, you must recognize *purpose*—the reason why the author writes. You must also be aware of *tone*—the expression of the author's attitude and feeling. Both purpose and tone are discussed in this chapter.

## PURPOSE

Authors write with a reason in mind, and you can better evaluate what is being said by determining what that reason is. The author's reason for writing is also called the *purpose* of a selection. Three common purposes are:

- **To inform**—to give information about a subject. Authors with this purpose wish to give their readers facts.

- **To persuade**—to convince the reader to agree with the author's point of view on a subject. Authors with this purpose may give facts, but their main goal is to promote an opinion.

- **To entertain**—to amuse and delight; to appeal to the reader's senses and imagination. Authors with this purpose entertain in various ways, through fiction and nonfiction.

Read each of the three paragraphs below and decide whether the author's purpose is to inform, to persuade, or to entertain. Write in your answers, and then read the explanations that follow.

1.  Using the present measurement system is as inefficient and old-fashioned as using Roman numerals. If more Americans realized how easy it is to convert milliliters to liters as opposed to converting tablespoons to quarts, the metric system would be adopted immediately.

    Purpose: _____

2.  About 113 billion people have lived and died in the history of our planet, according to scientific estimates. Of all these people, the names of about seven billion, or approximately 6 percent, are recorded in some way—on monuments or in books, manuscripts, and public records. The other 106 billion people are gone without a trace.

    Purpose: _____

3.  Because of the contrast between his medium-size wardrobe and his extra-large-size body, my brother has made a commitment to only three meals a day. His definition of a meal, however, is as broad as his belly. If we spot a pretzel salesman or a hot-dog stand on our way to an Italian restaurant, for example, he is not beyond suggesting that we stop. "It'll make a good appetizer," he says.

    Purpose: _____

In the first paragraph, the writer's purpose is to *persuade* the audience that Americans should change over to the metric system. That is clear because the author claims that our present system is "inefficient and old-fashioned," that conversions in the metric system are "easy," and that people would prefer the metric system. These are statements that are used to convince us rather than to inform us. The purpose of the second paragraph is to *inform*. The author is simply providing readers with information about the people who have lived and died on Earth. In paragraph three, the playful and exaggerated details tell us the author's main goal is to *entertain* with humor.

At times, writing may seem to blend two purposes. An informative article on losing weight, for example, may include comic touches, or a persuasive letter to the editor may contain factual information. Remember in such cases to focus on the author's primary purpose. Ask yourself, "What is the author's main idea?" That will help you determine his or her principal intention.

## ➤ *Practice 1*

Label each item according to its main purpose: to inform (**I**), to persuade (**P**), or to entertain (**E**).

_____ 1. In the 1886 baseball World Series, sixty-three errors were committed.

_____ 2. Nurses assigned to intensive care units should be given shorter shifts and higher pay because the work is unusually demanding and stressful.

_____ 3. It's easy to quit smoking; I've done it hundreds of times.

_____ 4. Shoparama has low, low prices, an outstanding selection of health and beauty products, and a convenient location near you.

_____ 5. The career of a professional athlete is usually quite short.

_____ 6. An artificial odor is added to natural gas so that people can tell whether or not gas is leaking.

_____ 7. Fred believes in a seafood diet: when he sees food, he eats it.

_____ 8. More women should get involved in local politics and support the growing number of female candidates for public office.

_____ 9. The best approach to take when you feel the urge to exercise is to lie down quickly in a darkened room until the feeling goes away.

_____ 10. In ancient Egypt, priests plucked all the hair from their bodies, including their eyebrows and eyelashes.

## ➤ *Practice 2*

Following are three passages: from a textbook, a humor book, and a collection of essays. Label each item according to its main purpose: to inform (**I**), to persuade (**P**), or to entertain (**E**).

_____ 1. We have all heard the story of how the young, impoverished Abraham Lincoln trekked miles to borrow books from a neighbor and then read them by firelight. We know that nineteenth-century readers would rush to the wharf to greet the ship carrying the latest chapters of a Dickens novel. Today, reading seems less urgent and less exciting to many of us. Worse, few people impart a passion for books to their children. Instead, they leave the children in front of the television and hope, weakly, that too much watching won't be bad for them. But we cannot afford to stop reading. Books shed a light that illuminates our problems and crises. They are also mirrors that reflect the truest image of ourselves.

_____ 2. Most of what I know about carpentry, which is almost nothing, I learned in Shop. You should know that I took Shop during the Eisenhower administration, when boys took Shop and girls took Home Economics—a code name for "cooking." Schools are not allowed to separate boys and girls like that anymore. They're also not allowed to put students' heads in vises and tighten them, which is what our Shop teacher, Mr Schmidt, did to Ronnie Miller in the fifth grade when Ronnie used a chisel when he should have used a screwdriver. (Mr. Schmidt had strong feelings abut how to use tools properly.) I guess he shouldn't have put Ronnie's head in the vise, but it (Ronnie's head) was no great prize to begin with, and you can bet Ronnie never confused chisels and screwdrivers in later life—assuming he made it to later life.

_____ 3. Studies of job satisfaction indicate that the vast majority of workers are at least somewhat satisfied with their jobs and would continue to work even if they didn't have to. The meaning of work varies from person to person. To some, it is a course of self-respect and life purpose. For others, work is a means of passing time. To still others, it is primarily a source of financial independence. Among women, available work is often less satisfying than home management. Yet, most women report increases in self-esteem when employed, especially if they experience support from their families.

## TONE

A writer's tone reveals the attitude he or she has toward a subject. Tone is expressed through the words and details the writer selects. Just as a speaker's voice can project a range of feelings, a writer's voice can project one or more tones, or feelings: anger, sympathy, hopefulness, sadness, respect, dislike, and so on. Understanding tone is, then, an important part of understanding what an author has written.

To appreciate the differences in tone that writers can employ, read the following versions of a murder confession:

"I just shot my husband five times in the chest with this .357 Magnum." (_Tone:_ matter-of-fact, objective.)

"How could I ever have killed him? I just can't believe I did that!" (_Tone:_ shocked, disbelieving.)

"Oh, my God. I've murdered my husband. How can I ever be forgiven for this dreadful deed?" (_Tone:_ remorseful, regretful)

"That dirty rat. He's had it coming for years. I'm glad I finally had the nerve to do it." (_Tone:_ revengeful, triumphant)

Below is a list of words commonly used to describe tone. Note that two different words may refer to the same tone or similar tones—for example, matter-of-fact and objective, or comic and humorous. Brief meanings are given in parentheses for some of the words.

*A List of Words That Describe Tone*

| | |
|---|---|
| straightforward | cheerful |
| matter-of-fact | joyous |
| objective | light-hearted |
| serious | amused |
| formal | humorous |
| informal | comic |
| solemn | playful |
| bitter | outspoken *(spoken boldly and freely)* |
| sorrowful | impassioned *(filled with passion and strong feeling)* |
| depressed | tolerant *(respecting of other views and behavior)* |
| distressed | remorseful *(filled with guilt over a wrong one has done)* |
| angry | outraged *(very angered)* |
| critical | sarcastic *(making sharp or wounding remarks; ironic)* |
| cruel | mocking *(ridiculing; sneering; holding up for scorn)* |
| hesitant | scornful *(looking down on someone or something)* |
| fearful | ironic *(meaning the opposite of what is expressed)* |
| anxious | arrogant *(conceited)* |
| alarmed | irreverent *(lacking respect)* |
| tragic | cynical *(believing the worst of others)* |
| self-pitying | indignant *(angry about something unfair or mean)* |
| disbelieving | revengeful *(wanting to hurt someone in return for an injury)* |
| surprised | vindictive *(very revengeful)* |
| regretful | malicious *(spiteful; intentionally harmful)* |
| sympathetic | contemptuous *(expressing great scorn and disgust)* |
| compassionate | ambivalent *(uncertain about a choice)* |
| loving | optimistic *(looking on the bright side of things)* |
| sentimental | pessimistic *(looking on the gloomy side of things)* |
| forgiving | desperate *(having a great desire or need for something)* |
| excited | grim *(harsh; dealing with unpleasant subjects)* |

## More About Tone

Below are five statements expressing different attitudes about a shabby apartment. Five different tones are used:

| | | |
|---|---|---|
| optimistic | tolerant | humorous |
| bitter | sentimental | |

Label each statement according to which of these five tones you think is present. Then read the explanation that follows.

_____ 1. This place may be shabby, but since both of my children were born while we lived here, it has a special place in my heart.

_____ 2. This isn't the greatest apartment in the world, but it's not really that bad.

_____ 3. If only there were some decent jobs out there, I wouldn't be reduced to living in this miserable dump.

_____ 4. This place does need some repairs, but I expect the landlord to get around to them any day now.

_____ 5. When we move away, we're planning to release three hundred cockroaches and two mice so we can leave the place exactly as we found it.

The tone of item 1 is *sentimental.* "It has a special place in my heart" expresses tender emotions. In item 2, the words "not really that bad" show that the writer is *tolerant,* accepting the situation while recognizing that it could be better. We could describe the tone of item 3 as *bitter.* The writer resents a situation that he blames for forcing him to live in a "miserable dump." Item 4 is *optimistic* since the writer is expecting the apartment to be improved soon. Finally, the tone of item 5 is *humorous.* Its writer claims to be planning a comic revenge on the landlord by returning the apartment to the intolerable condition it was in when the tenants moved in.

## A Note on Irony

One commonly used tone is that of *irony.* When writing has an ironic tone, it says one thing but means the opposite. Irony is found in everyday conversation as well as in writing. Following are a few examples; notice that the quotation in each says the opposite of what is meant.

If at the beginning of a semester you discover that one of your teachers is particularly demanding, you might comment, "This class is sure going to be a barrel of laughs!"

After seeing a terrible performance in a movie, someone might say about the actor involved, "Now there's a person with a great chance for an Oscar."

If a person is a klutz, someone might remark, "There goes an Olympic champion."

Irony also refers to situations in which what happens is the opposite of what we might expect. We could call it ironic, for example, if a man bites a dog. So another way for a writer to be ironic is to describe such situations. Here are a few more examples of this type of irony:

Helen won a lifetime supply of Marlboros a week after she quit smoking.

To get some quick extra cash, Elliot sold his stereo. For his birthday the next day, his girlfriend bought him the new Whitney Houston album.

Lenny, who adores basketball, is five feet five inches tall. His brother Frank, who plans on being a cartoonist and has no interest at all in sports, is six feet three.

## ➤ *Practice 3*

**A.** Below are five statements expressing different attitudes about a boss. Five different tones are used:

| | | |
|---|---|---|
| admiring | sympathetic | objective |
| ironic | critical | |

For each statement, write the tone that you think is present.

_____ 1. Tony is an excellent manager—the best one I've ever had.

_____ 2. I know Tony's boy has been sick. Naturally it's hard for him to concentrate on work right now.

_____ 3. Tony's too ambitious for his own good. That ambition may yet destroy him and the company.

_____ 4. Under Tony Robertson's leadership, sales in the appliance division have increased 30 per cent in the last six months.

_____ 5. Tony's wonderful, all right. He's gotten as far as he has without the slightest idea of how to manage a division.

**B.** The following conversation between a mother and son involves five of the tones shown in the box below. For each statement, write the tone that you think is present.

| | | | |
|---|---|---|---|
| threatening | joyful | solemn | straightforward |
| sympathetic | pessimistic | self-pitying | ironic |
| nostalgic | disbelieving | | |

_____  6. "Please take the garbage out on your way to school this morning."

_____  7. "Sure, Mom. I've been looking forward to that chore all morning."

_____  8. "Listen, young man, if you don't start fulfilling your responsibilities around this house, your father and I will start asking you for rent or to find your own place."

_____  9. "Okay, I'll take the garbage out. But you know it's not easy going to school full-time, working twenty hours a week, and just getting over a bad case of the flu."

_____  10. "I know, honey, this semester has been an especially difficult one for you."

## ➤ Practice 4

Each passage illustrates one of the tones in the box below. In each space, put the letter of the tone that best applies. Don't use any letter more than once.

Remember that the tone of a selection reflects the author's attitude. To find the tone of a paragraph, ask yourself what attitude is revealed by its words and phrases.

| | | | |
|---|---|---|---|
| a. arrogant | b. forgiving | c. worried | d. sorrowful |
| e. revengeful | f. affectionate | g. hypocritical | h. scornful |

\_\_\_\_\_  1. Spam—that slimy canned pork product—is surprisingly still around after more than fifty years. Despite its high fat content (more than three and a half teaspoons per two-ounce serving) and high calorie count (171 calories per serving), more than four billion cans have been sold since 1937. Spam's greasy, rubbery consistency and salty flavor have made it the butt of many jokes—such as David Letterman's suggestion of Spam-on-a-rope for people who want to eat and shower at the same time. Shareholders in George Hormel and

Company must be laughing all the way to the bank. More than three cans of Spam are consumed every second, despite its high cost—pound for pound it costs about the same as strip steak.

_____ 2. My grandfather lived with my family as I grew up, and some of my warmest early memories revolve around him. He was a sweet man with simple tastes. He liked Western movies, and when I was a preschooler, he often took me along to see them. After the movies, we would go to a nearby Bridgeman's ice-cream shop. He would order a hot chocolate. It always came with a couple of sugar cookies, which he would give to me to eat with my scoop of ice cream. Once I began school, he would go to the Westerns alone. But it wasn't unusual for me to come home from school and find those same sugar cookies waiting for me in a Bridgeman's napkin.

_____ 3. By the year 2000 there will be nearly ten million Americans over the age of eighty. Can we expect these people to be cared for by their relatives, who are themselves in their sixties? If the caregivers are retired, they may have more time to take care of older family members, but the costs of such care (especially in terms of retirement income) are high. As the retirees grow older, the task of caring for older people becomes harder. This is made more difficult by the fact that old age can be distressing because it is a time of continual loss. Too often adults take in ailing, elderly relatives without being aware that they are taking on an immense full-time job. Such caregivers should have somewhere to turn for help.

_____ 4. Are you on my list? If you know me, you may well be. See, I keep a record of everyone who's ever crossed me. Whether it's for making fun of my new dress or stealing my boyfriend, I believe in getting mad and getting even. It may take a while, but I settle the score with everyone on my list—the girl who made fun of my dress, for example. It took me a whole year to get back at her. Finally, one night a date took me to a party she gave. I took advantage of the opportunity and spilled red nail polish on the white rug in her powder room. That night, I took great satisfaction in crossing her name off my list.

_____ 5. My mother died a week after I had given birth to my first child. Mother and I had both wanted desperately for her to see little Emily. And Mom had managed to hang on for months, despite the cancer that was ravaging her body. I had just spoken to her the night before, and my plans were to bring Emily the fifty miles to see Mom that weekend. "I'm going to do it," Mom had said. "I'm going to hold my granddaughter before I die." But it was not to be.

## ➤ *Review*

To review what you've learned in this chapter, complete each of the following sentences about purpose and tone.

1. What is the purpose of each type of writing below? Label each according to its usual main purpose: to inform, to persuade, or to entertain.

    A news report: _____

    A mystery novel: _____

    An editorial: _____

2. *Complete the sentence:* The tone of a selection reveals the author's _____ toward his or her subject.

3. An ironic comment is one that means the _____ of what is said. For example, if everything goes wrong after a person gets up in the morning (there is no hot water for the shower, milk for the cereal is sour, a pool of oil is under the car, and so on), a person might ironically make which of the following statements: *(circle one letter)*
    a. "What a lousy start to the day."
    b. "What a great day this is going to be."
    c. "Good grief. What did I do to deserve this?"

# PURPOSE AND TONE: Test A-1

**A.** In the space provided, indicate whether the primary purpose of each sentence is to inform (**I**), to persuade (**P**), or to entertain (**E**).

_____ 1. The average dollar bill lasts about eighteen months.

_____ 2. With funerals so expensive, I'd better not die soon; I can't afford to.

_____ 3. Every car built in America should have air bags on both the driver and the passenger side.

_____ 4. Federal taxes must be raised so that we can afford a national health program.

_____ 5. The world's first ads were neither printed nor broadcast electronically; they were vocal, called out by street peddlers promoting their wares.

_____ 6. Instead of nagging my father to lose weight, my mother bought him an extra-large T-shirt imprinted with the message "This space for rent."

_____ 7. For our children's sake, TV networks should reduce the number of ads shown during children's programs.

**B.** Each of the following passages illustrates one of the tones named in the box below. In the space provided, write the letter of the tone that applies to the passage. Two tone choices will be left over.

| | | |
|---|---|---|
| a. revengeful | b. angry | c. sentimental |
| d. comic | e. matter-of-fact | |

_____ 8. Spicy foods such as those found in Indian, Thai and Mexican cuisine have become increasingly popular in recent years. If you like such foods, you may have discovered that drinking water does not take away the burning sensation they cause in your mouth—in fact, water may make it seem worse. That is because the hot flavorings in foods are oil-based. As you eat hot foods, spicy oils coat your tongue and throat. Water cannot break down and wash away that clinging layer of oil. Milk, however, because of its fatty content, breaks down the oil and relieves that burning sensation.

*(Continues on next page)*

_____ 9. Emperor penguins are among the most adorable animals in the world. Like all penguins, they look like cute little people dressed in tuxedos. They flap their wings and waddle into the water in an utterly charming way. The most enchanting thing they do is care for their sweet little babies. The newborn chick squats on its father's feet, where it is warmed by his body and cared for affectionately until its mother returns from a hunting trip to find food. Emperor penguins love their babies so much that they have been known to try to hatch blocks of ice if their own little ones die. This is a delightful testimony to the power of parental affection.

_____ 10. When I agreed in September to put out the newsletter, I wanted to create something that would unite our community. Now, due to lack of support from you, I must discontinue. I had assumed that residents would welcome and support the newsletter. Only one resident, Cindy Sherwood, answered my pleas for help with distributing the newsletter. I have been willing to volunteer a great deal of time to working on this project, yet no one was interested enough to meet with me and discuss it. There has been a total lack of response when I asked for ideas and input. It seems that I'm the only person in this community who really cares.

## PURPOSE AND TONE: Test A-2

**A.** Eight quotations in the story below are preceded by a blank space. Identify the tone of each italicized quotation by writing in the letter of one of these tones. (Two tone choices will be left over.)

| | | | |
|---|---|---|---|
| a. joyous | b. surprised | c. sarcastic | d. amused |
| e. curious | f. sympathetic | g. regretful | h. self-pitying |
| i. helpful | j. insulting | | |

Noreen and Ron were taking a coffee break together at work. Ron slumped over the table, looking depressed.

_____ 1.   *"Poor Ron,"* Noreen said. *"You still don't like working here, do you? It's written all over your face."*

_____ 2.   *"I guess I'm just unlucky with bosses,"* replied Ron. *"Since the day I arrived, nothing I've done has been quite right for Mr. Hunter."*

_____ 3.   "Well, why don't you give me some examples of what you mean?" said Noreen. "Maybe we can figure out how you and he can work together better."

_____ 4.   *"Just take my word for it,"* said Ron, *"the guy is a grade-A jerk."*

_____ 5.   Noreen's mouth fell open. *"I'm shocked to hear you say that, Ron."* She continued, "I've worked with Bob Hunter for six years, and the man is not a jerk."

_____ 6.   *"Oh, sorry!"* said Ron. *"I take it all back then! Mr. Hunter is actually the most wonderful human being I've ever met. I didn't realize you two were best buddies."*

Ron pushed his chair away from the table and stamped away. Shaking her head, Noreen watched him go. Then another co-worker, Emily, stopped by the table.

_____ 7. *"Gee, what's up with Ron?"* asked Emily. "He looks like a thunder-cloud."

_____ 8. *"It's a shame,"* Noreen said. *"Ron is a bright guy and he could do well in business. Instead, he works only half as hard as he should and then insists that everyone's out to get him. With his attitude, he's going to have trouble succeeding anywhere."*

*(Continues on next page)*

B. In the space provided, indicate whether the primary purpose of each passage is to inform (I), to persuade (P), or to entertain (E). (Remember that persuasive passages often contain facts—facts that support the author's views.)

_____ 9. All animals that move have home ranges. A "home range" is the area in which an animal finds food, mates, and cares for its young. Some animals are also territorial. This means that they claim certain areas for their use only. Other members of their species are excluded from their territory. Controlling territories singly or in pairs is the most efficient way to use an abundant and predictable food supply. Some birds and bottom-dwelling fish have this type of territory. On the other hand, group control of territories works best when the food supply is unpredictable or unevenly distributed. Baboons, wolves, hyenas, and lions have group territories.

_____ 10. Large, expensive high schools are a waste of the taxpayers' money. Helping to prove this point is Community High School, a small private Philadelphia school that teaches public school rejects and refugees. This is no high-tech heaven. Once a factory, the school has no labs or gym facilities. In fact, science is taught in the lunch room, and classes are large. But the school itself is small, with a friendly, caring staff. The school's size means that everyone there can know everyone else. Community High School is thus like a large, extended family. While a nearby, multi-million-dollar high school on a twenty-acre campus has a 66 percent attendance, Community's attendance averages 87 percent. In addition, of those students who make it past the first six months at Community, 90 percent graduate. Most graduates go on to a community college, the military or a job.

Write to your local politicians and school boards, and demand an end to large, impersonal high schools that are failing our children.

# PURPOSE AND TONE: Test A-3

This activity will give you practice in recognizing the purpose and tone of a selection. Read each of the paragraphs below. Then carefully consider the questions that follow and circle the best responses.

A.   According to memory experts, there are ways you can improve your chances of remembering the names of people you meet. One way is to make associations between a person's name and looks. For example, if you meet a man named Baker, you might picture him wearing a baker's hat. If the name is a difficult one, ask for the spelling and visualize the letters mentally. It's also useful to repeat the person's name as you converse, keeping your mental images in mind. And when your conversation ends, it is helpful to repeat the person's name as you say goodbye.

   1. The primary purpose of this paragraph is
      a. to inform.
      b. to persuade.
      c. to entertain.

   2. The overall tone of this paragraph can be described as
      a. critical and angry.
      b. obviously humorous.
      c. doubtful.
      d. straightforward and instructive.

B.   Columbus Day is meant to honor Christopher Columbus. But does he deserve that honor? Many believe that Leif Ericson discovered America much earlier. In addition, Columbus was cruel to many natives. Finally, how could he "discover" a land that was already populated by others? Isn't it time to get rid of a holiday that celebrates this type of person and achievement?

   3. The primary purpose of this paragraph is
      a. to inform.
      b. to persuade.
      c. to entertain.

   4. The tone of this paragraph can be described as
      a. anxious and fearful.
      b. playful and amused.
      c. serious and critical.
      d. detached and strictly factual.

*(Continues on next page)*

C. My memory is slipping away like a greased pig in a chute, which can be aggravating. This year, for instance, I forgot not only one of my grandchildren's birthdays but also my own. That was a big blunder because the only way my husband remembers my birthday is if I remember to call his secretary and remind her to remind him. In addition, last week, believe it or not, I drove the car to work and then took the bus home. Sometimes, however, a bad memory can be useful. For example, while forgetting my birthday may be a problem, forgetting my age is not.

5. The author's main purpose in writing this paragraph is
   a. to inform.
   b. to persuade.
   c. to entertain.

6. The tone of this paragraph can be described as
   a. worried and fearful.
   b. objective and factual.
   c. intense and complex.
   d. humorous and light.

D. I contend that walking is a more practical form of exercise than running. Walking a mile takes longer than running a mile, but it is nearly as good for the heart. Walking is also a "low-impact" exercise that does not subject bones and joints to the damage that can result from "high-impact" exercises such as running or playing basketball. In addition, walking is a way to get to know your neighborhood; you can pause to say hello to an acquaintance without breaking your rhythm or concentration. Furthermore, walking isn't as sweaty as other exercises. You can walk during your lunch break and not have to change your clothes or take a shower afterwards. Want a good, pleasant exercise? Take a walk!

7. The primary purpose of this paragraph is
   a. to simply inform readers of facts about walking and running.
   b. to persuade readers that walking is a more practical exercise than running.
   c. to entertain readers with amusing facts and opinions about walking and running.

8. The author's tone is
   a. understanding and compassionate.
   b. arrogant and outspoken.
   c. straightforward and enthusiastic.
   d. joyous but hesitant.

# PURPOSE AND TONE: Test B-1

**A.** In the space provided, indicate whether the primary purpose of each sentence is to inform (**I**), to persuade (**P**), or to entertain (**E**).

_____ 1. The best time to be in New York is in the spring. The warmer weather makes being mugged more pleasant.

_____ 2. The average human body is covered with 14 to 18 square feet of skin.

_____ 3. During World War II, entire sections of London were destroyed by German bombs.

_____ 4. Every family ought to install Sentry Smoke Detectors on each floor of their home.

_____ 5. Rachel says she eats a balanced diet by choosing items from the four major food groups: chips, soda pop, candy, and pastries.

_____ 6. By selling junk food like soda and candy in the lunchroom, public schools are teaching poor nutrition. Such "lessons" should not be allowed.

_____ 7. A cup of caramel popcorn has 7.1 grams of fat and 154 calories; a cup of plain popcorn has .3 grams of fat and 23 calories.

**B.** Each of the following passages illustrates one of the tones named in the box below. In the space provided, write the letter of the tone that applies to the passage. Two tone choices will be left over.

| | | |
|---|---|---|
| a. admiring | b. forgiving | c. distressed |
| d. sarcastic | e. hesitant | |

_____ 8. I can't thank Rob and Elsie sincerely enough for introducing me to Sheila. They promised me she was exactly my type, and how accurate they were—I've been yearning for a vain, shallow woman with the IQ of a turnip. Sheila and I hit it off immediately. When I picked her up in my Ford Escort, she wrinkled her adorable nose with exasperation and said, "I thought Elsie said you had a decent car." I took her to eat at Luigi's and was thrilled by the way she sneered and said, "You *are* a cheapskate, aren't you?" When I suggested we see a foreign film, and she announced that she never sees anything with subtitles because she hates to read, I wanted to marry her on the spot. I'll certainly have to think of some way to repay my dear friends for setting me up with such a marvelous girl.

*(Continues on next page)*

_____ 9. I believe Tina Turner is a terrific role model for anyone who thinks he or she cannot overcome obstacles early in life. Turner grew up in poverty, survived an abusive marriage, and dealt with dishonest business associates early in her career. Many people might have just given in at any point along the way. But Turner had the determination and inner strength to go it alone. Doing it her way, she first became a superstar when she was in her fortiess, when she finally received the money, the acclaim and the respect she always deserved but had been deprived of. Not only is Turner talented and tough-minded; she has proved that beauty and sex appeal can be ageless. Way to go, Tina!

_____ 10. It was about forty yards to the gallows. I watched the bare brown back of the prisoner marching in front of me. He walked clumsily with his bound arms, but quite steadily, with that bobbing gait of the Indian who never straightens his knees. At each step his muscles slid neatly into place, the lock of hair on his scalp danced up and down, his feet printed themselves on the wet gravel. And once, in spite of the men who gripped him by each shoulder, he stepped slightly aside to avoid a puddle on the path.

It is curious, but till that moment I had never realized what it means to destroy a healthy, conscious man. When I saw the prisoner step aside to avoid the puddle, I saw the mystery, the unspeakable wrongness, of cutting a life short when it is in full tide. This man was not dying; he was alive just as we were alive. All the organs of his body were working—bowels digesting food, skin renewing itself, nails growing, tissues forming—all toiling away. . . His nails would still be growing when he stood on the drop, when he was falling through the air with a tenth of a second to live. His eyes saw the yellow gravel and the grey walls, and his brain still remembered, foresaw, reasoned—reasoned even about puddles. He and we were a party of men walking together, seeing, hearing, feeling, understanding the same world; and in two minutes, with a sudden snap, one of us would be gone—one mind less, one world less.

## PURPOSE AND TONE: Test B-2

A. Eight quotations in the story below are preceded by a blank space. Identify the tone of each italicized quotation by writing in the letter of one of these tones. (Two tone choices will be left over.)

| | | | |
|---|---|---|---|
| a. sympathetic | b. straightforward | c. pleading | d. angry |
| e. superior | f. excited | g. depressed | h. scheming |
| i. curious | j. frightened | | |

The television reporter knocked on the door of the small row home. A woman opened the door.

_____ 1. *"My name is Tod Hunter,"* the reporter said. *"I'm with Action News, and I'd like to talk to the woman who lost her daughter in the school fire last night."*

"Oh, I'm sorry, but she's not much in the mood for visitors."

"I understand," the reporter said. "Please tell her that we only want a moment of her time."

While the woman was gone, the reporter turned to his crew.

_____ 2. *"You could shoot from this angle,"* he whispered, *"but let's try to get inside. If she's at all responsive to my questions, let's gradually move in through the doorway."*

Children in the neighborhood crowded around the TV crew.

_____ 3. *"Those are TV cameras!"* some shouted, laughing. *"Wow, real TV cameras!"*

_____ 4. Pausing to look at the crew standing outside the house, a passerby asked, *"What do you suppose happened there?"*

Then the mother of the fire victim appeared at the door, looking drawn and exhausted. "What do you want?"

_____ 5. *"I'm really very sorry for your great loss, Ma'am."* Hunter continued, "I'm here for Action News. Do you know what caused the fire?"

"Please, no interviews."

"Our viewers want to know about this awful fire."

_____ 6. *"The people can go to blazes! It's none of their business!"* Then the woman pointed at the reporter. *"It's none of your business, either, Mister!"*

_____ 7. *"Run! She's mad!"* shouted the children as they raced away.

_____ 8. *"All I want is two minutes,"* the reporter said. *"Please, just two minutes of your time."*

But the door had already slammed in his face. "Let's get out of here," the frustrated reporter said to his crew. "I'm starved."

*(Continues on next page)*

**B.** In the space provided, indicate whether the primary purpose of each passage is to inform (**I**), to persuade (**P**), or to entertain (**E**). (Remember that persuasive passages often contain facts—facts that support the author's views.)

_____ 9. Cats are allowed to roam just about wherever they please (try and stop them), and even dogs have the run of the house, or at least of a portion of the house. But pet birds are generally limited for most of their lives to the space defined by the four sides of a small cage. Yet birds are born to flap and swoop through wide spaces of sky, unlimited neither by walls nor ceilings. To keep a creature born with wings in a small space, unable to use its major natural means of transportation, is unfair. People who want birds as pets should at least find ways to allow the birds to fly freely within one or two rooms of the house.

_____ 10. Robert Todd Lincoln, the oldest son of President Abraham Lincoln, had the unhappy privilege of being present for three presidential assassinations. On April 14, 1865, Robert arrived home from college to see his parents. That night, his father was shot while attending the theater. Robert stayed with him through the night until President Lincoln died. Sixteen years later, Robert, then serving as secretary of war, traveled to a Washington train station to meet President James Garfield. He arrived just in time to see Garfield shot by an assassin. In 1901, Robert experienced yet another presidential assassination. He had taken his family to Buffalo, New York, to meet President William McKinley. As the Lincolns arrived, they were greeted with the news that McKinley had been shot.

# PURPOSE AND TONE: Test B-3

This activity will give you practice in recognizing the purpose and tone of a selection. Read each of the paragraphs below. Then carefully consider the questions that follow and circle the best responses.

A.  The list of birds that have become extinct includes the dodo, which has resulted in the expression "dead as a dodo." The world first learned about the dodo from a Dutch explorer who visited the Mauritius Islands, located in the Indian Ocean, in 1598. When he returned from the islands to Europe, he brought two of the odd-looking birds with him. The dodos were fat creatures about three times the size of turkeys. Their tiny wings did not permit them to fly; furthermore, the birds were unable to run or climb trees. In yet another blow to the dodo's chances of survival, the female laid just one egg each year. Once Dutch colonists on Mauritius, visiting sailors, and their domestic animals learned how easy it was to catch and eat the dodos and their eggs, they disappeared quickly. By 1681, the world's population of dodos was gone.

   1. The primary purpose of the passage is
      a. to inform.
      b. to persuade.
      c. to entertain.

   2. The tone of the passage can be described as
      a. amused.
      b. bitter.
      c. straightforward.
      d. cruel.

B.  Throughout history, people have suffered from ailments that could have been easily avoided if they had only been understood. For instance, it used to be common for hat-makers to be tortured by uncontrollable trembling, slurred speech, and mental confusion. (The condition led to Lewis Carroll's creation of the Mad Hatter in his book *Alice in Wonderland*.) Sadly, the hatters did not know that the mercury they used in creating felt hats was poisoning them, leading to their strange symptoms. Similarly, many of the world's greatest artists suffered from terrible depression. Today we know that the lead in their paint they used probably affected their mental state. How tragic that so many lives were destroyed for the want of a little knowledge.

   3. The primary purpose of the passage is
      a. to inform.
      b. to persuade.
      c. both of the above.

*(Continues on next page)*

4. The tone of the passage can be described as
   a. regretful.
   b. angry.
   c. alarmed.
   d. pessimistic.

**C.**   Strawberries are now available in the markets, and what a winning crop! In contrast to last year's berries, which were badly affected by poor weather conditions, these are plentiful, delicious, and relatively inexpensive. They will make a fine climax to any meal, whether under a dollop of sour cream laced with brown sugar or crushed over a scoop of vanilla ice cream. In fact, these luscious berries are so sweet, they can stand very well on their own. Strawberry lovers won't be disappointed.

5. The primary purpose of this paragraph is
   a. to inform readers about the virtues of this year's strawberry crop.
   b. to persuade readers to purchase strawberries.
   c. to amuse readers with details on strawberries.

6. The tone of this paragraph is best described as
   a. sentimental.
   b. detached.
   c. amused.
   d. enthusiastic.

**D.**   High schools should encourage young men to enroll in home economics classes. It's about time that boys learn to take care of themselves. More and more women have entered the work force, yet they are still expected to slave at home taking care of the male slobs in their lives. But women are beginning to rebel, so it's no longer realistic for boys to expect a woman to be both a wife and a mom. Furthermore, young men should be capable of living alone if they do not happen to marry. Being able to cook a meal, sew on a button and do the laundry will make it possible for them to live independent lives instead of having to bring their clothes home to Mommy and, to avoid starving, bring her food back to their homes.

7. The author of this paragraph wishes
   a. to inform readers about home economics courses.
   b. to persuade readers that boys should learn home economics skills.
   c. to entertain readers with amusing contrasts between boys and girls.

8. The tone of the paragraph can be described as
   a. amused and playful.
   b. unsure but straightforward.
   c. solemn and formal.
   d. outspoken and mocking.

# PURPOSE AND TONE: Test C-1

A. In the space provided, indicate whether the primary purpose of each sentence is to inform (**I**), to persuade (**P**), or to entertain (**E**).

_____ 1. Over the next fifty years, the number of elderly Americans is expected to grow from 26 million to over 66 million.

_____ 2. Every elementary school student ought to be taught how to use a computer.

_____ 3. Carob, a chocolate substitute, is made from the roasted and ground pods of the carob tree.

_____ 4. When a guest at the wedding was asked what he was giving the couple, he said, "About six months."

_____ 5. For the children's sake, everyone should get married before having children.

_____ 6. Between 93 and 95 percent of all fertile married couples choose to have children.

_____ 7. Seen on a bumper sticker: "Insanity is hereditary. You get it from your kids."

B. Each of the following passages illustrates one of the tones named in the box below. In the space provided, write the letter of the tone that applies to the passage. Two tone choices will be left over.

| a. caring | b. admiring | c. pessimistic |
| d. forgiving | e. ironic | |

_____ 8. Research on rats shows that when animals live in crowded conditions, they live disorderly, violent lives. Humans are no exception. Crowded inner cities are models of lawlessness; the crowded highways of Los Angeles encourage driver aggression and even shootings. As our urban areas continue to grow in population density, these types of problems will surely grow too. That means more family violence and more fighting over available resources. The American dream will become just that, only a dream.

*(Continues on next page)*

_____ 9. Those addicted to drugs and alcohol probably feel terrible about themselves—even if they don't show it—and harsh judgments only worsen their self-image. What these people need are programs to help rid themselves of their addictions. It is also important that we all open our hearts and minds to these troubled people. Their addiction does not make them any less "children of God" or at all deserving to be stripped of the dignity that is the birthright of every human being. We must strive to create an environment of hope and help for those who so desperately need it.

_____ 10. Eighth-grader Terry met his friend Ron in front of Ron's house on the first day of summer vacation. Ron looked at Terry's broad grin and remarked sympathetically, "I can't help noticing that you look utterly miserable. You can confide in me—what's the matter?"

Terry's smile expanded, but he sighed and replied, "Well, who wouldn't be bummed out. We have nothing to do but waste the most beautiful months of the year on unimportant pursuits like basketball, fishing, and bike riding."

"Yeah," sighed Ron, as the two ambled towards the nearby basketball court. "And the most depressing thing of all is that we don't get to see our valued colleague, Mr. Petersham, in the principal's office all summer."

"We must try to endure it with superior courage," Terry replied, and then he dashed onto the court for his first lay-up.

*Note:* Select the tone that describes the boys' conversation.

# PURPOSE AND TONE: Test C-2

**A.** Eight quotations in the story below are preceded by a blank space. Identify the tone of each italicized quotation by writing in the letter of one of these tones. (Two tone choices will be left over.)

| | | | |
|---|---|---|---|
| a. calming | b. bewildered | c. praising | d. matter-of-fact |
| e. threatening | f. sorrowful | g. remorseful | h. critical |
| i. pessimistic | j. grateful | | |

Tryouts for *The Wizard of Oz* were held Wednesday afternoon. The first student read for the part of Dorothy, the little girl who is swept away, along with her dog Toto, to the land of Oz.

_____ 1.    *"Toto!"* she read. *"Where are we? Everything looks so strange! I don't think we're in Kansas anymore!"*

_____ 2.    *"Very nice!"* said the teacher. *"You sound as if you've acted before!"*

Another student stepped up to read the lines of the Wicked Witch of the West.

_____ 3.    *"Just try to stay out of my way!"* the "witch" hissed at Dorothy. *"I'm going to get you, the ruby slippers, and your nasty little dog, too!"*

Next a student tried out for the part of the Tin Woodman, who wanted a heart more than anything.

_____ 4.    *"I'm just an empty kettle,"* he said with a sob. *"If the Wizard won't give me a heart, I might as well throw myself on the junk pile."*

While some students were reading for parts, others stood in the back of the room, whispering among themselves.

_____ 5.    *"That last guy who read for the Cowardly Lion was really terrible,"* said one student.

_____ 6.    *"I thought I'd try out for the part of Dorothy,"* a girl said, *"but I probably wouldn't have a chance. I don't think I'm nearly as good as the others who have read."*

After all the students who wanted to read had their chance, the drama teacher spoke to them once more before they left the room.

_____ 7.    *"Thank you all for coming. I really appreciate your interest in the drama department activities,"* she said with a warm smile.

_____ 8.    As they began to leave, she added, *"My choices for the parts will be posted on the bulletin boards Friday morning."*

*(Continues on next page)*

**B.** In the space provided, indicate whether the primary purpose of each passage is to inform (**I**), to persuade (**P**), or to entertain (**E**). (Remember that persuasive passages often contain facts—facts that support the author's views.)

_____ 9. The foundation of public education has always been reading, writing and arithmetic—the three "Rs." Yet the schools insist that students who have not mastered these fundamentals continue to take all the other subjects as well. What good does it do for young people to sit in on a history or science class if they can't read or calculate well? Schools ought to require students who are very behind in the fundamentals to devote all their time to the three Rs until they are at or near grade level.

_____ 10. Swollen glands can be uncomfortable, but they are a welcome sign that your body is working to defend itself. They are often associated with an illness such as mumps, German measles, a cold, or flu, but an insect bite or infected cut can also cause your glands to swell. A blocked duct in a salivary gland is another possible cause of a swollen gland. If swollen glands last more than a few days, they can be a sign of a serious illness, such as Hodgkin's disease.

## PURPOSE AND TONE: Test C-3

This activity will give you practice in recognizing the purpose and tone of a selection. Read each of the paragraphs below. Then carefully consider the questions that follow and circle the best responses.

A. Three people were killed because a man was angry that his girlfriend wanted to break up with him. Now the state is planning to kill him, and that's as it should be. Some may argue that taking a life is always wrong, that two wrongs don't make a right. But there is nothing right about taxpayers having to give free room and board to a person who killed innocent people— because of a disappointment experienced at some point by a large percentage of the population. And there's nothing right about putting such a dangerous person in prison, from which he will probably one day be released to again threaten society.

   1. The primary purpose of this paragraph is
      a. to inform readers of facts about the death penalty.
      b. to persuade readers that the death penalty has merit.
      c. to entertain readers with a description of an interesting problem.

   2. The overall tone of this paragraph can be described as
      a. angry and outspoken.
      b. insulting.
      c. compassionate and sentimental.
      d. excited and joyous.

B. My best school report was in first grade from Mrs. Varulo. First, she told my parents about my amazing physical energy: "Lisa never tires of chasing and punching her classmates." Next, she praised my class participation and active, questioning mind: "After every instruction—even one as simple as 'Please take out your pencils'—Lisa asks 'Why?'" Mrs. Varulo was so impressed with my vocabulary that she commented, "I don't know where Lisa has picked up some of the words she uses, certainly not in my classroom." Somehow she even knew I would become a famous fiction-writer. "More than any other student I have ever had," she wrote, "Lisa is a born liar."

   3. The primary purpose of this paragraph is
      a. to inform.
      b. to persuade.
      c. to entertain.

   4. The tone of this paragraph can best be described as
      a. enthusiastic and cheerful.
      b. annoyed and bitter.
      c. cheerful and nostalgic.
      d. ironic and humorous.

*(Continues on next page)*

C. People aren't the only creatures who respond to music. We have heard that music supposedly soothes the savage beast, but what about domesticated animals? A music therapist in Indiana wanted to test her theory that farm animals would respond best to country and Western tunes. She proceeded to play certain types of music for groups of cows during milking time to determine what type caused them to give more milk. She was encouraged when a cow group gave 6 percent more milk while listening to Beethoven, but disappointed when the same statistic held for rock music as well as country and Western tunes. She had to conclude that cows prefer music— any music—to silence.

5. The primary purpose of this paragraph is
   a. to inform.
   b. to persuade.
   c. to entertain.

6. The overall tone of this paragraph can be described as
   a. surprised.
   b. mysterious.
   c. matter-of-fact.
   d. critical.

D. Americans love parks and wildlife refuges, but the crowding they find there is a national disgrace. Parking lots are packed, and roadways through parks and refuges are often so jammed that they might as well be the parking lots. Playing fields and barbecue grills are claimed early in the day, and even on remote trails, voices can be heard from every direction. Americans badly need more land devoted to open space where nature walks, picnics, and camping can take place in uncrowded tranquility. Communities across the nation should establish parks and trails that provide free access to open space for everyone.

7. The primary purpose of this paragraph is
   a. to inform.
   b. to persuade.
   c. to entertain.

8. The overall tone of this paragraph can be described as
   a. straightforward.
   b. surprised and anxious.
   c. angry and revengeful.
   d. distressed and impassioned.

# PURPOSE AND TONE: Test D-1

**A.** In the space provided, indicate whether the primary purpose of each sentence is to inform (**I**), to persuade (**P**), or to entertain (**E**).

_____  1. More money should be spent on buying our city police officers up-to-date weapons.

_____  2. Mac's idea of healthy eating is to eat a double cheeseburger and large fries without putting any salt on them.

_____  3. For the sake of our already overcrowded schools, Paulsen City must reject the proposed housing development.

_____  4. During middle age, many people who previously have always had good vision require glasses to read comfortably.

_____  5. My father-in-law puts on his glasses and artificial leg, turns on his hearing aid, checks his pacemaker and says, "Okay—the Bionic Grandpa is ready to go."

_____  6. Have your eyes checked at the We Care Eye Care Center, where we sell glasses at a discount to families.

_____  7. The seeds of many fruits, including cherries, apples, plums, peaches and apricots, contain a form of the poison cyanide that can be deadly when eaten in large amounts.

**B.** Each of the following passages illustrates one of the tones named in the box below. In the space provided, write the letter of the tone that applies to the passage. Two tone choices will be left over.

| | | |
|---|---|---|
| a. self-mocking | b. joyous | c. alarmed |
| d. angry | e. matter-of-fact | |

_____  8. There has been a frightening increase in the numbers of suicidal teens in recent decades. The suicide rate for young people increased by a terrifying 400 percent between 1950 and 1980. Obviously, the pressures facing American teenagers are too much for many of them to bear. Broken families, the availability of drugs and alcohol, the breakdown of formerly close communities, and pressures to grow up too fast are creating circumstances so difficult to face that young people instead choose to end their lives. The situation will only grow worse if there are no substantial changes made in our society.

*(Continues on next page)*

_____ 9. Machines are complete mysteries to me, which has resulted in some embarrassing service calls at my home. For example, there was the time I called in a repairman because our refrigerator was too warm. Imagine my humiliation when he told me that the cause of the problem was a dirty filter, which I didn't know existed and therefore hadn't cleaned even once in the two years we owned the refrigerator. The best example of my brilliance with machines, however, has to be the time I called for someone to fix my washing machine. The repairman's solution was simply to put the plug back in the outlet, from which it had been jarred loose by the constant vibration of the washer.

_____ 10. Despite the publicity given to sex and birth control, many young people are still misinformed about the facts of conception. One national study showed that one-third of all adolescents believed that a girl could not get pregnant if she truly didn't want to have a baby. Few correctly understood the way in which the likelihood of pregnancy varies during a woman's menstrual cycle. In fact, more than half believed that a woman was most likely to become pregnant while she was menstruating.

# PURPOSE AND TONE: Test D-2

**A.** Eight quotations in the story below are preceded by a blank space. Identify the tone of each italicized quotation by writing in the letter of one of these tones. (Two tone choices will be left over.)

| | | | |
|---|---|---|---|
| a. disgusted | b. ashamed | c. outraged | d. appreciative |
| e. cheerful | f. understanding | g. straightforward | h. tragic |
| i. joyous | j. vengeful | | |

The scene is a busy restaurant on a Saturday evening.

_____ 1.  *"Good evening!"* a young waitress chirped to a table of diners. *"It's so nice to see you here tonight! My name is Annette, and I'll be your server this evening."*

_____ 2.  Meanwhile, across the room, a man stared at his food as he pushed it around with his fork. *"They call this 'ocean-fresh fish,'"* he muttered to his wife. *"I bet this fish hasn't been near an ocean in months."*

_____ 3.  But at the next table, a young man said to his friend, *"This great spaghetti really hits the spot. I was starved."*

_____ 4.  Nearby, in a dimly-lit corner of the restaurant, a young man and woman sat close together, smiling at the diamond ring on the woman's finger. *"Oh, darling,"* sighed the woman. *"This is the happiest night of my life. This restaurant will always be my favorite because this is where you asked me to marry you."*

_____ 5.  A conversation of a different sort was taking place at another table: *"I cannot believe you would do this!"* a woman hissed at her husband. *"What kind of man takes his wife into a public place to tell her he's having an affair with her best friend? What am I supposed to do now—order an appetizer?"*

_____ 6.  Back in the kitchen, the restaurant manager was instructing the staff. *"Annette, you cover tables one through four. Ben, you're responsible for five through eight. A party of sixteen people is coming in at eight o'clock; Lisa and Suzette will take care of them."*

"Well, we got passed over again, didn't we?" Ben remarked to Annette after the manager was gone. "Lisa and Suzette always get the big groups and the big tips. It makes me wonder why I try to do a good job here."

_____ 7.  *"Oh, I don't mind,"* Annette said. *"Lisa and Suzette do work a lot more hours than you or I do. I can see why the manager thinks they deserve the best assignments."* Then Annette walked out of the kitchen.

*(Continues on next page)*

_____ 8.    "Well, it's not okay with me," Ben muttered to himself. *"When I quit this lousy job, they're going to pay for the way they've treated me. I'll get back at them somehow."*

**B.** In the space provided, indicate whether the primary purpose of each passage is to inform (**I**), to persuade (**P**), or to entertain (**E**). (Remember that persuasive passages often contain facts—facts that support the author's views.)

_____ 9.    More and more elderly are turning to shared housing as a way to live more economically, more securely, and with more companionship. There are dozens of such projects around the country, including group homes in California, communes in Baltimore, and the "Share a Home" in Winter Park, Florida. While the latter includes 125 participants, a shared-housing project may involve only a few members. Most shared-housing projects have full- or part-time help, but members often share in such chores as shopping for food and cooking.

_____ 10.   Students should consider taking life-skills courses in addition to their usual classes. While the ordinary curriculum focuses on skills such as reading, writing, and mathematics, training in life skills teaches people what they need to know in order to live. Training is provided in four basic areas: identity, relationships, decision making, and health. Thus, life skills courses can help people find purpose in their lives, get along with others, solve problems, and lead healthy lives.

## PURPOSE AND TONE: Test D-3

This activity will give you practice in recognizing the purpose and tone of a selection. Read each of the paragraphs below. Then carefully consider the questions that follow and circle the best responses.

A.   The practice of tipping goes back thousands of years, at least to the times of the ancient Romans. You would think that by now the public would have refused to cooperate with such an unfair and bothersome habit. Who else besides restaurant owners can get away with underpaying their employees and expect their customers to make up the difference? It has gotten so that waiters no longer look at a tip as a reward for superior service. Instead, it is an expected part of their day's pay, to the point that even a waiter who has provided lousy service will demand a tip if a customer does not offer one. Restaurant customers should band together and demand the elimination of this ridiculous, unjust custom.

1. The primary purpose of this paragraph is
   a. to inform.
   b. to persuade.
   c. to entertain.

2. The tone of this paragraph can be described as
   a. cruel.
   b. revengeful.
   c. angry.
   d. alarmed.

B.   Sediment will sometimes accumulate in shower heads, causing the water to flow unevenly or completely clogging the shower head. Sometimes briskly opening and closing the adjustment mechanism a few times is enough to solve the problem. If this does not work, remove the shower head from the wall, holding onto the pipe while you unscrew the shower head so that you do not loosen the pipe inside the wall. Once you have removed the shower head, try cleaning it with a toothpick or wire. If necessary, take the shower head apart and soak it in water overnight to soften the mineral deposits.

3. The primary purpose of this paragraph is
   a. to inform.
   b. to persuade.
   c. to entertain.

4. The tone of this paragraph can be described as
   a. cheerful.
   b. matter-of-fact.
   c. hesitant.
   d. distressed.

*(Continues on next page)*

**C.**    On a hot Sunday morning, the church service had already gone far beyond its scheduled time when the pastor finally got up to deliver the sermon. Ignoring the lateness of the hour, the rising temperature in the room, and the restlessness of the congregation, he carefully arranged his notes in front of him. "Brothers and sisters," he said, his voice overflowing with emotion, "I have so much in my heart to say to you, I scarcely know where to begin." A helpful voice from the back of the room piped up to suggest, "Why don't you begin somewhere near the end?"

5. The primary purpose of this paragraph is
   a. to inform.
   b. to persuade.
   c. to entertain.

6. The tone of this paragraph could be described as
   a. amused.
   b. optimistic.
   c. joyous.
   d. sorrowful.

**D.**    When I hired Atlas Carpets to install a new wall-to-wall carpet in my living room, I relied on your firm's excellent reputation for quality work. However, as I have told you repeatedly on the telephone, I am deeply dissatisfied with the job you did in my home. In one corner near the fireplace, the carpeting is poorly fitted, and some of the flooring shows through. Some of the tacks are already coming loose, and I have had to hammer them in again myself, even though I have a bad back. Moreover, one of your workmen put a hot cup down on my coffee table, leaving a stain for which I hold you responsible. If we cannot agree to a reasonable adjustment promptly, I will turn the whole matter over to my lawyer, as well as tell all my friends about my exasperating experience with Atlas.

7. The primary purpose of this paragraph is
   a. to inform.
   b. to persuade.
   c. to entertain.

8. The tone of this paragraph can be described as
   a. remorseful.
   b. fearful.
   c. grim.
   d. angry.

## PURPOSE AND TONE: Test E-1

**A.** In the space provided, indicate whether the primary purpose of each sentence is to inform (**I**), to persuade (**P**), or to entertain (**E**).

_____ 1. Wintergreen Life Savers, if crunched vigorously between the teeth, will emit blue sparks.

_____ 2. I asked my boss for a raise, so he moved my office from the basement to the second floor.

_____ 3. Because of the number of fighters seriously injured or killed in the ring each year, professional boxing should be banned.

_____ 4. The Navajos have no native word for "reporter." To refer to a reporter in their own language, they use their word for "gossiper."

_____ 5. A bag of M&M candies contains about 60 percent dark brown candies, 30 percent yellow, and 10 percent other colors.

_____ 6. Since M&Ms are irresistible, don't keep them in the house if you want your children to eat a healthy diet.

_____ 7. My baby is so smart that he can make M&M candies melt in his hand, not in his mouth.

**B.** Each of the following passages illustrates one of the tones named in the box below. In the space provided, write the letter of the tone that applies to the passage. Two tone choices will be left over.

| | | |
|---|---|---|
| a. ironic | b. matter-of-fact | c. revengeful |
| d. pessimistic | e. indignant | |

_____ 8. The first radio advertisement was broadcast on August 28, 1922, on New York station WEAF. A real estate firm, Queensboro Corporation, bought a ten-minute segment for one hundred dollars in order to advertise its apartments. According to the advertisement, the apartment complex, Hawthorne Court, was named after the American author Nathaniel Hawthorne. The apartments were described as conveniently near the subway but also "right at the boundaries of God's great outdoors" near golf and tennis courts and other "pleasure-giving, health-giving activities." As a result of the advertisements, two apartments were sold, and commercial radio was born.

*(Continues on next page)*

_____ 9. Relentless greed and horrifying dishonesty characterized the treatment of Indians in the 1860s and 1870s, when massacres of native Americans were commonplace. The massacre at Sand Creek in Colorado in 1864 was sadly typical. The territorial governor had persuaded the Indians to gather there and had promised them protection. Despite this pledge, Colonel J. M. Chivington's militia attacked the defenseless Indian camp. They disregarded that sacred symbol, the American flag, and the white flag of truce that the Indians were flying at Sand Creek. Four hundred fifty peaceful Indians—men, women, and children—were slaughtered in what has been called "the foulest and most unjustified crime in the annals of America." This was only one of the heartless massacres that history records.

_____ 10. One way to lose weight is to go on a scientific weight-loss program. These are widely advertised in those newspapers that are sold at supermarket check-out lines, the ones with headlines like: BURT REYNOLDS FINDS CANCER CURE IN UFO RIDE WITH PRINCESS DIANA. You should buy one of these magazines and flip through the pages until you see a full-page advertisement with a headline that says, "WOMAN LOSES 240 POUNDS IN 30 SECONDS." Under the headline are two pictures of a woman's head: in the first picture the head is on top of what appears to be an industrial boiler wearing a 1952 bathing suit; in the second picture, the head is on top of Bo Derek's body.

# PURPOSE AND TONE: Test E-2

**A.** Eight quotations in the story below are preceded by a blank space. Identify the tone of each italicized quotation by writing in the letter of one of these tones. (Two tone choices will be left over.)

| | | | |
|---|---|---|---|
| a. arrogant | b. ambivalent | c. grim | d. embarrassed |
| e. self-mocking | f. optimistic | g. bitter | h. bored |
| i. comic | j. sentimental and nostalgic | | |

A group of friends were lounging around in junior Eileen Dawson's dorm room. Before them were college catalogs and class registration forms.

_____ 1.      Renee lay sleepily on a bed, gazing out the window. Her copy of the college catalog lay face down beside her. *"'Abnormal Psychology,' 'Literature of Victorian England,' 'Fundamentals of Marine Biology.' Everything sounds incredibly dull."*

"I know what you mean," Eileen responded.

_____ 2.      *"Maybe I should take a course on the abnormal psychology of marine life in Victorian England."* Renee smiled. *"Or how about a course in the normal psychology of guys majoring in marine biology?"*

_____ 3.      "Well, I've *already got a whole year's worth of courses picked out*," said Kay, stretching. *"The scholarship office insisted on getting my full schedule by this week. I sure hope I get straight A's again this year."*

_____ 4.      "Oh, look, you guys," said Marla, ignoring Kay's comment. *"'Introduction to American Lit.' Remember, that's where we all got to know each other. Gosh, we had a good time in that class. We were all so young and excited about being in college."*

_____ 5.      *"Yeah, we were young and excited, all right,"* laughed Eileen. *"You left out dumb. Do you remember who we spent our time mooning over that term? Do the names Arthur Peterson and Del Hunsberger ring a bell? Were we idiots or what?"*

_____ 6.      *"OOOhhh! Don't say those names!"* Renee howled, burying her head under her pillow. *"Please, please, never remind anyone that I had a crush on either of those two! Never remind me of it, either!"*

"Now, now, enough of this nonsense," Marla said. "Eileen, what are you going to sign up for this winter?"

*(Continues on next page)*

_____ 7.    *"Well, maybe I should get my final science and language requirements out of the way so I'm not frantic trying to squeeze them in next year,"* said Eileen. *"But there are some electives offered next term, like 'American Society and the Role of Women,' that sound really interesting. I'm not sure whether to be practical or adventurous. Which do you think I should do?"*

_____ 8.    *"I'm sure either choice would work out fine, Eileen,"* Marla replied. *"If you take the requirements now, you'll have a more relaxed senior year; but taking the electives would be good, too, because you'd be exploring interests that will last the rest of your life."*

"Is everything decided now?" asked Renee, lifting her head from the bed. "I'm starved from all that hard thinking. Let's go to lunch."

**B.** In the space provided, indicate whether the primary purpose of each passage is to inform (**I**), to persuade (**P**), or to entertain (**E**). (Remember that persuasive passages often contain facts—facts that support the author's views.)

_____ 9.    Until recently, many experts believed that people reach their mental peak by the time they're twenty. But lately, scientists have learned that our minds continue to grow long after our bodies are fully developed. Furthermore, some psychologists have expanded their notion of what makes up intelligence. A Yale University researcher, for example, outlines seven different areas of intelligence, including musical talent and self-knowledge.

_____ 10.   Prevention of mental illness is more important than its treatment. Yet few programs are devoted to prevention. Better education programs could lead to significant reductions in mental illnesses caused by poisons, poor nutrition, infections, and accidents. To promote mental health, I believe we must provide both short-term activities, such as crisis intervention counseling, and long-term programs in schools, businesses, and communities. You can help by writing to your local representatives and elected officials and requesting more and better programs.

# PURPOSE AND TONE: Test E-3

This activity will give you practice in recognizing the purpose and tone of a selection. Read each of the paragraphs below. Then carefully consider the questions that follow and circle the best responses.

A. Single, divorced, or widowed adults usually live either alone or with other family members. The idea of two unmarried adults joining forces in one household is one that has been too little explored in our society. When two divorced mothers and their children live together, everyone benefits. The adults can offer each other emotional support and practical assistance that isn't available in a single-parent household. The arrangement has similar advantages for unmarried or widowed persons. They can share expenses and household tasks while providing companionship for one another. Our commission should encourage such relationships by setting up a clearing house in which people can seek such partnerships.

1. The primary purpose of this paragraph is
   a. to inform.
   b. to persuade.
   c. to entertain.

2. The tone of this paragraph is
   a. solemn.
   b. ambivalent.
   c. straightforward.
   d. pessimistic.

B. Puberty causes the changing of considerably more than your sheets. I remember that puberty inspired me to brush my hair so hard that I almost exposed the area where my brains should have been. The moment my glands kicked in, I began to brush my hair a hundred times a day so that not a single strand was out of place for the girls I now wanted to impress. I shined my own shoes, I cut the tiny hanging strings off the frayed parts of my collar, and, in a stunning blend of vanity and vapidness, I even began to flaunt my eyelashes, which were particularly long. Before puberty, I had actually trimmed these lashes because women had said I looked like a girl; but now I was grooming them with a toothbrush and wondering if girls would prefer them from the front or the side.

3. The purpose of this paragraph is
   a. to inform.
   b. to persuade.
   c. to entertain.

4. The tone of the paragraph is
   a. regretful.
   b. encouraging.
   c. straightforward.
   d. self-mocking.

*(Continues on next page)*

C.   Consumers may be persuaded to buy an item not only by its price and quality, but also by the image it projects—and that image may be just that, only an image. For instance, consider the cases of Haågen-Dazs ice cream and its competitor, Frusen Glådje. Both are rich, so-called gourmet ice creams, and both cost considerably more than most other supermarket brands. Both appeal to the consumer through their Scandinavian-sounding names, which imply that they are imported and thus superior or special in some way. The Haågen-Dazs package even shows a map of Norway and Denmark, further suggesting a Scandinavian connection. But that special "imported" quality is wholly in the mind of the consumer: Haågen-Dazs is manufactured in New Jersey, and Frusen Glådje in Philadelphia.

5. The purpose of this paragraph is
   a. to inform.
   b. to persuade.
   c. to entertain.

6. The tone of the paragraph can be described as
   a. mainly matter-of-fact, with a bit of cynicism.
   b. largely optimistic, but somewhat unsure.
   c. angry, bitter, and greatly disappointed.
   d. strongly indignant and contemptuous.

D.   Increasingly, nursery schools are introducing schoolwork once thought appropriate for first and second grades. This is one of the practices that prove American educators are more interested in being trendy than in following sound educational principles. Preschool youngsters should not be forced to do academic work. High-pressure instruction for children who just need time to play is downright crazy, and the lunatics who are teaching young children academic skills are doing more harm than good. Attempting reading, writing, and arithmetic at too young an age can make small children feel like failures and lead to dislike (and even dread) of school. Activities that build independence and self-esteem are far more appropriate to nursery schools than stressful academics.

7. The primary purpose of this paragraph is
   a. to inform readers about the activities in today's nursery schools.
   b. to persuade readers that academic work doesn't belong in nursery schools.
   c. to entertain readers with anecdotes about children.

8. The tone of this paragraph can be described as
   a. optimistic
   b. chatty.
   c. revengeful.
   d. critical.

# 9

# Propaganda

What do you think is the main difference between the following two evaluations of a city?

> The weather isn't bad in Philadelphia, if you don't mind a few months of winter. And the city has wonderful museums and restaurants. But the streets are often dirty there, and state and city taxes keep going up.

> Philadelphia is the place to live! Once you experience its pleasant climate, its museums, and restaurants, you'll agree with Phillies baseball star Ken Greyson when he says, "Home base for me is Philadelphia. Living here is a ball!"

Did you notice that the first evaluation is an attempt to be objective about Philadelphia? It mentions both positive and negative points so the reader will get a balanced picture of the city. The second approach, however, includes only positive points. It was not meant to provide a balanced, objective view of the city. Instead, it was designed to influence people to come live in Philadelphia. When such biased information is methodically spread in order to promote or oppose a cause—whether the cause is a city, a political view, a product, or an organization—it is *propaganda*.

## PROPAGANDA TECHNIQUES

Propaganda may use one or more common techniques for convincing people by appealing to their emotions. Recognizing these techniques will help you separate the substance of a message (if there is any) from its purely emotional appeal. If you are not aware of the propaganda devices, you may make decisions as a result of emotional manipulation. This chapter will introduce you to seven of the more common propaganda techniques:

- Bandwagon
- Testimonial
- Transfer
- Plain Folks
- Name Calling
- Glittering Generalities
- Card Stacking

Once you have learned these techniques, you will recognize one or more of them in just about every advertisement you encounter.

## 1   Bandwagon

Old-fashioned parades usually began with a large wagon carrying a brass band. To "jump on the bandwagon," therefore, means to join a parade. For example, we are often told to buy a product or vote for a political candidate because, in effect, "everybody else is doing it." An ad for a cereal may claim that "Sugar-O's is Everybody's Favorite Breakfast." A political commercial may show people from all walks of life all saying they will vote for Candidate Harry Hogwash. The ads imply that if you don't jump on the bandwagon, the parade will pass you by.

Here are two examples of real TV ads that have used the *bandwagon* appeal:

To a background of appealing music, shots of many people wearing the sponsor's jeans appear on the screen.

On a beautiful day, almost everyone on the beach leaves in a hurry in order to attend the sponsor's sale.

## ➤ *Practice 1*

Circle the numbers of the two descriptions of ads that use the bandwagon appeal.

1. Famous actress Margo Lane explains that she loves to use a certain hair coloring.

2. Most of the people in a crowd at the ballgame are drinking the sponsor's cola beverage.

3. A very well-built man and woman in very tight exercise clothes demonstrate the sponsor's exercise equipment.

4. The tune of "God Bless America" is being played in the background as an announcer urges people to support the home baseball team by coming out to games.

5. An ad for a new movie shows people waiting to buy tickets in a line that extends halfway around the block.

## 2  Testimonial

Famous athletes often appear on television as spokespersons for all sorts of products, from soft drinks to automobiles. Movie stars make commercials endorsing products and political issues. The idea behind this approach is that the testimony of famous people influences the television viewers that admire these people.

What viewers must remember is that famous people get paid to endorse products. In addition, these people are not necessarily experts about the products or political issues they promote. This does not in itself mean that what they say is untrue. But realizing that celebrities receive money to recommend products that they may know little about should help consumers think twice about such messages.

Here are two examples of real ads that have used the appeal of *testimonials*:

A famous comedienne, now a senior citizen, promotes a cleaner for false teeth.

A popular singer with a wholesome image is spokesperson for a breakfast cereal.

## ➤ *Practice 2*

Circle the numbers of the two descriptions of ads that use a testimonial.

1.  Numerous people crowd around the department store door, waiting for the store to open.

2.  Famous actress Margo Lane explains that she loves to use a certain hair coloring.

3.  A grandmother, serving a canned vegetable soup to her grandson, says, "This has all the simple, healthy, and delicious ingredients I use in my own vegetable soup."

4.  A sports star talks about and laces on a particular brand of basketball sneakers.

5.  A cheerful mother announces that a day without a certain orange juice is like a day without sunshine.

## 3   Transfer

Ads that use the transfer technique associate a product with a symbol or image that people admire or love. The advertiser hopes that people's positive feelings for the symbol or image will *transfer* to the product. For example, calling an automobile "The All-American Car" appeals to would-be buyers' patriotism; the "All-American" image calls to mind all that is best in America. Or consider a recent real-life ad in which several nuns are surprised and impressed that the fresh-brewed coffee they think they are drinking is actually Folger's instant coffee. The qualities people associate with nuns—seeing them as honest, trustworthy, and highly selective in their worldly pleasures—are then associated with the product as well.

There is also a good deal of transfer value in good looks. Consumers *transfer* the positive feelings they have towards a sexy-looking person to the product being advertised. Many ads today use handsome men and beautiful women to pitch their products; more than ever, Madison Avenue seems convinced that "sex sells."

To summarize, the transfer technique depends upon the appeal value of two special categories:

1) admired and/or beloved symbols and images
2) sex appeal

Here are two examples of real ads that have used transfer:

An American eagle symbolizes the United States Post Office's Express Mail service.

A tanned blonde in a bikini is stretched out on the beach, holding in her hand a can of light beer.

## ➤ Practice 3

Circle the numbers of the two descriptions of ads that use the transfer approach.

1.   An announcer claims that a competitor's tires don't last as long as the sponsor's tires do.

2.   The tune of "God Bless America" is being played in the background as an announcer urges people to support the home baseball team by coming out to games.

3.   A very well-built man and woman in very tight exercise clothes demonstrate the sponsor's exercise equipment.

4.   Several ordinary, friendly-looking young men in jeans buy the sponsor's beer.

5.   "My opponent hasn't made up his mind about state taxes," says a candidate for mayor. "He's too wishy-washy to be mayor."

### 4   Plain Folks

Some people distrust political candidates who are rich or well-educated. They feel that these candidates, if elected, will not be able to understand the problems of the average working person. Therefore, candidates often try to show they are just "plain folks" by referring in their speeches to how poor they were when they were growing up or how they had to work their way through school. They also pose for photographs wearing overalls or buying a hot dog from a curbside vendor.

Likewise, the presidents of some companies appear in their own ads, trying to show that their giant enterprises are just family businesses. If a corporation can convince potential customers that it is run by people just like them, the customers are more likely to buy the corporation's product than if they felt it was run by ruthless millionaire executives. In other words, people using the *plain-folks* approach tell their audience, "We are ordinary folks, just like you."

Yet another plain-folks approach is for a company to show us a product being used and enjoyed by everyday types of people—persons just like ourselves. (In contrast, the propaganda technique of testimonial features famous people.)

Here are two examples of real ads that have used the appeal of plain folks:

A president of a fast-food hamburger chain, dressed in shirt sleeves, carries a food tray to a small table in one of his restaurants, all the while pitching his burgers to the viewer.

Average-looking American kids are shown trying and enjoying a cereal.

### ➤ *Practice 4*

Circle the numbers of the two descriptions of ads that use the plain folks approach.

1.   Two ordinary, friendly-looking young men in jeans buy the sponsor's beer.

2.   A famous baseball player wears the sponsor's jeans.

3.   A man leaves a theater after seeing a play with a big smile on his face. Then his chauffeur pulls up in a Cadillac to take him home.

4.   "Drink our soda," says the announcer. "It's the real thing."

5.   A grandmother, serving a canned vegetable soup to her grandson, says, "This has all the simple, healthy, and delicious ingredients I use in my own vegetable soup."

## 5 Name Calling

*Name calling* is the use of emotionally loaded language or negative comments to turn people against a rival product, candidate, or movement. An example of name calling would be a political candidate's labeling an opponent "uncaring," "radical," or "wimpy." Or a manufacturer may say or imply that a competing product is "full of chemicals," though in reality everything is made up of chemicals of one kind or another. Or one group may call another group's beliefs "un-American" when all they mean is that they disapprove of them.

Here are two examples of name calling taken from real life:

In the early days of the "cold war" with the Soviet Union, in the 1950s, an exaggerated concern about communism in this country brought charges of un-Americanism against many.

A fast-food chain accuses a competitor of selling a seaweed burger simply because the competitor used a seaweed extract to keep its burger moist.

➤ *Practice 5*

Circle the numbers of the two descriptions of ads that use name calling.

1. "Drink our soda," says the announcer. "It's the real thing."

2. "Brand X's spaghetti sauce tastes like Mom used to make," says a man to his wife. "And you know what a lousy cook she was." Then he suggests trying the sponsor's brand.

3. A cheerful mother announces that a day without a certain orange juice is like a day without sunshine.

4. "My opponent has lived in our state for only two years," says a candidate for state senator. "Let's not put an outsider into state office."

5. An ad for cigarettes shows a beautiful woman in a strapless gown smoking the sponsor's product and being admired by several handsome men.

## 6   Glittering Generalities

A *glittering generality* is an important-sounding but unspecific claim about some product, candidate, or cause. It cannot be proved true or false because no evidence is offered to support the claim. Such claims use general words that different people would define differently, such as "progress," "great," and "freedom."

"Simply the best," an ad might say about a certain television set. But no specific evidence of any kind is offered to support such a generality. "Janet Mayer has the Right Stuff! Vote Mayer for Congress," a campaign slogan might claim. But what seems like "the right stuff" to her campaign manager might seem very wrong to you. The point is that the phrase sounds good but says nothing definite.

Here are two examples of ads that use glittering generalities:

A car ad claims, "It just feels right."

A canned-food ad boasts of "nutrition that works."

➤ *Practice 6*

Circle the numbers of the two descriptions of ads that use glittering generalities.

1.   "For a forward-looking government," says the announcer, "vote for Ed Dalton for governor."

2.   A well-known astronaut says that he uses the sponsor's aspirins.

3.   "Millions of satisfied customers can't be all wrong," says the announcer of an ad for grass seed.

4.   "My opponent attends Alcoholics Anonymous meetings," says a candidate for city council. "Do you want him to represent you on the council?"

5.   A cheerful mother announces that a day without a certain orange juice is like a day without sunshine.

## 7 Card Stacking

*Card stacking* refers to stacking the cards in your favor and presenting only the facts and figures that are favorable to your particular side of the issue. It could also be called the "Too-Good-to-Be-True Technique" or the "Omitted Details Technique."

Part of every writer's job is to choose what information to include and what to omit. This right to choose also carries a responsibility. When making a case, writers are occasionally tempted to omit facts that oppose their arguments. Writers should face those facts and either explain why they do not apply, or, if that proves impossible, modify their original arguments. But the temptation to take a short cut and ignore unpleasant facts is sometimes too strong to resist.

In legal language, deliberately leaving out inconvenient facts is called "concealing evidence." In advertising, such evidence may be concealed in the interests of selling a product. For example, advertisements for the drug Tylenol call it "the pain reliever hospitals use most," and this statement is perfectly true. What these advertisements fail to mention is that the manufacturer of Tylenol offers hospitals large discounts. Since other drug companies may not offer similar discounts, or did not in the past, most hospital administrators have chosen to buy Tylenol. The advertising campaign depends on people jumping to the conclusion, "Hospitals use more Tylenol than any other pain reliever. They must consider it the best drug of its kind available." In fact, other drugs with the same pain reliever as Tylenol might work just as well.

Read the following passage and then the list of omitted details below it. Then decide which of the missing details you think Credit Information Services deliberately left out of its ad.

For only forty dollars, Credit Information Services will provide a copy of your credit report. Haven't you been wondering what information a potential lender gets when you apply for a loan? Now you will have all the information you need for a single low yearly fee.

Missing fact:

a. Each additional use of this service will cost only thirty-five dollars.
b. Credit Information Services already has 300,000 customers nationwide.
c. Federal law gives you the right to find out what is in your credit report —free.

Answer: _____

If you chose *c*, you are right. If you know this detail, you are not likely to send forty dollars to Credit Information Services.

## ➤ *Practice 7*

Which missing details does the reader need to know in order to avoid being tricked? Circle the letter of the important fact that has been purposely omitted from each paragraph.

1. Congratulations! You have just won an all-expenses-paid three-night vacation to Atlantic City, New Jersey. You will dine at glamorous restaurants, enjoy stage shows, and swim in the beautiful Atlantic Ocean—all free. This free trip has been awarded to only a handful of selected winners in your area.

   a. The voucher for your free trip will arrive by registered mail within two weeks of your acceptance of this offer.
   b. You may stay at your choice of two casino hotels: Trump's Castle or Resorts International.
   c. You must pay $399 to join a travel club before you become eligible for your free trip.

2. For a set fee you can make as many long-distance calls as you wish at special times. This is your chance to get back in touch with all the family members and friends you've been meaning to call. Now you can afford the pleasure of talking regularly with the people who mean the most to you. Talk as long as you wish to anyone in the continental United States for only one hundred dollars a month.

   a. Merely dial the number you want. You need not dial extra access numbers.
   b. The service is available now in your area.
   c. Calls can be made only between 10 P.M. and 6 A.M.

3. Sunnyside College offers a wide choice of majors, ranging from liberal studies to high technology. On its beautiful campus students can take advantage of up-to-date laboratory equipment, an Olympic-sized swimming pool, and a new four-story library. The faculty are well-known for their commitment to students.

   a. More than 80 percent of the students are from the northeastern part of the country.
   b. Only 5 percent of the graduates that apply to graduate school are accepted.
   c. More people major in high technology than in liberal studies.

## ➤ *Review*

To review what you've learned in this chapter, complete each of the following sentences about propaganda.

1. Propaganda is usually intended to appeal to our (*logic, emotions*)

   _____.

2. An important difference between a testimonial and a plain folks appeal is

   that testimonials feature (*famous, ordinary*) _____ people.

3. The (*transfer, plain folks*) _____ technique associates a
   product with symbols and images that people respect.

4. (*Glittering generalities, Card stacking*) _____ is
   the technique of making dramatic but unspecific and unsupported claims.

# PROPAGANDA: Test A-1

A. In each pair of the fictional ads that follow, the first ad does *not* illustrate a propaganda technique, but the second one does. On each line, write the letter of the propaganda technique used in the *second* ad.

As a reminder, brief explanations of the propaganda techniques are given in the box below.

> Bandwagon—*Buy me or vote for me because everyone's doing it; jump on the bandwagon.*
> Testimonial—*Buy me or vote for me because famous people endorse me.*
> Transfer—*Buy me or vote for me because I'm associated with a symbol or image that people admire or love.*
> Plain folks—*Buy me or support me because I'm used by—or I am—an everyday kind of person, just like you.*
> Name calling—*Buy me or vote for me because my competitors have negative qualities.*
> Glittering generalities—*Buy or vote for me because of some important-sounding—but unspecific—claims.*

_____ 1. • Sureguard sunglasses filter out harmful ultraviolet rays.

       • "Sureguard sunglasses flatter my looks while they protect my eyes," says actress Judy Winsor. "You'll love them too."

       a. Testimonial          c. Plain folks
       b. Transfer             d. Name calling

_____ 2. • Olson's pizzas are lower in fat and calories.

       • Bailey's Pizza doesn't care about your health.

       a. Plain folks         c. Glittering generalities
       b. Name calling      d. Transfer

_____ 3. • Protect your teeth with sturdy Gordon's dental floss.

       • Buy Gordon's dental floss, the official floss of the American space program. Protect your teeth the way the astronauts do.

       a. Plain folks         c. Glittering generalities
       b. Bandwagon        d. Transfer

_____ 4. • West's Tall Men's Store sells well-tailored suits in all tall sizes.

       • Buy your next suit at West's Tall Men's Store, and you'll be walking tall.

       a. Plain folks         c. Testimonial
       b. Name calling      d. Glittering generalities

*(Continues on next page)*

_____ 5. • Barron's Department Store is holding its annual storewide sale.

• All across town, people are hurrying to Barron's annual storewide sale. Hurry in now, before the best buys are gone!

a. Testimonial          c. Bandwagon
b. Name calling         d. Transfer

_____ 6. • Radio Station-KFGB plays country and Western music all day and night.

• Listen up to Station-KFGB, music for honest working folks like you!

a. Name calling         c. Transfer
b. Testimonial          d. Plain folks

**B.** The following fictional ad involves card stacking—in some way, it is too good to be true. Circle the letter of the important detail that has intentionally been omitted.

7. With your purchase of a new Cadillac, you will win a free five-day vacation in Disneyland.
   a. The vacation package doesn't include coupons to other tourist attractions.
   b. The company also offers vacations in New Orleans and New York City.
   c. The hotel stay and meals are free, but you have to pay the round-trip air fare to Disneyland.

**C.** Read the fictional ad below, and then circle the letter of the best answer to each question.

> Try Mrs. Green's new Lite Line Cereals. We use only vegetable oils—and no animal fats at all! Try all of our new bright lites—Grandma's Granola, Tropical Wheat Flakes, and Nutty Nut Bran. True to its name, Tropical Wheat Flakes contains coconut and the finest coconut oil, and Nutty Nut Bran has more nuts per bite than any other cereal.

8. Which propaganda technique is probably the reason for the name "Grandma's Granola"?
   a. Bandwagon              c. Testimonial
   b. Glittering generalities d. Plain folks

9. Which propaganda technique is illustrated by the phrase "bright lites"?
   a. Plain folks             c. Name calling
   b. Glittering generalities d. Bandwagon

10. Which of the following facts has the advertiser purposely omitted?
    a. Butter is an animal fat.
    b. Animal fats are known to raise cholesterol levels.
    c. Coconut oil is known to raise cholesterol levels.
    d. Nuts are high in protein.

## PROPAGANDA: Test A-2

**A.** Each fictional ad that follows illustrates a particular propaganda technique. On the line next to each ad, write the letter of the main technique being used.

As a reminder, brief explanations of the propaganda techniques are given in the box below.

---

Bandwagon—*Buy me or vote for me because everyone's doing it; jump on the bandwagon.*
Testimonial—*Buy me or vote for me because famous people endorse me.*
Transfer—*Buy me or vote for me because I'm associated with a symbol or image that people admire or love.*
Plain folks—*Buy me or support me because I'm used by—or I am—an everyday kind of person, just like you.*
Name calling—*Buy me or vote for me because my competitors have negative qualities.*
Glittering generalities—*Buy or vote for me because of some important-sounding—but unspecific—claims.*

---

_____ 1. Liberty Bell Airlines flies anywhere in this great land, from sea to shining sea. We proudly hail America's finest: Liberty Bell.

   a. Plain folks           c. Transfer
   b. Testimonial           d. Name calling

_____ 2. Cast your vote next Tuesday for Larry Lewis for representative. He pledges to better conditions and to bring you closer to the fulfillment of your highest dreams.

   a. Transfer              c. Bandwagon
   b. Glittering generalities   d. Name calling

_____ 3. Join your neighbors and friends in a massive protest against the proposed landfill. People from all walks of life are forming the overwhelming opposition to this project.

   a. Testimonial           c. Bandwagon
   b. Transfer              d. Name calling

_____ 4. "Out here in farm country I work hard and live simply," says a farmer. "I don't look for fancy, but I do require quality. That's why, for everyday down home toughness, I drive a Wellbilt pickup truck."

   a. Name calling          c. Bandwagon
   b. Transfer              d. Plain folks

*(Continues on next page)*

_____ 5. Every stereo we sell at Stereo World comes with an extended-care warranty included in the purchase price. But at Super Sound Stereo, every extended-care warranty costs you big extra bucks. That doesn't sound so super to us. Maybe they should call it So-So Sound Stereo?

    a. Glittering generalities      c. Bandwagon
    b. Name calling      d. Transfer

_____ 6. The most beautiful hair this season has shape, style, and a luxuriant, natural feel. "Flirt softens my hair and gives it great body," television actress Leslie Langtree says. "Thanks to Flirt, my hair has never looked better."

    a. Name calling      c. Bandwagon
    b. Transfer      d. Testimonial

**B.** The following fictional ad involves card stacking—in some way, it is too good to be true. Circle the letter of the important detail that has intentionally been omitted.

7. For only $255 per month, you can live in this roomy, two-bedroom, second-floor apartment in the heart of the city. Very close to convenient transportation.
    a. The apartment has one full bathroom and one powder room.
    b. Every few minutes, trains pass by on the tracks right outside your window.
    c. Apartments aren't easy to find in this part of the city.

**C.** Read the fictional ad below, and then circle the letter of the best answer to each question.

[1]Butter is the enemy of your heart and diet, loaded as it is with saturated fats and calories. [2]Cream cheese has only half the calories of butter, and its delicate taste is the perfect complement to bagels, muffins, and many other favorite foods. [3]Cream cheese is a delicious recipe ingredient as well. [4]Join the other diet-conscious Americans who are making the switch from butter to cream cheese. [5]Remember—it's time for cream cheese.

8. What propaganda technique is used in sentence 1?
    a. Bandwagon      c. Name calling
    b. Transfer      d. Plain folks

9. Which propaganda technique is used in sentence 5?
    a. Plain folks      c. Transfer
    b. Glittering generalities      d. Testimonial

10. Which fact has the advertiser intentionally omitted?
    a. Cream cheese is an important ingredient in many cheesecakes.
    b. Cream cheese and butter are both sold in the dairy section of supermarkets.
    c. Consumers typically put about twice as much cream cheese on their bagels and muffins as butter.
    d. Like butter, cream cheese is available in both bricks and tubs.

# PROPAGANDA: Test A-3

**A.** Below are descriptions of *actual* ads. On each line, write the letter of the main propaganda technique described. Each technique is represented once.

---

**a** Bandwagon—*Buy me or vote for me because everyone's doing it; jump on the bandwagon.*

**b** Testimonial—*Buy me or vote for me because famous people endorse me.*

**c** Transfer—*Buy me or vote for me because I'm associated with a symbol or image that people admire or love.*

**d** Plain folks—*Buy me or support me because I'm used by—or I am—an everyday kind of person, just like you.*

**e** Name calling—*Buy me or vote for me because my competitors have negative qualities.*

**f** Glittering generalities—*Buy or vote for me because of some important-sounding—but unspecific—claims.*

---

_____ 1. An ad for Progresso Soup shows a family sitting down to dinner. The announcer says that Progresso provides "all the goodness of home."

_____ 2. In an ad for Purina O·N·E dog food, actor Robert Urich is quoted as saying, "To me, there are two kinds of dog food. Purina O·N·E, and the rest."

_____ 3. "There's a brownie's worth of fat in every spoonful of Hellmann's. But new Kraft Free is fat-free," states a Kraft ad.

_____ 4. Watch Your Grades Go From B's, C's, and D's To Straight A's! Let the *To Get an "A" or Not to Get an "A"* booklet show you how! Hundreds of thousands of students have gone from B's, C's and D's to straight A's and so can YOU!

_____ 5. "How do you make something taste so fattening when it's at least 98% fat free?" asks an ad for Sara Lee low-fat baked products. "Make it 100% Sara Lee" is the answer.

_____ 6. A picture of a can of Budweiser Beer covers more than half of a full-page ad in a campus paper. Smaller pictures include a map of the U.S. and an eagle. The ad says, "You won't believe what this can can do. . . . Recycling this can reduces litter, saves energy, and provides important income for non-profit groups and others. So pitch in, recycle, and help keep America clean. . . . A Pledge and a Promise. Anheuser-Busch Companies."

*(Continues on next page)*

**B.** The actual product promotion described below involves card stacking—in some way, the promotion is not all that it seems. Circle the letter of the important detail that the advertiser has intentionally omitted.

7. Bounty came out with a new package of paper towels at the old price. A roll of the new paper towels carried the impressive announcement "New! More Absorbent Than Ever."
   a. The new towels are 10 percent more absorbent than before.
   b. The new roll has fewer sheets of towels than before.
   c. Bounty often advertised its paper towels on television.

**C.** Read the description below of an actual ad, and then circle the letter of the best answer to each question.

> [1]Music plays as television viewers see a man, woman and dog running through the rain, up some steps, and into a house. [2]The man sets down a grocery bag, the woman squeezes out her dripping shirt, and the dog shakes the rain off his coat. [3]A voice says, "In over half the homes in America, people come home to Kenmore appliances."

8. Which propaganda technique is used in the scenes described in sentences 1 and 2?
   a. Testimonial                    c. Transfer
   b. Bandwagon                      d. Plain folks

9. Which propaganda technique is used in sentence 3?
   a. Testimonial                    c. Bandwagon
   b. Glittering generalities        d. Name calling

10. Which words are the key to the propaganda technique used in sentence 3?
    a. "over half the homes in America"
    b. "come home"
    c. "Kenmore appliances"

# PROPAGANDA: Test B-1

**A.** In each pair of the fictional ads that follow, the first ad does *not* illustrate a propaganda technique, but the second one does. On each line, write the letter of the propaganda technique used in the *second* ad.

As a reminder, brief explanations of the propaganda techniques are given in the box below.

---

Bandwagon—*Buy me or vote for me because everyone's doing it; jump on the bandwagon.*
Testimonial—*Buy me or vote for me because famous people endorse me.*
Transfer—*Buy me or vote for me because I'm associated with a symbol or image that people admire or love.*
Plain folks—*Buy me or support me because I'm used by—or I am—an everyday kind of person, just like you.*
Name calling—*Buy me or vote for me because my competitors have negative qualities.*
Glittering generalities—*Buy or vote for me because of some important-sounding—but unspecific—claims.*

---

_____ 1. • I'm voting for Jones because he has had ten years of experience on the Senate's Committee on International Affairs.

 • I'll bet my French poodle and German shepherd know more about foreign affairs than Smith does. My vote goes to Jones.

 a. Bandwagon          c. Transfer
 b. Name calling       d. Glittering generalities

_____ 2. • Many shoppers find Cheese Bits to be good and economical.

 • Home Town Cheese Bits taste just like the down-to-earth snacks at your local diner. You don't need fancy snacks at fancy prices, just simple, delicious food.

 a. Testimonial        c. Name calling
 b. Plain folks        d. Bandwagon

_____ 3. • Two recent polls suggest that Dick Levy may win next week's election.

 • Add your vote to the landslide victory Dick Levy will win in next week's election.

 a. Bandwagon          c. Transfer
 b. Testimonial        d. Name calling

_____ 4. • Mimi's Mango-Guava Juice is sweet and rich in vitamins.

 • Drink Mimi's Mango-Guava juice, the official juice of the U.S. Olympic team. Start *your* day like America's best!

 a. Name calling       c. Transfer
 b. Plain folks        d. Glittering generalities

*(Continues on next page)*

_____ 5. • The Falcon is designed to provide sports-car handling at an affordable price.

   • As a top-ranking tennis pro, Susan Gibbs knows performance. "That's why I drive a Falcon," she says.

   a. Bandwagon          c. Testimonial
   b. Glittering generalities   d. Transfer

_____ 6. • We hope you'll find Choco-Chip Cookies the best you've ever tasted.

   • Try Choco-Chip Cookies—the cookies with goodness that doesn't quit.

   a. Name calling       c. Plain folks
   b. Testimonial        d. Glittering generalities

_____ 7. • Our Presidential candidate supports our country's farmers.

   • The Presidential candidate has her own small farm, so she knows the farmers' concerns.

   a. Plain folks        c. Glittering generalities
   b. Testimonial        d. Name calling

**B.** The following fictional ad involves card stacking—in some way, it is too good to be true. Circle the letter of the important fact that has intentionally been omitted.

   8. Our wonderful new line of extra light cakes is made without any fats at all.
   a. The cakes come in six flavors.
   b. The cakes have the same number of calories as the cakes that aren't called "light."
   c. The cakes cost almost as much as the cakes that aren't called "light."

**C.** Read the fictional promotion below, and then circle the letter of the best answer to each question.

   [1]You probably know many people who are constantly on a diet, starving themselves and yearning for forbidden hot fudge sundaes. [2]Did you know that at least 95 percent of the weight that is lost through all this effort is regained? [3]A new movement is based on the belief that the cycle of losing and regaining weight is worse for people than maintaining a stable (yet plump) weight. [4]Thousands of people are joining Roberta Rice, a champion of this new cause, in the pledge, "I'll never diet again." [5]True, Miss Rice weighs much more than the vain models whose sickly thin thighs are displayed in fashion magazines. [6]But she is attractive, self-confident, and delighted with her role in the new movement. [7]She even reports that after she lost her obsession with food, she lost some weight.

   9. Which propaganda technique is used in sentence 4?
   a. Name calling        c. Bandwagon
   b. Transfer            d. Glittering generalities

   10. Which propaganda technique is used in sentence 5?
   a. Bandwagon appeal    c. Name calling
   b. Testimonial         d. Glittering generalities

# PROPAGANDA: Test B-2

**A.** Each fictional ad that follows illustrates a particular propaganda technique. On the line next to each ad, write the letter of the main technique being used.

As a reminder, brief explanations of the propaganda techniques are given in the box below.

> Bandwagon—*Buy me or vote for me because everyone's doing it; jump on the bandwagon.*
> Testimonial—*Buy me or vote for me because famous people endorse me.*
> Transfer—*Buy me or vote for me because I'm associated with a symbol or image that people admire or love.*
> Plain folks—*Buy me or support me because I'm used by—or I am—an everyday kind of person, just like you.*
> Name calling—*Buy me or vote for me because my competitors have negative qualities.*
> Glittering generalities—*Buy or vote for me because of some important-sounding—but unspecific—claims.*

_____ 1. One of the hottest trends this season is shorter skirts. In the office, on the street, in restaurants—everywhere you look, increasing numbers of women are switching to this new look.

    a. Name calling          c. Transfer
    b. Testimonial           d. Bandwagon

_____ 2. At BeWell Health Plan, your health and satisfaction is our chief concern. Our competitors, on the other hand, are apparently more interested in how much paperwork they can wring out of you.

    a. Testimonial           c. Bandwagon
    b. Name calling         d. Plain folks

_____ 3. We've got plenty of style and color at Candy's Styles, so come see how our fashions can bring out the rainbow in you.

    a. Bandwagon           c. Glittering generalities
    b. Name calling         d. Plain folks

_____ 4. Senator Bob Curren's rough-hewn manners and casual style reflect his small-town background. This down-to-earth candidate has down-to-earth solutions.

    a. Plain folks            c. Glittering generalities
    b. Name calling         d. Testimonial

*(Continues on next page)*

_____ 5. Feel like a princess on your wedding day! The Royal Bridal Shop features stunning brides' dresses as beautiful as those worn by Great Britain's royal brides, Lady Di and Fergie.

   a. Transfer
   b. Glittering generalities
   c. Plain folks
   d. Name calling

_____ 6. James Oliver, the former star of *Avenue A*, is currently talking to kids across America about the dangers of drug addiction. "You don't want drugs," he says. "They can ruin your life and even kill you."

   a. Glittering generalities
   b. Testimonial
   c. Transfer
   d. Bandwagon

**B.** The following fictional ad involves card stacking—in some way, it is too good to be true. Circle the letter of the important fact that has intentionally been omitted.

7. Congratulations, Ms. Kerr; you are among the finalists for the National Magazine Club's Ten Million Dollar Lottery.
   a. The ten million dollars will be split among several winners.
   b. There are several million other people who are also among the finalists.
   c. The company has sponsored lotteries for twenty years.

**C.** Read the fictional ad below, and then circle the letter of the best answer to each question.

> [1]The dazzling book *Early America* can now be yours for only $2.95. [2]This beautifully illustrated, 356-page volume ordinarily sells for $34.95. [3]To receive your copy, just fill in the card below and send it to the Library of History Book Club. [4]Join the thousands who already enjoy membership, which carries no obligation.

8. Which of the following is a glittering generality?
   a. "dazzling"
   b. "356-page volume"
   c. "illustrated"
   d. "ordinarily sells for $34.95"

9. Which propaganda technique is used in the first part of sentence 4?
   a. Plain folks
   b. Testimonial
   c. Transfer
   d. Bandwagon

10. Which of the following facts has been purposely omitted?
   a. All books sold to members are printed in special editions for the club and offered at reduced prices.
   b. Members will be charged for each month's special selection unless they return a card indicating that they do not want the selection.
   c. The Library of History sells both paperback and hardcover books.
   d. The club does not sell children's books.

# PROPAGANDA: Test B-3

**A.** Below are descriptions of *actual* ads. On each line, write the letter of the main propaganda technique described. Each technique is represented at least once.

> **a** Bandwagon—*Buy me or vote for me because everyone's doing it; jump on the bandwagon.*
> **b** Testimonial—*Buy me or vote for me because famous people endorse me.*
> **c** Transfer—*Buy me or vote for me because I'm associated with a symbol or image that people admire or love.*
> **d** Plain folks—*Buy me or support me because I'm used by—or I am—an everyday kind of person, just like you.*
> **e** Name calling—*Buy me or vote for me because my competitors have negative qualities.*
> **f** Glittering generalities—*Buy or vote for me because of some important-sounding—but unspecific—claims.*

_____ 1. Actress Lindsay Wagner tells how roomy and convenient a Ford station wagon is.

_____ 2. An ad states that Carlton cigarettes have "a taste that's right."

_____ 3 From an ad for the Plymouth Sundance: "The Sundance is also the lowest-priced car in the world with an air bag. Civic, Tercel, and Escort don't offer you the protection of a driver's-side air bag."

_____ 4. An ad for an "instant memory" course offered by The Institute of Advanced Thinking claims the course has been used "by over 200,000 for insight, creativity, knowledge, and profit."

_____ 5. In a Tanqueray Gin advertisement, a beautiful woman in a sexy bikini is lying on the beach, her eyes closed. She is deeply tanned, but light untanned areas on her belly create a replica of the Tanqueray Gin label. The caption reads: "The perfect tan."

_____ 6. An ad for Citrus Hill Lemonade shows a picture of a little boy selling lemonade near his home while his mom looks over the fence. The headline reads, "Mom and Citrus Hill gave my business a healthy start."

_____ 7. An ad for a Canon personal copier features a photo of television actor and sleight-of-hand magician Harry Anderson. Anderson is quoted as saying, ". . . now, bingo, I'm knocking out clean, crisp copies on everything from business cards to . . . transparencies, faster than a three-handed card dealer."

*(Continues on next page)*

**B.** The actual ad described below involves card stacking—the product is not all the ad makes it seem to be. Circle the letter of the important fact that the advertiser has intentionally omitted.

8. An ad for a shaving gel for woman claimed, "New Soft Sense Moisturing Shave Gel with Vitamin E." It went on to say, "You've never shaved so soft."

The advertiser has purposely omitted
a. what the scent of the gel is like.
b. whether or not vitamin E has been proven to moisturize well, or at all.
c. the percentage of women who have decided not to shave their legs at all.

**C.** Read the fictional ad below, and then circle the letter of the best answer to each question.

Are you tired of big impersonal banks that treat you like a number? At HomeTown Savings and Loan Bank, you aren't a code in a giant computer somewhere. Here, you're a valued customer, a member of the community we're a part of. As lending officer Janet Morris says, "At HomeTown Savings Bank, I can assist my neighbors, people like me."

9. Which propaganda technique is used in the first sentence?
a. Bandwagon      c. Transfer
b. Name calling      d. Testimonial

10. Which propaganda technique is used in the last sentence?
a. Transfer      c. Plain folks
b. Name calling      d. Glittering generalities

## PROPAGANDA: Test C-1

A. In each pair of the fictional ads that follow, the first ad does *not* illustrate a propaganda technique, but the second one does. On each line, write the letter of the propaganda technique used in the *second* ad.

As a reminder, brief explanations of the propaganda techniques are given in the box below.

---

Bandwagon—*Buy me or vote for me because everyone's doing it; jump on the bandwagon.*
Testimonial—*Buy me or vote for me because famous people endorse me.*
Transfer—*Buy me or vote for me because I'm associated with a symbol or image that people admire or love.*
Plain folks—*Buy me or support me because I'm used by—or I am—an everyday kind of person, just like you.*
Name calling—*Buy me or vote for me because my competitors have negative qualities.*
Glittering generalities—*Buy or vote for me because of some important-sounding—but unspecific—claims.*

---

_____ 1. • A college degree opens up job doors, and there's no better college than Western College.

• Comedian Bill Groff says, "A college degree opens up job doors, and there's no better college than Western College."

a. Name calling          c. Transfer
b. Testimonial           d. Bandwagon

_____ 2. • Olsen Paint has rich color and lasts for years.

• A man in painter's overalls is dipping his brush into a can of Olsen Paint. "Most of the week I'm president of Olsen Paint Company," he says. "On Saturdays, I'm a housepainter myself. So I know what people look for in a quality housepaint."

a. Transfer              c. Bandwagon
b. Name calling          d. Plain folks

_____ 3. • You can make a deal at Dave's Auto Dealership.

• Come early so you won't have to stand in line—because everyone knows you can make a deal with Dave and save.

a. Name calling          c. Testimonial
b. Transfer              d. Bandwagon

_____ 4. • Come to Ace Autos for warrantied cars at competitive prices.

• They say, "When life gives you lemons, make lemonade." But I say when you paid $11,000 for the lemon at Wheelers' Car Dealers, you should demand your money back and come see me at Ace Autos.

a. Bandwagon             c. Testimonial
b. Name calling          d. Plain folks

*(Continues on next page)*

_____ 5. • Lynda Byrne will make an impressive mayor; as deputy mayor and state senator, she convinced many that she is an excellent speaker, a hard worker, and a capable administrator.

   • Linda Byrne will make an impressive mayor; she's a natural wonder.

   a. Bandwagon              c. Glittering generalities
   b. Testimonial            d. Transfer

_____ 6. • Frosty Diet Cola has no calories.

   • An attractive couple in bathing suits stop at a soda stand. "What are you drinking?" the man asks. "Frosty Diet Cola, of course," she answers as she slips her hand around the man's waist.

   a. Transfer                c. Name calling
   b. Glittering generalities  d. Testimonial

**B.** The following fictional ad involves card stacking—in some way, it is too good to be true. Circle the letter of the important fact that has intentionally been omitted.

7. Not only is our new fruit punch delicious, but bottle for bottle, it costs less than the leading brand.
   a. The punch comes in assorted flavors.
   b. The punch is in a 6-ounce bottle; the leading brand is in an 8-ounce bottle.
   c. The punch includes a mixture of more fruit juices than the leading brand.

**C.** Read the fictional ad below, and then circle the letter of the best answer to each question.

> ¹Have you ever wondered why the prices at Broad Street Cameras are always lower than many of our competitors'? ²Our magnificent discounts and amazing low prices are possible because of our wise policy. ³That policy is to buy our products from independent importers who charge less than the companies that others choose as their offical importers. ⁴As a result, we pay less than many of our competitors, and so we charge less. ⁵Our warehouse is fully stocked now with cameras, computers, and video equipment, so don't buy until you see us. ⁶Remember, if you buy from our competitors, you'll probably pay too much.

8. Which is a glittering detail?
   a. "lower than many of our competitors'"   c. "independent importers"
   b. "magnificent discounts"                 d. "video equipment"

9. Which propaganda technique is used in sentence 6?
   a. Bandwagon              c. Name calling
   b. Plain folks            d. Transfer

10. Which of the following facts has the advertiser intentionally omitted?
    a. Broad Street Cameras' goods come with English-language instructions.
    b. The company sells both German and Japanese cameras.
    c. Companies not officially chosen as importers are still legitimate businesses.
    d. Goods not ordered from manufacturers' official importers do not have a manufacturer's U.S. warranty.

## PROPAGANDA: Test C-2

**A.** Each fictional ad that follows illustrates a particular propaganda technique. On the line next to each ad, write the letter of the main technique being used.

As a reminder, brief explanations of the propaganda techniques are given in the box below.

> Bandwagon—*Buy me or vote for me because everyone's doing it; jump on the bandwagon.*
> Testimonial—*Buy me or vote for me because famous people endorse me.*
> Transfer—*Buy me or vote for me because I'm associated with a symbol or image that people admire or love.*
> Plain folks—*Buy me or support me because I'm used by—or I am—an everyday kind of person, just like you.*
> Name calling—*Buy me or vote for me because my competitors have negative qualities.*
> Glittering generalities—*Buy or vote for me because of some important-sounding—but unspecific—claims.*

_____ 1. "I wear Form Fit jeans—if I wear anything at all," whispers a shapely model in tight jeans and low-cut T-shirt.

   a. Bandwagon      c. Transfer
   b. Name calling      d. Glittering generalities

_____ 2. An Arnold Autofocus camera is the camera of your dreams. This delightful camera will make all your photography a pleasure. You'll love your new Arnold Autofocus.

   a. Testimonial      c. Bandwagon
   b. Glittering generalities      d. Name calling

_____ 3. "I'll sing for my supper, when the supper is a Farm Fresh chicken," warbles opera great Lucy Edwards. "Plump, delicious Farm Fresh chicken puts a song in my heart and great food on my table."

   a. Transfer      c. Testimonial
   b. Plain folks      d. Name calling

_____ 4. "I shop for my family's wardrobe at Wilson's Department Store. I want good values, not necessarily designer labels," says Anna Hendricks, bank clerk and homemaker.

   a. Plain folks      c. Transfer
   b. Name calling      d. Glittering generalities

_____ 5. Senator Bernita Walters does not know the most elementary facts about how to represent her state. To call her a legislator is exaggeration. Vote for Karen Dow for state senate.

   a. Glittering generalities      c. Testimonial
   b. Name calling      d. Transfer

*(Continues on next page)*

_____ 6. A small group comes onto a crowded beach carrying buckets of Deep Southern brand fried chicken. Other people nearby notice the group, leave, and come back with buckets of Deep Southern fried chicken. Soon everyone on the beach is either eating Deep Southern or going to get some.

a. Glittering generalities     c. Transfer
b. Name calling     d. Bandwagon

_____ 7. An ad brochure for a restaurant is titled, "Cavanaugh's & Tradition. It's a Family Affair." Inside, the brochure features biographical sketches of hard-working Cavanaugh's employees and repeatedly refers to them as "family." One featured individual is Danitra Barnett, a "wife and mother, who is expecting her second child shortly."

a. Glittering generalities     c. Plain folks
b. Name calling     d. Bandwagon

**B.** The following fictional ad involves card stacking—in some way, it is too good to be true. Circle the letter of the important detail that has intentionally been omitted.

8. "As President," says a candidate, "I will do everything in my power to keep income taxes from rising."
   a. The candidate was governor of a large state for two terms.
   b. The candidate played basketball in college.
   c. The candidate is in favor of raising sales taxes.

**C.** Read the fictional ad below, and then circle the letter of the best answer to each question.

> ¹First America Bank offers a remarkable protection plan for lost or stolen credit cards. ²For only $15, you can buy credit card protection that covers your losses up to $10,000. ³Isn't this impressive guarantee worth the small yearly fee? ⁴Losing a credit card naturally causes some anxiety, but First America's protection plan frees you from needless worry. ⁵We notify your credit card company, and we cover your losses, all for one astonishingly low fee. ⁶Remember, First America Bank is as sound as the country it serves so well.

9. Which propaganda technique is used in sentence 6?
   a. Plain folks     c. Bandwagon appeal
   b. Transfer     d. Testimonial

10. Which of the following facts has the advertiser intentionally omitted?
    a. Federal law limits a card owner's legal responsibility for lost or stolen credit cards to fifty dollars.
    b. The First America protection plan covers no more than twenty credit cards.
    c. A lost or stolen credit card should be reported within forty-eight hours.
    d. The bank offers its own Red, White, and Blue Bank Card to members in the plan.

# PROPAGANDA: Test C-3

A. Below are descriptions of *actual* ads. On each line, write the letter of the main propaganda technique described. Each technique is represented at least once.

> **a** Bandwagon—*Buy me or vote for me because everyone's doing it; jump on the bandwagon.*
> **b** Testimonial—*Buy me or vote for me because famous people endorse me.*
> **c** Transfer—*Buy me or vote for me because I'm associated with a symbol or image that people admire or love.*
> **d** Plain folks—*Buy me or support me because I'm used by—or I am—an everyday kind of person, just like you.*
> **e** Name calling—*Buy me or vote for me because my competitors have negative qualities.*
> **f** Glittering generalities—*Buy or vote for me because of some important-sounding—but unspecific—claims.*

_____ 1. Adults—a teacher and a businesswoman—confess that they like the taste of Sugar Frosted Flakes.

_____ 2. Actress and comedienne Martha Raye (known for her large mouth) appears on an ad for a denture adhesive. "Take it from a big mouth," she says, "it really works."

_____ 3. A print ad for Toyota Corolla states: "Millions of people have fond memories of a Toyota Corolla."

_____ 4. An ad for Black Velvet Canadian Whiskey includes a large photo of a beautiful, sexy-looking blonde woman dressed in a strapless black velvet dress and gold jewelry. In the corner of the ad is a small picture of the whiskey.

_____ 5. An ad for Gallo wine reads: "It's time for a change to Gallo."

_____ 6. Philadelphia Eagle Keith Byars tells the radio audience that he caught more passes than any other "back" in the National Football League last year. He goes on to say, "But building up good-enough yardage really builds up my appetite, and I tackle it with Swanson's Hungry Man dinners."

_____ 7. A Pennsylvania state senatorial campaign ad for Dick Thornburgh included pictures of Harris Wofford, Thornburgh's opponent in the election. At one point the ad states: "Be careful of Mr. Wofford. He'll say anything to get elected."

*(Continues on next page)*

**B.** The actual ad quoted below involves card stacking—the product is not all that the ad makes it seem to be. Circle the letter of the important fact that the advertiser has intentionally omitted.

8. "The California Avocado. It's a rich source of vitamins and minerals. 17 to be exact. It also has lots of potassium. And contains absolutely no cholesterol. So when it comes to adding nutrition to your daily routine, the delicious California Avocado is a natural."
   a. A California avocado is 90 percent fat.
   b. A California avocado has a small amount of sodium.
   c. Half of a California avocado provides a quarter of the Recommended Daily Allowance of vitamin C.

**C.** Read the fictional ad below, and then circle the letter of the best answer to each question.

> [1]Get off of that sofa, thunderthighs! [2]Drag your tired, shapeless body to Norman's Sporting Goods in time for our exercise bike and treadmill sale. [3]Join the multitude of former slobs like yourself who are now fit, trim, and energetic, thanks to a regular program of exercise on one of our quality home workout machines. [4]You can be like our customer James Woodall, a plumber, who says, "I shed forty pounds and cut my cholesterol level in half after purchasing one of Norman's affordable exercise bikes."

9. Which is the main propaganda technique used in sentence 3?
   a. Bandwagon                          c. Transfer
   b. Glittering generalitires           d. Testimonial

10. Which is the main propaganda technique used in sentence 4?
   a. Name calling                       c. Plain folks
   b. Testimonial                        d. Glittering generalities

# PROPAGANDA: Test D-1

**A.** In each pair of the fictional ads that follow, the first ad does *not* illustrate a propaganda technique, but the second one does. On each line, write the letter of the propaganda technique used in the *second* ad.

As a reminder, brief explanations of the propaganda techniques are given in the box below.

> Bandwagon—*Buy me or vote for me because everyone's doing it; jump on the bandwagon.*
> Testimonial—*Buy me or vote for me because famous people endorse me.*
> Transfer—*Buy me or vote for me because I'm associated with a symbol or image that people admire or love.*
> Plain folks—*Buy me or support me because I'm used by—or I am—an everyday kind of person, just like you.*
> Name calling—*Buy me or vote for me because my competitors have negative qualities.*
> Glittering generalities—*Buy or vote for me because of some important-sounding—but unspecific—claims.*

_____ 1. • Miami offers its residents several advantages, from warm weather to spectator sports.

• "I love Miami," says Dolphins' star George Raymond. "The fans here are great, and I recommend Miami as a wonderful place to live."

    a. Plain folks              c. Name calling
    b. Bandwagon            d. Testimonial

_____ 2. • As a young man, Candidate Alan Wilson had a variety of jobs working in a department store and in his family's TV station.

• As a young man, Candidate Alan Wilson learned what it means to work hard by spending long hours  lifting boxes and sweeping floors.

    a. Name calling           c. Plain folks
    b. Bandwagon            d. Glittering generalities

_____ 3. • Twin Oaks is a residential development near Des Moines, Iowa.

• There's nothing else quite like Twin Oaks, an exclusive residential community where you will be proud to live.

    a. Bandwagon            c. Transfer
    b. Testimonial          d. Glittering generalities

_____ 4. • Markey's Used Cars will be open on the Fourth of July.

• A patriotic march plays, and a giant American flag waves over a used car lot. "Celebrate your freedom of choice on the Fourth of July!" says the announcer. "At Markey's, we'll honor the holiday by making some star-spangled deals."

    a. Testimonial           c. Bandwagon
    b. Name calling         d. Transfer

*(Continues on next page)*

_____ 5. • Cheesy Pizza is delicious.

• Al's Pizza is like the thick cardboard we use to wrap take-home orders of Cheesy Pizza. Eat Cheezy Pizza if you're a pizza lover; eat Al's if you love cardboard.

a. Name calling      c. Testimonial
b. Glittering generalities      d. Plain folks

_____ 6. • The Pineapple II GS Computer Co. offers educational programs designed to improve children's skills in reading, math, and science.

• Don't let your children lag behind! Join the thousands of smart parents who are investing in their children's future with a Pineapple II GS Computer and Programs.

a. Name calling      c. Bandwagon
b. Testimonial      d. Glittering generalities

_____ 7. • A modern convention center should draw more conventions to our city.

• A stunning new convention center would be just what's needed to usher us into the twenty-first century.

a. Plain folks      c. Name calling
b. Glittering generalities      d. Bandwagon

**B.** The following fictional ad involves card stacking—in some way, it is too good to be true. Circle the letter of the important fact that has intentionally been omitted.

8. The Kellogg's Corn Pops box explains that an ounce of Corn Pops (once called *Sugar Pops*) contains less sugar than an apple, a banana, or two pancakes with syrup.
   a. Corn Pops contains less sugar than cola drinks.
   b. Corn Pops can be eaten out of the box like a snack.
   c. Many people eat more than an ounce of Corn Pops for breakfast.

**C.** Read the fictional ad below, and then circle the letter of the best answer to each question.

[1]"The Tri-County Regional Craft Festival is an event our family never misses," said Belinda Groffman, famous folk singer. [2]"It's a weekend all of us look forward to all year," added her singing partner and husband Bob. [3]"Not only do we enjoy the best in crafts from all over the region, but the other activities are so much fun—from puppet shows to magicians and jugglers. [4]This year, join the thousands of families who have already discovered how much fun they can have at the Tri-County Folk Festival."

9. Which is the main propaganda technique used in this passage?
   a. Plain folks      c. Name calling
   b. Transfer      d. Testimonial

10. Which is the main propaganda technique used in sentence 4?
    a. Name calling      c. Testimonial
    b. Bandwagon      d. Transfer

## PROPAGANDA: Test D-2

**A.** Each fictional ad that follows illustrates a particular propaganda technique. On the line next to each ad, write the letter of the main technique being used.

As a reminder, brief explanations of the propaganda techniques are given in the box below.

> Bandwagon—*Buy me or vote for me because everyone's doing it; jump on the bandwagon.*
> Testimonial—*Buy me or vote for me because famous people endorse me.*
> Transfer—*Buy me or vote for me because I'm associated with a symbol or image that people admire or love.*
> Plain folks—*Buy me or support me because I'm used by—or I am—an everyday kind of person, just like you.*
> Name calling—*Buy me or vote for me because my competitors have negative qualities.*
> Glittering generalities—*Buy or vote for me because of some important-sounding—but unspecific—claims.*

_____ 1. "Sure, I'm a professional basketball player," says Torpedo star center Mitch Jacobson. "But playing basketball isn't all that life's about. That's why I like to read *Newsweek* to learn more about life outside the court."

     a. Name calling       c. Transfer
     b. Testimonial       d. Plain folks

_____ 2. You can be part of the growing number of people who are saying "no" to drugs and "yes" to achievement. Be part of the crowd that makes a difference.

     a. Glittering generalities       c. Testimonial
     b. Name calling       d. Bandwagon

_____ 3. The U. S. Heritage Committee has selected Bubble-O as the official soft drink of the Heritage Celebration to be held in six major American cities this summer. Bubble-O: an important part of your heritage.

     a. Testimonial       c. Transfer
     b. Bandwagon       d. Name calling

_____ 4. The nitwits that make up City Council have created a real crisis in town. Instead of working together, these political clowns spend all their time feuding with each other. Let's vote the incumbents out.

     a. Plain folks       c. Bandwagon
     b. Name calling       d. Testimonial

*(Continues on next page)*

_____ 5. "We can work magic with your children," says Edna of Edna's Nanny Service. "We have the best nannies in the world."

    a. Glittering generalities      c. Bandwagon

    b. Name calling      d. Testimonial

_____ 6. Monroe Archer is a millionaire and the president of Monroe Vans, yet he has never lost touch with his small-town roots. He still likes returning to his hometown—in a Monroe Van, of course—to enjoy a summer band concert and a simple supper at Charley's Diner.

    a. Name calling      c. Plain folks

    b. Bandwagon      d. Testimonial

**B.** The following fictional ad involves card stacking—in some way, it is too good to be true. Circle the letter of the important fact that has intentionally been omitted.

    7. If your request for a loan has been turned down by your local bank, don't worry—no matter what your credit rating is like, we will lend you money.

    a. The lending company charges a far higher interest rate than banks.

    b. You can reach the lending company by calling a toll-free number.

    c. The lending company has been in business since 1976.

**C.** Read the fictional ad below, and then circle the letter of the best answer to each question.

    At Build-Rite Furniture, we know that Do-it-Yourself is the traditional American way. Build-Rite carries a fantastic variety of exceptional home furnishings that only await your finishing touches. Just follow the simple instructions and, in no time, you've assembled a magnificent patio set or charming night table. Join the millions of Americans who take pleasure and pride in creating their own homes with Build-Rite Furniture, the right furniture to buy.

    8. Which propaganda technique is used in the opening sentence?

    a. Testimonial      c. Glittering generalities

    b. Name calling      d. Transfer

    9. Which fact has the advertiser intentionally omitted?

    a. Build-Rite's "do-it-yourself" furniture is cheaper than furniture assembled by a manufacturer.

    b. Build-Rite does not sell electronic equipment.

    c. Build-Rite's furniture does not come with the tools necessary for assembly.

    d. Build-Rite's furniture comes in a variety of woods and plastics.

    10. Which of the following is _not_ a glittering generality?

    a. "exceptional home furnishings"      c. "the right furniture to buy"

    b. "millions of Americans"      d. "magnificent patio set"

# PROPAGANDA: Test D-3

**A.** Below are descriptions of *actual* ads. On each line, write the letter of the main propaganda technique described. Each technique is represented at least once.

---

**a** Bandwagon—*Buy me or vote for me because everyone's doing it; jump on the bandwagon.*
**b** Testimonial—*Buy me or vote for me because famous people endorse me.*
**c** Transfer—*Buy me or vote for me because I'm associated with a symbol or image that people admire or love.*
**d** Plain folks—*Buy me or support me because I'm used by—or I am—an everyday kind of person, just like you.*
**e** Name calling—*Buy me or vote for me because my competitors have negative qualities.*
**f** Glittering generalities—*Buy or vote for me because of some important-sounding—but unspecific—claims.*

---

_____ 1. "You buy cheap, you get cheap . . . there's only one reason a tire costs less than a Michelin—it deserves to," states a Michelin Tires ad.

_____ 2. An announcer states that "one very special number" is always available: General Electric's Appliance Service Center. A worried mother comes on the line, saying her son put marbles in the referigerator ice maker. "Don't worry, ma'am," a reassuring voice says.

_____ 3. An ad for a new model of Mercury Sable reads: "The New, Remarkably Sophisticated Sable."

_____ 4. "Two million retirement investors have already chosen Fidelity for a full range of plans and services," states an ad for Fidelity Investments.

_____ 5. In a drawing, a bottle of Grand Marnier Liqueur is nestled in the bank of a frozen pond. White doves are breaking out of the icy pond and circling the bottle. The caption reads, "Peace. The grandest wish of all."

_____ 6. An ad for Advil pain-reliever features a large photo of pitcher Nolan Ryan and states, "Every fifth day, Nolan Ryan rears back his 44-year-old arm and throws 75 fastballs about 90 miles per hour. So, it's not surprising that after the last out is made, the muscle aches begin for Nolan Ryan. Of course that's just about the time Nolan reaches for Advil. Advil is all the relief he needs."

_____ 7. An ad for Pierre Cardin men's cologne shows a handsome young man in a tuxedo lifting a laughing young woman, blonde and attractive, up into the air. The woman is wearing a low-cut red evening dress and a necklace of large pearls.

*(Continues on next page)*

B. The actual advertising described below involves card stacking—the product is not all that the advertising make it seem to be. Circle the letter of the important detail that the advertiser has intentionally omitted.

8. The front of boxes of Fibbers High Fiber Cookies includes these claims: "All Natural, No Cholesterol, Low in Saturated Fat."
   a. Fiber helps to lower cholesterol.
   b. The cookies come in flavors.
   c. Though low in saturated fat, each Fibbers cookie has more total fat than two Oreo cookies.

C. Read the fictional ad below, and then circle the letter of the best answer to each question.

> [1]Hurry into Wellco Electronics this week to buy an Avoid 'Em Radar Detector at 20 percent off the suggested retail price! [2]With an Avoid 'Em mounted on your automobile's dashboard, you will never be subject to speeding tickets from overly ambitious police officers. [3]Before they clock your car's speed, you'll—Avoid 'Em! [4]Join the millions of smart drivers who don't have time to waste on speed traps—buy an Avoid 'Em at Wellco Electronics today!

9. Which fact has the advertiser intentionally omitted?
   a. Wellco Electronics carries two other brands of radar detectors.
   b. The Avoid 'Em Radar Detector is manufactured in Japan.
   c. The use of radar detectors is illegal in some states.
   d. Drinking and driving is a major cause of highway deaths.

10. What is the main propaganda technique used in sentence 4?
    a. Transfer               c. Testimonial
    b. Glittering generality  d. Bandwagon

## PROPAGANDA: Test E-1

A. In each pair of the fictional ads that follow, the first ad does *not* illustrate a propaganda technique, but the second one does. On each line, write the letter of the propaganda technique used in the *second* ad.

As a reminder, brief explanations of the propaganda techniques are given in the box below.

> Bandwagon—*Buy me or vote for me because everyone's doing it; jump on the bandwagon.*
> Testimonial—*Buy me or vote for me because famous people endorse me.*
> Transfer—*Buy me or vote for me because I'm associated with a symbol or image that people admire or love.*
> Plain folks—*Buy me or support me because I'm used by—or I am—an everyday kind of person, just like you.*
> Name calling—*Buy me or vote for me because my competitors have negative qualities.*
> Glittering generalities—*Buy or vote for me because of some important-sounding—but unspecific—claims.*

_____ 1. • MoneyReady credit-card company has a 24-hour telephone number to call if a card is lost or stolen.

   • A young woman with her arms around two small children says, "When my credit card was stolen while we were at Disneyland, I thought our vacation was ruined. Instead, after just one phone call, the company canceled my old card number and issued me a new one. Thanks, MoneyReady."

   a. Plain folks                  c. Bandwagon
   b. Glittering generalities      d. Name calling

_____ 2. • Rep. Snark has served six terms in the House of Representatives.

   • Six-term incumbent Representative Snark is part of the pampered Washington crowd now, out of touch with the people who elected him.

   a. Testimonial                  c. Transfer
   b. Glittering generalities      d. Name calling

_____ 3. • Clear Image copy machines come with a full 90-day warranty.

   • Join the thousands of other top executives who insist upon Clear Image quality for your office copier.

   a. Testimonial                  c. Bandwagon
   b. Plain folks                  d. Name calling

_____ 4. • Zesty Zip frozen fruit concentrate is made from five tropical fruits.

   • "I get each day off to a roaring start with Zesty Zip," says two-time Indy 500 winner Lonnie Milles.

   a. Testimonial                  c. Bandwagon
   b. Plain folks                  d. Name calling

*(Continues on next page)*

_____ 5. • At Triple A Technical School, you can learn skills needed to become a plumber, mechanic or electrician.

   • Set the world on fire with skills you learn at Triple A Technical School!

   a. Glittering generalities     c. Bandwagon
   b. Name calling     d. Transfer

_____ 6. • Come to Smith's Carpets' spring sale.

   • We cannot tell a lie—we honor America's Presidents with beauty and savings. Come to Cherry Tree Carpets to see the great quality and discounts at our Presidents' Day Sale.

   a. Bandwagon     c. Transfer
   b. Name calling     d. Plain folks

_____ 7. • Kiddy Kare is the largest day-care center in town.

   • Kiddy Kare's competitor's day-care center is more concerned about profits than children.

   a. Bandwagon     c. Testimonial
   b. Transfer     d. Name calling

**B.** The following fictional ad involves card stacking—in some way, it is too good to be true. Circle the letter of the important fact that has intentionally been omitted.

8. For only $25, Employment Education, Inc. will send you complete information on how to earn money stuffing envelopes at home.
   a. It is not difficult to stuff envelopes.
   b. The company also sells information on learning to type.
   c. Very few people are ever hired to stuff envelopes at home.

**C.** Read the viewpoint below; then circle the letter of the best answer to each question.

Air bags in automobiles definitely save lives—it's been proven through research and statistics. Still, the ever-greedy American automotive industry has dragged its feet in providing this simple, effective safety feature in its vehicles. Most companies, callous even when actual human lives are at stake, are installing the first air bags in their most expensive models only. Apparently wealthy people's lives are more valuable than the lives of lower-income people. Drivers, too, are evidently valued more than passengers: most companies have plans to install only driver's-side air bags . . . when they get around to it.

9. Which is the main propaganda technique used in this passage?
   a. Name calling     c. Bandwagon
   b. Testimonial     d. Plain folks

10. Which words are being used in that technique?
   a. "air bags" and "models"     c. "proven" and "companies"
   b. "research and statistics"     d. "greedy" and "callous"

# PROPAGANDA: Test E-2

A. Each fictional ad that follows illustrates a particular propaganda technique. On the line next to each ad, write the letter of the main technique being used.

As a reminder, brief explanations of the propaganda techniques are given in the box below.

---

Bandwagon—*Buy me or vote for me because everyone's doing it; jump on the bandwagon.*
Testimonial—*Buy me or vote for me because famous people endorse me.*
Transfer—*Buy me or vote for me because I'm associated with a symbol or image that people admire or love.*
Plain folks—*Buy me or support me because I'm used by—or I am—an everyday kind of person, just like you.*
Name calling—*Buy me or vote for me because my competitors have negative qualities.*
Glittering generalities—*Buy or vote for me because of some important-sounding—but unspecific—claims.*

---

_____ 1. Use Today's Liquid Soap to feel cleaner than clean!

    a. Glittering generalities        c. Bandwagon
    b. Testimonial                   d. Plain folks

_____ 2. They say that Abraham Lincoln walked miles to return a nickel to a customer. We admire Honest Abe here at Garrity's Discount Furniture, and we'll try to give you that same kind of presidential service.

    a. Bandwagon             c. Testimonial
    b. Transfer                 d. Name calling

_____ 3. There's no more popular phone service than Ringaling Telephone Co. Why don't you join our rapidly growing list of customers?

    a. Glittering generalities        c. Transfer
    b. Name calling              d. Bandwagon

_____ 4. Those noisy environmentalists are anti-progress. They're afraid of modern technology. They'd rather hug a tree, or a whale, than make a real contribution to society.

    a. Name calling           c. Testimonial
    b. Bandwagon             d. Plain folks

_____ 5. The best way to warm up on those cold winter days? Ask Olympic skier Mark Terril. "There's nothing like a good hot cup of Myer's Soup to take the chill off," says Mark. "Delicious Myer's makes me feel warm all over."

    a. Bandwagon             c. Testimonial
    b. Glittering generalities    d. Plain folks

*(Continues on next page)*

_____ 6. A man interviews a worker at a construction site and a waitress and diner at a coffee shop. They say they think Senator Harley's done a good job and that they plan to vote to re-elect him.

   a. Transfer
   b. Glittering generalities
   c. Testimonial
   d. Plain folks

_____ 7. A Suzuri Pacekeeper minitruck is climbing a dirt road in the desert. "Pacekeeper, from Suzuri," says the announcer. "Freedom for the 90s."

   a. Plain folks
   b. Glittering generalities
   c. Bandwagon
   d. Name calling

B. The following fictional ad involves card stacking—in some way, it is too good to be true. Circle the letter of the important fact that has intentionally been omitted.

8. This new laptop personal computer is so easy to use that you can be a pro in just two hours!
   a. The laptop computer weighs three pounds.
   b. You can be a pro in two hours by taking an expensive training program.
   c. Laptop computers are convenient to use while traveling or otherwise working away from your desk.

C. Read the viewpoint below, and then circle the letter of the best answer to each question.

> The idea that doctors should be able to sell the medications they prescribe to their patients is outrageous. The current situation, in which patients take prescriptions from their doctors to their pharmacists, provides a check on doctors' greed. Some doctors claim they want to make acquiring drugs more convenient for their patients, but they are definitely involving themselves in a situation of conflict of interest. What prevents doctors from prescribing unnecessary drugs in order to improve their practice's profitability? Drug salespeople tempt doctors to enter this racket by promising increased profits of $30,000 to $50,000 a year. The greedy doctors in this country are hearing the cash registers ringing, but shouldn't they be keeping their minds on the Hippocratic oath they took when they entered their profession?

9. What is the main propaganda technique used in this paragraph?
   a. Bandwagon
   b. Name calling
   c. Testimonial
   d. Plain folks

10. Which words are used in that technique?
   a. "Current situation"
   b. "Greedy doctors"
   c. "Drug salespeople"
   d. "their profession"

# PROPAGANDA: Test E-3

**A.** Below are descriptions of *actual* ads. On each line, write the letter of the main propaganda technique described. Each technique is represented at least once.

> **a** Bandwagon—*Buy me or vote for me because everyone's doing it; jump on the bandwagon.*
> **b** Testimonial—*Buy me or vote for me because famous people endorse me.*
> **c** Transfer—*Buy me or vote for me because I'm associated with a symbol or image that people admire or love.*
> **d** Plain folks—*Buy me or support me because I'm used by—or I am—an everyday kind of person, just like you.*
> **e** Name calling—*Buy me or vote for me because my competitors have negative qualities.*
> **f** Glittering generalities—*Buy or vote for me because of some important-sounding—but unspecific—claims.*

_____ 1. An ad for *The Book of Waves* states that it is "A worldwide best-seller."

_____ 2. An ad for Superslims cigarettes features a super-slim, beautiful and sexy woman relaxing with a Superslim cigarette.

_____ 3. An advertisement for Hanes Gloves includes this claim: "Nothing else feels so right."

_____ 4. A friendly-looking young man in a sweatshirt is pictured in an ad for AT&T Long Distance. The ad tells us his name is Nick Joost and that he's from Austin, Texas. The ad reads in part: "My Daddy always had a saying—he said, 'Don't ever be afraid to buy the best. You'll always be happy with it.' So I did."

_____ 5. Actress Connie Sellecca walks through a wind-swept desert scene, her hair blowing in the wind. We see that she is on a movie set as she explains that Professional Formula hair-care lotion helps keep her hair looking beautiful even in the toughest conditions.

_____ 6. A Mutual of Omaha Insurance ad states: "Adapting to change isn't easy. Maybe that's why so many insurance companies don't even try . . . . If your insurance company hasn't changed in years, maybe it's time to change your insurance company."

_____ 7. Jenny Craig Weight Loss Center advertises its program with the small wedding photograph of a heavy woman beside a large picture of her new slim self. "Laura Ybarra-Beck lost 57 lbs." it says. The ad continues with Laura's words: "Jenny Craig made it easy for me to travel and still stick to my food plan."

*(Continues on next page)*

**B.** The actual advertising described below involves card stacking—the product is not all the advertising makes it seem to be. Circle the letter of the important fact that the advertiser has intentionally omitted.

8. Carnation Breakfast Bars are promoted with the claims that a bar "helps provide a nutritious start for the day"; that a bar has "balanced nutrition"; and that "with milk," a bar "provides 18 vitamins and minerals and all the protein of a nutritionally complete breakfast."
   a. The bars come in chocolate chip and peanut butter flavors.
   b. Most of the protein calculated for the "nutritionally complete breakfast" comes from the milk mentioned.
   c. The company also sells numerous other products, including powdered and condensed milk.

**C.** Read the description below of an actual ad, and then circle the letter of the best answer to each question.

A mail-order course called "Successful Investing & Money Management" claims to offer "a unique, completely practical course and successful method of acquiring wealth." The ad includes some examples of ordinary people who have increased their wealth since they took the course.

9. Which propaganda technique is illustrated by the examples of people who increased their wealth since taking the course?
   a. Transfer                                  c. Glittering generalities
   b. Name calling                              d. Plain folks

10. The advertiser has probably stacked the cards by omitting
   a. the fact that the first lesson is free.
   b. the fact that the first lesson is written by tax specialists.
   c. the percentage of people who have taken the course and have not significantly increased their wealth.
   d. a statement of how long the company has been in business.

# 10

# Argument

Many of us enjoy a good argument. A good argument is not an emotional experience where people's feelings get out of control, leaving them ready to start throwing things. Instead, it is a rational discussion where each person advances and supports a point of view about some matter. We might argue with a friend, for example, about where to eat or what movie to go to. We might argue about whether a boss or a parent or a teacher is acting in a fair or unfair manner. We might argue about whether certain performers or sports stars deserve to get paid as much as they do. In a good argument, the other person listens carefully as we state our case, waiting to see if we really have solid evidence to support our point of view.

Argumentation is, then, a part of our everyday dealings with other people. It is also central to many of the papers that we write, and it is a basic structure in much of the material that we read. Very often the two most important things we must do as *writers* are to:

1 Make a point.
2 Support the point.

Very often the two most important things we must do as *readers* are to:

1 Recognize the point.
2 Recognize the support for the point.

The essence of a good argument is this: a clear point and evidence that truly backs up that point. Clear and logical thinkers are persons who can advance a point and provide valid evidence to support that point.

This chapter will be divided into two parts. In the first part, you will practice the basics of a good argument: making a clear point and solidly supporting that point. In the second part, you will learn to recognize common errors in reasoning that prevent clear and logical thinking.

## THE BASICS OF ARGUMENT: POINT AND SUPPORT

A good argument is one in which you make a point and then provide persuasive and logical evidence to back it up. Here is a point:

**Point:** The Beef and Burger Shop is a poor fast-food restaurant.

This statement hardly discourages us from visiting the Beef and Burger Shop. "Why do you say that?" we might legitimately ask. "Give your reasons." Support is needed so we can decide for ourselves whether a valid point has been made. Suppose the point is followed by these three reasons:

1. The burgers are full of gristle.
2. The roast beef sandwiches have a chemical taste.
3. The fries are lukewarm and soggy.

Clearly, the details provide solid support for the point. They give us a basis for understanding and agreeing with the point. In light of these details, our mouths are not watering for lunch at the Beef and Burger Shop.

We see here, then, a small example of what clear thinking in an argument is about: making a point and providing support that truly backs up that point. (Another way to describe a valid argument is: stating a conclusion and providing logical reasons to support the conclusion.)

Let's look at another example:

**Point:** My neighbors are inconsiderate.

We don't really yet know if the neighbors are inconsiderate. We might trust the opinion of the person who made the statement, but we don't know for sure until supporting details enable us to see and judge for ourselves. Here are details:

1. They play their stereo very loud late at night.
2. They let their children play on my front lawn.
3. They don't stop their dog from running into my back yard.

Again, the solid support convinces us that a logical point has been made.

In everyday life, of course, people don't simply say, "Here is my point" and "Here is my support." Nor do writers of material that you read state their basic ideas so directly. Even so, the basic structure of point and support is still at work beneath the surface, and you will benefit enormously from developing the ability to discover it. In particular, to become a more skilled reader and thinker, you should learn to analyze what you read. You want to be able to determine whether a given selection really does have a logical foundation, based on a clear point and logical support for that point.

To help you distinguish, first of all, between a point and support for that point—or a conclusion and reasons for that conclusion—do the following activity.

➤ *Practice*

In each group of statements, one statement is the point, and the other statement or statements are support for the point. Identify each point with a **P**, and identify each statement of support with an **S**.

*Hint:* If you can insert the word *because* in front of a sentence, you probably have a statement of support.

1. \_\_\_\_\_ I can't keep my eyes open any longer.

\_\_\_\_\_ I'd better take a nap.

2. \_\_\_\_\_ That traffic light has stayed red for at least five minutes.

\_\_\_\_\_ That traffic light must be broken.

3. \_\_\_\_\_ His face looks tight and he seldom smiles.

\_\_\_\_\_ He's smoking more than usual.

\_\_\_\_\_ When asked how he is, he quickly changes the subject.

\_\_\_\_\_ Something must really be bothering Craig.

4. \_\_\_\_\_ The library should be kept open on Sundays and holidays.

\_\_\_\_\_ Many students save their studying for days when they do not have classes.

\_\_\_\_\_ Library facilities are already overcrowded on weekdays.

\_\_\_\_\_ It's difficult to find research materials during the week; other students are often using the books.

5. \_\_\_\_\_ The dialogue sounded like junior high school jokes.

\_\_\_\_\_ The monsters belonged in a salad, not a laboratory.

\_\_\_\_\_ *Invasion of the Asparagus People* is a terrible science fiction movie.

\_\_\_\_\_ The ending just didn't make sense. Who's ever heard of bacteria that like to eat asparagus?

## Using Informal Outlines to Evaluate Arguments

An excellent way to develop your skill at thinking clearly is to do informal outlines. In an informal outline, you identify the basic point and the basic support of a selection. Such outlines are invaluable, whether for a paper you plan to write, a speech you plan to give, or a reading selection you want to understand and study. The outline helps you think about the point that is being made and about whether the point has been adequately and logically supported.

Consider the following point. It is followed by six items of support, only three of which logically back up the point. See if you can circle those three items.

**Point:** My dog Otis does not appear to be very bright.

1. He's five years old and doesn't respond to his name yet.
2. He cries when I leave for work every day.
3. He always gets excited when visitors arrive.
4. He often attacks the back yard hedge as if it's a hostile animal.
5. He gets along very well with my neighbor's cat.
6. I often have to put food in front of him because he can't find it by himself.

Now read the following comments on the six items to see which ones you should have circled and why.

1. Most dogs know their names, so Otis's unfamiliarity with his own name reveals a weak memory, one aspect of intelligence. You should have circled the number to this item.
2. Even an intelligent dog might be sad when its companions leave the house.
3. Both bright and not-so-bright dogs are happy to see old and new human friends.
4. The inability to distinguish between a bush and an animal—friendly or hostile—suggests a lack of analytical skills. *Four* is the second number you should have circled.
5. Contrary to the comic book stereotype, dogs of all degrees of intelligence have been known to be friendly with cats.
6. Since most dogs recognize food much more often than their owners would like them to, Otis's inability to find food clearly indicates poor problem-solving skills. You should also have circled the number of this item.

## ➤ Practice

Each point below is followed by six items, three of which logically support the point and three of which do not. In the spaces provided, write the letters of the three items that logically support each point.

1.   **Point:** My neighbors are weird folks.
    a. Each family member, including the males, has purple fingernails.
    b. They call me if their dog gets loose.
    c. They have lived in the house for the past two years.
    d. They keep cows and goats inside the house.
    e. On nights with a full moon, they sit on lawn chairs placed on their roof.
    f. Each member of the family has his or her own car.

    Items that logically support the point: _____  _____  _____

2. **Point:** Alcohol and tobacco are among the most dangerous drugs that Americans use.

   a. Cancer from cigarette smoking kills a number of Americans every year.

   b. During Prohibition, liquor bootleggers fought one another as drug dealers do today.

   c. About half of all fatal traffic accidents are due to drunk driving.

   d. Nothing is more annoying than trying to enjoy a restaurant meal when the people at nearby tables are smoking and drinking heavily.

   e. We often don't think of alcohol and tobacco as "drugs," because they are legal.

   f. Alcohol abuse causes many people to become more aggressive and violent.

   Items that logically support the point: _____  _____  _____

3. **Point:** Halloween trick-or-treating should be abolished.

   a. The holiday encourages vandalism in older children.

   b. Summer would have been a better time for Halloween because it stays light longer then.

   c. Children who wear vision-obstructing masks and dark, hard-to-see costumes are in danger of being struck by cars.

   d. Thanksgiving is a lot more meaningful than Halloween.

   e. Some local business people overcharge for Halloween costumes and candy.

   f. More and more incidents of poisoned treats are occurring.

   Items that logically support the point: _____  _____  _____

4. **Point:** There should be a limit on how much can be spent for political campaigns.

   a. The television networks profit greatly from the ads for local and national elections.

   b. Elected officials could spend more time on their jobs and less on raising money.

   c. Once and for all, candidates should stop using personal attacks in their campaigns.

   d. Candidates with less money would have a more fair chance of competing.

   e. Citizens must learn to evaluate political campaigns in a logical manner.

   f. Elected officials would be less likely to be influenced by rich contributors to their campaigns.

   Items that logically support the point: _____  _____  _____

## MORE ABOUT ARGUMENTS: ERRORS IN REASONING

Learning about some common errors in reasoning will help you to spot weak points in arguments. The rest of this chapter will familiarize you with some of those errors, also known as *fallacies*. Specifically, you'll look at these unsound reasoning patterns:

Four Fallacies That Ignore the Issue:

- Changing the Subject
- Circular Reasoning
- Personal Attack
- Straw man

Four Fallacies that Overgeneralize or Oversimplify Issues:

- Hasty Generalization
- False Cause
- False Comparison
- Either-Or Fallacy

Following are explanations of these eight common types of fallacies. Exercises throughout give you practice in spotting them.

### Fallacies That Ignore the Issue

#### Fallacy 1. Changing the Subject

This method of arguing tries to divert the audience's attention from the true issue by presenting evidence that actually has nothing to do with the argument. You have already had experience with this method in the activity on pages 388-389, where you had to separate relevant support from support that was beside the point. Here are two more examples:

> I think you should buy a bird, not a dog. Many dogs shed all over the house.
> (Saying that many dogs shed is beside the point; it is possible to buy a dog that does not shed.)

> The congressman is clearly an able leader. He has a warm family life and attends church every Sunday.
> (Mention of the congressman's family and church life sidesteps the issue of just how able a leader he is.)

This fallacy is also called a *red herring*. In a fox hunt, drawing a red herring across the dogs' path causes them to lose the scent, allowing the fox to escape. Someone who changes the subject when arguing may hope the audience will lose track of the real point of the argument.

Now read the following paragraph and try to find the sentence that does *not* support the point, which is in the first sentence.

Sigmund Freud was one of the most important scientists of the twentieth century. He was among the first to study mental disorders, such as hysteria and neurosis, in a systematic way. He developed the theory of the unconscious and showed how people's behavior is greatly affected by forgotten childhood events. His discoveries are the basis of psychoanalysis, a method of treating mental illness that is still important today. He was highly regarded by scientists of his time.

The point of this argument is that Freud "was one of the most important scientists of the twentieth century." Any statement that doesn't help prove this point is irrelevant. The manner in which the scientists of his day viewed Freud isn't a logical reason for his being one of the most important scientists of this century. Many scientists have been highly regarded in their time without being very important. Thus the last sentence is irrelevant to the argument.

## ➤ Practice 1

One sentence in each paragraph below does not support the point of the argument. Read the paragraph, and then decide which sentence is not relevant to the argument. To help you decide if a sentence is irrelevant or not, ask yourself, "Does this have anything to do with the point that is being proved?"

1.  [1]Soon, the personal computer will be as necessary to every American home as the telephone is today. [2]Every family member will be able to use the computer in some way. [3]Parents will find a computer of value for keeping family information such as tax records and recipe collections. [4]Software programs now exist even for such annoying chores as balancing the family checkbook. [5]Of course, banks are already beginning to offer a computer service that balances customers' checkbooks for them. [6]In addition, children's grades will improve when they use a computer to master a subject or write an English paper. [7]And everyone will enjoy taking a break with one of the popular computer games.

Which of the following statements does not contribute to the author's conclusion that soon every American home will have a personal computer?

a. Sentence 3          c. Sentence 5
b. Sentence 4          d. Sentence 6

2.    ¹The proposed new highway linking Interstate 95 with the turnpike is a disaster. ²The plans for this highway were drawn over thirty years ago, when the affected area was lightly settled. ³Now, a generation later, the area has become developed, and hundreds of families would lose their homes if the highway were built. ⁴There are already too many forces weakening the American family structure these days. ⁵The environment will also be negatively affected by the construction of a new superhighway. ⁶Hundreds of thousands of birds and small animals, including several endangered species, will lose their natural habitats and may die out.

Which of the following is not a sound argument in support of the author's conclusion that the proposed highway is a disaster?

a.  Sentence 2                    c.  Sentence 4
b.  Sentence 3                    d.  Sentence 6

### Fallacy 2. Circular Reasoning

Part of a point cannot reasonably be used as evidence to support it. That type of argument is called *circular reasoning*, also known as *begging the question*. A simple and obvious example of such reasoning is: "Mr. Green is a great teacher because he is so wonderful at teaching." The supporting reason given in this point itself ("he is so wonderful at teaching") is really the same as the conclusion ("Mr. Green is a great teacher"). We still do not know why he is a great teacher. No real reasons have been given—the statement merely has repeated itself.

Can you spot the circular reasoning in the following arguments?

1.  Vitamins are healthy, for they improve your well-being.
2.  Since people under 21 are too young to vote, the voting age shouldn't be lowered below age 21.
3.  Abortion is an evil practice because it is so wrong.

Let's look more closely now at these arguments:

1.  The word *healthy*, which is used in the conclusion, conveys the same idea as *well-being*.
2.  The author uses the idea that people under 21 are too young to vote as both the conclusion *and* the reason of the argument. No real reason is given for *why* people under 21 are too young to vote.
3.  The claim that abortion is wrong is simply a restatement of the idea that it is an *evil practice*.

In all these cases, the reasons merely repeat an important part of the conclusion. The careful reader wants to say, "Tell me something new. You are reasoning in circles. Give me supporting evidence, not a repetition."

## ➤ *Practice 2*

Circle the number of the one item that contains an example of circular reasoning.

1. Why support Ray O'Donnell's highway safety proposal? He's got the biggest collection of speeding tickets in the district.
2. The government should lower our taxes because taxes are entirely too high.
3. Our football team is going to be number one this year. We have a new stadium to play in, and the half-time show is better than ever.
4. The people who are in favor of gun control are obviously not concerned about criminals taking control of this fine country.

### Fallacy 3. Personal Attack

This fallacy often occurs in political debate. Here's an example:

Senator Snerd's opinions on public housing are worthless. He can't even manage to hold his own household together, having married and divorced three times already.

Senator Snerd's family life may or may not reflect a weakness in his character, but it has nothing to do with the value of his opinions on public housing. This kind of fallacy ignores the issue under discussion and concentrates instead on the character of the opponent.

Sometimes personal attacks take the form of accusing people of taking a stand only because it will benefit them personally. For instance, here's a personal attack on a Congressman who supports the Equal Rights Amendment (ERA): "He doesn't care about the ERA. He only supports it in order to get more women to vote for him." This argument ignores the Congressman's detailed defense of the ERA as a way to insure equal rights for both men and women. The key to recognizing personal attack is that it always involves an opponent's personal life or character, rather than simply his or her public ideas.

## ➤ *Practice 3*

Circle the number of the one item that contains an example of personal attack.

1. Why support Ray O'Donnell's highway safety proposal? He's got the biggest collection of speeding tickets in the district.
2. The government should lower our taxes because taxes are entirely too high.
3. Our football team is going to be number one this year. We have a new stadium to play in, and the half-time show is better than ever.
4. The people who are in favor of gun control are obviously not concerned about criminals taking control of this fine country.

### *Fallacy 4. Straw Man*

An opponent made of straw can be defeated very easily. Sometimes, if one's real opponent is putting up too good a fight, it can be tempting to build a scarecrow and battle it instead. For example, take the following passage from a debate on the death penalty.

> Ms. Collins opposes capital punishment. But letting murderers out on the street to kill again is a crazy idea. If we did that, no one would be safe.

Ms. Collins, however, never advocated "letting murderers out on the street to kill again." In fact, she wants to keep them in jail for life rather than execute them. This fallacy suggests that the opponent favors an obviously unpopular cause—when the opponent really doesn't support anything of the kind.

### ➤ *Practice 4*

Circle the number of the one item that contains an example of straw man.

1.   Why support Ray O'Donnell's highway safety proposal? He's got the biggest collection of speeding tickets in the district.
2.   The government should lower our taxes because taxes are entirely too high.
3.   Our football team is going to be number one this year. We have a new stadium to play in, and the half-time show is better than ever.
4.   The people who are in favor of gun control are obviously not concerned about criminals taking control of this fine country.

## Fallacies That Overgeneralize or Oversimplify

### *Fallacy 5. Hasty Generalization*

To be valid, a point must be based on an adequate amount of evidence. Someone who draws a point or conclusion on the basis of insufficient evidence is making a *hasty generalization*. This is a very common fallacy. It is not unusual, for instance, to hear an argument like this one:

> The Chinese people have a natural talent for art. Two Chinese girls took an art course with me last semester, and they were the best students in the class.

Forming a conclusion about the quarter of a billion Chinese people in the world based on two examples is an illogical jump.

   In the argument on the next page, three supporting reasons are given, followed by four possible points. Three of the points are hasty generalizations which cannot logically be drawn from the small amount of evidence given. The fourth is a valid conclusion. Choose the one point you think is valid and put a check mark beside it. Then read the explanation that follows.

- The first time I went to that beach, I got a bad case of sunburn.
- The second time I went to that beach, I couldn't go in the water because of the pollution.
- The third time I went to that beach, I stepped on a starfish and had to go to the emergency room to have the spikes removed from my foot.

Which of the following is a valid conclusion that can be drawn from the evidence above?

____ a. That beach is unsafe and should be closed.

____ b. I've had a string of bad experiences at that beach.

____ c. Beaches are not safe places.

____ d. We're never going to get this planet cleaned up.

The correct answer is *b*. Answer *a* is simply not supported by three isolated instances; we'd need many more reports of dangerous conditions before considering having the beach closed. Answer *c* is even more poorly supported. We'd need many, many reports of dangerous conditions at beaches worldwide to come to the conclusion stated in *c*. Answer *d* is supported in part by the reference to pollution in the second statement, but the other two statements (about sunburn and starfish) are not examples of pollution.

## ➤ *Practice 5*

Check the sentence that states a valid point based on the supporting evidence in each group below. Remember that the point, or conclusion, should follow logically from the evidence. Do not jump to a conclusion that is not well-supported.

### *Group 1*

- My grandmother's cottage is in the country.
- The only sounds we hear are bird calls and the wind rustling in the pine trees.
- On Grandmother's front porch, we often enjoy watching the sunset over the lake.

Check the one valid conclusion that can be drawn from the evidence above:

____ a. The speaker would rather be at his grandmother's cottage than anywhere else.

____ b. His grandmother often invites him to her cottage.

____ c. His grandmother's cottage is the most peaceful place he's ever been.

____ d. His grandmother's cottage at the lake is very peaceful.

### Group 2

- Some people put off writing or calling a friend because they feel they did not have time to do it right, but a quick note or call is often better than nothing.
- Sometimes it makes sense to do a routine chore quickly rather than perfectly in order to save time for something more important.
- Even a desk and office need not be perfectly neat; sometimes cleaning them up is just an excuse for putting off more important work.

Check the one valid conclusion that can be drawn from the evidence above:

___ a. Perfection is not always a worthwhile goal.

___ b. People who aim for perfection never get around to important tasks.

___ c. You can be better organized if you plan each day more carefully.

___ d. Getting things done haphazardly is always better than not getting them done at all.

### Fallacy 6. False Cause

You have probably heard someone say as a joke, "I know it's going to rain today because I just washed the car." The idea that someone can make it rain by washing a car is funny because the two events obviously have nothing to do with each other. However, with more complicated issues, it is easy to make the mistake known as the fallacy of *false cause*. The mistake is to assume that because Event B follows Event A, Event A has *caused* Event B.

Cause-and-effect situations can be difficult to analyze, and people are often tempted to oversimplify them by ignoring other possible causes. To identify an argument using a false cause, look for alternative causes. Consider this argument:

> The Macklin Company was more prosperous before Ms. Williams became president. Clearly, she is the cause of the decline.

> (*Event A:* Ms. Williams became president.
> *Event B:* The Macklin Company's earnings declined.)

What other possible causes could have been responsible for the decline? Perhaps the policies of the previous president are just now affecting the company. Perhaps the market for the company's product has changed. In any case, it's easy but dangerous to assume that just because A *came before* B, A *caused* B.

## ➤ *Practice 6*

Circle the number of the one item that contains an example of false cause.

1. You'll either have to get a good job soon or face the fact that you'll never be successful.
2. Cincinnati has terrible weather. I visited there for a week last summer, and the sun didn't shine even once.
3. After visiting Hal today, I came home with a headache. I must be allergic to his dog.
4. Of course the legalization of prostitution will work in America. It's worked in European countries, hasn't it?

### Fallacy 7. False Comparison

When the poet Robert Burns wrote, "My love is like a red, red rose," he meant that both the woman he loved and a rose are beautiful. In other ways—such as having green leaves and thorns, for example—his love did not resemble a rose at all. Comparisons are often a good way to clarify a point. But because two things are not alike in all respects, comparisons (sometimes called *analogies*) often make poor evidence for arguments. In the error in reasoning known as *false comparison*, the assumption is that two things are more alike than they really are. For example, read the following argument.

It didn't hurt your grandfather in the old country to get to work without a car, and it won't hurt you either.

To judge whether or not this is a false comparison, consider how the two situations are alike and how they differ. They are similar in that both involve a young person's need to get to work. But the situations are different in that the grandfather didn't have to be at work an hour after his last class. In fact, he didn't go to school at all. In addition, his family didn't own a car he could use. The differences in this case are more important than the similarities, making it a false comparison.

## ➤ *Practice 7*

Circle the number of the one item that contains an example of false comparison.

1. You'll either have to get a good job soon or face the fact that you'll never be successful.
2. Cincinnati has terrible weather. I visited there for a week last summer, and the sun didn't shine even once.
3. After visiting Hal today, I came home with a headache. I must be allergic to his dog.
4. Of course the legalization of prostitution will work in America. It's worked in European countries, hasn't it?

## *Fallacy 8. Either-Or*

It is often wrong to assume that there are only two sides to a question. Offering only two choices when more actually exist is an *either-or fallacy*. For example, the statement "You are either with us or against us" assumes that there is no middle ground. Or consider the following:

People opposed to unrestricted free speech are really in favor of censorship.

This argument ignores the fact that a person could believe in free speech as well as in laws that prohibit slander or that punish someone for yelling "Fire!" in a crowded theater. Some issues have only two sides (Will you pass the course, or won't you?), but most have several.

## ➤ *Practice 8*

Circle the number of the item that contains an example of the either-or fallacy.

1. You'll either have to get a good job soon or face the fact that you'll never be successful.
2. Cincinnati has terrible weather. I visited there for a week last summer, and the sun didn't shine even once.
3. After visiting Hal today, I came home with a headache. I must be allergic to his dog.
4. Of course the legalization of prostitution will work in America. It's worked in European countries, hasn't it?

## ➤ *Review*

To review what you've learned in this chapter, complete each of the following sentences about evaluating arguments.

1. Often the two most important things we must do when we read are to identify the _____ of a selection and also the _____ that backs it up.

2. A valuable step in reading, writing, or speaking clearly is to first prepare a(n) _____.

3. A fallacy is an error in (*reading, reasoning, changing the subject*) _____ that makes an argument illogical.

4. The fallacies of personal attack and straw man are specific versions of (*circular reasoning, changing the subject, hasty generalization*) _____ because they present evidence that is beside the point.

5. Assuming that there are only two sides to a question is called the (*false cause, false comparison, either-or*) _____ fallacy.

# ARGUMENT: Test A-1

A. 1-3. In each of the following groups, one statement is the point, and the other statements are support for the point. (Put another way, one statement is the conclusion, and the other statements are the reasons for the conclusion.) Identify the point of each group with a check.

### Group 1

_____ a. I'd better look for another pre-school for my son.

_____ b. My son says he hates his pre-school teacher.

_____ c. Yesterday he hid under his bed when it was time to go to pre-school.

### Group 2

_____ a. If workers go on strike, they now may lose their jobs to replacement workers.

_____ b. Conditions in the workplace are tougher than they used to be.

_____ c. In many industries, workers have had to take wage cuts.

### Group 3

_____ a. The roaches seem to be taking over this apartment.

_____ b. My apartment is no longer a good place to live.

_____ c. The landlord refuses to fix the leaky faucet.

_____ d. The people upstairs make a lot of noise.

B. Each of the two points below is followed by six statements—three of the statements logically support the point, and three do not. In the spaces provided, write the letters of the three statements that logically support each point.

**Point:** My old car is ready for the junkpile.

  a. The body has rusted through, and water trickles down on me if I drive it in the rain.
  b. The car is painted a particularly ugly shade of green.
  c. I've saved up enough to buy a much better car.
  d. My mechanic says its engine is too worn to be repaired, and the car isn't worth the cost of a new one.
  e. I never really did like that car very much.
  f. Its brakes are shot.

4-6. Statements that logically support the point: _____   _____   _____

*(Continues on next page)*

**Point:** Our town diner is an unsanitary health hazard and ought to be closed down.

    a. Some of the food is high in fat, cholesterol, or both.

    b. The last time I ate at the diner I got food poisoning and was sick for a week.

    c. For the prices the diner charges, the food ought to be better than it is.

    d. The city inspector found roaches in the kitchen at the diner.

    e. Most of the customers at the diner are a shabby, untidy lot.

    f. The cook has been seen using the end of a mop to stir the soup.

7-9. Statements that logically support the point: _____ _____ _____

C. Circle the letter of the sentence that does not support the point of the argument.

> [1]Most people who have trouble with schoolwork don't lack intelligence—instead they are tripped up by their own attitudes towards the work. [2]One attitude that gets in many students' way is the "I can't do it" syndrome. [3]Instead of making an honest effort to do the work, the "I can't do it" type gives up before he begins. [4]This type often also has trouble on the job. [5]Then there's the "I'm too tired" excuse. [6]Students with this problem give in to the temptation to nap whenever there is work to be done. [7]Another common excuse for low achievement is "The instructor is boring." [8]These students expect every course to be highly entertaining and claim they can't be expected to learn anything otherwise.

10. Which of the following does *not* support the author's conclusion that people who have trouble with school work are tripped up by their own attitudes rather than a lack of intelligence?

    a. Sentence 2

    b. Sentence 3

    c. Sentence 4

    d. Sentence 7

## ARGUMENT: Test A-2

**A.** Circle the letter of the one sentence in the paragraph that does not support the point of the argument.

1.  [1]Short-term goals encourage self-discipline better than distant aims. [2]For instance, dieters lose more weight by attempting to shed two pounds a week than by worrying about a total of twenty pounds or more. [3]Low-fat diets are another help for dieters. [4]Also, students who try to increase study time by a half hour each day do better than those who think only about compiling straight A averages. [5]And alcoholics and drug addicts achieve more lasting recovery when they deal with their problems one day at a time.

    Which statement is *not* relevant to the author's conclusion that short-term goals are better for will power than long-term goals?

    a.  Sentence 2
    b.  Sentence 3
    c.  Sentence 4
    d.  Sentence 5

2.  [1]Every high school student should be required to take a class in parenting skills. [2]The absence of such classes shows how little our schools do for young people. [3]Far too many young people today are bearing children without having the least idea of how to be a good parent. [4]Many of them have grown up in families where poor parenting was the norm. [5]Well-planned parenting classes could give future parents at least an idea of what responsible parenting is all about. [6]The classes might then reduce future problems, including child abuse.

    Which statement is *not* relevant to the author's conclusion that every high school student should take a class in parenting skills?

    a.  Sentence 2
    b.  Sentence 3
    c.  Sentence 4
    d.  Sentence 6

*(Continues on next page)*

**B.** Check the conclusion that is best supported by the evidence in each group below.

### Group 1

- • I used to eat junk food all the time, but now I almost never touch the stuff.
- • I only have dessert on special occasions now.
- • Now I eat fresh vegetables almost every day.

3. Which of the following conclusions is best supported by the evidence above?

___ a. The speaker must be a vegetarian.

___ b. The speaker has become a pretty good cook.

___ c. The speaker's diet must be healthier now than it used to be.

___ d. The speaker probably bicycles or jogs five days a week.

### Group 2

- • The instructions for my new VCR might as well be written in Greek.
- • When I try to tape a show, I get either nothing but "snow" or else I record the wrong channel.
- • I have given up trying to record one show while watching another.

4. Which of the following conclusions is best supported by the evidence above?

___ a. The speaker doesn't know how to deal with any mechanical gadgets.

___ b. VCRs are a waste of money.

___ c. The speaker doesn't know how to use many of his VCR's features.

___ d. It's better to subscribe to cable TV than to rent movies.

**C.** Circle the letter of the fallacy contained in the argument below.

5. A month after the governor took office, my company fell on hard times, and I got fired. I'll certainly never vote for him again.

a. False cause *(the argument assumes that the order of events alone shows cause and effect)*

b. False comparison *(the argument assumes that the things being compared are more alike than they really are)*

c. Either-or *(the argument assumes that there are only two sides to a question)*

## ARGUMENT: Test A-3

**A.** The point below is followed by six statements—three of the statements logically support the point, and three do not. In the spaces provided, write the letters of the three statements that logically support the point.

**Point:** Convenience stores live up to their name.

    a. Convenience stores are close to home.
    b. Small local businesses should be supported by the community.
    c. Some convenience store chains sell products under their own brand name.
    d. Convenience stores are open till late or all night.
    e. Parking is right outside the convenience store's door.
    f. The produce at most of our supermarkets is usually terrible.

1-3. Statements that logically support the point: _____ _____ _____

**B.** After reading the passage below, circle the letter of the best answer to each question that follows.

> [1]Public high schools should require their students to wear uniforms. [2]The change to a simple, attractive uniform for all students would benefit schools, students, and parents. [3]Students now spend far too much time worrying about dressing stylishly for school. [4]Many act more interested in the latest rock music and dance fads than in getting an education. [5]They are also distracted from their studies by the competition to wear the sharpest clothes. [6]Teachers often complain that their classes are more like fashion shows than places of learning. [7]Students who cannot afford the latest styles may feel left out and lose interest in doing well at school. [8]And parents have to pay for their children's constant wardrobe demands. [9]If school uniforms aren't required, this generation will become uneducated slaves to fashion.

4. Which sentence is *not* relevant to the author's argument that schools should require students to wear uniforms?
    a. Sentence 3
    b. Sentence 4
    c. Sentence 5
    d. Sentence 7

5. A conclusion that is *not* logically supported by the passage is that
    a. students' clothing can be very expensive.
    b. many high school students tend to judge one another largely by appearances.
    c. many students are in favor of school uniforms.
    d. school uniforms are more economical than most other school wardrobes.

*(Continues on next page)*

6. Which sentence contains an either-or fallacy?
   a. Sentence 3
   b. Sentence 7
   c. Sentence 8
   d. Sentence 9

C. Check the conclusion that is best supported by the following evidence.

   - My father often takes out books from the public library.
   - There is often an open book in his hands.
   - Right now he's reading a history of the American railroad.

7. Which of the following conclusions is best supported by the evidence above?

   ___ a. The speaker's father is probably a retired railroad worker.

   ___ b. The speaker's father is fond of reading.

   ___ c. The speaker's father would rather read than talk.

   ___ d. The speaker's father must be a college graduate.

D. In the space provided, write the letter of the fallacy contained in each argument. Choose from the three fallacies shown in the box below. Each fallacy is used once.

---

**a** Circular reasoning (*a statement repeats itself rather than providing a real supporting reason to back up an argument*)
**b** Personal attack (*the argument shifts to irrelevant personal attack*)
**c** Straw man (*an argument is made by claiming an opponent holds an extreme position and then opposing that extreme position*)

---

_____ 8. Earl will make a lousy class treasurer because he's just a conceited jerk.

_____ 9. I feel my salary should be higher because it is too low.

_____ 10. George wants the firm to hire more women and minorities. He doesn't seem to care how qualified our workers are.

## ARGUMENT: Test B-1

**A. 1-3.** In each of the following groups, one statement is the point, and the other statements are support for the point. (Put another way, one statement is the conclusion, and the other statements are the reasons for the conclusion.) Identify the point of each group with a check.

### Group 1

_____ a. Cats refuse to learn silly tricks just to amuse people.

_____ b. Cats seem to be more intelligent than dogs.

_____ c. Dogs will accept cruel mistreatment, but if a cat is mistreated, she will run away.

### Group 2

_____ a. I need to pass math this quarter if I want to graduate on time.

_____ b. I'm having trouble understanding my teacher and the math textbook.

_____ c. I should make an appointment to see a math tutor.

### Group 3

_____ a. Chefs work on their feet most of the day.

_____ b. A chef's job can be very difficult.

_____ c. Some chefs put in long hours, as many as 15 a day.

_____ d. Even in the most air-conditioned of restaurants, the kitchen is uncomfortably hot.

**B.** Each of the two points below is followed by six statements—three of the statements logically support the point, and three do not. In the spaces provided, write the letters of the three statements that logically support each point.

**Point:** Boxing should be banned.

    a. Promoters make too much money.

    b. Boxers have died from injuries received in the ring.

    c. The sport of boxing began even more violently in ancient Greece.

    d. The main point of boxing is for opponents to badly hurt each other.

    e. Only a handful of boxers are very financially successful.

    f. Boxers have been permanently brain-damaged from the constant blows to the head.

**4-6.** Statements that logically support the point: _____ _____ _____

*(Continues on next page)*

**Point:** The 55-miles-per-hour speed limit should be maintained.

   a. Efforts to get drunk drivers off the road have increased recently.

   b. The chance of a fatal crash doubles when speeds go above 60 miles per hour.

   c. States that enforce the 55-miles-per-hour limit have lower highway death rates.

   d. The police shouldn't ticket people driving 57 miles an hour in a 55-mile-per-hour zone.

   e. Driving at 55 miles per hour saves fuel.

   f. Speeders should be punished with large fines.

7-9. Statements that logically support the point: \_\_\_\_\_  \_\_\_\_\_  \_\_\_\_\_

C. Circle the letter of the sentence that does not support the point of the argument.

> [1]Statistics show that people travel more safely in airplanes than in cars. [2]For that reason, it seems foolish to be afraid of flying and not be concerned about safety in a car. [3]The figures are clear—planes are safer than cars, per passenger mile. [4]But statistics do not tell the whole story. [5]Automobile accidents usually involve only a few people per occurrence and kill or injure only some of the victims. [6]They involve situations which drivers believe they can avoid through skill or caution. [7]On the other hand, airplane accidents usually involve large numbers of people and high death rates. [8]One hundred percent is not uncommon. [9]Surviving an airplane accident requires luck, not skill or caution, and passengers are totally dependent upon their crew. [10]And to add insult to injury, passengers have paid unreasonably high amounts for tickets for this unsafe type of transportation. [11]There's no question about it: when driven by a safe and sober driver, a car is a safer bet than an airplane.

  10. Which of the following is *not* relevant to the author's conclusion that when driven by a safe and sober driver, a car is a safer bet than an airplane?

     a. Sentence 5

     b. Sentence 8

     c. Sentence 9

     d. Sentence 10

# ARGUMENT: Test B-2

**A.** Circle the letter of the one sentence in the paragraph that does not support the point of the argument.

1.  [1]Proms are one traditional part of the high school experience that should be discontinued. [2]For one thing, proms are just too expensive. [3]Between the girl's dress, the guy's tuxedo, flowers, tickets, and probably dinner in a restaurant, it's way too much money for an average high school couple to spend. [4]Rich parents, however, are glad to show off their wealth by supporting such expensive occasions. [5]Secondly, proms encourage destructive forms of social competition. [6]Teenagers get caught up in worrying about who has the best-looking date, who spends most on a dress, or who arrives in a rented limousine. [7]And finally, proms often turn into excuses for underage drinking-and-driving excursions.

    Which sentence is *not* relevant to the author's conclusion that high school proms should be discontinued?

    a. Sentence 2
    b. Sentence 3
    c. Sentence 4
    d. Sentence 5

2.  [1]In addition to highways and airlines, America should have a high-speed rail system. [2]We have let our highway system reach a point where repairs are badly needed. [3]And the French have shown that trains can operate safely at speeds over 160 miles per hour. [4]Over distances up to several hundred miles, such trains, running downtown-to-downtown, would actually get you there faster than jetliners that have to fly from outlying airports. [5]Trains, powered by electricity, produce less pollution and also save oil. [6]Developing an American high-speed rail system would also be a boost to American industry.

    Which sentence is *not* relevant to the author's conclusion that the U.S. should build high-speed trains?

    a. Sentence 2
    b. Sentence 3
    c. Sentence 4
    d. Sentence 5

*(Continues on next page)*

B. Check the conclusion that is best supported by the evidence in each group of statements.

### Group 1

- Many day-care facilities have health and safety standards that are barely satisfactory.
- Long waiting lists exist at most good day-care centers.
- Day-care centers can't get enough qualified help.

3. Which of the following conclusions is best supported by the evidence above?

_____ a. Day care is unreasonably expensive.

_____ b. Mothers with young children should not work.

_____ c. Our present birth rate must be drastically reduced.

_____ d. Our present day-care system is inadequate.

### Group 2

- Janis Chavez served three terms on the city council.
- Ms. Chavez was head of the local planning commission for several years.
- She has also served as a special assistant to the mayor.

4. Which of the following conclusions is best supported by the evidence above?

_____ a. Janis Chavez is the best qualified candidate for mayor.

_____ b. Janis Chavez has broad experience in city government.

_____ c. Ms. Chavez has devoted her entire life to public service.

_____ d. Janis Chavez has always worked for the voters' best interests.

C. Circle the letter of the fallacy contained in the following argument.

5. Aretha Franklin is the best soul singer alive because her singing is so great.

a. Circular reasoning (*a statement repeats itself rather than providing a real supporting reason to back up an argument*)

b. False comparison (*the argument assumes that the things being compared are more alike than they really are*)

c. Straw man (*an argument is made by claiming an opponent holds an extreme position and then opposing that extreme position*)

## ARGUMENT: B-3

**A.** The point below is followed by six statements—three of the statements logically support the point, and three do not. In the spaces provided, write the letters of the three statements that logically support the point.

**Point:** My boss is a very unpleasant man to work for.

    a. He barks orders and never asks for an employee's opinion.

    b. His fashion-plate wife is said to be even nastier than he is.

    c. He's so heavy that he can't even fit into most of the company's desk chairs.

    d. Even when he invites employees out to lunch, he expects them to pick up their own checks.

    e. He changes his mind so often than an employee who pleased him on Friday can be in the doghouse by Monday.

    f. He once accumulated so many parking tickets that the police actually came to his home to arrest him.

1-3. Statements that logically support the point: _____    _____    _____

**B.** After reading the passage below, circle the letter of the best answer to each question that follows.

    [1]Today it is not uncommon for men, as well as women, to purchase products for themselves at a cosmetics counter. [2]Similarly, men are having their hair professionally permed in ever greater numbers. [3]Men are also using a variety of skin products and getting facials to improve their skin tone. [4]These products and services are often less expensive for men than for women. [5]Also, men are increasingly coloring their hair to conceal the gray. [6]Obviously, men have become more concerned with their appearance.

    4. Which sentence is not relevant to the author's conclusion that men are taking more interest in their appearance?

        a. Sentence 1

        b. Sentence 2

        c. Sentence 3

        d. Sentence 4

5-6. Which *two* of the following conclusions are best supported by the passage? (Circle two letters.)

        a. Men are outspending women on cosmetic purchases.

        b. Professional salons are catering to the needs of men and women.

        c. It will soon be common for men to use eye makeup.

        d. Some men are quite open about their use of cosmetics.

*(Continues on next page)*

C. Check the conclusion that is best supported by the evidence below.

- Unprotected engine systems freeze at very low temperatures.
- Cold temperatures cause worn automobile belts and hoses to break.
- Weak batteries go dead in very cold weather.

7. Which of the following conclusions is best supported by the evidence above?

___ a. One should buy new automotive belts and hoses every year or two.

___ b. Improperly maintained cars are likely to break down in the winter.

___ c. It's best to walk or take buses and taxis in very cold weather.

___ d. Car repairs cost more in the winter than in the summer.

D. In the space provided, write the letter of the fallacy contained in each argument. Choose from the three fallacies shown in the box below.

> **a** Circular reasoning (*a statement repeats itself rather than providing a real supporting reason to back up an argument*)
> **b** Personal attack (*the argument shifts to irrelevant personal attack*)
> **c** Straw man (*an argument is made by claiming an opponent holds an extreme position and then opposing that extreme position*)

_____ 8. Mr. Collins supports the idea of sex education in junior high school. Maybe he think's it's okay for 13-year-olds to be having babies, but I don't agree.

_____ 9. Pollution is wrong because it dirties the environment.

_____ 10. Congressman Nagel's policy on welfare is nonsense. What do you expect from a man known to cheat on his wife?

## ARGUMENT: Test C-1

**A.** 1-3. In each of the following groups, one statement is the point, and the other statements are support for the point. (Put another way, one statement is the conclusion, and the other statements are the reasons for the conclusion.) Identify the point of each group with a check.

### Group 1

_____ a. The anchors on Channel 1 spend more time on small talk than those on Channel 2.

_____ b. Channel 2's newscasts are better than Channel l's.

_____ c. Channel 1 emphasizes sensational stories, such as local fires and highway accidents. Channel 2 features important local and world issues.

### Group 2

_____ a. Laws should be passed to reduce acid rain.

_____ b. Scientists have proven that acid rain harms trees and bodies of water.

_____ c. The damage done by acid rain is hard or impossible to undo.

### Group 3

_____ a. I feel dread every time I sit down to take our Friday math quiz.

_____ b. During the math midterm, I "froze" and didn't even try to answer most of the questions.

_____ c. I'm a good example of someone who has "math anxiety."

_____ d. I turned down a salesclerk job because I would have had to figure out how much change customers should get back.

**B.** Each of the two points below is followed by six statements—three of the statements logically support the point, and three do not. In the spaces provided, write the letters of the three statements that logically support each point.

**Point:** It makes sense to give alternative sentences, not jail, to some nonviolent offenders.

a. The courts have a huge backlog of cases.
b. Alternative sentences cost less than jail.
c. The crime rate goes up every year.
d. Prisons are overcrowded.
e. Everyone is entitled to legal representation.
f. Evidence suggests that alternative sentences offer a better chance of rehabilitating the offender.

4-6. Statements that logically support the point: _____  _____  _____

*(Continues on next page)*

**Point:**   Selling cigarettes ought to be against the law.

    a. Cigarette smoking kills many more people than all illegal drugs combined.

    b. Today, tobacco growing is actually supported by government subsidies.

    c. Smoking makes clothing smell bad and stains teeth.

    d. Alcohol is another legal drug that kills numerous Americans every year.

    e. Non-smokers are endangered by breathing the smoke from others' cigarettes.

    f. Tobacco is one of the most addictive of all drugs.

7-9.  Statements that logically support the point:  _____   _____   _____

C. Circle the letter of the sentence that does not support the point of the argument.

> [1]Hollywood's obsession with big-budget "action" movies has harmed the careers of women in film. [2]Even top-rated actresses like Meryl Streep or Kathleen Turner are paid only about half as much as male action performers such as Arnold Schwartzeneggar. [3]In addition, they are offered fewer good roles. [4]In most big action movies, women exist only as decorations or as victims to be rescued. [5]Some of these costly, violent action movies have also been major-league box office flops.

  10. Which sentence does *not* support the author's point that Hollywood denies opportunities to women?

    a. Sentence 2

    b. Sentence 3

    c. Sentence 4

    d. Sentence 5

# ARGUMENT: Test C-2

A. Circle the letter of the one sentence in the paragraph that does not support the point of the argument.

1.  [1]Renting a movie for a VCR makes much more sense these days than going to see a movie at a theater. [2]First of all, the large selection of video movies will always be many times greater than the available choices at all the neighborhood theaters. [3]The rental stores even offer cassettes of made-for-television movies, foreign films, and classics like the legendary comedies of Charlie Chaplin. [4]Also, the low cost of film rental is well below the price of admission to a movie these days. [5]And you won't have to put up with noisy patrons drowning out the sound track with their personal conversations or comments on the action on the screen. [6]These ill-mannered moviegoers should be ejected from a theater when they create a disturbance.

    Which of the following statements does *not* support the author's conclusion that renting movies makes more sense than going to see movies at a theater?

    a. Sentence 3
    b. Sentence 4
    c. Sentence 5
    d. Sentence 6

2.  [1]Keeping up with the news is an important part of good citizenship. [2]First of all, it's only by watching the policies of our elected officials that we can make judgments about their performance. [3]If we are not satisfied, we can then write them letters to try to influence them. [4]We can also use what we learn about their performance to determine how we vote in the coming elections. [5]Knowing about current events can also make us more interesting conversationalists. [6]Finally, we can occasionally learn from the news about how we can be useful to society. [7]Perhaps we can serve a family in need of help by sending a few dollars or offer to volunteer at a shelter for the homeless that we learn is opening nearby.

    Which of the following statements does *not* support the author's conclusion that keeping up with the news contributes to good citizenship?

    a. Sentence 4
    b. Sentence 5
    c. Sentence 6
    d. Sentence 7

*(Continues on next page)*

**B.** Check the conclusion that is best supported by the evidence in each group of statements.

### Group 1

- Dolphins appear to be able to talk to one another through a language of squeals and grunts.
- There have been reports of dolphins helping people who were lost at sea.
- Dolphins in captivity have learned to perform sophisticated tasks, such as fetching objects in a particular order.

3. Which of the following conclusions is best supported by the evidence above?

___ a. There are no other animals as intelligent as dolphins.

___ b. Dolphins appear to be highly intelligent animals.

___ c. Dolphins are better off in captivity.

___ d. Dolphins are good parents.

### Group 2

- Music is often effective in  helping emotionally disturbed children communicate.
- Music can help relieve anxiety in patients about to undergo surgery.
- Music can help relieve persistent arthritis pain.

4. Which of the following conclusions is best supported by the evidence above?

___ a. Every one should listen to music each day.

___ b. Music has been used successfully in the treatment of physical and emotional ailments.

___ c. More and more people are entering the field of music therapy.

___ d. Music can probably help relieve headaches and backaches.

**C.** Circle the letter of the fallacy contained in the following argument.

5. Students must choose between a career that will help their fellow human beings and one that will earn them a decent living.

a. False cause *(the argument assumes that the order of events alone shows cause and effect)*

b. False comparison *(the argument assumes that the things being compared are more alike than they really are)*

c. Either-or *(the argument assumes that there are only two sides to a question)*

## ARGUMENT: Test C-3

**A.** The point below is followed by six statements—three of the statements logically support the point, and three do not. In the spaces provided, write the letters of the three statements that logically support the point.

**Point:** Chocolate is enormously popular.

a. The price of chocolate candy varies enormously.

b. There is an American magazine devoted entirely to chocolate.

c. Numerous chocolate treats can be bought in every drugstore, supermarket, candy store, bakery, and ice cream store in the country.

d. Not many people are allergic to chocolate.

e. Many cookbooks are available that include nothing but chocolate recipes.

f. Despite claims to the contrary, it has not been proven that chocolate causes complexion problems.

1-3. Statements that logically support the point: _____ _____ _____

**B.** After reading the passage below, circle the letter of the best answer to each question that follows.

> [1]The death penalty is popular with voters, who are frightened of violent crime, but it is not very effective in reducing the murder rate. [2]In the 1960s and 1970s, the death penalty was hardly ever used, yet murder rates were lower than today. [3]Even today, the states that most often impose the death penalty also often have the highest murder rates. [4]In addition, every death sentence costs taxpayers hundreds of thousands of dollars in appeals and lawyers' fees.

4. Which sentence does *not* support the author's argument that the death penalty is not very effective in reducing the murder rate in America?

a. Sentence 2

b. Sentence 3

c. Sentence 4

5-6. Which *two* of the following conclusions are *not* supported by the passage? (Circle two letters.)

a. The death penalty is more widely used in America today than it was 20 years ago.

b. We could lower murder rates substantially by eliminating the death penalty.

c. The death penalty is costly to impose.

d. The death penalty is more costly than life imprisonment.

*(Continues on next page)*

C. Check the conclusion that is best supported by the evidence below.

- Electric train sets have become popular again in recent years.
- Simple dolls are among the favorite girls' toys today.
- Sales of computer games have dropped off lately.

7. Which of the following conclusions is best supported by the evidence above?

___ a. Parents are more careful about their money when they buy toys.

___ b. Old-fashioned playthings have come back into fashion.

___ c. Kids don't like to play computer games any more.

___ d. Parents buy the toys they themselves would like to play with.

D. In the space provided, write the letter of the fallacy contained in each argument. Choose from the three fallacies shown in the box below.

> **a** Circular reasoning (*a statement repeats itself rather than providing a real supporting reason to back up an argument*)
> **b** Personal attack (*the argument shifts to irrelevant personal attack*)
> **c** Straw man (*an argument is made by claiming an opponent holds an extreme position and then opposing that extreme position*)

_____ 8. A high-fat, low-fiber diet isn't healthy because it is damaging to the body.

_____ 9. The senator's support for lowering the capital gains tax can't be taken seriously. She supports the bill only because she stands to benefit from it.

_____ 10. Supporters of state lotteries apparently don't think that anyone should work hard for what he gets. They believe the ridiculous idea that it's better to get something for nothing.

## ARGUMENT: Test D-1

**A.** 1-3. In each of the following groups, one statement is the point, and the other statements are support for the point. (Put another way, one statement is the conclusion, and the other statements are the reasons for the conclusion.) Identify the point of each group with a check.

### Group 1

_____ a. Food sources such as leaves, seeds, and fruits are greatly reduced when the trees are bare.

_____ b. Cold temperature and wind are felt more severely when leaves are absent.

_____ c. When the leaves are shed in fall, the animal community has more difficulty surviving.

_____ d. Once the leaves have fallen, animals must reduce their activity level by taking longer winter naps.

### Group 2

_____ a. Dinosaur fossils teach us about animals that are now extinct.

_____ b. Fossils have "recorded" much about the past of the earth and its inhabitants.

_____ c. Fossils of ferns found in the Arctic suggest climatic changes.

_____ d. Seashell fossils found high in the mountains indicate that those areas were once covered by salt water.

### Group 3

_____ a. Often you'll wait half an hour for a Route 27 bus, and then three will show up at once.

_____ b. Sometimes Route 27 buses will roar right past you at a bus stop, even though they aren't full.

_____ c. Route 27 seems to be assigned the oldest buses, ones that rattle and have broken seats.

_____ d. It is wise to avoid the Route 27 bus as much as possible.

*(Continues on next page)*

**B.** Each of the two points below is followed by six statements—three of the statements logically support the point, and three do not. In the spaces provided, write the letters of the three statements that logically support each point.

**Point:** Sunbathers should be careful to avoid excessive exposure to solar rays.

    a. In recent years, the sun has been particularly active in producing harmful rays.

    b. Beachgoers should also be aware of water pollution.

    c. Air pollution has destroyed some of the ozone in the atmosphere, which protects against solar rays.

    d. Too much exposure to the sun can lead to skin cancer.

    e. Sun hats are not expensive and can be very attractive.

    f. Other countries have stricter laws against air pollution.

4-6. Statements that logically support the point: _____    _____    _____

**Point:** The "newest thing" might be something old that has made a comeback.

    a. Some cities that tore out their streetcar lines years ago are now putting them back.

    b. The basic black dress has never really gone out of fashion.

    c. Miniskirts, a 1960s fashion, became popular again in the 1980s.

    d. Fashions are more varied today than ever before.

    e. Many recent buildings have a 1930s look to them.

    f. The work of architect and designer Frank Lloyd Wright is still admired today.

7-9. Statements that logically support the point: _____    _____    _____

**C.** Circle the letter of the sentence that does not support the point of the argument.

    [1]The level of personal service is deteriorating in the American marketplace. [2]Yesterday I waited for nearly five minutes at a cash register while two clerks complained bitterly to one another about how much they hated their jobs. [3]I have heard workers in restaurants groan loudly when customers walked in too close to quitting time. [4]Operators taking telephone orders for a catalog have snapped at me in exasperation when I can't find the customer identification number on my catalog. [5]They don't realize that there are too many numbers on the address label anyway. [6]Even when I ask for assistance in finding a product in a store, clerks sometimes shrug their shoulders and walk away.

10. Which of the following does *not* support the author's conclusion that the level of personal service is deteriorating in the American marketplace?

    a. Sentence 3

    b. Sentence 4

    c. Sentence 5

    d. Sentence 6

# ARGUMENT: Test D-2

**A.** Circle the letter of the one sentence in each paragraph that does not support the point of the argument.

1.  ¹Individual and family stress would be lessened if household responsibilities were assigned more evenly among family members. ²Often wives who work fulltime also do most of the work around the house, which makes their lives more stressful than necessary. ³This stress certainly creates tension between husbands and wives, thereby certainly contributing to our high divorce rate. ⁴America's husbands have always been too self-centered. ⁵If household work was more fairly divided between wives, husbands, and children, everyone's lives would undoubtedly be improved.

    Which of the following sentences does *not* support the author's point that household responsibilities should be assigned more evenly among family members?

    a. Sentence 2
    b. Sentence 3
    c. Sentence 4

2.  ¹Sexual harassment in the workplace must be recognized for the serious problem it is. ²Too many people make light of the problem, believing sexual harassment to be nothing more than pleasant flirtation between co-workers. ³Many women, and even some men, have been driven to quit their jobs because of unwanted sexual attention from their supervisors. ⁴An employer can more or less subtly pressure employees to grant sexual favors in order to keep their jobs. ⁵Even employers who do not demand sex can make their employees miserable through unwelcome remarks about their bodies or dress. ⁶Supervisors who sexually harass their employees must have a need to feel important or powerful. ⁷All degrees of sexual harassment have the effect of creating a hostile and degrading atmosphere in the workplace. ⁸To protect people from having to work in such an environment should be the aim of laws against sexual harassment.

    Which of the following sentences does *not* support the author's conclusion that sexual harassment in the workplace is a problem that should be taken seriously?

    a. Sentence 3
    b. Sentence 4
    c. Sentence 5
    d. Sentence 6

*(Continues on next page)*

**B.** Check the conclusion that is best supported by the evidence in each group below.

*Group 1*

- The Tempora Cheetah has a top speed of 180 miles per hour.
- The Tempora Cheetah has a fuel-injected, six-cylinder, 280 horsepower engine.
- The Tempora Cheetah can do zero-to-sixty in four seconds.

3. Which of the following conclusions is best supported by the evidence above?

___ a. Young people should not be allowed to drive the Tempora Cheetah.

___ b. The Tempora Cheetah is designed for high speed and performance.

___ c. The Tempora Cheetah is the car of the twenty-first century.

___ d. The Tempora Cheetah should not be allowed on our highways.

*Group 2*

- There's been a Shrimp Boat seafood restaurant on Thayer Street for about five years.
- Last week, two new Shrimp Boats opened in local shopping malls.
- A display ad in the classified section reads, "Shrimp Boat: Franchises Available in Top Money-Making Locations."

4. Which of the following conclusions is best supported by the evidence above?

___ a. Shrimp Boat serves the best seafood in town.

___ b. The Shrimp Boat chain is probably expanding.

___ c. People who work for Shrimp Boat can expect to make a lot of money.

___ d. Anyone who wants to can open a Shrimp Boat restaurant.

**C.** Circle the letter of the fallacy contained in the following argument.

5. A local association wants to establish a home in our neighborhood for retarded people. But the neighbors oppose the home; they say they don't want dangerous psychopaths roaming our streets.

a. Circular reasoning *(a statement repeats itself rather than providing a real supporting reason to back up an argument)*

b. False comparison *(the argument assumes that the things being compared are more alike than they really are)*

c. Straw man *(an argument is made by claiming an opponent holds an extreme position and then opposing that extreme position)*

# ARGUMENT: Test D-3

**A.** The point below is followed by six statements—three of the statements logically support the point, and three do not. In the spaces provided, write the letters of the three statements that logically support the point.

**Point:** Information on food packaging is often misleading.

 a. The label "light" doesn't mean that a product is lower in calories.
 b. The print on labels is often so small that it is difficult for many people to read.
 c. Half of all consumers depend on labels to help them decide which foods to buy.
 d. Manufacturers often adjust serving size in the label information to their advantage.
 e. False health claims appear on many products.
 f. Products like meat and poultry don't require labels at all.

1-3. Statements that logically support the point: _____ _____ _____

**B.** After reading the passage below, circle the letter of the best answer to each question that follows.

[1]Much of America's drug problem could actually be eliminated by legalizing drugs. [2]Harsh drug laws have not ended drug use. [3]And we already sell many drugs over the counter as cold and flu medicines. [4]If drugs were legal, illegal street dealers would swiftly go out of business. [5]Most drug-related crimes are not actually due to the drugs themselves, but to the need for money to buy drugs (which would be affordable if legal) or to turf battles between dealers. [6]Legalized drugs would also positively affect the problem of addiction because profits from drug sales could be taxed to support drug treatment and education programs.

4. Which sentence does *not* support the author's conclusion that drugs should be legalized?
 a. Sentence 3
 b. Sentence 4
 c. Sentence 5
 d. Sentence 6

5. Which sentence supports the argument that drug legalization would reduce crime?
 a. Sentence 2
 b. Sentence 3
 c. Sentence 5
 d. Sentence 6

*(Continues on next page)*

6. Which of the following statements is best supported by the passage?
   a. Legalizing drugs would reduce alcoholism in this country.
   b. Laws should never be passed that tell people what they can or cannot take for recreational or health purposes.
   c. The question of whether something should be legal is different from the question of whether it is good for you.
   d. It is impossible to influence private behavior with laws.

C. Check the conclusion that is best supported by the evidence below.

   • Stevie Wonder, a blind pianist, singer and composer, won several Grammy Awards, including one for his album "Songs in the Key of Life."
   • Franklin Delano Roosevelt, the popular U.S. president who was elected for four terms, was paralyzed by polio.
   • Beethoven, one of the greatest musical composers who ever lived, was completely deaf in his later years—even when he wrote and conducted his famous *Ninth Symphony*.

7. Which of the following conclusions is best supported by the evidence above?

   ___ a. If you want to be really successful, you must have a handicap.

   ___ b. Individuals with disabilities can achieve greatness.

   ___ c. Handicapped people become more famous than equally talented people who aren't handicapped.

   ___ d. One hundred years ago, people with disabilities couldn't be famous—now they have more opportunities.

D. In the space provided, write the letter of the fallacy contained in each argument. Choose from the three fallacies shown in the box below.

> **a** Circular reasoning (*a statement repeats itself rather than providing a real supporting reason to back up an argument*)
> **b** Personal attack (*the argument shifts to irrelevant personal attack*)
> **c** Straw man (*an argument is made by claiming an opponent holds an extreme position and then opposing that extreme position*)

___ 8. The mayor wants to allow liquor stores in our town. He may not mind having all those drug pushers around, but I certainly do.

___ 9. Watering new grass is important since a lot of water is beneficial for new lawns.

___ 10. Who can take Jake Green's argument for raising the sales tax seriously? Judging by the age of his wardrobe and car, the man hasn't paid a sales tax himself in decades.

# ARGUMENT: Test E-1

A. 1-3. In each of the following groups, one statement is the point, and the other statements are support for the point. (Put another way, one statement is the conclusion, and the other statements are the reasons for the conclusion.) Identify the point of each group with a check.

### Group 1

_____ a. Profits Unlimited has been the target of many complaints to the Better Business Bureau.

_____ b. The company's advertising tells you that you can get rich quick—by sending them a check for a thousand dollars.

_____ c. The company is very likely a fraudulent "scam" business.

_____ d. The owner served time for fraud in state prison.

### Group 2

_____ a. The original *Star Trek* TV shows were kept on the air because of a support campaign by its viewers.

_____ b. There have been six *Star Trek* movies made.

_____ c. *Star Trek* is a true pop-culture phenomenon.

_____ d. *Star Trek: The Next Generation* is a highly successful TV series— twenty-five years after the debut of the original show.

### Group 3

_____ a. Congress should enact a comprehensive highway program.

_____ b. Some of the numerous accidents, injuries, and fatalities on our nation's roads can be attributed to poor highway design.

_____ c. There is an urgent need for bridge construction and maintenance throughout this country.

_____ d. This nation needs programs to alleviate traffic jams.

*(Continues on next page)*

**B.** Each of the two points below is followed by six statements—three of the statements logically support the point, and three do not. In the spaces provided, write the letters of the three statements that logically support each point.

**Point:** Feeling guilty is not all bad.

    a. Some people feel guilty because they can't do everything others ask of them.

    b. Feelings of guilt can encourage a person to think about his behavior and act differently the next time.

    c. People who feel guilt are less likely to commit a crime than those who feel no guilt for their wrongdoings.

    d. People often feel guilty even when they have done nothing wrong.

    e. Parents often feel guilty when their children, even their adult children, do something wrong.

    f. People who feel guilt have more understanding and compassion for other people's imperfections.

4-6. Statements that logically support the point: _____ _____ _____

**Point:** Religion is a powerful force in modern American life.

    a. The main religion in America is Christianity.

    b. Television evangelists can gather millions of dollars from contributors.

    c. Religious leaders are often influential voices on public issues in America.

    d. One of the fundamental principles of America is the separation between church and state.

    e. The Pilgrims came to America seeking religious freedom.

    f. Public opinion polls show that a majority of Americans consider religion personally important to them.

7-9. Statements that logically support the point: _____ _____ _____

**C.** Circle the letter of the sentence that does not support the point of the argument.

> [1]The annual highway death rate has dropped 40 percent since the late 1970s primarily because of the safety features now available in vehicles. [2]Seat belts automatically present themselves, encouraging drivers and passengers to use them. [3]Air bags inflate instantly during impact, preventing deaths in many circumstances. [4]Automatic braking systems often allow drivers to avoid an accident because the car can stop in a shorter distance with greater control. [5]Fog lights improve a driver's visibility and make it easier for oncoming drivers to see the vehicle. [6]Campaigns against drunk driving may also be making a dent in traffic accidents.

10. Which of the following does *not* support the author's conclusion that new vehicle safety features are helping to reduce highway deaths.

    a. Sentence 2

    b. Sentence 3

    c. Sentence 5

    d. Sentence 6

# ARGUMENT: Test E-2

**A.** Circle the letter of the one sentence in the paragraph that does not support the point of the argument.

1. [1]America's top corporate executives are often greatly overpaid. [2]They use their enormous incomes to support a lavish lifestyle that only makes them more greedy. [3]Some corporate bosses make nearly a hundred million dollars a year—thousands of times more than what some of their employees are making. [4]American corporate heads are paid several times what top Japanese managers get—yet the Japanese often seem to do a better job. [5]Some corporate executives have gotten multi-million-dollar bonuses even though their companies lost money.

   Which sentence is *not* relevant to the the author's conclusion that corporate executives are often overpaid?

   a. Sentence 2
   b. Sentence 3
   c. Sentence 4
   d. Sentence 5

2. [1]People are so lazy today that they'd rather complain about a problem than actually participate in a solution. [2]However, community governments and citizens must join together for an all-out effort to make recycling work. [3]Recycling is necessary to conserve precious energy and other natural resources. [4]It is necessary to save our land from the burden of additional landfills. [5]It is necessary to give our children and grandchildren a clean environment, one not littered with the discarded junk of previous generations.

   Which of the following sentences does *not* support the author's implied point that recycling is an important goal?

   a. Sentence 1
   b. Sentence 3
   c. Sentence 4
   d. Sentence 5

*(Continues on next page)*

**B.** Check the conclusion that is best supported by the evidence in each group of statements below.

*Group 1*

- Under airline deregulation, one airline may have, for all practical purposes, a monopoly on air service to many cities.
- Since the airlines were deregulated, airline fleets have become older and maintenance standards have slipped.
- Airline deregulation has produced airline fares that are so confusing and complicated that even professional travel agents can't always figure them out.

3. Which of the following is best supported by the evidence above?

_____ a. Deregulation of an industry is always a bad idea.

_____ b. Airline deregulation has had some negative consequences.

_____ c. Flying is now extremely dangerous.

_____ d. Travel agents earn more money than they're worth.

*Group 2*

- Vitamin C is not stored in the body fat like some other vitamins.
- Any vitamin C not used by the body is excreted within a few hours.
- In addition, vitamin C is an acid, and thus it's best not to take large doses of it on an empty stomach.

4. Which of the following conclusions is best supported by the evidence above?

_____ a. Everyone should take supplemental doses of vitamin C.

_____ b. For people who take vitamin C pills, it is more efficient to take one pill a day.

_____ c. People should spread out vitamin C intake through the day.

_____ d. It is not necessary to include vitamin C in one's diet if vitamin C pills are taken.

**C.** Circle the letter of the fallacy contained in the following argument.

5. We'd never have all those wonderful synthetic fabrics without chemicals, so what's wrong with using plenty of chemicals on our farms?

a. False cause *(the argument assumes that the order of events alone shows cause and effect)*

b. False comparison *(the argument assumes that the things being compared are more alike than they really are)*

c. Either-or *(the argument assumes that there are only two sides to a question)*

# ARGUMENT: Test E-3

**A.** The point below is followed by six statements—three of the statements logically support the point, and three do not. In the spaces provided, write the letters of the three statements that logically support the point.

**Point:** Dolores spends money rather carelessly.

a. When all her socks were dirty, she bought a few new pairs rather than do a load of laundry.

b. She charges most of what she buys with her Visa or Master card.

c. She bought a dress without trying it on, and when it didn't fit, she hung it in the back of her closet instead of returning it.

d. Last year she bought an almost-new Toyota.

e. Although she shops at a grocery store that will double the value of customers' coupons, she says it's too much bother to use coupons at all.

f. She keeps a hundred-dollar bill in the top drawer of her bureau in case of an emergency.

1-3. Statements that logically support the point: _____   _____   _____

**B.** After reading the passage below, circle the letter of the best answer to each question that follows.

> [1]Despite what many parents say, video games aren't all that bad for children. [2]Educational psychologists believe that video games aid problem-solving skills by challenging children to reason a solution. [3]Children must constantly use their thinking ability to respond to a rapidly changing game screen. [4]Also, at least video games don't impose on children the worthless plots of Saturday morning cartoons. [5]Another advantage to playing video games is that operating the keys and controls can increase a child's manual dexterity. [6]And many authorities feel that video games enable children to learn that they can master and control technology.

4. Which of the following is *not* relevant to the author's conclusion that there are benefits to having children play video games?

a. Sentence 2

b. Sentence 3

c. Sentence 4

d. Sentence 6

5. A valid conclusion that can be drawn from this passage is that children who play video games

a. may transfer the skills they learn to real-life situations.

b. never have time to read books.

c. forget to do their homework.

d. spend all their money on new games.

*(Continues on next page)*

6. Another valid conclusion that can be drawn from this passage is that children who benefit from playing video games
   a. are more likely to be male.
   b. rarely watch television.
   c. will be more likely to enjoy using computers.
   d. have no limits placed on the amount of time they spend on the games.

C. Check the conclusion that is best supported by the following evidence.

   - By 1860 (just before the Civil War began), one person out of every four in the U.S. lived in a city.
   - By 1890, one out of every three people in the U.S. lived in a city.
   - Half of all the people living in the U.S. in 1910 lived in a city.

7. Which of the following conclusions is best supported by the evidence above?

   ___ a. Following the Civil War, people began flocking to the cities.

   ___ b. At the end of the 1800s and the beginning of the 1900s, people felt safer living in a city.

   ___ c. By the early part of the 20th century, people no longer wished to settle in the West.

   ___ d. Since 1910, numerous people have gone back to rural America.

D. In the space provided, write the letter of the fallacy contained in each argument. Choose from the three fallacies shown in the box below.

---

**a** Circular reasoning (*a statement repeats itself rather than providing a real supporting reason to back up an argument*)
**b** Personal attack (*the argument shifts to irrelevant personal attack*)
**c** Straw man (*an argument is made by claiming an opponent holds an extreme position and then opposing that extreme position*)

---

   _____ 8. Of course Mel supports giving large malpractice rewards to patients. As a lawyer specializing in malpractice, his only interest is in big fees.

   _____ 9. You can always trust an animal lover because people who like animals are more trustworthy than other people.

   _____ 10. Mary asked if she could have a couple of friends sleep over on her birthday. Her father said no because he didn't want a house full of screaming girls.

## COMBINED SKILLS: Test A-1

After reading the paragraph, circle the letter of the best answer to each question.

[1]If you feel a tingling sensation on your neck on a hot and humid August night, chances are it's a female mosquito. [2]You have no need to worry about the male, who devotes his time to drinking nectar from flowers and helping to propagate more mosquitoes. [3]The female is the biter; she needs blood to nourish the hundreds of eggs she will breed in the month or two that she lives. [4]The mosquito has probably been drawn to you by a stream of exhaled carbon dioxide "downwind" from your sleeping place. [5]She has followed your carbon dioxide scent to its source, where she circles until she finds a good landing place on which to do her bloody work. [6]If you have been asleep, you may be stirred by her rapid wingbeat as this little swooping helicopter settles in on you. [7]The noise is your last chance of escape, for she will land on you so gently you will probably not feel her.

[8]As she drives her pointy snout into your skin, she injects a small amount of saliva into the puncture to keep your blood from coagulating. [9]It is the remains of this saliva that leaves you with an itching welt after she has made her departure. [10]The itch may wake you up, but by then it is too late. [11]You have been the victim of the female mosquito's search and attack.

1. In sentence 2, the word *propagate* means
   a. share with.
   b. produce.
   c. compete with.
   d. bite.

2. The passage indicates that a female mosquito is attracted to
   a. body warmth.
   b. carbon dioxide.
   c. body movement.
   d. the sound of breathing.

3. The mosquito's saliva
   a. punctures skin.
   b. mixes with carbon dioxide.
   c. nourishes the insect's eggs.
   d. causes itching welts.

*(Continues on next page)*

4. From the passage, you can assume that to mosquito eggs, human blood is
   a. healing.
   b. nourishing.
   c. sweet.
   d. the only acceptable blood.

5. On the basis of the passage, one could conclude that the female mosquito
   a. is easily avoided.
   b. is feared by the male.
   c. is a sophisticated creature.
   d. lives a long and useful life.

6. The author's primary purpose is
   a. to inform.
   b. to persuade.
   c. to entertain.
   d. to predict.

7. The tone of this passage is
   a. formal.
   b. sentimental.
   c. informal.
   d. alarmed.

8. Which is an appropriate title for this selection?
   a. The Differences Between the Male and Female Mosquito
   b. Why the Mosquito Bites
   c. A Female Mosquito's Search and Attack
   d. The Mosquito's Life Cycle

## COMBINED SKILLS: Test A-2

After reading the paragraph, circle the letter of the best answer to each question.

[1]Johnny Appleseed, one of the gentlest and most beloved of American folk heroes, was born in 1774 in Leominster, Massachusetts. [2]His real name was John Chapman. [3]Chapman's early life was full of misfortune. [4]First, his father left home to fight in the Revolutionary War. [5]Then John's mother and baby brother died before John's second birthday. [6]However, John's fortunes improved when his father returned and remarried, and by the time John was in his teens, he had ten brothers and sisters.

[7]As a young man, John began traveling west on foot, stopping to clear land and plant the apple seeds he always carried with him. [8]Settlers who followed John's path were delighted to find young apple orchards dotting the landscape.

[9]John was a friendly fellow who often stopped to visit with families along his way, entertaining them with stories of his travels. [10]Tales of his exploits followed him through Pennsylvania, Ohio, and Indiana. [11]Many of the stories were true. [12]For instance, John really did travel barefoot through the snow, lived on the friendliest of terms with Indian tribes, and refused to shoot any animal. [13]Other tales about John, however, were exaggerations. [14]Settlers said, for example, that he slept in the treetops and talked to the birds or that he had once been carried off by a giant eagle. [15]Johnny Appleseed never stopped traveling until his death in Fort Wayne, Indiana, in 1845.

1. As used in sentence 6, the word *fortunes* means
   a. wealth.
   b. possessions.
   c. luck.
   d. health.

2. The details in sentences 4 and 5 support the point or points in
   a. sentence 1.
   b. sentence 2.
   c. sentence 3.
   d. sentence 6.

3. The relationship between sentences 3 and 6 is one of
   a. contrast.
   b. addition.
   c. cause and effect.
   d. comparison.

*(Continues on next page)*

4. We can conclude that Johnny Appleseed
   a. provided apples for numerous settlers.
   b. was quickly forgotten by the settlers.
   c. grew wealthy from selling his apple trees.
   d. left home because of problems with his family.

5. The passage suggests that Johnny Appleseed
   a. grew weary of traveling.
   b. had great respect for other people and animals.
   c. lived a very short but rich life.
   d. planted many trees other than apple trees.

6. Sentence 1 is a statement of
   a. fact.
   b. opinion.
   c. fact and opinion.

7. The tone of the passage is
   a. pessimistic.
   b. bitter and impassioned.
   c. loving and compassionate.
   d. straightforward with a touch of admiration.

8. Which is the most appropriate title for this selection?
   a. The Planting of American Apple Orchards
   b. Folk Heroes of America
   c. Settlers Recall Johnny Appleseed
   d. The Life and Legends of John Chapman

## COMBINED SKILLS: Test A-3

After reading the passage, circle the letter of the best answer to each question.

[1]Mary was watching a mystery on television. [2]The end of the movie was near, and she was totally engrossed. [3]Then her baby started crying. [4]She shouted at him to shut up. [5]His response was intensified crying. [6]Mary got angry and shook him. [7]The baby cried even louder. [8]In the meanwhile, the mystery's conclusion took place, and Mary missed it. [9]Angrily, she slapped her son's face. [10]In this situation, someone was pursuing a goal—seeing the end of a suspenseful television show. [11]But something happened to block the achievement of that goal. [12]The person thus became frustrated, anger built up, and direct aggression occurred.

[13]Aggression is not always aimed at the original frustrator. [14]For example, consider a businessman who had a hard day at the office. [15]He was about to close a deal with a client when his boss clumsily interfered and lost the sale. [16]On the way home in his car, the frustrated businessman blew his horn angrily at a car ahead when it didn't pull immediately away from a stoplight. [17]As he entered his home, his dog jumped up on him, only to receive a quick kick. [18]He then shouted at his wife during supper. [19]All these aggressive behaviors are examples of displaced aggression. [20]Aggression against the person who caused the original frustration can often be harmful. [21]In this case, assaulting or swearing at the boss could cost the businessman his job. [22]When the original frustrator has status and power over the frustrated person, aggression may be displaced onto a less threatening target, who may have nothing at all to do with the original frustration.

1. In sentence 2 of the passage, the word *engrossed* means
   a. involved.
   b. alone.
   c. charmed.
   d. bored.

2. The first paragraph deals with
   a. aggression.
   b. direct aggression.
   c. displaced aggression.
   d. frustration.

3. Aggression is more likely to be displaced if the original frustrator
   a. is a family member.
   b. has power over the frustrated person.
   c. is angry at the frustrated person.
   d. is unfair to the frustrated person.

*(Continues on next page)*

4. The relationship between sentences 11 and 12 is one of
   a  general idea and example.
   b. comparison.
   c. contrast.
   d. cause and effect.

5. The organizational pattern of *each* paragraph is
   a. a series of steps in a process.
   b. a contrast of events.
   c. illustration and explanation of a general concept.
   d. a comparison of two or more events.

6. The writer's main purpose in writing this selection is to
   a. predict how aggression influences relationships.
   b. inform readers about two types of aggression.
   c. persuade readers to be careful not to take out their aggression on the wrong people.
   d. entertain readers with dramatic anecdotes about aggressive behavior.

7. What is the best title for the selection?
   a. Aggression
   b. The Causes of Aggression
   c. Direct and Displaced Aggression
   d. Displaced Aggression

8. Which sentence best states the main idea of the selection?
   a. A great deal of frustration is aimed against family members.
   b. When frustration and anger build up, direct or displaced aggression may occur.
   c. Sometimes a frustrator may have a great deal more power or status than the person who is frustrated.
   d. Direct aggression is more satisfying than indirect aggression.

## COMBINED SKILLS: Test B-1

After reading the passage, circle the letter of the best answer to each question.

[1]The large, gleaming refrigerator is the focal point of most American kitchens. [2]It holds enough food to last many days. [3]It is cold enough to preserve that food well. [4]Its advantages are clear. [5]But that big refrigerator has its drawbacks as well, although they are not usually recognized. [6]First of all, the large refrigerator encourages the hoarding of food and leads to obesity and other eating problems. [7]Also, it has destroyed the pleasant custom, still common in Europe, of going to market each day. [8]Picking out one's fresh produce daily while chatting with friends and neighbors is no longer a part of our lives. [9]In addition, people's desire to buy huge amounts of groceries just a few times a month has encouraged the growth of supermarkets and destroyed local grocery stores. [10]Other victims of the giant refrigerator have been small local farmers, who can't compete against the mega-producers favored by the supermarkets.

1. The prefix *mega-* in sentence 10 means
   a. small.
   b. large.
   c. farmer.
   d. new.

2. According to the author, two victims of the "giant refrigerator" are
   a. healthy food and varied food.
   b. local grocery stores and small farms.
   c. convenient locations and low-cost shopping.
   d. low utility costs and kitchen space.

3. What is the relationship of sentence 10 to sentence 9?
   a. Time
   b. Addition
   c. Contrast
   d. Illustration

4. The organizational pattern used in this passage is
   a. steps in instructions.
   b. a sequence of events.
   c. a definition and examples.
   d. lists of advantages and disadvantages.

*(Continues on next page)*

5. From this passage, you could infer that many Europeans
   a. are more economical shoppers than Americans.
   b. are better cooks.
   c. enjoy eating more.
   d. don't have "giant" refrigerators.

6. Sentence 7 is a statement of
   a. fact.
   b. opinion.
   c. fact and opinion.

7. The author's tone in this passage is mainly
   a. cheerful.
   b. depressed.
   c. critical.
   d. optimistic.

8. Which of the following statements best expresses the main idea of the passage?
   a. Shopping patterns in Europe have advantages.
   b. Large, modern refrigerators have disadvantages as well as advantages.
   c. Fresh, healthy produce and daily meetings with friends are preferable to the convenience of a refrigator.
   d. Modern kitchen appliances are not as wonderful as they may seem.

## COMBINED SKILLS: Test B-2

After reading the paragraph, circle the letter of the best answer to each question.

¹Little League baseball in its present form should be abolished. ²For one thing, the pressure that children are put under to succeed may harm them more than help them. ³One mother discovered her son taking Maalox tablets from the medicine chest whenever a game approached. ⁴He explained that they helped relieve the stomach burn he would feel during the game. ⁵Other children have been found taking tranquilizers. ⁶Another drawback to today's Little League baseball is that some parents take the game too seriously and set a bad example for their children. ⁷Recently, a disillusioned coach said, "At our field, we put the bleachers way back from the dugout where the players are. ⁸That way, parents can't be hissing down advice to their children all the time and getting them upset." ⁹A final reason Little League should be abolished is that it doesn't offer enough success to most players. ¹⁰Instead, the game revolves around the more developed kids who are able to hit and throw the ball harder than the smaller children. ¹¹In one recent game, most of the batters were clearly afraid of the speed of the hardball, which was pitched by a boy bigger than many of the other players. ¹²A viable alternative to Little League hardball would be lob-pitch softball. ¹³The ball is pitched slowly and underhand and offers a high level of success to kids without a high level of ability. ¹⁴Lob-pitch softball should get more children involved in the game, and help people remember that it *is* a game—not an adult arena where one is branded with success or failure.

1. In sentence 12, the word *viable* means
   a. dangerous.
   b. workable.
   c. impractical.
   d. professional.

2. According to the author, one advantage of lob-pitch softball is
   a. the ball's weight.
   b. the lesser degree of skill required.
   c. the field size.
   d. the players' ages.

3. The relationship of sentence 6 to the sentences that come before it is one of
   a. time.
   b. addition.
   c. contrast.
   d. comparison.

*(Continues on next page)*

4. Sentence 1 is a statement of
   a. fact.
   b. opinion.
   c. fact and opinion.

5. From the passage, you can conclude the author would agree with the idea that
   a. it's not whether you win or lose; it's how you play the game.
   b. competition in baseball helps prepare people for competition in life.
   c. children's games should imitate adults' games.
   d. sports should help children learn that there are winners and losers in life.

6. The author's main purpose is
   a. to inform.
   b. to persuade.
   c. to entertain.
   d. to predict.

7. What is the most appropriate title for this selection?
   a. The Pressures on Today's Children
   b. Lob-Pitch Softball
   c. Let's Reform Little League
   d. Sportsmanship in Baseball

8. The main idea of the passage is best stated in
   a. sentence 1.
   b. sentence 2.
   c. sentence 9.
   d. sentence 12.

## COMBINED SKILLS: Test B-3

After reading the passage, circle the letter of the best answer to each question.

[1]Most people dislike bats, and surely the most feared of all the species is the dreaded vampire bat. [2]Vampires live up to their horror-story reputation as greedy and efficient stealers of blood.

[3]Depending upon its type, the vampire bat may prefer to dine on the blood of mammals (including humans) or birds. [4]The bat begins its meal by circling above its usually sleeping target for several minutes, probably to allow heat-sensitive patches on its face to determine where best to bite. [5]It then inflicts a small wound with its teeth, which are so razor-sharp as to make the incision virtually painless. [6]The wound bleeds freely as long as the bat continues feeding, thanks to a substance in the bat's saliva that prevents clotting. [7]As many as half a dozen of the bat's fellows may join it to feed from one wound.

[8]Vampire bats have such great appetites for blood that they may drink more than their own weight at one feeding, thus making it briefly impossible to fly. [9]A single vampire drinks about twenty-five gallons of blood in its lifetime. [10]Although vampire bats are sometimes responsible for the death of humans or animals, those deaths are not due to blood loss. [11]Rather, the deaths are caused by rabies or other diseases spread by the creatures.

1. In sentence 5, *incision* means
   a. heat-sensitive patch.
   b. cut.
   c. blood.
   d. saliva.

2. Sentence 8 expresses relationships of
   a. contrast.
   b. cause and effect.
   c. addition.
   d. comparison.

3. The main patterns of organization of the second paragraph are
   a. contrast and cause and effect.
   b. comparision and list of items.
   c. time order and cause and effect.
   d. time order and definition/example.

*(Continues on next page)*

4. We can conclude that vampire bats use their heat-sensitive patches
   a. for personal temperature control.
   b. to find where blood is close to their victims' skin.
   c. to find sleeping victims.
   d. to find out which potential victims have the best blood.

5. The passage suggests that
   a. there's only one type of vampire bat.
   b. all vampire bats have rabies.
   c. vampire bats intend to kill their victims.
   d. vampire bats prefer victims that lie still.

6. The author's main purpose is to
   a. inform.
   b. persuade.
   c. entertain.
   d. predict.

7. On the whole, the tone of the passage is
   a. fearful.
   b. objective.
   c. disbelieving.
   d. playful.

8. Which is the most appropriate title for this passage?
   a. Blood-Sucking Bats
   b. Vampire Bats Spread Disease
   c. Bats Feed in Social Groups
   d. Bat's Saliva Keeps Blood Flowing

# COMBINED SKILLS: Test C-1

After reading the passage, circle the letter of the best answer to each question.

[1]The Peace Corps has come a long way since it was founded in 1961 by President John F. Kennedy. [2]The corps, whose mission it is to improve the environment and economic conditions of various nations, initially had 750 volunteers. [3]It now boasts approximately 6,000 members, with additional growth projected. [4]At first, corps volunteers were almost exclusively young, white and male. [5]Today, there are many older volunteers, as well as both men and women representing a wide range of ethnic backgrounds. [6]The corps is also constantly updating and shifting the emphasis of the various services and skills it offers. [7]For example, a greater effort is being made to teach English to host nations. [8]"The language of commerce, science, computer technology and aviation is English," explains a Peace Corps director. [9]"Eastern European nations say, 'Send us English instructors—and fast.'"

1. The word *mission* in sentence 2 means
   a. name.
   b. growth.
   c. purpose.
   d. membership.

2. The relationship of sentence 7 to sentence 6 is one of
   a. illustration.
   b. addition.
   c. time.
   d. contrast.

3. The overall pattern of organization for this passage is
   a. series of steps.
   b. contrast.
   c. definition and example.
   d. cause and effect.

4. Sentence 2 is a statement of
   a. fact.
   b. opinion.
   c. fact and opinion.

*(Continues on next page)*

5. The passage implies that
   a. the Peace Corps was a good idea in 1961, but has outlived its usefulness.
   b. young white males make the best Peace Corps volunteers.
   c. the corps is not doing enough to update the services it offers.
   d. some changes in the Peace Corps reflect changes in our society.

6. The author implies that Eastern European residents
   a. want to learn English mainly to converse with American visitors.
   b. have little interest in the modern world.
   c. need English to master modern commerce, science, and technology.
   d. prefer to work with older Peace Corps volunteers.

7. The author's tone in this passage is largely
   a. sentimental.
   b. critical.
   c. objective.
   d. amused.

8. Which is an appropriate title for this passage?
   a. President Kennedy's Vision for the Peace Corps
   b. Eastern Europe's Hunger for English Teachers
   c. The Typical Peace Corps Worker Has Changed
   d. Changes in the Peace Corps

# COMBINED SKILLS: Test C-2

After reading the passage, circle the letter of the best answer to each question.

[1]Social psychologist Philip Zimbardo set out to test the theory that the anonymity of city life encourages crime. [2]He arranged to have automobiles abandoned in two different locations: New York City and Palo Alto, California, a medium-sized suburban community. [3]The cars' license plates were removed and their hoods were raised to signal that the autos were abandoned. [4]Then each car was secretly watched for sixty-four hours.

[5]The person assigned to watch the New York car did not have long to wait:

[6]Within ten minutes the 1959 Oldsmobile received its first auto strippers—a father, mother, and eight-year-old son. [7]The mother appeared to be a lookout, while the son aided the father's search of the trunk, glove compartment, and motor. [8]He then handed his father the tools necessary to remove the battery and radiator. [9]Total time of destructive contact: seven minutes.

[10]This, however, was only the first "contact." [11]By the end of the sixty-four hours, the car had been vandalized twenty-four times, often by well-dressed, seemingly middle-class adults. [12]What remained when the experiment was over was a useless hunk of metal. [13]In contrast, the Palo Alto car was approached only once: when it started to rain, a passerby stopped to lower the hood.

[14]According to Zimbardo, the crucial factor in the different fates of the two cars was anonymity. [15]In a large city, where the chances of being recognized outside one's own neighborhood are extremely slim, even "upstanding citizens" can afford a temporary turn at thievery. [16]In a smaller community, on the other hand, the higher probability of being recognized and caught keeps people honest.

1. In sentence 14, *crucial* means
   a. least interesting.
   b. most important.
   c. most unlikely.
   d. most helpful.

2. According to the passage, Zimbardo's main purpose was
   a. to illustrate a point.
   b. to test a theory.
   c. to catch thieves.
   d. to teach honesty.

*(Continues on next page)*

3. The pattern of organization in sentences 6 through 9 is one of
   a. time order.
   b. list of items.
   c. comparison.
   d. contrast.

4. The relationship between sentences 15 and 16 is one of
   a. time.
   b. comparison.
   c. contrast.
   d. cause and effect.

5. Sentence 13 is a statement of
   a. fact.
   b. opinion.
   c. fact and opinion.

6. The passage suggests that
   a. old Oldsmobiles are especially popular among thieves.
   b. New Yorkers are more dishonest than people in most other big cities.
   c. social pressure promotes honesty.
   d. the car used in Palo Alto was probably newer than the car in New York City.

7. The tone of the passage can be described as mainly
   a. objective.
   b. doubtful.
   c. alarmed.
   d. scornful.

8. Which statement best states the main idea of the passage?
   a. Philip Zimbardo is a creative social psychologist.
   b. People are now more dishonest than ever.
   c. In big cities, ordinary people's chances of being recognized outside of their neighborhood are quite slim.
   d. Zimbardo's experiment suggests that the anonymity of city life encourages crime.

## COMBINED SKILLS: Test C-3

After reading the passage, circle the letter of the best answer to each question.

[1]We live in an era in which more women are entering formerly male-dominated professions, demanding equal pay for equal work, and generally rejecting the societal double standard which has held them back from reaching their full potential. [2]Yet many women are still bound by old-fashioned and harmful ideas about sexuality. [3]An epidemic of "date rapes" on college campuses is evidence that warped beliefs about sexuality are barriers that women—as well as men—need to break in order to achieve a full human partnership. [4]As many as 25 percent of all college women may become victims of rape or attempted rape. [5]Women at the beginning of their college careers are especially vulnerable to date rape. [6]They may be living in coed dorms with men whom they assume they can trust. [7]They are eager to appear cool, sophisticated, not paranoid or uptight. [8]Most destructively of all, many women still subscribe at least subconsciously to the belief that they "owe" sexual favors to a man they date. [9]After a sexual attack by a date, many women are racked with guilt rather than anger. [10]Were they to blame, they ask themselves, because they drank too much? [11]Because they wore a short skirt? [12]Similarly, men have grown up in a culture which suggests that once they have spent "good money" entertaining a date, they are owed sex in return.

1. In sentence 8, the words *subscribe . . . to* mean
   a. describe.
   b. agree with.
   c. ignore.
   d. argue with.

2. The relationship of sentence 2 to sentence 1 is one of
   a. addition.
   b. illustration.
   c. contrast.
   d. comparison.

3. The relationship of sentence 12 to sentences 9-11 is one of
   a. time.
   b. contrast.
   c. comparison.
   d. cause and effect.

*(Continues on next page)*

4. You can conclude that the author believes
   a. many men and women should change their attitudes about sexuality.
   b. attitudes about rights in the workplace must be easier to change than attitudes about sexuality.
   c. victims of date rape often feel responsible for having been attacked.
   d. all of the above.

5. The main purpose of this passage is
   a. to inform readers about interesting sexual attitudes.
   b. to use facts to argue that sexual attitudes need improving.
   c. to entertain readers with dramatic sexual images.
   d. to predict the future of the American sex scene.

6. The author's tone can be described as
   a. sarcastic.
   b. optimistic.
   c. arrogant.
   d. distressed.

7. The point made in sentence 2 is best supported by
   a. sentence 1.
   b. sentence 4.
   c. sentence 8.
   d. sentence 12.

8. The main idea of the passage is that
   a. women are now close to reaching their full potential.
   b. societal attitudes toward sexuality are old-fashioned and harmful.
   c. colleges should provide better security in coed dorms.
   d. men's sexual attitudes are strongly in need of change.

# COMBINED SKILLS: Test D-1

After reading the passage, circle the letter of the best answer to each question.

[1]The general public may still think of Girl Scouts as pigtailed lasses who earn merit badges for learning to apply tourniquets that stop bleeding. [2]However, such an image is dated. [3]Girl Scouts today are more likely to be talking about making career choices or dealing with sexual pressure than about building campfires or knitting afghans.

[4]In recent years, the New York City-based Girl Scouts organization has been bombarded with criticism that its programs were no longer relevant to today's young females. [5]In response, Girl Scouts began overhauling the merit badge programs and updating its guidebooks for members. [6]Drugs, sex abuse, and teen pregnancy are all topics dealt with in Girl Scout books published since 1987. [7]Girls today can earn merit badges reflecting issues of the '90s. [8]For example, badges are available for Girl Scouts who demonstrate their understanding of eating disorders such as anorexia and bulimia. [9]The result of these changes is that the Scouts organization helps members become more realistically prepared to deal with their lives.

1. The relationship of sentence 7 to sentence 8 is one of
   a. contrast.
   b. time.
   c. illustration.
   d. comparison.

2. The relationship between sentence 9 and the rest of the passage is one of
   a. illustration.
   b. comparison.
   c. cause and effect.
   d. contrast.

3. The passage suggests that activities formerly associated with Girl Scouts include
   a. applying tourniquets.
   b. making career choices.
   c. understanding eating disorders.
   d. learning about teen pregnancy.

4. From the passage, one could conclude that
   a. Girl Scouts leaders were unconcerned by criticism of their organization.
   b. criticism of the Girl Scouts organization was unfair.
   c. most people preferred the old-style Girl Scouts organization.
   d. Girl Scouts leaders agreed that their organization needed updating.

*(Continues on next page)*

5. Sentence 6 is a statement of
   a. fact.
   b. opinion.
   c. fact and opinion.

6. The author's main purpose is
   a. to inform.
   b. to entertain.
   c. to persuade.
   d. to predict.

7. The passage supports the point that
   a. change begins from within.
   b. constructive criticism can lead to change.
   c. the old values are the best values.
   d. criticism is pointless and cruel.

8. The main idea of this passage is that
   a. the Girl Scouts are an outdated organization.
   b. eating disorders are common problems among members of the Girl Scouts.
   c. the Girl Scouts have made changes to adapt to modern times.
   d. the Girl Scouts would not have survived long without making some changes.

# COMBINED SKILLS: Test D-2

After reading the passage, circle the letter of the best answer to each question.

[1]In the eighteenth century, warfare never affected the whole populace. [2]Armies were small, and combat could be conducted in war zones away from population centers. [3]The Civil War, however, touched nearly every American life. [4]Families gave fathers and sons to the armed services; and women assumed the management of farms or moved to the cities and took jobs to keep factories going in the production of war goods. [5]Hundreds of women, more rigidly segregated from combat than had been the case at the time of the War for American Independence, became nurses, and they fought to save thousands of lives.

[6]Serving the fallen was grim work at best. [7]Too often hospitals were centers of filth and death. [8]Women like Dorothea Dix, superintendent of Union army nurses, and Clara Barton, who later founded the American Red Cross (1881), put up with enormous personal privation to comfort those in pain. [9]Still, they could hardly relieve the suffering. [10]Medicine was too primitive to cope with the killer diseases, such as typhoid fever and malaria, that swept through camps and cut down thousands of soldiers. [11]In fact, fewer Union troops died in battle than from bouts of diarrhea and dysentery.

[12]Because doctors had no sense of the importance of sterilization, germs spread rapidly as surgeons cut off arms and legs to save wounded soldiers from gangrene poisoning. [13]Troops on both sides would have agreed with the Alabama private who wrote in 1862: "I beleave the doctors kills more than they cure." [14]For those who survived the crude surgery of the times, only a small portion recovered in the type of clean, well-managed hospital run by Sally L. Tompkins in Richmond. [15]Indeed, Confederate leaders did not officially permit the use of female nurses until the autumn of 1862; once they did, they found that death rates were lower than in hospitals employing only male nurses.

1. The word *privation* in sentence 8 means
   a. solitude.
   b. lack of basic comforts.
   c. primitive medicine.
   d. confusion.

2. According to the author, the Civil War
   a. caused women to become more dependent upon their menfolk.
   b. affected more people than previous wars had.
   c. gave doctors the chance to develop successful surgical methods.
   d. led to the last major typhoid epidemic in the U.S.

*(Continues on next page)*

449

3. Civil War nurses were often
   a. sacrificing.
   b. unable to help much.
   c. male.
   d. all of the above.

4. The relationship of sentence 3 to sentences 1 and 2 is one of
   a. comparison.
   b. contrast.
   c. illustration.
   d. time.

5. The general pattern of organization of paragraph 2 is
   a. list of items.
   b. comparison.
   c. time order.
   d. definition and example.

6. The passage implies that during the Civil War,
   a. deaths from disease were more common than in any other war.
   b. males preferred to serve in combat rather than to serve as nurses.
   c. women took on new roles.
   d. Confederate leaders were the first to recognize the value of women in the war effort.

7. Sentence 15 is a statement of
   a. fact.
   b. opinion.
   c. fact and opinion.

8. The main idea of the second paragraph is stated in
   a. sentence 6.
   b. sentence 9.
   c. sentence 10.
   d. sentence 11.

# COMBINED SKILLS: Test D-3

After reading the passage, circle the letter of the best answer to each question.

[1]It would be a mistake to assume that primitive societies are mentally backward—unable to benefit from their environments or understand how to cope effectively with them. [2]Given the general level of technology available, they do adapt to and manipulate their environment in a sophisticated and understanding manner. [3]Countless examples can be cited to illustrate this point. [4]Among some Eskimo groups, wolves are a menace—a dangerous environmental feature that must be dealt with. [5]They could perhaps be hunted down and killed, but this involves danger as well as considerable expenditure in time and energy. [6]So a simple yet clever device is employed. [7]A sharp sliver of bone is curled into a springlike shape, and seal blubber is molded around it and permitted to freeze. [8]This is then placed where it can be discovered by a hungry wolf, which, living up to its reputation, "wolfs it down." [9]Later, as this "time bomb" is digested and the blubber disappears, the bone uncurls and its sharp ends pierce the stomach of the wolf, causing internal bleeding and death. [10]The job gets done! [11]It is a simple yet fairly safe technique that involves an understanding of the environment as well as wolf psychology and habits.

1. As used in sentence 6, the word *employed* means
   a. hired.
   b. recognized.
   c. used.
   d. known.

2. The relationship between the two parts of sentence 5 is one of
   a. time.
   b. comparison.
   c. contrast.
   d. addition.

3. For this passage, the author uses the organizational pattern of
   a. listing a series of details that support a point.
   b. narrating a sequence of events.
   c. defining and illustrating a term.
   d. using a specific example to support a general statement.

4. The author implies that among primitive societies, the Eskimos' cleverness is
   a. superior.
   b. typical.
   c. rare.
   d. inferior.

*(Continues on next page)*

5. The author implies that certain societies are considered "primitive" because of their
   a. attitude toward animals.
   b. level of technology.
   c. creative ability.
   d. understanding of their environment.

6. In sentence 9, the author uses the term "time-bomb" because the bone and blubber weapon
   a. gives the wolf some extra time to live.
   b. is an efficient way of eliminating the wolf.
   c. has a delayed action.
   d. takes little time to prepare.

7. Which is an appropriate title for this selection?
   a. Mentally Backward Societies
   b. Dangerous Environmental Features
   c. Intelligence in Primitive Societies
   d. Land of the Eskimos

8. Which sentence best expresses the main idea of the passage?
   a. There are no greater challenges to a society than that of controlling one's environment.
   b. Eskimos are able to control wolves.
   c. With increased technology, primitive societies should be able to cope even more effectively with their environment.
   d. Primitive societies can deal shrewdly and effectively with the demands of their environment.

# COMBINED SKILLS: Test E-1

After reading the passage, circle the letter of the best answer to each question.

¹Earlier in this century, Halloween was a night when roving gangs (usually boys) played elaborate tricks on their neighbors. ²These tricks more closely resembled practical jokes than vandalism. ³For example, the boys might lift an outhouse off its foundations and move it to someone else's yard, or they might remove a screen door from its hinges and leave it on the owner's roof. ⁴Such tricks required skill and planning, and the victims were usually neighbors or relatives. ⁵Thus, Halloween was a night when adolescents took their "revenge" on adults in a way that was, for the most part, tolerated by the community.

⁶Today, the holiday mischief has degenerated into destructive vandalism, such as tire-slashing and window-breaking. ⁷These kinds of actions require no skill or intelligence. ⁸In addition, instead of the small offerings—an apple or a piece of cake—meant to be given in exchange for protection from practical jokes, trick-or-treaters demand bagfuls of commercial candy bars from the numerous people, many of them strangers, on a collection route. ⁹But the most alarming and repulsive aspect of the new Halloween combines evildoing and food in the worst way—now criminals insert pins into candy bars and razors into apples. ¹⁰Thus Halloween has been transformed into an event not of harmless fun, but of greed, vandalism, and occasional terror.

1. Earlier in the century, children celebrated Halloween by
   a. committing vandalism.
   b. begging for candy bars.
   c. working for the community.
   d. playing practical jokes.

2. On the whole, the relationship between the two paragraphs is one of
   a. comparison.
   b. contrast.
   c. cause and effect.
   d. definition and example.

3. The words *these kinds of actions* in sentence 7 refer to
   a. holiday mischief.
   b. tire-slashing and window-breaking.
   c. trick-or-treaters demanding bagfuls of candy.
   d. taking "revenge" on adults.

*(Continues on next page)*

453

4. The author's attitude toward today's Halloween is
   a. sympathetic.
   b. critical.
   c. doubtful.
   d. unrealistic.

5. The author would probably agree with the idea that
   a. today, Halloween brings out some of our worst qualities.
   b. collecting for UNICEF is merely a different form of begging.
   c. tire slashing is simple adolescent mischief.
   d. teenage boys are responsible for the change in Halloween.

6. From the passage you could conclude that earlier in this century,
   a. children in effect bribed people to give them treats.
   b. holidays were more fun than they are now.
   c. girls never participated in the Halloween tricks.
   d. children had a sense of humor and pride about their Halloween tricks.

7. What is the most appropriate title for this selection?
   a. Halloween: A Change for the Worse
   b. A Traditional Holiday
   c. Halloween Terror
   d. The Charm of the Past

8. Which statement best expresses the main idea of the passage?
   a. Halloween celebrations should be banned.
   b. Children today don't want to work for their rewards.
   c. Halloween has deteriorated into a time of greed and terror.
   d. Halloween is an event when adolescents are allowed to take their revenge on adults.

## COMBINED SKILLS: Test E-2

After reading the passage, circle the letter of the best answer to each question.

[1]The concept of adopting a child to raise as one's own is a relatively modern phenomenon. [2]While there have always been instances of families taking in unrelated children to raise for a variety of reasons, most had more to do with helping the children of a dead or disabled relative or securing cheap labor than adding a new member to the family.

[3]A remarkable chapter in American history that began in 1853 helped to sow the seeds of modern adoption practices. [4]The story began when Charles Loring Brace, a wealthy Connecticut man, visited New York City. [5]He was appalled by the number of orphans and abandoned children he found living in the streets there. [6]In response, Brace organized the Children's Aid Society, dedicated to finding loving homes for such children. [7]Its method was to send trainloads of orphaned children into Western states, where community leaders would encourage friends and neighbors to adopt a child "to treat in every way as a member of the family."

[8]The Children's Aid Society was a remarkable success. [9]By the time its program ended in 1929, "orphan trains" had carried almost 100,000 children to new homes. [10]The orphans grew up to make solid contributions to their communities; many became respected farmers, while others went on to practice law or medicine. [11]One of the orphans became governor of North Dakota; another, governor of Alaska.

1. In sentence 5, the word *appalled* means
   a. annoyed.
   b. unmoved.
   c. excited.
   d. horrified.

2. The relationship between sentences 5 and 6 is one of
   a. cause and effect.
   b. addition.
   c. comparison.
   d. general idea and illustration.

3. Sentence 11 expresses
   a. fact.
   b. opinion.
   c. fact and opinion.

*(Continues on next page)*

4. The passage suggests that the success of the Children's Aid Society was due in part to
   a. the attractiveness of the children.
   b. the participation of well-known citizens in the communities the trains went through.
   c. the national reputation of Charles Loring Brace.
   d. none of the above.

5. The author's main purpose in writing this selection is to
   a. predict future adoption practices.
   b. inform readers about a significant chapter in American history.
   c. persuade readers to consider adopting orphans or abandoned children.
   d. entertain readers with stories of the "orphan train."

6. The author's tone in this passage is largely
   a. approving.
   b. critical.
   c. regretful.
   d. pessimistic.

7. The main idea of the third paragraph is stated in
   a. sentence 8.
   b. sentence 9.
   c. sentence 10.
   d. sentence 11.

8. Which sentence best states the main idea of the selection?
   a. Charles Loring Brace was appalled by the number of orphans and abandoned children he found living in the streets of New York City.
   b. Individuals can make a great impact on society, for both good and bad.
   c. The initial success of the Children's Aid Society contributed to modern adoption practices.
   d. The orphans placed by the Children's Aid Society made numerous worthwhile contributions to their communities.

## COMBINED SKILLS: Test E-3

After reading the passage, circle the letter of the best answer to each question.

[1]In 1948, during the re-election campaign of Senator Claude Pepper of Florida, large numbers of leaflets with an unsigned message were circulated throughout the state just before election day. [2]The message was as follows:

[3]Are you aware that Claude Pepper is known all over Washington as a shameless extrovert? [4]Not only that, but this man is reliably reported to practice nepotism with his sister-in-law, and he has a sister who was a thespian in wicked New York City. [5]Worst of all, it is an established fact that Mr. Pepper, before his marriage, habitually practiced celibacy.

[6]In a literal sense, the statements were not false. [7]However, the words *extrovert* (a person who is active and expressive), *nepotism* (favoritism to relatives), *thespian* (an actor) and *celibacy* (not being sexually active) were used in contexts that seemed threatening to people who did not know the meanings of these uncommon words.

[8]A very clever and dishonest writer had purposely selected words that gave the impression that Senator Pepper was a very immoral person. [9]The effect was very damaging. [10]Senator Pepper was defeated at the polls by George Smathers, who denied that he was involved in this political "dirty trick." [11]However, the damage could not be undone.

1. In sentence 6, *literal* means
   a. based on imagination.
   b. marital.
   c. not understood.
   d. according to actual word meanings.

2. The relationship of sentence 7 to sentence 6 is one of
   a. addition.
   b. cause and effect.
   c. comparison.
   d. contrast.

3. The pattern of organization of sentences 3 through 5 is
   a. time order.
   b. list of items.
   c. comparison/contrast.
   d. cause and effect.

*(Continues on next page)*

4. Overall, the passage is about
   a. a general idea and a list of examples.
   b. a comparison and a contrast.
   c. a cause and effect.
   d. a definition and example.

5. The passage implies that Senator Pepper
   a. probably did not deserve to be elected.
   b. was in reality a very shy person who never practiced celibacy.
   c. may have lost the election because of a "dirty trick."
   d. had been an excellent senator.

6. You could conclude from the passage that
   a. the writer of the leaftlet assumed many readers would not know some uncommon words.
   b. Claude Pepper never showed favoritism to his sister-in-law nor had a sister who was an actor.
   c. the writer of the leaflet did not understand the psychology of the average voter.
   d. George Smathers was later elected governor of Florida.

7. The author of this passage would probably agree with which of the following statements?
   a. Honest political campaigns don't succeed.
   b. Political tricks have ruined Florida's politics.
   c. Unsigned leaflets are a fair way to spread valuable information.
   d. When the truth is told deceitfully, it can do as much damage as a lie.

8. Which of the following statements best expresses the main idea of the passage?
   a. Dishonesty is a major problem in Florida's political campaigns.
   b. Florida's citizens are easily fooled.
   c. A "dirty trick" that twisted the truth damaged a political campaign.
   d. Claude Pepper should have run a better senatorial campaign.

# Limited Answer Key

*An Important Note*: To strengthen your reading skills, you must do more than simply find out which of your answers are right and which are wrong. You also need to figure out (with the help of this book, the teacher, or other students) *why* you missed the questions you did. By using each of your wrong answers as a learning opportunity, you will strengthen your understanding of the skills. You will also prepare yourself for the reviews and the mastery tests, for which answers are not given here.

## ANSWERS TO THE PRACTICES

### 1 Vocabulary in Context

*Practice 1*

1. Example: *only a spoonful of rice and a few beans*; a
2. Examples: *The TV is talking to them, others can steal their thoughts*; a
3. Examples: *What sign are you? How do you like this place? You remind me of someone*; b
4. Examples: *gardening, long-distance bike riding*; a
5. Examples: *two heads, webbed toes*; c

*Practice 2*

1. Synonym: *a person who habitually postpones doing things*
2. Synonym: *carefully examine*
3. Synonym: *practical*
4. Synonym: *isolating infected patients to prevent their diseases from spreading*
5. Synonym: *mercy-killing*

*Practice 3*

1. Antonym: *great wealth*; c
2. Antonym: *long, vague*; a
3. Antonym: *openly*; b
4. Antonym: *weak*; c
5. Antonym: *decorated plainly*; b

*Practice 4*

1. c
2. b
3. a
4. b
5. c

## 2   Main Ideas

*Practice 1*

1. Topic: c; Main Idea: b
2. Topic: a; Main Idea: d
3. Topic: c; Main Idea: c
4. Topic: d; Main Idea: d

*Practice 2*

Group 1.  a. SD
          b. SD
          c. T
          d. MI

Group 2.  a. SD
          b. T
          c. SD
          d. MI

Group 3.  a. SD
          b. T
          c. SD
          d. MI

Group 4.  a. T
          b. SD
          c. MI
          d. SD

*Practice 3*

A. 1
B. 4
C. 2
D. 1, 5

*Practice 4*

1. b
2. b
3. c

*Practice 5*

The implied main ideas may be stated in various ways, including the following:

1. Many commonly held beliefs about sleepwalking are not true.
2. Being an only child is not as great a privilege as people think it is.
3. There are benefits to watching television.

## 3   Supporting Details

*Note:* Wording may vary throughout these practices.

*Practice 1*

**Group 1**

(The order of points a. and b. may vary.)

1. Bad location
2. Poor advertising
   a. Relied on word of mouth
   b. No display ad in Yellow Pages
3. a. Unexpected rise in wholesale prices
   b. High salaries for workers

**Group 2**

Missing minor details under "Substitutes for high-fat dairy products": Skim milk instead of whole milk; Yogurt instead of sour cream.

Missing second major detail: Substitutes for fats.

Missing third major detail: Substitutes for high-fat meats.

Missing minor details under "Substitutes for high-fat meats": Ground turkey breast instead of ground beef; Boiled ham instead of bacon.

*Practice 2*

1. Missing minor detail under "Sports addicts": Summer: focus is baseball, golf, tennis.

   Missing second major and minor details: Television—Flip on television as soon as they get home; Schedule much of their lives around favorite shows.

   Missing third major detail: Love

2. Main idea: Animals open their mouths for several reasons besides hunger.

   1. To warn an intruder away
      Examples: Lizards and fish threaten by opening their mouths.

Bears and wolves show their teeth before attacking.
2. To quiet aggression
Example: Lions yawn to distract other lions that may want to fight.
3. To get their teeth clean
Example: The crocodile opens to let little birds eat leftover food off its teeth.
4. To signal an interest in the opposite sex
Example: Open beaks are part of the penguin's court-ship dance.

*Practice 3*

1. serious depression?
   a. A change in sleep patterns
   b. Abnormal eating patterns
   c. A general feeling of hopeless-ness
2. What simple steps can drivers take to prevent car theft?
   a. Lock all valuables in the trunk or glove compartment.
   b. Park in the middle of the block on a busy, well-lighted street.
   c. Always lock the car and take the keys.

*Practice 4*

A. 1. b
2. a
3. c
4. They can undo complicated bolts on gates.
5. c
B. 6. c
7. shipping them out of the country.
8. witches or possessed by the devil.
9. punishing the mentally ill.
10. c

# 4   Transitions

Answers to some of these exercises may vary.

*Practice 1*

1. also
2. First of all
3. In addition
4. Finally
5. third

*Practice 2*

1. After
2. Then
3. during
4. before
5. while

*Practice 3*

1. Although
2. in contrast
3. but
4. in spite of
5. Nevertheless

*Practice 4*

1. Similarly
2. like
3. in the same way
4. In like manner
5. Just as

*Practice 5*

1. For example
2. such as
3. To illustrate
4. For instance
5. For example

*Practice 6*

1. Because
2. as a result
3. Since
4. Consequently
5. therefore

## 5 Patterns of Organization

Wording will vary throughout these practices.

### Practice 1a

Main idea: The 1960s were a time of turmoil and change in America.
1. Assassination of President Kennedy depressed the country.
2. Urban riots brought out the issue of racial equality.
3. Anti-war protests spread across the country.

### Practice 1b

Main idea: There are several steps to remembering your dreams
2. Put a pen and notebook near your bed.
3. Turn off alarm and wake up gradually.
4. Write down any dream you remember before you get out of bed.

### Practice 2

1. Number of items: 3
   Type of item: Advantages to children of owning a pet
2. Number of items: 3
   Type of item: Ways to be an active listener

### Practice 3

A. Comparison; 1. Mysteries, 2. Science fiction
B. Contrast; 1. Government's role in society 2. Journalists' role in society (in relation to their attitudes toward secrecy)

### Practice 4

A. 1. Cause: late spring freeze
   Effect: poor Florida orange crop
2. Cause: Mr. Coleman's compulsive gambling
   Effect: Mr. Coleman's bankruptcy
3. Cause: I slipped and fell on a patch of ice
   Effect: I twisted my ankle
4. Cause: Linda's new boss not appreciating her excellent work habits
   Effect: Linda's work became careless

B. 5. Uncontrolled high blood pressure: cause
   Stroke: effect
   Heart attack: effect
6. Valid objection: cause
   Thrown-out evidence: effect
   Dismissed case: effect
7. Ammunition was low: cause
   Food supplies were low: cause
   The general surrendered: effect
8. A study schedule: cause
   Tonia's better grades: effect
   Not going out on weeknights: cause

C. 9. Inability to listen carefully all the time: effect
   Message overload: cause
   Preoccupation with personal concerns: cause
   Surrounding noise: cause
10. Meditation: cause
    Decrease or elimination of drug use: effect
    Cardiovascular improvements: effect
    Stress relief: effect

### Practice 5

A. Definition: 1    Example: 2
B. Definition: 2    Example 1: 5
                    Example 2: 7

### Practice 6

1. b    4. c
2. c    5. c
3. a

## 6    Fact and Opinion

### Practice 1

1. F
2. F+O
3. F
4. F+O
5. F
6. F
7. F
8. F+O
9. F
10. F+O

### Practice 2

1. F
2. O
3. F
4. O
5. O
6. F
7. O
8. F
9. F
10. O

### Practice 3

1. O
2. F
3. F+O
4. F+O
5. O
6. F
7. O
8. F
9. F+O
10. O

### Practice 4

1. O
2. F+O
3. O
4. F
5. F

## 7    Inferences

### Practice 1

1. c
2. c
3. a
4. c
5. d

### Practice 2

1. c
2. b
3. b
4. c
5. b

### Practice 3

1, 6, 8

### Practice 4

1. c
2. c
3. b
4. a
5. c
6. c
7. b
8. b
9. b
10. c

## 8    Purpose and Tone

### Practice 1

1. I
2. P
3. E
4. P
5. I
6. I
7. E
8. P
9. E
10. I

### Practice 2

1. P
2. E
3. I

*Practice 3*

A. 1. admiring
   2. sympathetic
   3. critical
   4. objective
   5. ironic
B. 6. straightforward
   7. ironic
   8. threatening
   9. self-pitying
  10. sympathetic

*Practice 4*

1. h
2. f
3. c
4. e
5. d

## 9   Propaganda

*Practice 1*

2, 5

*Practice 2*

2, 4

*Practice 3*

2, 3

*Practice 4*

1, 5

*Practice 5*

2, 4

*Practice 6*

1, 5

*Practice 7*

1. c
2. c
3. b

## 10   Argument

*Practice, page 387*

1. S, P
2. S, P
3. S, S, S, P
4. P, S, S, S
5. S, S, P, S

*Practice, pages 388-389*

1. a, d, e
2. a, c, f
3. a, c, f
4. b, d, f

*Practice 1*

1. c
2. c

*Practice 2*

2

*Practice 3*

1

*Practice 4*

4

*Practice 5*

Group 1: d
Group 2: a

*Practice 6*

3

*Practice 7*

4

*Practice 8*

1

# Acknowledgments

Baker, Russell, Excerpt from *Growing Up*. Copyright © 1982 by Russell Baker. Published by St. Martin's Press, Inc. Excerpt from "The Plot Against People." Copyright © 1968 by the New York Times Company.

Barry, Dave. Selections on pages 284, 308, and 340. Reprinted by permission.

Cosby, Bill. Selection on page 343. From *Love and Marriage*. Copyright © 1989 by Bill Cosby. Reprinted by permission of Doubleday, a division of Bantam, Doubleday, Dell Publishing Group, Inc.

Crane, Stephen. "I Stood Upon a High Place," from *Works of Stephan Crane: Volume 10: Poems and Literary Remains*. Published in 1975 by the University Press of Virginia.

Davies, W. H. "The Example," from *The Complete Poems of W. H. Davies*. Published in 1965 by the Wesleyan University Press.

Krents, Harold. Excerpt from the essay "Darkness at Noon," from *The New York Times*, May 26, 1976, Op-Ed. Copyright © 1976/84 by The New York Times Company.

Lester, Julius. Excerpt from "Being a Boy," which originally appeared in *Ms.* magazine. Reprinted by permission of Julius Lester.

Lurie, Alison. Excerpt from *The Language of Clothes*. Copyright © 1981 by Alison Lurie. Published by Random House.

Orwell, George. Excerpt from "A Hanging," from *Shooting an Elephant and Other Essays*. Copyright © 1945, 1946, 1949, 1950 by Sonia Brownell Orwell; renewed 1973, 1974 by Sonia Orwell. Published by Harcourt Brace Jovanovich, Inc. Selection on page 322.

Robinson, Edwin Arlington. "Richard Cory," from *The Children of the Night*. Published in New York by Charles Scribner's Sons, 1897.

Roth, Philip. Excerpt from *Goodbye Columbus*. Copyright © 1959 by Philip Roth. Reprinted by permission of Houghton Mifflin.

Sandburg, Carl. "Grass," from *The Complete Poems of Carl Sandburg*. Published in 1970 by Harcourt Brace Jovanovich.

# Index

Addition, words that show, 136-137; 180
Antonyms, as context clues, 9-10
Argument, 385-428
    basics of: point and support, 386-387
    evaluating with informal outlines, 387-389
    fallacies that ignore the issue, 390-394
    fallacies that overgeneralize or
        oversimplify, 394-398
    mastery tests for, 399-428
    review, 398

Bandwagon propaganda technique, 346

Card stacking propaganda technique, 352-353
Cause and effect
    pattern of organization, 184-188
    words that show, 142-143; 185
Changing the subject fallacy, 390-392
Circular reasoning fallacy, 392-393
Combined skills mastery tests, 429-458
Comparison and/or contrast pattern of
    organization, 182-184
Comparison, words that show, 140-141; 183
Context clues
    antonyms, 9-10
    examples, 6-8
    general sense of the sentence or
        passage, 10-11
    synonyms, 8-9
Contrast, words that show, 139-140; 183

Definition and example pattern of
    organization, 189-190
Definitions, textbook, 12
Details, supporting, 91-134

Either-or fallacy, 398
Examples
    as context clues, 6-8
    with definitions, 12; 189-190
    words that show illustration, 142; 190

Fact
    definition, 224
    points about, 225-227
Fact and opinion, 223-262
    mastery tests for, 233-262
    review, 232
False cause fallacy, 396-397
False comparison fallacy, 397
Fallacy, definition of, 390
Fallacies that ignore the issue, 390-394
    changing the subject, 390-392
    circular reasoning, 392-393
    personal attack, 393
    straw man, 394
Fallacies that overgeneralize or oversimplify,
    394-398
    either-or, 398
    false cause, 396-397
    false comparison, 397
    hasty generalization, 394-396

General sense of the passage, as context clue, 10-11
Glittering generalities, 351


Hasty generalization fallacy, 394-396
Illustration, words that show, 141-142; 190
Implied main ideas, 55-59
Inferences, 263-304
  in everyday life, 263-266
  in literature, 269-274
  in reading, 266-269
  mastery tests for, 275-304
  review, 274
Informal outlines, using to evaluate arguments, 387-389
Irony, a note on, 310-311


Limited answer key, 459-464
List of items pattern of organization, 180-182


Main ideas, 43-90
  and topic, 44-48
  definition, 44
  implied, 55-59
  in topic sentence, 48-55
  mastery tests for, 61-90
  review, 60
Maps, 95


Name calling propaganda technique, 350

Opinion
  definition, 224
  points about, 225-227


Patterns of organization, 175-222
  cause and effect, 184-188
  comparison and/or contrast, 182-184
  definition and example, 189-190
  list of items, 180-182
  mastery tests for, 193-222
  review, 192

  time order, 176-179
  topic sentences and, 191-192
Performance Chart, inside back cover
Personal attack fallacy, 393
Plain folks propaganda technique, 349
Point and support, in arguments, 386-387
Propaganda, 345-384
  bandwagon, 346
  card stacking, 352-353
  definition, 345
  glittering generalities, 351
  mastery tests for, 355-384
  name calling, 350
  plain folks, 349
  review, 354
  techniques, 345-346
  testimonial, 347
  transfer, 348
Purpose, 305-308
Purpose and tone, 305-344
  mastery tests for, 315-344
  review, 314


Reading carefully, 101-104


Sense of the passage, as context clue, 10-11
Straw man fallacy, 394
Supporting details, 91-134
  identifying, 91-104
    by asking questions, 99-101
    in reading carefully, 101-104
  major and minor, 91-99
  mastery tests for, 105-134
  review, 104
Synonyms, as context clues, 8-9


Testimonial propaganda technique, 347
Time, words that show, 137-139; 177
Time order pattern of organization, 176-179
  series of events or stages, 177-178
  series of steps (directions), 178-179
Tone, 308-313
  list of words that describe, 309
Topic, 44-48

Topic sentences
    and patterns of organization, 191-192
    definition, 48
    locations of, 51-55
    that cover more than one paragraph, 54-55
Transfer propaganda technique, 348
Transitions, 135-174
    mastery tests for, 145-174
    review, 144
    that show addition, 136-137
    that show cause and effect, 142-143
    that show comparison, 140-141
    that show contrast, 139-140
    that show illustration, 141-142
    that show time, 137-139


Vocabulary in context, 5-42
    antonyms, 9-10
    examples, 6-8
    general sense of the sentence
        or passage, 10-11
    mastery tests for, 13-42
    review, 12
    synonyms, 8-9